FEMINISM, MULTICULTURALISM, AND THE MEDIA

FEMINISM, MULTICULTURALISM, AND THE MEDIA

GLOBAL DIVERSITIES

EDITED BY

ANGHARAD N. VALDIVIA

SAGE Publications
International Educational and Professional Publisher
Thousand Oaks   London   New Delhi

For information address:

 SAGE Publications, Inc.
2455 Teller Road
Thousand Oaks, California 91320
E-mail: order@sagepub.com

SAGE Publications Ltd.
6 Bonhill Street
London EC2A 4PU
United Kingdom

SAGE Publications India Pvt. Ltd.
M-32 Market
Greater Kailash I
New Delhi 110 048 India

Printed in the United States of America

Library of Congress Cataloging-in-Publication Data

Main entry under title:

Feminism, multiculturalism, and the media: Global diversities /
    edited by Angharad N. Valdivia.
        p. cm.
    Includes bibliographical references and index.
    ISBN 0-8039-5774-2 (alk. paper). — ISBN 0-8039-5775-0 (pbk. :
alk. paper)
    1. Mass media and women. 2. Feminism. 3. Pluralism (Social
sciences) I. Valdivia, Angharad N.
P94.5.W65F45 1995
302.23'082—dc20   95-8204

95 96 97 98 99 10 9 8 7 6 5 4 3 2 1

Sage Production Editor: Astrid Virding   Typesetter: Christina M. Hill

Contents

Acknowledgments

This book would not have been possible without the assistance of many individuals and institutions. The impetus for the book came from the relative lack of materials available for a class on gender, race, and the media that I was assigned to teach upon arriving at Penn State in 1989. Conversations with others who taught similar classes, notably H. Leslie Steeves at the University of Oregon, convinced me of the need to do this project now.

Once I decided to go ahead and put this book together, I had the good fortune of having close friends and colleagues whose suggestions, conversations, and support were indispensable. Jeanne Brady and I had long conversations about all of the themes in this book and life in general. Without her friendship, company, and support I couldn't have finished it. Nina Gregg was also a constant source of encouragement and clarification. A diasporic network of colleagues and friends, including Benedicte Monicat, Steve Hanson, Mary Ellen Brown, and Aida Barrera, helped me sort out many of the relevant issues.

I had the additional good fortune of having truly incredible research assistance. In particular, Víctor Rivera went well beyond the call of duty to help me with the manuscript. His expert knowledge of computer matters, his brilliant and sharp critique of critical theory in general and feminism in particular, his untiring dedication to the project, and his lighthearted singing in Spanish and English enabled me to finish faster than I would have thought possible. As well, Lisa Sanmiguel and Colleen Reagan were very helpful.

I also want to thank my students in the Women, Minorities and the Media class. It was their feedback and questions that kept me convinced that this was an important project. In particular, I wish to thank Isabel Molina Guzmán, Shannon Kokoska, Kristen Lambertin, Kelly Lengel, and Jessica Hartshorn for their inspiring questions, challenges, and actions.

This project was begun at the School of Communications at The Pennsylvania State University, continued at the Department of Communications at the University of California at San Diego, and finished at the Institute of Communications Research at the College of Communications at the University of Illinois—whose generous financial support in terms of equipment and research assistance underscores its commitment to issues and scholarship of diversity.

Last but not least, I want to thank Rhiannon and Tobin for their support and inspiration, and for always reminding me that we owe it to our children to engage in interventions that will make their lives more meaningful.

—ANGHARAD N. VALDIVIA

PART I

The Production of Interventions

One of the major areas of study in mass communications theory is production. In this area we consider overlapping and often inextricable levels of analysis. As McQuail (1987) notes, these levels are theoretical and methodological models for the purposes of intellectual examination, but most of us live these levels simultaneously and inseparably. Thus in the study of production we have institutional, organizational, and individual levels of analysis. At the institutional level of analysis we study the norms and values that govern a particular institution. In the case of media studies we have the mass media as the overarching if evanescent institution, but we also have more specific ones, such as the press. Institutions, if I may be allowed to simplify matters a bit, have no address, no building where we can find them. On the other hand, the organizational level of analysis refers to the conventions and practices that govern a particular organization. Here, we can find these places on the map. For example, the *New York Times* is one such organization, with practices such as timeliness and objectivity that govern the production of the daily newspaper. Similarly, NBC, MTV, Paramount, Sony, and others are all organizations with buildings and addresses wherein rules, written or unwritten, govern the steady and repeated production of mass media. At the individual level of analysis, we study the particular producer who functions within an organization that in turn more or less obeys values and norms at the institutional level. Although it is important to consider the socioeconomic makeup of individual producers—that is, their gender, class background, race and/or ethnicity, sexual orientation, age, national origin, and physical ability—we cannot forget

1

that these individuals function within organizations with established practices that, in turn, respond to institutional norms and values.

All three levels overlap, and chapters in this section explore some of the issues and contradictions facing the production of media from a feminist multiculturalist perspective. While other parts of the book focus on textual analysis (Part II) and the combination of approaches (Part III), the chapters in this first section privilege the area of production.

Consistent with the comments made in Chapter 1, the issue of identity politics, for example, is lived by sociohistorical subjects at all three levels. At the individual level of analysis, multicultural subjects often face double, triple, or multiple binds as they attempt to negotiate, consciously or unconsciously, their individual goals and needs with those of their organizations and their institutions. This is why identity politics strategies cannot be successful from an individual level alone. Organizational practices, most of which were developed and adopted prior to the explicit consideration of multiculturalism, are not sensitive to these issues of identity. Similarly, the norms and values that govern media institutions do not include multiculturalism. Quite the contrary, as Chapter 1 notes, the binary approach that underscores much of Western intellectual thought precludes multiculturalism.

Isabel Molina Guzmán (Chapter 2) illustrates the binds and contradictions faced by a multiculturalist feminist subject as she navigates the individual, organizational, and institutional issues in the setting of higher education. At the individual level of analysis, Molina faces attitudes and comments from both fellow students and teachers that underscore her otherness from their perspective. Molina also faces and challenges organizational pedagogical practices that would mute her experience. As a feminist woman of color, Molina has to wait until her senior year in college to study issues that seem pertinent to her lived experiences. It is not, as some critics charge of the multiculturalist project, that Molina demands that her experiences be the only basis for the educational curriculum, but rather that inclusion of multiculturalist experiences be integrated throughout the curriculum rather than singled out as aberrant and other. The curriculum is not set up to include the study of everyone's multicultural identity. At the institutional level of analysis, both the organizational practices and individual attitudes reflect the fact that higher education as an institution does not value multiculturalism. From the system of rewards and promotions to overarching "universal" values, multiculturalism falls between the cracks. It is thus only too easy for a feminist woman of color to continually face challenge after challenge or to drop out of the field altogether. Similarly, as her mini case study suggests, Molina demonstrates that a minor intervention, such as Chino Wilson's in the *Daily Collegian,* is met with strong and concerted resistance for it challenges individual attitudes, organizational practices, and institutional values. It is not so much that Wilson challenged the cherished value of objectivity, which is held at all three levels of analysis, but that he revealed just how limited that notion is from the perspective of multiculturalism, and that is why the reaction is so virulent.

Lorna Roth, Beverly Nelson, and Kasennahawi Marie David (Chapter 3) explore the intervention of three differently situated women in a moment of geographic and cultural struggle. Here we encounter a basic production issue—namely who will speak for whom. In this case, the news value of the confrontation between a First Nation community and the Canadian government lures the attention of national and international news agencies. The only ones present at the site, however, are two women and their outside contact, another woman. This chapter highlights the agenda-setting role of the media, and the battle over the terms that will be used to refer to the confrontation and the people who will be allowed to cover the confrontation. Clearly, these three women make a difference as individual producers of media. They do so partly because of their own tenacity and endurance but also, due to their access to a more or less independent community radio station, at the organizational level of analysis. Finally, at the institutional level of analysis, the cultural clash was multiple, involving not just two communities with different norms and values, but gender issues as well. Though gender issues were different in the Mohawk and Québequois communities, they nevertheless existed in both. One could also see the similarity in terms of women's socialized roles that teach us to value community and oral communication, both of which were central to the continued operation of the radio station. As an intervention, these women showed that in times of crisis, the struggle over meaning and production presents barriers and opportunities.

In Chapter 4, Marina Heung discusses the intervention of Asian American female filmmakers. While Asian chic appeared to be the rage, especially after *The Joy Luck Club,* Heung finds that Hollywood film still draws on time-worn stereotypes for Asians in general and Asian women in particular. She then explores mostly independent films made by Asian American women. Again, as in the previous chapter, what appears to make the difference is the combination of individual intervention outside of an organizational structure that limits or predefines the possibilities for a particular multicultural group, in this case feminist Asian American filmmakers. The filmmakers use narrative and stylistic innovations to represent themselves. Under these conditions, filmmakers can challenge and possibly alter or modify organizational practices (e.g., what constitutes a good shot) as well as long-held values and norms at the institutional level (e.g., do multiculturalist subjects make worthwhile cinema). The change can be aimed at Hollywood film in particular and media production in general. The task is all the more onerous, given the long history of global influence enjoyed by Hollywood film, an influence that extends to our very imagination, and, as Heung notes, to the imagination of both Asian American film scholars and film producers.

Finally, Carolyn M. Byerly (Chapter 5) provides a study of the Women's Feature Service (WFS). Whereas the previous two chapters focused on bottom-up interventions, this chapter analyzes the top-down style of the United Nations, an organization that has attempted or contributed to many such undertakings with varying degrees of success. Although the United Nations possesses resources unavailable to the independent producers in the previous two chapters, the incipient news organizations nevertheless encounter resistance from mainstream individuals and organizations because of the WFS's challenge of cherished institutional norms and values. Expanding the news to include women challenges the basic premise of news as the arena of public, mostly male, events. Expanding the focus beyond Western parameters to developing countries pushes the boundaries even further. As such, the WFS intervention goes beyond creating an alternative news agency for and by women by challenging the current definition of news. It is not surprising then, that even with the support of the United Nations, some of the agencies did not become self-supporting organizations and therefore did not survive. On the other hand, as WFS headquarters moves to India and continues to be run by Third-World women, it promises to be a long-lasting intervention. None of this, of course, would be possible without the commitment of individuals such as Anita Anand and the many other journalists who keep WFS going.

The five chapters in this first section give the reader a taste of the possibilities of interventions in the area of media production. Though apparently different, all chapters demonstrate the interrelatedness of the three levels of analysis. Although independent media production seems to offer more possibilities for challenge and creativity, major global organizations such as the United Nations also contribute to the challenges and challengers. It is hoped that these challenges will not remain at the margins, that at the institutional level the challenges will become the norm and feminist multicultural intervention will not be challenging by definition.

Reference

McQuail, C. (1987). *Mass communication theory: An introduction* (2nd ed.). London: Sage.

1 Feminist Media Studies in a Global Setting

Beyond Binary Contradictions and Into Multicultural Spectrums

ANGHARAD N. VALDIVIA

Multicultural feminist media research is quite a mouthful. In both practical and theoretical terms there is so much to consider, so much to discuss. This book strives to provide a map with some of the major signposts for this discussion. The map is neither static, two-dimensional, nor complete, for there is no monolithic vision for multicultural feminist media studies. As Jesús Martín Barbero (in Rowe & Schelling, 1991, p. 13)[1] has noted, this "map is nocturnal because the terrain has still to be made visible." The reader is encouraged to fill in the gaps and to see them as "instigations for future work" (p. 13). The gaps will be extensive, because we are just beginning to draw it. Conditions and locations that may have been ignored or considered unimportant will rise to new prominence, making this map a living document of our emerging knowledge about our multicultural identity and the media's role in it. Think of it as a living map, one with active volcanic eruptions, with no clear beginnings or ends. This book is a nocturnal map to some of the eruptions marked by media.

I want to acknowledge that *feminism* and *multiculturalism* are highly contested concepts. It is beyond the scope of this book to engage in the history, debate, and resolution of these terms. Rather, the book begins from an assumption that these are worthy areas of study and that the reader has a cursory background of the conversation surrounding these concepts. *Feminism* in this book is broadly understood as the theoretical study of women's oppression and the strategical and political ways that all of us, building on that theoretical and historical knowledge, can work to end that oppression. It should be a given or an understood component that we simultaneously mean the oppression of all women while acknowledging that there are differences among women. That has not been the case, however, so we have to engage in what is now known as *multicultural* studies, thus specifically naming and addressing the fact that ours is a multicultural situation. Needless to say, this step should not even be necessary in a truly multicultural situation, but it underscores the fact that tendencies in a dominant culture serve to obscure the multiculturalism that is present in nearly every setting. By *multiculturalism* we mean not just a spectrum of race, ethnicities, class, global regions, and sexual orientation but the different cultural settings that we encounter as we traverse through our lives. Thus one of the cultural settings that is relevant to this book would undoubtedly be the area of media production. Another is the area of media reception—how do we encounter media products and with whom? Yet another would be the production of knowledge about media studies. We encounter media and media studies in the family, within a diverse spectrum of formations, the street, our work, and our friends. The cultures in all of these are quite different.

Because the study of mass communications is central to the contemporary condition, it is not surprising that media studies research yields provocative answers or paths to the understanding and discussion of multicultural feminist issues. In fact, Betty Friedan's groundbreaking book, *The Feminine Mystique* (1963), privileged the mass media as an indicator and site of struggle over gender politics. Lessons about diversity and multiculturalism have not been easy to learn, however. In the more than three decades since Friedan's book was published, feminists have learned much about the pervasiveness of sexist patterns, the difficulty of changing these patterns, and the media's role in the establishment, continuity, and breaking of these patterns. To make matters more complex but infinitely more realistic, a major additional lesson learned by dominant culture feminist scholars, or one that, as Haraway (1987) notes, they "were forced kicking and screaming to notice" (p. 11), was that the term *women* applied to differently situated individuals. Women occupy a spectrum of identities as well as positions of power. Or as de Lauretis (1987) reminds us, the subject of feminism must be positioned in relation to social relations other than gender. Nevertheless, as Rakow (1992) notes, despite the many spaces opened up by a broad range of diversity focused groups, "feminist scholarship as a collective and public endeavor in the field has been by and about white women" (p. 4).

On the other hand, there is a growing amount of work on race and ethnic studies. Much like feminist work has focused largely on white women, ethnic and race studies have focused primarily on African Americans, and within that group the focus is usually on men. By omission, much of this work generalizes the race experience across genders. Recent readers include chapters addressing both race and gender (e.g., Friedman, 1991; Gonzales, Houston, & Chen, 1994), but these remain in the minority. To be sure, there are some commonalities about being an African American person as opposed to a Native American or Caucasian. However, we can also say that there are some commonalities to being women. Nevertheless these caveats do not obviate the need to study and understand some of the specific issues surrounding multicultural women and media studies. This book addresses such a need.

Recent work promises to expand the boundaries of previous scholarship, boundaries that have already been exploded by feminist multiculturalist scholars in many other disciplines (e.g., Moraga & Anzaldúa, 1981). The reader also should note that though Moraga and Anzaldúa's work dates back to 1981, multicultural feminist scholarship cited in this chapter is quite recent, most of it published in the past 3 years. Feminist work in communications has tended to simplify the multicultural experience. Although most authors begin their work by acknowledging that race, ethnicity, class, sexuality, age, and global issues intersect with the topic of gender and the media, the vast majority of books and articles available on this topic focus primarily on white, middle-class, heterosexual, Western women. For example, Pribram's (1988) elegant collection of women and film contains but two chapters on women of color, and both of these chapters are about African American women. Granted, one of the wonderful aspects of Pribram's book is that the two chapters do not present a unified approach to African American issues. In fact, the two authors differ extensively on strategies for and about black women and film. Many readers on women and the media (e.g., Creedon, 1989; Rush & Allen, 1989), however, either had the occasional chapter on and by African American women or did not discuss race (e.g., Baehr & Dyer, 1987; Brown, 1990). Rakow's 1992 collection stood alone as the sole example of a book that expanded the color spectrum beyond white and black. Recent anthologies (e.g., Gonzales et al., 1994) demonstrate greater sensitivity, if not a total focus on diversity issues. In addition, another notable exception is the work of Nakayama (1994) and Peñaloza and Nakayama (1993), which considers the intersection of more than one form of oppression, namely gender, race, and sexuality.

Another vector of oppression that remains largely unexplored is the issue of class. Press (1990, 1991) stands nearly alone in exploring issues of class in feminist media studies. Gregg (1992) also considers class issues when discussing workplace organizing. As contributors to this book note (see Paul & Kauffman, Chapter 8), class analysis is missing from both feminist discussions and media representations. We neither hear from nor about working-class women. Furthermore, as Cuklanz (Chapter 7 in this volume) suggests, when studying ethnic minorities one often finds that issues of class overlap with issues of race and gender. In fact, this is one of the major points of reference for multicultural scholars. Issues of class always overlap with issues of race and gender. It's only the power afforded by membership in dominant culture that allows some to pretend that none of these vectors are the stuff of everyday life or of media representation and production. As Shohat (1991a) comments about ethnicity and race, these issues are "culturally ubiquitous and textually submerged" (p. 215), present not just when they are on the "epidermic" surface of the text.

In addition, we must take into consideration a global perspective to bring gender and minority studies into the international communications debate. As teachers we need to explore with our students the tools for understanding how gender intersects with other forms of oppression in media production and consumption. Integrating issues of race, ethnicity, class, and global outlook into courses and research allows us all to name our multicultural identity. Issues that may appear to be local or national affect people throughout the world. Similarly, issues that may seem exotic or "other" affect our everyday lived experience. By exploring intersecting variables of oppression as they are articulated by mass media, we propose that issues of gender, race, class, sexual orientation, global origin, and ethnicity affect the coverage, portrayal, and media production of everyone.

Although there is a wealth of work on international media studies, little of it focuses on gender and race. Feminist scholars (Gallagher, 1981; Mahoney, 1991; Roach, 1991) have given us the outlines of some of the major issues facing women in/and international media studies. As they note, issues of access and representation remain paramount, whether these refer to old or new technologies. While the focus of international feminist media studies has remained largely on the macro level of analysis, it provides a fertile ground for international scholars who want to study issues of multicultural feminism and for feminist scholars who want to study global issues. Feminist readers are beginning to include global issues as a component of a multicultural focus. For example, Rush and Ogan (1989) included several contributions from around the world on local and global issues. Rakow (1992), as well, includes chapters on international case studies (Valdivia, 1992) and postcolonial theory (Ganguly, 1992). Previously, the extent of an international focus in feminist media studies was accomplished through the contributions of British scholars, who usually wrote about England (see Baehr & Dyer, 1987; Pribram, 1988). The connections between multicultural and international work were not usually highlighted. The expansion to other regions and other women enables the making of connections that will allow us to understand the prevalence and specificities about multicultural feminist studies.

Herein lies the crux of this book. The nocturnal map previously mentioned marks a spectrum of eruptions. Furthermore, these eruptions compose the lifeblood of this terrain. There is a range of possibilities as far as the beginning and the development of eruptions. Besides, eruptions influence each other. There are no clear binary situations, subjects, or histories. Multiculturalism is at once global and local. To paraphrase Anzaldúa (1990), there is a spectrum of possibilities that includes coalitions, collusions, and collisions. In fact, "it is only by understanding the *contradictions* inherent in women's location within various structures that effective political action and challenges can be devised" (Mohanty, 1991, p. 66). This is in large part the multiculturalist project. In this process, media and cultural products are often the vehicle if not the tool for bridges, drawbridges, sandbars, or islands of power (see Anzaldúa, 1990). All contributors to this volume explore the media's response to the contradictions that multicultural subjects—that is, all of us—face as consumers and/or producers of media.

From Binary Contradictions
to Multicultural Spectrums

Though issues of diversity, multiculturalism, and feminism are neither mutually exclusive nor equivalent and interchangeable, they continue to be treated mostly in two possible ways. The first way is denial.[2] These issues are marginalized for they extend, push, and explode familiar binary oppositions. They interfere with a preset order. They represent disorder. It's just too difficult to consider a range of options. Not that these options are foreign to most of us, especially those of us who experience contradictions daily (see Molina, Chapter 2 in this volume), but somehow we have managed either to walk around eruptions or to pretend they are not happening. While for some of us it's a little more difficult to ignore these eruptions, this should not obscure the fact that we all encounter them throughout our lives. Denial eventually has to be faced. If, however, diversity, multiculturalism, and feminism are not marginalized, a second "natural" option is to fit these issues into binary oppositions. Thus we have issues set in "black or white" frameworks. We have rich or poor, male or female, masculine or feminine, gay or straight, rational or irrational, local or global, nature or culture, multicultural or monocultural. In this process, issues of diversity are fitted into a preexisting framework of analysis foregrounded by binary oppositions.

Of course, the above two options are but two of many possibilities for the discussion of multicultural feminist issues. Neither technology nor cultural forms predetermine the relative openness or closure of the mass media. The same technology that is used for transmission of news by CBS can be used by revolutionaries in the mountains of Nicaragua, El Salvador, or Guatemala, by miners in Bolivia, by feminists in Chile, and by disenchanted teenagers in suburban landscapes, wherever these may be.[3] Likewise, the same *fotonovela* that can carry imperialist and gendered messages can be used by the agricultural workers' union to express the concept of quotas during the Sandinista revolution and by the Immigration and Naturalization Service (INS) of the United States to dissuade border crossers. The possibilities for both technologies and cultural forms are great, though not infinite. Nevertheless, there is a range of possibilities that may be difficult to predict, map, and study but no less important because of the perceived difficulty. As Colin MacCabe (1987) asserts, "Difficulty is . . . an ideological notion. . . . Within our ascriptions of difficulty lie subterranean and complex evaluations" (p. ix). Thus to consider a range of possibilities may appear difficult because we are used to binary oppositions, but by labeling something as difficult we engage in ideological marginalization. On the other hand, if we look carefully at marginality we face "a suspicion that what is at the center often hides repression" (Spivak, 1987, p. 104). That suspicion largely fuels feminism. De Lauretis (1987) argues that feminism enables us to begin articulating that which masculinist modes of articulation almost preclude, voicing the representation of discursive possibilities beyond the status quo. Undoubtedly, precisely because the status quo makes it easier to articulate some visions and not others, we must expand the terrain of articulation. The contributors to this book honor suspicion and consider the repressed stories, subjects, and histories, whether these be textual or organizational, hiding behind a variety of *simple* cultural forms.

Once we move onto a framework of analysis that includes spectrums and continuums, contradictions fade away. Contradictions occur when one attempts to analyze multiplicity within linear, binary frameworks. Thus a central component of multicultural studies is the exploration of contradictions through spectrums. This is very difficult in a culture so heavily influenced by binary oppositions. The dualities that form the core of much of our intellectual and commonsense thought prevent us from thinking in terms of spectrums. Dichotomization of the world makes it difficult to study race, class, and gender; sexual orientation; and postcolonial issues of oppression. Seldom are multicultural issues clear cut, though this does not prevent much of media coverage and academic analysis from suggesting such simplicity.

As Spivak (1987, p. 144) maintains, undermining the binary opposition of public and private spheres underlies the very basis of all feminist activity. This, however, is not the only binary opposition to be undermined. Feminism problematizes the binary division of genders. Multiculturalism is about the rejection of binary oppositions of high and low culture as well as white and black culture, both of which complement the public and private one so central to liberal philosophy. Dating back at least to Friedan's book in 1963, feminist media scholars have rejected the division between personal and political issues, suggesting that we need to study both individual and institutional forms of oppression as well as public and private issues. This remains a central component of feminist scholarship and activism, one that remains contemporary and crucial to multicultural work, as recent ethnographic and testimonial literature will attest. In addition, the tendency within an intellectual system of binary oppositions is to set all oppositions as equivalent. Thus the private sphere is gendered, and the public sphere is racialized. The contributors to this book explore the additive process of dividing the world into two categories and the inadequacies of that process.

A discussion of the deconstruction of binary oppositions would be incomplete without some cursory comments about liberal philosophy. For liberalism simultaneously highlights the role of the press and by extension all other modern mass media, as well as overemphasizes the importance of individual agency. Individuals are theorized to communicate through the press, and the role of the press and mass media is positioned in the public sphere. Thus one binary opposition piggybacks on another. Individual workers in the mass media document the public experiences of individuals. Personal or domestic experience as a domain, should, within this formulation, fall outside the scope of the mass media. As well, institutional analysis becomes nearly irrelevant when the individual is assumed to be the sole agent of society. In a sense the liberal media reflect this perceived irrelevance by focusing on individuals and seldom scrutinizing institutions (see Bagdikian, 1990; Herman & Chomsky, 1988). It must be noted, however, that critical scholars, although acutely aware of class issues, are nearly blind to issues of gender and race. Thus even though Herman and Chomsky (1988) present an elegant propaganda framework that highlights the avoidance of class as an issue within a capitalist system, they do not mention gender and race, which should really be their sixth filter at the institutional level of analysis.

As all of the authors in this volume suggest, individuals have agency, but they also operate within ideological formations and organizations with long histories and traditions. From a pedagogical perspective, this is a difficult lesson to share with our students. Not that agency is irrelevant, and none of the authors in this volume suggest so, but all agree that individual agency needs to be channeled toward systemic change and studied within a context of limits and possibilities. As McCarthy (1993) explains, if we focus solely on individuals' attitudes, we falsely assume "that negative white attitudes towards minorities will change if these prejudiced individuals are exposed to sensitivity training in human studies relations and ethnic studies programs" (p. 292). Institutional and organizational change at both national and global levels (see McQuail, 1994) involves more than attitudinal reforms. Yes, being nice and inclusive is important, but that is not enough. The case studies in this book explore some of the limits and possibilities of individual agency vis-à-vis institutional explorations.

Contributors to this volume present us with several interventions that question the usefulness of private/public and individual/social binary oppositions. Gaunt (Chapter 13 in this volume) reminds us that African American girls' play was dismissed because it occurred in the private sphere. Furthermore, as women enter the gendered world of rap music and bring domestic or personal concerns into their lyrics, they disrupt and reformulate the possibilities of rap as a narrative. Still, they operate within a prescribed set of morals, not being able, for example, to explore issues and possibilities of sexual freedom without fear of being labeled as whores. The sexual double standard still reigns across class and racial lines. Female rappers have entered the public sphere, yet they encounter preconceived notions that cannot be ignored. A similar process has already occurred to a certain extent within the Western press, wherein the women's movement has achieved a degree of success in disrupting that division of private and public spheres. Issues such as child and spousal abuse, rape, and reproductive rights are now discussed in the press as public issues. Luthra (Chapter 10 in this volume) presents a classic example of previously private issues about reproduction being discussed in the public world of the press. Here, however, we must temper optimism with the fact that U.S. media has a history of willingness to treat issues of sex and sexuality of postcolonial women when fearing to tread in similar discussions about U.S. women (e.g., Shohat, 1991b). Furthermore, part of the silence that postcolonial women are forced to occupy stems, at least partly, from the Western press's inability to envision such women as speaking subjects on public issues. Finally, Paul and Kauffman (Chapter 8 in this volume) document the representation of many working-class women as individual and private. This strategy serves the function of depoliticizing class issues, a necessary move from the perspective of a capitalist media system (Herman & Chomsky, 1988). Given that the private/public binary opposition is functional in our current political and social system, feminist multiculturalist studies are inherently revolutionary for they begin from the rejection of such a binary system.

Binary oppositions abound in all of Western intellectual work. In particular, one of the most important binary oppositions is that of separating the world into traditional and modern spheres (Lerner, 1958; Rostow, 1964; Schramm, 1964). In the work of these germinal scholars, the Third World embodies tradition whereas the Western industrialized nations, especially Great Britain and the United States, embody modernity. In this volume, both

Luthra and Byerly (Chapters 10 and 5, respectively, in this volume) explore the contradictions that women face through the modern media, either as producers or as represented subjects. Here we encounter another set of binary oppositions that piggybacks on the previous ones—for the mass media embody modernity, whereas women embody tradition. Thus it appears that when the framework of modern media encounters traditional women, we get a nearly inevitable underrepresentation or absence at the level of artifact because conceptually women are precluded from modernity. In this vein, Frith (Chapter 9 in this volume) explores some of the basic concepts as they are represented in binary descriptions of nature. In this type of media we encounter a collapse of the major binary categories: Nature and tradition are gendered feminine and ripe for the advance of masculine modern culture. Finally, that label of "traditional" is used in the Cuklanz case study when referring to Luso Americans' views about rape. Given that tradition is gendered feminine, one way of devaluing ethnic communities' values is by labeling them traditional and thus robbing them of much of their legitimacy and credibility.

Identity Issues and Media Possibilities

Another fertile area of feminist multicultural studies is the exploration of identity. Although some scholars define *identity politics* as "discourses and movements organized around questions of religious, ethnic and national identity" (Moghadam, 1994, p. 3), central to this book is the notion that we all have multicultural identities, but some of us have to mark our components as "difference" while others mark theirs as "normal." Simply put, some women's identity puts them/us closer to dominant culture than others'. This, in turn, means that some women are more likely to be close to or to gain from strategies to make them closer to avenues of power despite the fact that in a patriarchal system, all women are oppressed vis-à-vis their male counterparts because of their gender. Strategies using the mass media have benefited some women but not others. Multicultural feminist strategies seek to achieve gains for women within a broad spectrum of identities.

Of course, identity is not something that one entirely chooses. Here again we encounter the liberal notion of individual self-determination and the need to consider organizational practices and institutional norms that circumscribe the freedom of individuals. Certain aspects of identity formation, as some postmodern scholars and particular theorists of sexual orientation suggest, might be a matter of choice. Over other aspects, however, we have little control. Among these are class, race, ethnicity, physical ability, age, and global origin. Although educational opportunities, travel, and contemporary technology may allow some to change or alter our class, race, ethnicity, and gender, for most these variables are fixed. The closer these components of identity situate us to the mainstream, the closer to power we are *and* the more we can delude ourselves that our identity is unitary—that is, we do not identify ourselves as multicultural subjects. For example, a young, white, middle-class, heterosexual, physically able Western woman might[4] feel oppressed only by gender whereas a poor, Third World, lesbian woman of color could experience oppression from a number of fronts, most of which are unidentifiable at any given moment, thereby making it difficult for her to address her oppression. The former can identify her oppression as one of gender. The latter can't narrow it down to gender, or to any individual factor for that matter, and has to follow a multipronged analysis of and strategy to end that oppression. A multipronged analysis in a culture replete with binary explanatory frameworks is contradictory, as anyone involved in that experience will tell you. Who to identify with—gender or race peers? What if identification on the basis of gender antagonizes one's race community? What if solidarity with one's socioeconomic class sets one apart from one's occupational goals? How to carry all of these considerations as one experiences media or as one produces it? Identity politics can have a tyranny of their own if not conceptualized within a framework of spectrums.

To begin with issues of identity as they are influenced by race and ethnicity, a black or white approach effaces all that falls between and beyond these two markers. For example, what about Latinas? This is not as easy as saying, "Well, that would be brown," for Latinas come in all different colors. Some of us are Caucasian and this is sometimes, though not always, related to upper-class standing. Some of us are of African descent. Still others, most of us, have some combination of indigenous roots, whether they be Mapuche, Araucanian, Incan, Mayan, Quiche, or others. Nearly all of us are *mestizas*—that is, we can trace our racial and ethnic heritage to two or more groups. Among the languages we natively speak are Spanish, Aymara, Quiche, English, Portuguese, and French. When speaking English, as most of us have to do when living and working in the United States or aspiring to take part in a global academic discourse, some of us have an accent that is labeled as "Latino," others speak with a British or French intonation, and I am told that I am either Italian or Yugoslavian! Along another vector of oppression, Lorde (1991) discusses the uneasy reception among Latino publishing houses to lesbian Latinas, as if this would somehow disrupt or soil some mythical type of Latina-ness they seek to preserve. A black or white approach to the study of ethnic identity would miss Latinas altogether, not to mention the rich variety of Latinas, some of which I've mentioned above. A multicultural perspective would include Latinas in the study of women of color *plus* would also consider the spectrum of Latina-ness. Indeed, a multicultural perspective includes Latinas in the study of women just as it problematizes the study of whiteness as anything but natural.

Kray (Chapter 11 in this volume) urges us to consider the issue of "whiteness," for it can serve to hide minorities that are not visible to the eye. Just as not all Latinas are brown, not all white women are Christian. Yet given the undeniably high level of participation of Jewish men in media industries, how do we account for the nearly virtual exclusion of Jewish female representations? How do we study an ethnicity that is not visible but nevertheless quite present? How does the media, in this case U.S. mainstream television, portray Jewish women? What does their exclusion say about their male counterparts?

As Negrón-Muntaner (Chapter 12 in this volume) warns us, however, we don't mean to "imply, as identity disclosures often attempt to suggest, that if there were more images, writings, and institutions created by _____ for _____" we would not turn to another group's practices. Feminist multicultural studies do not suggest a frozen type of identity, as if, as Negrón-Muntaner continues, having already conquered one's own terrain, one could recognize the locations and possibilities as one's own. Feminist multicultural interventions depend on contacts with others in ways that "may invoke practices and discourses of solidarity and community in a larger social context." Thus the urgency of studying Latinas, to use the above mentioned example, is not only for Latinas to have access to interpellation possibilities with media texts, but also for a particular set of voices to be included in the struggle and contestation over culture, a set of voices that will enrich our understanding of ourselves and others.

Thus far we have two major aspects of a multicultural strategy: the relations of identity to power and the spectrum approach. A third component is the fluidity of identity, one's relation to power and spectrums. Clearly one's identity changes as one becomes more or less powerful. Part of the logic behind Negrón-Muntaner's previously mentioned argument is that even in the presence of Latina images, many of us would not necessarily recognize ourselves, for our identity depends on so much more than race or ethnicity, and it is not fixed in either time or space. A recent theme of discussion is that most women are one man away from lack of health coverage. One's position on proposed health care reforms is largely influenced by how much health care one has and who is paying for it. In this discussion, vectors of gender, race, class, age, and sexual orientation are paramount. Power enables one to challenge and possibly overcome oppression at both individual and institutional levels or to take it for granted and pretend it's not there. Conversely, as one travels downward on the socioeconomic ladder, a trip many have taken in a period of growing inflation and unemployment as well as corporate retrenchment, one experiences a loss of power and the acknowledgment of a new identity. One's awareness of one's changing power affects one's identity.

Identity and the perception of oppression change with our access to power. Yolanda in *How the Garcia Girls Lost Their Accent* provides a perfect example of this postmodern subjectivity. In the Dominican Republic she is a member of one of the country's elite families, yet she is also a girl destined to marry and become a society housewife. In the United States she is simultaneously another "Hispanic" to her neighbors and an exotic Latina to her gringo boyfriend, yet she forges a more independent gender path of higher education and sexual freedom. Her identity changes as she travels between her country and the different spaces she occupies in the United States. Our global or geographical location influences our ethnic and gender identity. Moving from one community to another—especially, but not necessarily, if these are in different countries and/or hemispheres—changes our identity, because the definitions of who we are, mostly by others, shift. Thus a Latina can go from being white in Chile to being brown in Pennsylvania to being "Italian" in Southern California, though her skin color remains the same. An Indian woman can go from being Black in Britain to being Asian in New Jersey. Conversely, an African American woman can tour England with two South African women who hate "Negroes" yet do not recognize her as such.[5]

Spectrums change not just in space but also in time. Thus what was once considered "Indian" in Central America is now considered "Nicaraguan." We can also use particular components of race and ethnicity. Full lips, which were once considered and used to depict a stereotype of African Americans, are the height of high fashion and beauty—with models and others paying nearly $500 every 6 weeks for the painful lip enlarging operation. Though most of us may not be able to afford this type of surgery, we cannot avoid being faced, throughout our encounters with the mass media, with the results of that new component of the ideal of beauty. Moritz (Chapter 6 in this volume) traces the discourse of *lesbian chic* to the media's attempt not only to "deny lesbians a real voice in the culture but also to construct them in the same sexualized and sexist ways that women in general have been formulated." This includes a focus on appearance and beauty. All of a sudden lesbians are *chic,* but just as quickly lesbians can disappear from mainstream cultural representation. The changing spectrums of whiteness and beauty speak to the relational aspect of multiculturalism (see Shohat, 1991a). Race, ethnicity, gender, and class cannot make sense without comparison to other races, ethnicities, genders, and classes. Multiculturalist research seeks to understand the relational aspect of oppression at specific times and spaces. A basic assumption is that these relational aspects change. One major area of research becomes understanding that change so that we might possibly use that knowledge to end contemporary forms of oppression. Of course, the media figure prominently as a component of a strategy to end oppression and recognize the multicultural identity of individuals and society at large. Just as our identities change, media products can have different meanings for different people in different situations. As well, portraying changing identities presents a challenge to media producers. Consideration of multicultural issues could be easier with input from people with explicitly multiculturalist identities.[6]

Production! Not Just Consumption

As well, another theme in this volume, and one that has already been repeatedly mentioned, is the need to focus on consumption *and* production. Political economic approaches are too often missing from multicultural studies. On the one hand, we could take care of political economy quite briefly— namely, we could note that women and minorities have little ownership and control of mainstream media production. That, however, would be both true and overly simplistic. Some women have achieved a degree of input and control in today's media environment. Oprah Winfrey and Roseanne Barr come to mind. Also, we should not lapse into essentialist arguments that assume women would make a feminist difference and men would be antifeminist. There are many women in decision-making positions in media who are not particularly sensitive to gender issues. In fact, some of them have been promoted to those positions *precisely* because they have demonstrated their adherence to organizational practices and institutional norms that are not sensitive to issues of gender or race.

On a representational level, there is the tendency to have people of color represent caricatured stereotypes. For example, Rosie Perez cannot seem to get away from playing the tacky, overly emotional Latina in such movies as *White Men Can't Jump* and *It Could Happen to You*. It remains to be seen whether she is cast into these roles or whether she chooses to exploit that stereotype. To make matters more complex, this isn't a simple issue of individual choice, either on the director's or the actress's part. Quite often the choice is premade in terms, for example, of portrayal, or in terms of the range that a Latina can portray, so that deciding on a multiculturalist strategy might very well mean unemployment for the actress and/or the director. The double bind facing people in such a situation is to shut up and put up or to speak out and lose one's job—not much of a choice.

Conversely, and still trying to distance ourselves from essentialist arguments, a few men have tried to expand the stereotypes and limitations of gender portrayals within mainstream representations. Clearly one of the goals of feminist multiculturalism would be to get to the point where media producers possess a sensitivity to issues of diversity in media production. This, however, returns us to a whole other set of issues—namely, the need to expand the base of access to production. As Margaret Spillane suggests (in Moore, 1992) though many are asking questions about the relative merits of government funding a particular project or other, not many are asking more fundamental questions about "who gets to produce art to begin with?" Other relevant questions include "who gets to make art, become an artist, envision themselves as an artist, tell their story through art?" Once we replace the word *art* with *mass media,* we can appreciate the relevance of such an argument. For if we don't consider issues of basic access, the argument could become, "let the usual people do the diversity thing." One example that immediately comes to mind is Steven Spielberg. He has done the topic of African American women in *The Color Purple* and the holocaust in *Schindler's List*. Although neither of those efforts is unproblematic, it would not be unrealistic to expect that Spielberg could do a movie about lesbian Latinas and another about working-class Asian Americans, to choose a couple of random possibilities. Spielberg's successful mainstream Hollywood films differ drastically, however, from many of the examples given to us by Heung (Chapter 4 in this volume). We are not talking about silencing Spielberg, but rather about opening a space for other interventions. To argue otherwise would be the media equivalent of the political correctness debate wherein multicultural groups' attempt for inclusion in the curriculum are treated as if they were attempts to do away with the canon. We are proposing the expansion of themes, voices, and perspectives—an expansion rather than a rejection of the canon.

Studying reception and interpretation issues is of crucial importance, but we need to situate these studies within concrete historical and material contexts. Issues of access, both of media producers and media subjects, are essential to multiculturalist studies. Accordingly, we must study the interventions made by oppressed groups and individuals in the production process. What are the possibilities and limitations of certain types of interventions? What are some alternative funding sources? In a situation of inherent contradictions, what are some of the compromises and challenges that can and have been made by multicultural subjects? Who counts as a source and when? How are the validity, legitimacy, and credibility of sources influenced by contradictions in people's multiple identities? How does the media deal with such shifting identities and perceptions? Can movies, TV shows, music videos, popular music, and news represent identity spectrums? It is undoubtedly much easier to fall back on predictable and stereotypical binary oppositions. This, however, leads to inevitable eruptions in an age when multicultural subjects are no longer willing to be ignored or blatantly misrepresented.

Interventions

Although the contributors to this book do not tackle all issues of oppression at once, there are some overlaps among the chapters. We have tried to provide a diversity of contributions in as many aspects as possible. For example, we have tried to provide a spectrum of racial and ethnic analyses. Thus we have Latina (Molina; Negrón-Muntaner), Asian American (Heung), African American (Gaunt; Negrón-Muntaner), Native American/First Nation (Roth, Nelson, & David), Jewish American (Kray), and Portuguese (Luso) American (Cuklanz). We also have chapters on global aspects, notably Luthra on postcolonial region women in whose name the population control debate is carried; and Byerly on the establishment of an alternative news agency for women. Paul and Kauffman focus primarily on the issue of class. Moreover, both Luthra and Cuklanz also find that class is inextricably a part of the global population debate and the rape case in Massachusetts. As well, issues of sexual orientation are foregrounded in Moritz's chapter on lesbian chic and in

Negrón-Muntaner's chapter on the appropriation of cultural texts by oppressed groups. We admittedly lack chapters focusing on age and on ability, but this omission is not meant to suggest that these issues are not important. On the contrary, we hope that scholarship to fill these blank spots on our nocturnal map is forthcoming.

In terms of media, we also tried to include as broad a range as possible. Analyses of news (Luthra; Cuklanz; Byerly; Molina; Moritz), advertising (Frith); film (Heung; Paul & Kauffman); television (Kray; Moritz); music (Gaunt); video (Negrón-Muntaner); community radio (Roth, Nelson, & David); and the academy (Molina) show that multicultural feminist studies can inform us about each and every medium. Again, there are more media that we may have missed, but we gladly admit that the spectrum needs to be explored.

In addition, many of the authors also focus on issues of access and production. For example, Byerly explores the possibility of alternative yet parallel news agencies run by and for women. Similarly, Heung considers the difference in content as a result of production by Asian American women. Gaunt urges us to re-vision the role of African American women who produce rap music in particular and the ways in which oppressed women produce culture in general. Roth, Nelson, and David (Chapter 3 in this volume) elucidate the conditions in which two First Nation women found themselves as the sole transmitters of information in a situation of conflict. Access to production and control is a major component of a feminist multicultural strategy. The authors in this volume, by presenting case studies of moments of intervention, provide us with some of the issues to be considered.

We also have diversity in terms of methodological approach. Most of the contributors choose some form of textual analysis. As Reinharz (1992) acknowledges, "contemporary feminist scholars of cultural texts are likely to see meaning as mediated, and therefore examine both the text and the processes of its production" (p. 145). For example, Luthra analyzes international news and the U.S. *Congressional Record*. Negrón-Muntaner explores the intertextuality between a novel and a film. Heung focuses mainly on film, both Hollywood and alternative. Cuklanz focuses on local news coverage of a bar rape case. Frith analyzes a collection of ads for themes about the nature/culture of binary opposition. Units of analysis range from that of news, magazine, television, or musical text or lyrics, to photographs and text of an ad, to that of musical instruments and background grooves. While not all of the above authors choose the same approach for textual analysis, for here as well there is a spectrum of possibilities, they all find media content a useful indicator of the volcanic eruptions generated by feminist multicultural issues.

True to the spectrum focus of the entire book, most authors analyze a variety of media using a combination of methodologies. For example, Gaunt examines different types of narratives—ranging from street verse to rap to original poetry to classic poetry—to weave a chapter about women in rap. In addition, she combines textual analysis with discussions about spectatorship and fandom (what is more commonly known as *audience* research in media studies) and a little bit about production. Molina combines an individual framework of analysis based on identity politics with a case study of the Chino Wilson case, which involves both textual analysis and cultural reception work. In fact, though this volume is not a cultural studies reader per se, multicultural research embodies the diversity in methodology approach so common to that body of work. It is as if when speaking of the intersection of race, gender, class, and sexual orientation, one single method or focus is just not enough. Linear approaches are inadequate to the task of analyzing multiple and multiplying positions.

Accordingly, these chapters highlight the issue of multivocality (Roth, Nelson, & David use the term *polyvocality*) in the sense that more so than a dialogue, which implies response and integration, we listen to parallel voices so that we can integrate ourselves, putting ourselves in the active role of integrators rather than in the more passive role of readers of an integrated narrative. Multivocality is one of the responses to the immense debate of who shall speak for whom. Democratic access to the production and circulation of knowledge is one of the ways to ensure multivocality. Another is usage of an expansive variety of materials and narratives. Furthermore, Gaunt and Roth, Nelson, and David present unparaphrased narratives, providing us with the raw material for us to formulate our vision of the events and issues.

One of the many types of media is books, and thus this effort qualifies as an intervention. I began to put this book together as a result of teaching a course entitled "Women, Minorities and the Media" at The Pennsylvania State University. When I first was assigned this course there were no books that approached the issues of gender, diversity, and media in an integrated manner. So far there is still no such book, although this book attempts to provide a number of useful case studies for such a class. I am aware that many other universities have such a course or are in the process of instituting such a course and am often in touch with other students and instructors about possible readings and other curricular materials. This collection aims to make a variety of readings and voices available so that the reader can make connections across diversity issues. Normatively we should hope that as our curriculum and our media include issues of diversity at an integral level, there will be no need for books such as this one. At this point, however, we need to focus on issues of diversity, ways of noticing them, and ways of studying them so that we can formulate an informed strategy to include them in our overall approaches to education, media production, and public policy.

Having decided to produce this book, to do it in a multivocal manner, and to have it cover a broad range of topics, other issues surfaced. It is more difficult to engage in a multivocal project because technological, economic, and professional practices that sustain a linear order work against a spectrum approach. First, though the utopian potential of new technologies should allow us to produce an ever-increasing variety of texts and formats, few of us are trained to do so. At most, we all know one or two word processing programs. Fewer of us are acquainted with graphics or statistical packages. In reference to Roth, Nelson, and David's chapter, the formatting of the text in three columns presented us with many obstacles. Neither Lorna nor I used the same software, and transferring from one to another required specialized advice so that we could transfer these files between systems.

Second, from an economic perspective, publishers and recording companies make it difficult for scholars, or anybody trying to engage in popular culture criticism, to quote or reproduce material without paying copyright fees—which can present formidable barriers to publishing. Through the legal stratagem of intellectual property, publishers, recording companies, and any other major institutions that hold the rights to media content, charge for the use of material. This was particularly relevant to Gaunt's and Frith's chapters. Seeking permission to quote or reproduce previously circulated material, for educational purposes, can present substantial barriers to publishing. Quite often one feels like deleting or omitting a special quote or image rather than continuing with the process of gaining copyright clearance. What usually happens is that one reverts to a more conventional academic style, integrating and paraphrasing, thereby once more not doing multivocality.

Third, from a professional standpoint all sorts of conventions and traditions mitigate against the possibility of multivocality. For example, multivocal narrative, whether it be three columns (Roth, Nelson, & David) or a mixture of personal narrative, poems, and song lyrics (Gaunt) just doesn't fit APA

(American Psychological Association) format. How does one represent a multivocal narrative, one that draws from music, video, and different types of written narratives, in the reductionist form of academic prose? Furthermore, and in terms of professional survival, will such an effort count in one's professional career? That is, will multivocal narratives pass the test of legitimacy in a promotion and tenure process?

A related set of issues is the tendency toward tokenism and canonization. No doubt there are many scholars engaged in the task of feminist multiculturalist research. In the field, however, is the tendency to think of that one particular person who does feminism; that other one who does African American women; that other one who explores lesbian issues, and so on. Although it is certainly a step in the right direction to have these particular scholars in mind, the tokenization smacks of enlightened racism. The underlying assumption behind that seemingly liberal approach is that all we need is that one particular person to speak for the whole range of issues affecting that particular group. This is the homogenizing approach to diversity. It assumes that dominant culture is rich enough to have many different scholars using a variety of different approaches but that just one person can speak for an entire community of oppressed people. Furthermore, this process restricts the diversity of academic voices, those who can participate in the intellectual feminist multiculturalist conversation, debate, and struggle.

Finally, finding the contributors to this volume was a pleasurable task. It was mostly through a diasporic network that these authors came together here. Artificial divisions in the field of media studies keep many of us from learning about each other's work. For example, film scholars usually publish and present papers in different venues than do feminists focusing on news or television issues. As Shohat (1991a, 1991b) suggests, however, the narrative conventions are really not much different in film than they are in mainstream news. The culture of gender and empire abounds in both. Nevertheless, when approached some film scholars did not understand why they were being asked to participate in a media studies project. Similarly, status divisions get in the way of a full exchange of information. The contributors to this book range from undergraduate students to senior scholars. One of the components of the multiculturalist project is creating a space for participatory democracy. Furthermore, given the relative newness of this area of studies, the bulk of the work is being done by students as they come through the higher education establishment. This may well be the first generation of scholars who had access to multiculturalist classes and other curricular materials in the form of textbooks and readers at the undergraduate and graduate levels.

Conclusion

I began this introduction with the metaphor of the nocturnal map. As readers explore the different sections and chapters in this book, we hope that they will come up with new ways of looking at media studies issues. Expanding our framework of analysis from binary oppositions to spectrums enables us to look behind apparent contradictions and into situations that speak to the complexity of our experiences and the media's role in those experiences. In the spirit of filling out the nocturnal map, we hope that the gaps will inspire readers to engage in the conversation as active contributors. We also hope that the exploration of the intersecting vectors of gender, race, ethnicity, class, and sexual orientation will lead to a media practice that is much more inclusive than the present one. Most important, readers are not only encouraged to join the conversation about media but to join in the production of mass media. For, given the diversity of our culture and the incredible technological resources available to us, there is really no reason why we should not try to produce media that speaks to the richness of our experiences.

Notes

1. Though Jesús Martín Barbero writes about the study of Latin American popular culture, a very similar statement can be made about feminist multiculturalist media studies.

2. See Creedon (1993) for an elegant discussion of denial at the individual and institutional levels of analysis.

3. I acknowledge that because of a different level of resources, CBS will have at its disposal personnel, technology, and other capital that far surpasses that of all of the other groups mentioned in this example. I am, however, referring to the basic technology of radio, which with basic materials enables one to transmit and receive over-the-air information.

4. I use the word *might* because there are a number of possibilities, even within this construction. First, this woman might be one of the lucky ones who is reaping the benefits of affirmative action policies and has, for example, broken through the glass ceiling. Second, this woman might be at an age when she has yet to experience oppression, given her privileged class and race status. She has yet to hit the glass ceiling or encounter sexual harassment. Third, this woman has internalized oppression—that is, blamed herself for failures that are beyond her control—and will not identify herself as being oppressed. These are some of the possibilities.

5. All of these examples are based on experiences of my own and those of some friends.

6. This is a rather awkward way of acknowledging that we are all multicultural subjects. Yet some of us know this explicitly while others, by virtue of their proximity to dominant culture, see multiculturalism as something that applies only to others.

References

Anzaldúa, G. (1990). Bridge, drawbridge, sandbar, or island lesbians-of-color: Hacienda Alianzas. In L. Albrecht & R. M. Brewer (Eds.), *Bridges of power: Women's multicultural alliances* (pp. 216-231). Philadelphia: New Society Publishers.

Bagdikian, B. (1990). *The media monopoly.* Boston: Beacon.

Baehr, H., & Dyer, G. (Eds.). (1987). *Boxed in: Women and television.* London: Pandora.

Brown, M. E. (Ed.). (1990). *Television and women's culture: The politics of the popular.* London: Sage.

Creedon, P. (1989). (Ed.). *Women in mass communication: Challenging gender values.* Newbury Park, CA: Sage.

de Lauretis, T. (1987). *Technologies of gender: Essays on theory, film, and fiction.* London: Macmillan.

Friedan, B. (1963). *The feminine mystique.* New York: Dell.

Friedman, L. D. (Ed.). (1991). *Unspeakable images: Ethnicity and the American cinema.* Urbana: University of Illinois Press.

Gallagher, M. (1981). *Unequal opportunities: The case of women and the media.* Paris: UNESCO.

Ganguly, K. (1992). Accounting for others: Feminism and representation. In L. F. Rakow (Ed.), *Women making meaning* (pp. 60-82). New York: Routledge.

Gonzales, A., Houston, M., & Chen, V. (1994). *Our voices: Essays in culture, ethnicity, and communication.* Los Angeles: Roxbury Publishing Group.

Gregg, N. (1992). Telling stories about reality: Women's responses to a workplace organizing campaign. In L. F. Rakow (Ed.), *Women making meaning* (pp. 263-288). New York: Routledge.

Haraway, D. (1985). A manifesto for cyborgs: Science, technology, and socialist feminism in the 1980s. *Socialist Review, 80*(2), 65-108.

Herman, E., & Chomsky, N. (1988). *Manufacturing consent: The political economy of the mass media.* New York: Pantheon.

Lerner, D. (1958). *The passing of traditional society.* New York: Free Press.

Lorde, A. (1990, August 1). What is at stake in lesbian & gay publishing today?—1990 Bill Whitehead lecture. *Lambda Book Report,* pp. 11-12.

Mahoney, E. (1991). Women, development and media. *Media Development, 38*(2), 13-17.

McCarthy, C. (1993). After the canon: Knowledge and ideological representation in the multicultural discourse on curriculum reform. In C. McCarthy & W. Crichlow (Eds.), *Race, identity, and representation in education* (pp. 289-305). New York: Routledge.

MacCabe, C. (1987). Foreword. In G. C. Spivak (Ed.), *In other worlds: Essays in cultural politics* (pp. ix-xi). New York: Methuen.

McQuail, D. (1994). *Mass communication theory* (3rd ed.). London: Sage.

Moghadam, V. M. (1994). *Identity politics and women: Cultural reassertions and feminisms in international perspective.* Boulder, CO: Westview.

Mohanty, C. T. (1984). Under western eyes: Feminist scholarship and colonial discourses. *Feminist Review, 30,* 61-88.

Moraga, C., & Anzaldúa, G. (1981). *This bridge called my back: Writings by radical women of color.* New York: Kitchen Table Press.

Moore, D. (1992, Summer). White men can't program: The contradictions of multiculturalism. *Afterimage*, pp. 3, 23.

Nakayama, T. K. (1994). Show/down time: "Race," gender, sexuality, and popular culture. *Critical Studies in Mass Communication, 11*, 162-179.

Peñaloza, L., & Nakayama, T. K. (1993). Madonna T/Races: Music videos through the prism of color. In C. Swichtenberg (Ed.), *The Madonna connection* (pp. 39-56). Boulder, CO: Westview.

Press, A. (1990). Class, gender and the female viewer. In M. E. Brown (Ed.), *Television and women's culture: The politics of the popular* (pp. 158-182). London: Sage.

Press, A. (1991). *Women watching television: Gender, class, and generation in the American television experience.* Philadelphia: University of Pennsylvania Press.

Pribram, E. D. (Ed.). (1988). *Female spectators.* London: Verso.

Rakow, L. F. (Ed.). (1992). *Women making meaning.* New York: Routledge.

Reinharz, S. (1992). *Feminist methods in social research.* New York: Oxford University Press.

Roach, C. (1991). The movement for a New World Information and Communication Order: A second wave? *Media, Culture and Society, 13*(3), 283-307.

Rostow, W. W. (1964). *The stages of economic growth: A non-communist manifesto.* Cambridge: Cambridge University Press.

Rowe, W., & Schelling, V. (1991). *Memory and modernity: Popular culture in Latin America.* London: Verso.

Rush, R. R., & Allen, D. (Eds.). (1989). *Communications at the crossroads: The gender gap connection.* Norwood, NJ: Ablex.

Rush, R. R., & Ogan, C. L. (1989). Communication and development: The female connection. In R. R. Rush & D. Allen (Eds.), *Communication at the crossroads: The gender gap connection.* Norwood, NJ: Ablex.

Schramm, W. (1964). *Mass media and national development.* Stanford, CA: Stanford University Press.

Shohat, E. (1991a). Ethnicities-in-relation: Toward a multicultural reading of American cinema. In L. D. Friedman (Ed.), *Unspeakable images: Ethnicity and the American cinema.* Urbana: University of Illinois Press.

Shohat, E. (1991b). Gender and the culture of empire: Toward a feminist iconography of the cinema. *Quarterly Review of Film and Video, 13*(1-3), 45-84.

Spivak, G. C. (1987). *In other worlds: Essays in cultural politics.* New York: Methuen.

Valdivia, A. (1992). Women's revolutionary place. In L. F. Rakow (Ed.), *Women making meaning: New feminist directions in communication* (pp. 167-190). New York: Routledge.

2 Living Theory Through Practice

Race, Gender, and Class in the
Everyday Life of a Graduate Student

ISABEL MOLINA GUZMÁN

I am frustrated by the binary opposition you make between the intellectual and the underclass, because I feel myself to be both working in the underclass in many ways and an intellectual. So that I feel all the more like an outsider here, at this conference that seems to be so much a mirroring of the very kinds of hierarchies that terrorize and violate. The problem is we can't even dialogue in this space. The challenge to us here is to try and disrupt and subvert and change that and not just sit here and be passively terrorized. We need to actualize the politics that we are trying to evoke as being that radical moment in cultural studies.

bell hooks (quoted in Fiske, 1992, p. 171).

bell hooks's feelings of rage, isolation, and silence resonate deeply. I too have felt frustrated by the schizophrenia of identities imposed on me as a working-class *Puertorriqueña* graduate student at the prestigious Annenberg School for Communication in Philadelphia, PA: The complexity of my identity quickly simplified into one category—minority student. I too have felt like an outsider at this predominantly "white"[1] institution. I too have felt terrorized and violated by the systematic silencing of my voice. So silently I let out a scream, and I wonder if losing my self-sanity is a sacrifice worth an Ivy League education. The following account is an echo of that scream and an attempt to create a dialogic space.

Frustrated (by) Binary Opposition

Throughout Western scholarship—more often than not—race, gender, and class have been treated as essential categories existing in mutual exclusivity from one another. As Spelman (1988) so eloquently argues:

> I wish to suggest that much of Western feminist theory has been written from a viewpoint not unlike that of Uncle Theo: that is, as if not just the manyness of women but also the differences among us are disturbing, threatening to the sweet intelligibility of the tidy and irrefutable fact that all women are women. From the Uncle Theo view, the theocratic view, the view of the ultimate purveyor of intelligibility, this fact about women is more important than those facts about us that distinguish us from one another. (p. 2)

In de-emphasizing our differences and privileging our similarities we inevitably begin to conceptualize race, gender, and class as essential categories—essential categories often studied in isolation and opposition to each other. The study of women thus becomes the study of "white" women: "White feminist scholars pay hardly more than lip service to race as they continue to analyze their own experiences in ever more sophisticated forms" (Brooks-Higginbotham, 1992, p. 252). Unable and often unwilling to break away from their positions of racial and class privilege, critiques of race are often subjugated to gender. When race is studied, it is more often than not the study of "blackness":[2]

> In the realm of categories, black is always marked as colour (as the term "coloured" egregiously acknowledges), and is always particularizing; whereas white is not anything really, not an identity, not a particularizing quality, because it is everything—white is no colour because it is all colours. (Dyer, 1988, p. 4)

Academic discussions of race become synonymous with academic discussions of "blackness." And in the midst of the debate, "whiteness" remains unexamined and all other categories remain unnamed.

Likewise, the study of class has throughout the "his"tory of the social sciences been largely invisible:

> We also should consider that women in academe are not necessarily touched by the same problems that haunt the lives of non-professional working-class women. Our lives are not typical, so we must consciously see to develop a theoretical as well as practical understanding of the intersection of race, gender and class. (Matabane, 1989, p. 119)

As Spelman and others recognize, the interrelationship between race, gender, and class cannot be ignored because "a woman's race and class, for example, will influence her 'place' along with her gender" (Spelman, 1988, p. 5).

Unfortunately, far too many communication scholars and students still fail to recognize the existence of alternative social positions for understanding— racialized, classed, and gendered "realities" that radically alter the way we position ourselves and experience this world. Whether in the classroom or in the lecture hall, in a journal article or in a book, race, gender, and class continue to be set up and treated as mutually exclusive categories. The fact is all of us experience these realities simultaneously.

In my second year of graduate school, I am still shocked to read scholarly articles and books and find that a researcher has looked at gender without analyzing the implications of race and class, or looked at race and class without analyzing the implications of gender, or failed to look at or acknowledge any of these issues at all. I am shocked not because this type of ignorance still exists, but because journal editors and publishers continue to legitimate this type of scholarship so that it continues unchecked. I am also tired of special issues on gender, class, and/or race when these issues should be an intrinsic part of intellectual pursuit. I wonder if sometimes articles are rejected because the upcoming issues do not focus specifically on "otherness"?

In the classroom, I experience a similar phenomenon. I remain dumbfounded that at the graduate level I am still receiving syllabi that classify the readings regarding gender and race as separate but equal topics—that is, when those topics are dealt with at all. So that, dutifully, we spend 2 hours one week discussing gender, and 2 hours another week discussing race. Never is time allotted to discussing their intimate relatedness. And when we as students who demand to have our racial, gender, and class positions recognized, raise our voices in protest, our comments are perceived as anomalous and often quickly discarded. Our positions are held tenuous and vehemently attacked. Our positions are seen as personal and anecdotal whereas dominant culture positions are perceived as social and theoretical.

Within the academic curricula this separation in the study of race, gender, and class is a residual effect of the rigid, essentially bipolar oppositional thinking encouraged by a European-centered academic system that valorizes monologic discourses:

> The result is that women of color and women from working-class backgrounds have few opportunities to become part of the networks that produce and monitor knowledge in women's studies. In addition, those who have the advantage of being researchers and gatekeepers are primarily located at privileged institutions, where they get little exposure to working-class and ethnically diverse students. As a result they tend to develop and teach concepts divorced from the realities of women of color and working-class women's lives. (Zinn, Cannon, Higginbotham, & Dill, 1990, p. 31)

This disciplinary division is the result of a European-centered academy that imposes a hierarchical system of organization so that areas of study are organized in opposition to each other and rewarded for maintaining their separability and individuality. As Lana Rakow (1989) explains: "Underlying our society are a structure and set of values that emphasize individualism, competition, the transcendence of property rights over other rights, hierarchy, the separation of public and private activities and moralities, and a reliance upon science for problem solving" (p. 300).

Scholarly collaboration and integration across departments becomes difficult, if not impossible, for its students and teachers as the department chairpersons struggle to compete for funding, faculty, and administrative recognition.

More telling, however, is the silence that pervades most communication courses, the silence that falls upon the classroom when race, gender, and class are seldom constructively examined and interrogated—as if the communicative process and communication institutions existed in a social and political vacuum outside of the intersections of race, gender, and class. It is this absence, the absence of race, gender, and class from communication scholarship and teaching, that is most specious.

When race, gender, and class are talked about in terms of their insepara-bility in these courses, they are usually brought into the discussion by a student whose everyday existence with his or her race, gender, class, and sexual orientation does not afford him or her any other course of action. For many of us, our positions in this society demand that we live at the crossroads of theory and of our everyday experiences with race, gender, and class through the practice of our everyday lives as students, educators, scholars, media practitioners, and human beings. So often, for me, my everyday life is struc-tured by the mutual existence of multiple shifting subjectivities across a multidimensional grid of race, gender, class, and sexual orientation.

Hierarchies That Terrorize and Violate

When I studied at The Pennsylvania State University as an undergraduate student of Mass Media Research and Theory, I felt like an outsider. When I was invited to join the *Daily Collegian,* the independent Penn State student newspaper, I felt like an outsider. When I began my graduate studies at The Annenberg School for Communication at the University of Pennsylvania, I felt like an outsider. Outside of, marginal, de-centered, peripheral, expend-able—these are descriptors that have been historically and politically in-scribed on the bodies of women of color, descriptors of how people within racial, gender, and class hierarchies terrorize and violate those they wish to keep outside of, on the margins of, on the periphery of power.

Undergraduate School

I attended The Pennsylvania State University, one of the largest land-grant universities, situated in rural central Pennsylvania. Despite having lived in predominantly "white" suburban situations throughout most of my adoles-cent life, none of my life experiences prepared me for the types of everyday otherings I would come to face in higher education and in "Happy Valley." This was the case for minority students in general at Penn State. The university has had difficulty in recruiting and retaining students of color precisely because of the removed "white" situation.

In my first semester on the staff of the *Daily Collegian,* Penn State's independent student newspaper and one of the major forms of news media in central Pennsylvania, I was confronted by the subtle forms of daily indignities that remind us, women of color, that we are "not"-white. For my first assignment as a candidate reporter, I approached the metro editors about doing a story on Latino enrollment at the university—focusing on the issue of whether Penn State was recruiting and enrolling predominantly working-class Latino students from the state or recruiting and enrolling predominantly upper-class Latino students from outside of the continental United States. Many Latino students wanted to know the specific enrollment breakdown in order to determine the university's commitment to recruiting working-class Latino students from rural and urban cities in Pennsylvania. To me it was a seemingly innocuous story with important news value. For the "white" woman who was then the metro editor, however, the story assignment clashed with her ethical values as a journalist. She believed that it would be a conflict of interest to have a Latina student cover a Latino issue. That is, she saw my ethnic and racial identity as a dangerous marker of difference that would jeopardize the newspaper's journalistic integrity.

Never did she question the practice of having "white" students cover and report on the activities and issues of "white" students every day. Never— because her racial and ethnic position was not in question, yet mine was. Despite the fact that the managing editor summarily ruled on my behalf, that was the first signal to me that I was not going to be treated like everyone else, that I was trespassing in foreign territory, that I was not one of "them."

These feelings of marginalization transcended not only my work at the *Collegian,* they also crossed into my experiences as a Penn State Latina undergraduate student, in my coursework. Throughout most of my classes at Penn State I was subjected to an academic curriculum that symbolically annihilated my social position as a working-class woman of color. Every semester I looked around me and saw "whiteness"—"white" scholars on course syllabi, "white" students seated around me, and "white" professors teaching me about "white" history, sociology, and philosophy as if it were the only history, sociology, and philosophy. Most of the time I was exposed to a curriculum that remained unintegrated in terms of class, gender, race, and sexuality. Furthermore, my choice of a theoretical major instead of the more professional journalism major was challenged by some of my professors. I lived not only the contradictions of a journalist woman of color but also that of a journalist scholar.

Throughout my 4 years at the *Collegian* I continued to challenge the boundaries of journalistic norms: first as a reporter covering people of color, women, and gay men, lesbians, and bisexual issues; second as an editor encouraging the diversification of our staff and coverage. For the most part, although I was encouraged by my editors to pursue the topics I found relevant and essential to my existence and reality as a Latina student at Penn State, there were some students within the organization that saw my work as special-interest coverage, as non-objective, and as non-important.

It was not until late in my undergraduate coursework that I was exposed to the discursive tools necessary to give a voice to the sensations of marginalization and alienation that I was experiencing. Finally, the professors teaching me were women, women of color, queer women. Women like me—women with similar experiences. And the curriculum they taught was a multicultural curriculum—a curriculum composed of scholars from various class, gender, racial, and sexual backgrounds. For the first time I was provided the opportunity to read about myself, to give a voice to my life experiences. These women were my media research and theory professors at the School of Communication. Through their curricula, they helped me to make the connections between the theoretical frameworks I was learning about in class and the reality I was living as a student-journalist. The clearest example of this intersection between reading theory and living theory occurred during my last year of undergraduate school. My personal, professional, and classroom experiences all proved useful in confronting this crisis of hegemony.

In the spring of 1992, Chino Wilson, an African American sports reporter, wrote, and the *Collegian* published, a column that many Penn State community members interpreted as advocating violence against "white" people (see Figure 2.1). Partly because two white males picketed the student newspaper for the visual convenience of a local television news reporter and partly because the incident so clearly fit into the "political correctness" debate of the time, Wilson's column gained national attention, eventually appearing on the Cable News Network and in the *New York Times*. The adverse reactions of the university administration, faculty, students, and community members were emblematic of the double standard often placed on discourses about race, gender, and class. Although the Penn State administration refused to discipline or speak out against James Whitehead—a student who in 1989 on the campus electronic network system called for the explicit extermination of all gay men, lesbians, and bisexuals—it was the first one to call for the self-disciplining of Wilson and all editors involved in the decision to publish the column.[3] The administration fell short of suggesting censorship, thus avoiding inevitable First Amendment debates. The message sent by the Penn State administration was clear: It is all right to attack certain groups but not others. It is acceptable for those in social and political positions of power verbally to threaten and harass those of us outside of that matrix—that constitutes the exercise of freedom of speech. But it is not acceptable for those of us outside of the power matrix to question, to challenge the social and political formations privileged by upper- to middle-class, "white," heterosexual males—that is construed as irresponsible journalism. The Chino Wilson incident provided one instance in which a woman of color was in a position of social power and control. Thus, perhaps part of the virulent reaction—by the Penn State administration, faculty, and students—was influenced by the threat that I posed as a woman of color and editor in chief in control of one of the community's main information media. To many, my position and the resulting publication of the Wilson column demonstrated that people of color could not be "objective"—objectivity, of course, being defined by a white standard.

Despite the rhetoric of those politicians and academicians who argue against multiculturalism, who say that "political correctness" is stifling the freedom of ideas at college campuses, the Chino Wilson incident illustrates that "whiteness" still remains a privileged category protected by predominantly "white" social, educational, and political institutions. Because when the situation is reversed, when a "white" student argues for the genocide of an underrepresented people, the same people who would have Wilson's speech punished are the first ones rallying around the First Amendment. The social double standard is experienced as a double bind by a woman-of-color journalist.

For instance, in 1993 members of the undergraduate African American community at the University of Pennsylvania in Philadelphia staged a protest against its independent student newspaper, the *Daily Pennsylvanian,* for what was perceived as insensitive coverage. Earlier that year a feature photograph displayed as dominant art on the front page was published with the following headline and cutline: "Welcome to West Philadelphia: West Philadelphia homeless enjoys a shot of Wild Turkey beneath the hot sun." The following semester the *Pennsylvanian* continued its pattern of "white"-centered coverage by publishing on the opinions page a bimonthly column by a "white," undergraduate male student who believed that all "minority" students were on affirmative-action scholarships, and that all "minority" students were accepted at the University of Pennsylvania without having adequate credentials (whatever those credentials might be), and that celebrating Martin Luther

King's birthday was synonymous with celebrating the birthday of a communist, womanizing alcoholic. At the center of his attacks on these marginalized student groups was an attack on "political correctness"—the boogeyman of the radical right. What often goes unrecognized in these debates is that the policies, the issues at the cross of the debate are not "politically correct" but "politically imperative" to destabilizing patriarchal privilege in the academy. It is true that the critique implies a change in business as usual, but only because the current situation is unjust. The "politically correct" debate inverts the logic of the argument, suggesting that radical people of color are out to make a just system unjust.

When some members of the African American community protested this consistent form of racially biased coverage by emptying all the available newspaper dispensers of their products, the dominant issue raised by the University of Pennsylvania administrators, faculty, and students centered around "theft of these newspapers." Unlike the reaction to the Chino Wilson column at Penn State, the academic community couched its reaction in terms of loss of property, thereby avoiding any link with freedom-of-speech issues. The official response suggested the administration was not necessarily concerned about the content of the newspaper, but with whether or not the African American students who participated in the protest had committed a crime punishable by university regulations. Rather than framing the protest by these students as an expressive political act protected by the First Amendment, the act committed by these African American students was framed in terms of property rights violations. Effectively erased from the popular discourse surrounding the student protest was the original issue of race and racially biased coverage in the newspaper, and replaced as the focus of the debate was the issue most threatening to the privilege of the "white" academic community—the loss of its voice, particularly as a tool of the dissemination of discursive power.

As a Latina journalist and student caught in the storm of the Chino Wilson controversy, the entire event became for me emblematic of what occurs when someone on the social, political, and economic margins of society challenges the dominant ideological order of race, class, and gender. Wilson's column did not cause so much controversy because it called "white" people "devils." It stirred debate because its message was aimed at the center of the mechanisms by which social order is maintained, a social order that benefits the privileged class, by placing disempowered groups, like African Americans, at a socioeconomic and political disadvantage. Wilson's remarks, taken out of context, were used as evidence of the chaos and disorder that the "political correctness" debate could bring to a civilized university community.

The discomfort caused by Wilson's column may best be epitomized by the reactions of many mainstream journalists and journalism educators, reactions that inscribe them and their organizational practices within the racially and gendered hegemonic class of our present "white"-patriarchal social order. Their virulent defense of such notions as objectivity, truth, and reality—concepts used in the daily practice of journalism to set up boundaries that reify the conventions that help preserve the status quo—exemplify their professional and personal investment in maintaining this order.

At that time, one of my mass media and research professors, who was teaching a course on women, minorities, and the media, began encouraging me to look at joining the academy as a way for contesting and critiquing the hierarchical structures of oppression that I was encountering as an undergraduate student. Not only was she the first professor to mentor me in this way, but this was the first time I begin seriously considering the thought that this was indeed a viable option. As Grunig (1989) suggests in her analysis of the status of women mass communication students:

> Without taking classes from women professors who have managed to get hired in predominantly male university faculties, female graduate students may not believe that such entree to what has been called a "bastion of male clubiness" (Rohter, 1987) is possible at least for the ordinary student. (p. 133)

Her invaluable mentorship led me to examine the academy as a place where I could critically question basic journalistic concepts—concepts like objectivity, truth, and reality—concepts that are consistently used to conserve the imbalance of power by those who benefit most from it. With the assistance, mentorship, and encouragement of my mass media research and theory professors, I became a student at The Annenberg School for Communication in fall 1992.

Graduate School

Walking into The Annenberg School for Communication is an experience I have lived through many times but never before felt so dramatically. The cold, angular, white exterior of the school building—and its similar interior— marked with signs of wealth, prestige, power, and Ivy League "whiteness." Its predominantly white faculty and students about as warm and inviting as the building itself. This section begins with the statement that this is an event experienced by me many times throughout my life, because walking into "white" public and private spaces is something I am constantly required to do. Never, however, have the distinctions and intersections between race, gender, and class been so lucidly illustrated by the administrators, faculty, staff, and students as what I experienced at this institution.

In this territory of "white" privilege, all but one of the security personnel are people of color. And most of the maintenance personnel are people of color. By contrast there is one African American faculty member and two white women faculty members. Despite having been a student at Annenberg for more than 2 years, I still feel awkward walking past all those faces that look like my own, past those faces that remind me of both my racial and class roots, to sit in a predominantly white classroom at an economically and academically privileged university and to talk about theoretical abstractions far removed from the life I lead. The day-to-day otherings we (myself and the other students of color) receive from those around us—from the students and the faculty—often make it difficult to fight off those feelings of isolation, marginalization, and inferiority.

Among our own student peers, we are constantly forced to acknowledge the silent backlash of what is perceived by some of our "white" colleagues as financially unfair affirmative-action policies. It is a silent disapproval that demarcates us as outsiders treading on the border of a territory that until recently belonged only to upper- and middle-class, "white," heterosexual males. It is a silence that vociferously asks: "What are we doing here?" "Are we qualified to be here?" "Do we belong here?" It is the silence heard when our colleagues speak to us, as one "white" female student shared with me: "Did you hear they took away funding from several students? All of them were white males." The silent subtext being: "But you are still here." What often goes unrecognized is that so are "they." Annenberg, like the majority of academic institutions, continues to be predominantly "white" in the makeup of its students, faculty, administration, and curriculum.

Not only do many of us think that we have to work twice as hard to produce academic products that are twice as "good" in order to be considered on a par with our "white" peers, but we also feel like we have to perform as educators, as informants to the "white" academic community, about those worlds they are often afraid of or unwilling to trespass—classed, sexualized, gendered, and racialized worlds. In such an atmosphere it becomes an acceptable and even expected behavior to view us as monolithic representations of our various communities, thus making it permissible for one "white" student to ask an African American student about her hair: "How did it grow to be so long?" "How did she wash it?" "How did she style it?" These are the types of daily otherings, of daily alienations that make us feel like outsiders in our own environments.

The students are not alone, however. These forms of otherings occur not only at the informal social level but also at the formal classroom level. For example, one African American student was told by a professor during a question-answer session that questions regarding the use of the word *black* instead of *African American* in survey methodology were completely irrelevant. In another instance, a professor, after being challenged by students about the Eurocentric bias of the syllabus, responded flatly that race would not be directly addressed in the course. Another professor under a similar challenge replied that he had no knowledge of Afrocentric research applicable to the course material. The questioning student was able to cite several sources from memory.

Perhaps the most insidious form of othering experienced in daily academic interactions with students and faculty is the everyday usage of the dominant, generalizable *Our*, or what Gloria Anzaldúa (1990) terms "selective reality": "Failure to empathize with . . . another's experience is due, in part, to what I call 'selective reality,' the narrow spectrum of reality that human beings select or choose to perceive and/or what their culture 'selects' for them to 'see' " (p. xxi). So it is that the slippage caused by the presumption that the word *Our* in daily academic discourse—our media, our society, our history— assumes to describe the experiences of all women, people of color, gay men, lesbians, or bisexuals. Some students and faculty are so deeply inscribed within their social positions as determined by race, class, and gender that they unknowingly—and at times willingly—fail to recognize that the world they have selectively come to privilege is often not the world of marginalized peoples.

When we as students challenge theoretical constructions or academic analyses that question the unproblematic conceptual usage of a monolithic culture, the reaction is often hostile and always conflictual. This is illustrated best by a classroom interaction between an African American student who objected to a faculty member's premise that nationally distributed newspapers, such as the *New York Times,* represent the record keepers of "our" U.S. history and culture. After the student corrected the faculty member several times, the professor quickly moved on to another point, dismissing her objections as irrelevant to the class discussion. These types of everyday elisions work together to render people outside of the matrix of social and political power at least uncomfortable and at most invisible.

When one is constantly placed in a position to make one's visibility and vocality acknowledged,[4] to defend one's presence and one's academic interest, it is many times easier to walk away. Describing a similar experience, Anzaldúa (1990) writes:

> Like many *mujeres*-of-color in graduate school, she felt oppressed and violated by the rhetoric of dominant ideology, a rhetoric disguised as good "scholarship" by teachers who are unaware of its race, class and gender "blank spots." It is a rhetoric that presents its conjectures as universal truths while concealing its patriarchal privilege and posture. It is rhetoric riddled with ideologies of Racism which hush our voices so that we cannot articulate our victimization. (p. xxiii)

The emotional and psychological violence that is inflicted is often too difficult to withstand. And I have seen more brothers and sisters of color than I care to remember lost physically and spiritually in the fight to survive in the world of the academy. Unable to find the answers to such self-annihilating questions as "Why are we here?" "Are we qualified to be here?" "Do we belong here?" and "How are we helping our communities?", my brothers and sisters of color have left for more supportive environments. This applies to faculty as well as graduate students.

Challenge/Disrupt/Subvert/Change

It is only after much introspection that I am able to face and answer these questions for myself. The double bind that is caused by diversifying the academy without instituting fundamental changes to the structures that conserve its "white," patriarchal, and heterosexist mechanisms, is one that provides disempowered people the opportunity to enter spaces previously denied to us, but only at immeasurable cost.

When one looks at the marginalization of gender and race studies within the academy, the processes by which racial and gender inequalities are sustained become effortlessly clear. The lack of resources available for scholarship in these areas as well as the lack of recognition bestowed on faculty and students working in these areas is immense. Neither the candidacy nor the tenure and promotion processes are very sensitive to the extra labor required to survive and prosper in an adversarial setting.

Unlike many of my graduate student colleagues, I know that I am going to have to invest a lot of extra time finding the academic support and resources that I require and legitimizing the study of those issues and communities most relevant to my existence as a human being. The extra time, the extra work, the extra effort required to survive academically help keep "those hierarchies that terrorize and violate" in place. Furthermore, the devaluing of these issues and the sparse financial and scholarly support within the academy continue to send the message to scholars of color that we are "tolerated but not desired" here.

In her study, "The 'Glass Ceiling' Effect on Mass Communication Students," Lisa Grunig (1989) found that "the main source of inequality seems to be the small numbers and powerlessness of women on the typical faculty" (p. 127). Consequently, the small number of women faculty and even smaller number of faculty of color results in female students of color having few same-sex role models, fewer same-sex role models of the same racial background, and practically no mentors.

At Annenberg we learned to survive by creating a support network in which we not only look out for ourselves, the students, but also the staff who are mostly comprised of people of color. We help each other in looking for research opportunities; in networking with other students, staff, and faculty members who share similar interests; in finding funding opportunities; and in offering emotional support. In this space—often our offices, more often our homes—we speak to each other in our own empowering discourse as women of color.

But this group of women offers more than support—in many ways we act like a watchdog. When the only African American member of the computer staff was fired, we as a group questioned the decision of the administration—raising obvious concerns regarding racism and sexism. Although the administrative decision stood, at least those issues were vocalized and those questions asked. In many ways our very existence within the academy, much

African Americans should not

My Opinion

Chino Wilson

Why are my people so gullible? I know that we're a peaceful and loving race but sometimes it borders on the ridiculous. The most heartbreaking thing, though, is how we'll trust white people over our own in a minute.

The first month of 1992 alone brought two glaring examples. In the City College tragedy in New York, where nine people were trampled to death, "Negro" Mayor David Dinkins praised the white police for "heroic" behavior. What? Nine of our brothers and sisters perished because the police, according to News 4 New York, cancelled seven calls to the Emergency Medical Services. Consequently, it took 35 minutes for EMS to enter the building. Needless to say, it was too late. This doesn't surprise me. The police figured, "It's only niggers. Let 'em kill each other."

The other example is the recent African-American heritage dinner in honor of our esteemed brother, Rev. Martin Luther King Jr. The dinner was farcical, stereotypical and racist. Barbecue ribs, smothered chicken, red beans, rice, candied sweet potatoes, collard greens, corn, biscuits, honey butter, cornbread, pound cake and fried fruit pies. Next

time, remember the watermelon, chitlins, hamhocks, pig feet and grits. In order to certify this lie, they had to have Lawrence Young legitimate it. I respect Mr. Young but keep in mind that white folks will use anything and anyone to achieve their goals.

What will it take for us to wake up and fight? I often ask myself, "If white people died tomorrow, could we prosper as a people?" The only answer is no. As a people, we lack self-respect and love for our race. There is no reason for us to trust white people yet we continue to depend upon them for emotional, physical, economic, political and cultural support.

Now I'm not condemning all white

"White people have raped, deceived and tricked every ever come in contact with."

folks. There are definitely some decent white people out there. The vast majority, by that I mean 85-90 percent, however, are devout racists. I don't care, overt or covert, it's all the same. While I acknowledge that there may be some well-meaning white folks in the land of the thief, home of the slave, I'm looking at it from a holistic point of view. For once, it would be nice if our "Negro" brothers and sisters could put their love for white people aside for just a minute and look at my "radical, militant" viewpoint. Let's break down the reasons why we shouldn't trust white people:

1) History — God will bear me witness that white people are the most violent race ever to inhabit the Earth. Wherever white people have gone in this world, hell, misery and chaos have been the results. They raped and slaughtered our benevolent "Indian" brothers and sis-

Figure 2.1. Chino Wilson's Column
SOURCE: © Collegian Inc., reprinted from the *Daily Collegian* by permission.

less our often vocal resistance inside and outside of the classroom, presents a challenge to those "hierarchies that terrorize and violate."

Likewise, those faculty members who themselves have been marginalized due to their gender, class, race, or sexual orientation and who themselves have had to combat—sometimes winning and sometimes losing—the nexus of upper- to middle-class, "white," male, heterosexual privilege often extend the power they have achieved and the experience they have accrued to provide an academic space of resistance. At Annenberg, my academic advisor not only has provided me with the scholarly support necessary to complete my master's project, but he also has allowed me to create a space for myself where I can explore issues of race without having to prove its legitimacy. It is a space that extends into the classroom through his use of a carefully integrated syllabus that takes into account the multiplicity of social positions and realities and

trust 'devilish' white people

murdered, plundered, race that they have

ters. After committing these heinous acts, these gray people stole their land and forced them onto reservations, where they live in the most abominable conditions.

That was only the beginning. After deciding that their race was superior to ours, they kidnapped our Afrikan ancestors out of mother Africa. Everyone always talks about the Holocaust, but what about the Black Holocaust? An estimated 50-100 million Afrikans died as a result of the slave trade but we never hear about that. Kidnapping our brothers and sisters wasn't enough so they proceeded to rape, plunder, murder, lynch and dehumanize our ancestors. After all of this, we're supposed to trust white people?

2) AIDS — I wrote two years ago that this killer disease was created as part of a diabolical plot to exterminate black people. Now I've got the proof. In "Black Men, Obsolete, Single, Dangerous?" Haki

Madhubuti states: "Dr. Theodore A. Strecker, a white man, has unearthed evidence that the AIDS virus was created in a laboratory at Fort Detrick, Maryland from smallpox and Hepatitis B vaccines. It is now certain that the World Health Organization introduced the vaccine that contaminated east and central Africa with the AIDS virus ... Dr. William Campbell Douglass wrote, "the world was startled when the London Times reported on its front page, May 11, 1987 that WHO had "triggered" the AIDS epidemic in Africa through the WHO smallpox immunization program. The only people in the free world not surprised by the London Times front page exposé were the Americans — because they never heard about it."

This shouldn't really surprise you since the Tuskegee Experiment — in which 400 black men were injected with the most virulent form of syphilis, then allowed to spread the disease and die — proves that it's been done before.

After looking at all of the evidence there is only one conclusion: white people are devils. Since they've inculcated black people with these values, it's not surprising that some of us run around acting like devils

today. They have raped, murdered, plundered, deceived and tricked every race that they have ever come in contact with. My "Negro" brothers and sisters cannot name one black-white relationship that has ever been productive.

White people have made it clear that they intend to hold on to their power. I believe that we must secure our freedom and independence from these devils by any means necessary, including violence. Remember, the devil doesn't play by the rules. He makes up his own. White people are irredeemable racists, who have never loved or cared about black people. I refuse to fall victim to their treachery and devilishness. To protect ourselves we should bear arms (three handguns and two rifles, maybe an M-16) immediately and form a militia to defend our property, our beautiful black women, men and children. The next time a white person physically threatens us we should send that person to the cemetery.

So black people, let us unite, organize and execute.

Chino Wilson is a senior majoring in journalism and a wrestling reporter for The Daily Collegian.

pedagogical practices that encourage diversity. It is from these faculty members, who still must continue to resist in order to survive, that we have learned the importance of transforming the structures of the academy as women of color, as students, and as faculty. It is from these mentors that we have learned how to negotiate or not to negotiate, to maintain or not to maintain the dominant ideologies or race, class, and gender present in today's academy.

In order to "challenge, disrupt, subvert, and change" the hegemonic structures of the academy we must engage not in a multiculturalism but in a "multicentric perspective":

in order for the "multicultural paradigm" to amount to more than still another warmed-over version of cultural pluralism, the entire culture and national project need to be conceived from a "multicentric perspective." It is at the border, where diversity is concentrated, that diversity as a fact of cultural life may be most readily and profoundly perceived and expressed. (Flores & Yudice, 1990, pp. 78-79)

By virtue of our positions at the margins, we are used to living a pluralistic existence consisting of multiple identities. Because of the multiple cultural possibilities existing at the borders, Rosaldo (1989) argues that it is there that we may find the potential for "new forms of human understanding" (p. 216). So it is that we must engage in a recentering of the curriculum, of the academy, of methods for gathering and disseminating information that privilege our everyday experiences.

Notes

1. I place the word *white* in quotation marks because I believe that "white" and "black" as racial categories are social constructions predicated on the privileging of a biological discourse. I wish to question and challenge this discourse with its racialized notions of "whiteness" and "blackness" and the invisibility of everything else.

2. The study of "whiteness" remains largely unexamined as it continues to be naturalized by academic, political, and scientific discourses (see Dyer, 1988).

3. Although the university administration spoke out in favor of the self-disciplining of Wilson and the responsible editors, it did recognize the independence of the students' newspaper and the administration's inability to pursue any disciplinary action.

4. I choose this use of words for it is not that I and other women of color are either invisible or silent, but rather that the dominant culture is unable or unwilling to notice or listen to us. To suggest invisibility or silence would be tantamount to acknowledging a passive posture, and oppressed groups are nearly always in an active resistant posture.

References

Anzaldúa, G. (1990). Haciendo Caras, una entrada. In G. Anzaldúa (Ed.), *Making face, making soul: Haciendo Caras* (pp. xv-xxviii). San Francisco: Aunt Lute Foundation.

Brooks-Higginbotham, E. (1992). African-American women's history and the metalanguage of race. *Signs: Journal of Women in Culture and Society, 17*(2), 251-272.

Dyer, R. (1988). White. *Screen, 29*, 44-65.

Fiske, J. (1992). Cultural studies and the culture of everyday life. In L. Grossberg, C. Nelson, & P. A. Treichler (Eds.), *Cultural studies*. New York: Routledge.

Flores, J., & Yudice, G. (1990). Living borders/Buscando America. *Social Text: Theory/Culture/Ideology, 8*, 57-84.

Grunig, L. S. (1989). The "glass ceiling" effect on mass communication students. In P. J. Creedon (Ed.), *Women in mass communication: Challenging gender values* (pp. 125-147). Newbury Park, CA: Sage.

Matabane, P. (1989). Strategies for research on Black women and mass communication. In P. J. Creedon (Ed.), *Women in mass communication: Challenging gender values* (pp. 117-122). Newbury Park: Sage.

Rakow, L. (1989). A bridge to the future: Re-visioning gender in communication. In P. J. Creedon (Ed.), *Women in mass communication: Challenging gender values* (pp. 299-312). Newbury Park: Sage.

Rohter, L. (1987, January 4). Women gain degrees but not tenure. *New York Times,* p. E9.

Rosaldo, R. (1989). *Truth and culture: The remaking of social analysis.* Boston: Beacon.

Spelman, E. (1988). *Inessential woman: Problems of exclusion in feminist thought.* Boston: Beacon.

Zinn, M. B., Cannon, L. W., Higginbotham, E., & Dill, B. T. (1990). The costs of exclusionary practices in women studies. In G. Anzaldúa (Ed.), *Making face, making soul: Haciendo Caras* (pp. 29-41). San Francisco: Aunt Lute Foundation.

3 Three Women, a Mouse, a Microphone, and a Telephone

Information (Mis)Management During the Mohawk/Canadian Governments' Conflict of 1990

LORNA ROTH
BEVERLY NELSON
KASENNAHAWI MARIE DAVID

Dialogical modes are not, in principle, autobiographical;
they need not lead to hyper self-consciousness or self-ab-
sorption. As Bakhtin (1981) has shown, dialogical processes
proliferate in any complexly represented discursive space.
. . . Many voices clamor for expression. Polyvocality was
restrained and orchestrated in traditional ethnographies by

AUTHORS' NOTE: We would like to thank Susan Oke and Valerie David for their invaluable input and support in "jarring our molecules." We are grateful to Elizabeth Sacca and her secretary Marylou Matthews for their generous contribution toward transcribing our discussion notes in preparation for this chapter. Also, a heartfelt thanks to Thelma and Walter David, Sr., for all the teachings that they have passed on to their immediate and extended family; to Dan Doane for his help with formatting; to Thierry Le Brun for his ongoing cheerful support and discussions during the writing process; to Valerie Alia and Angharad Valdivia for their editorial suggestions; and to Conway Jocks for contributing the map.

giving to one voice a pervasive authorial function and to others the role of sources, "informants," to be quoted or paraphrased. Once dialogism and polyphony are recognized as modes of textual production, monophonic authority is questioned, revealed to be characteristic of a science that has claimed to *represent* cultures. The tendency to specify discourses—historically and intersubjectively—recasts this authority, and in the process alters the questions we put to cultural descriptions.

Clifford (1986, p. 15)

There are four distinct voices[1] in this chapter on the Mohawk/governments' crisis in Canada in 1990. Our choice to divide our voices one from the other is based on our desire to convey more than a distant historical chronology and descriptive analysis of these events. Rather, we are offering a series of impressionistic reflections on the Canadian media from both "insider" and "outsider" perspectives during what has come to be known here as the Oka "crisis." Separating our narratives to show "who is saying what" is our strategy for ensuring the integrity of our personal story versions and interpretations.

The "crisis" itself revolved around a land conflict between the Mohawks of Kanehsatake (a small community approximately 40 kilometers west of Montréal, Québec) and the governments of Oka,[2] Québec, and Canada. From early March until the end of September, the Mohawks of Kanehsatake firmly opposed Oka municipality developers' plan to expand a golf course onto Mohawk land, on which the sacred burial ground and the only community Commons are located. They occupied the contested territory by setting up protest barricades and were, in turn, surrounded by the Québec Provincial Police, the *Surété Québec* (SQ), and Canadian military forces. On July 11, the tragic death of an SQ officer, Corporal Lemay, occurred as a result of the Québec Police's surprise armed raid on the Mohawk-protected lands. The confrontation soon escalated when nearby Kahnawake Mohawks sympathetically closed down the Mercier Bridge linking Montréal to the south shore, resulting in the inconvenient increase in hours of travel to residents/commuters. The armed occupation and negotiation process lasted 78 days. The Mohawks (25 men—including 3 teenage boys, 1 of whom is non-native, and 2 spiritual advisors; 18 women; and 6 children), resisted arrest by remain-

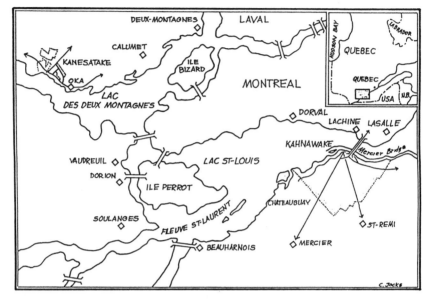

Figure 3.1. Map of Quebec

ing at an Addiction Treatment Center close to the contested land inside the barricades. On September 26, they agreed to stop the protest. They were arrested and indicted for "obstruction of justice," bearing firearms, using firearms in a threatening manner, wearing a disguise, death threats, participating in a riot, and other charges. They have subsequently been tried for these charges; all but 3 were found "not guilty."

The two confrontations at Kanehsatake and Kahnawake also marked the beginning of a public relations war between the First Nations and non-native communities in Canada, as the struggle over native land rights in urban regions escalated. That summer, the Kanehsatake and Kahnawake communities became internationally scrutinized focal points for all outstanding and residual grievances among Indians and non-native governments in Canada. What initially appeared to be a contained, local conflict eventually became redefined as a much larger battleground on which Indian land, cultural, political, and economic rights were struggled over. The year of 1990 is considered a turning point in First Nations cross-cultural relations in Canadian society.

The community radio stations on the Kanehsatake and Kahnawake territories rapidly became pivotal sources of information during the confrontation. They were contacted by local, regional, national, and international media for "their side of the story." The evolution of events at Kahnawake and the ways in which they were covered by and debated in the media have been written about elsewhere (see Roth, 1992, 1993). This chapter focuses exclusively on the conflict as experienced by two Kanehsatake Mohawk women— Marie David (Column 2) and Beverly Nelson (Column 3)—who breathed, ate, slept, and awoke to the experience of a state of siege while living at the local community radio station, CKHQ, between July 11 and September 29; and by me (Column 1), a non-native, Jewish Canadian. I had been involved in a community-radio training program sponsored by CEGEP *Jonquière*[3] just prior to the commencement of the confrontation and kept in touch with the two women on a regular basis throughout the course of the dramatic summer. I am also an academic and concerned with finding new ways of speaking and writing that take into account the complexity and multiplicity of perceptions around this historical event.

Since 1990, I have heard the "stories" we are about to tell from varied sources—official and unofficial, mainstream, alternative, and oppositional.[4] I have also told and retold them many times from multiple narrative and analytical positions—in personal conversations and in different media. All of these accounts were oral, textured with the metacommunicative subtleties of my own and others' voices.

When I recently sat down to produce a formal written narrative, I realized that much of the complexity lived during the "Indian summer" could not be captured in conventional social science or communications discourse on "media and crises" in which issues of gender and race are seldom considered.[5] Accounts of the events and background about the issues could not adequately be analyzed and/or synthesized in an "objective," neutral fashion, as the mainstream media had tried and abysmally failed to do during that summer. To do a traditional scholarly content analysis of the coverage would not reveal the essence of the two women's roles in representing the community to the outside world. Nor would it have addressed the interrelationships between their lived experiences of the crisis from the inside and my own perceptions from the outside. Even more important, it would not touch upon the ways in which mainstream media coverage mediated our experiences and reports about the crisis.

I also wanted to show the important telephone connections we had built in a time of restricted mobility. Through our daily telephone "barometer comparisons" on inside/outside information, the particular significance of this electronic link emerged.[6] How could I write the texture of these summer conversations into an essay form?

I explored and experimented with modes of presentation. This led to a "literary" approach, which employs several "positioned" accounts of the summer's events. Bev and Marie generously offered their "insider" voices to contrast with my "outsider" version of the ways in which public information was (mis)managed. They are in a unique position. They both *heard* the mainstream media versions of what we are about to narrate, and *produced* some of the key definitional statements about these events <u>for</u> *the mainstream media.* Their insights complement my more distanced and academic perspectives.

The complex realities of the Mohawk/governments' confrontation required thoughtful and sensitive reporting and analysis. Journalistic coverage of the events that unfolded that summer clearly showed large cultural, racial, gender, and territorial distances and distortions between the Mohawk peoples' understanding of the events and that of non-native community representatives in Canada. To make things more problematic, much of what reporters and academics have written *about the event* since the summer of 1990 is based on newspaper and magazine clippings and broadcast coverage, including sound bytes. This first-generation writing presents an even more difficult problem—the question of who was chosen *to speak for* the community by mainstream journalists, an issue raised in the early analysis of newswork (Tuchman, 1978) and currently debated by feminists and others involved with issues of cultural appropriation (Clifford, 1986; *Fuse Magazine,* 1993; hooks, 1992; Minh-ha, 1989; Spivak & Adamson, 1990; Spivak & Gunew, 1990).

The 1990 coverage raised serious ethical concerns about the cultural representation of a community by outsiders, as well as insiders, that mainstream journalists in Canada can no longer afford to ignore. Who, in and out of the community, should have the option of choosing insider spokespersons? What happens when a minority community's notion of representativeness, dialogue, and gender roles differ in essence from those of the dominant community? It is precisely because of these distinctions that the choice of spokes-women and Bev's and Marie's decision to woman the station are so revolutionary (Angharad Valdivia, personal correspondence, January 27, 1994).

How then can an outside journalist assess the appropriateness or representativeness of her or his sources? Underlying the possible answers to this question is the need for an honest acknowledgment of the degree to which mainstream journalists have been and continue to be (in)capable of dealing with the cross-cultural complexity of First Nations issues, given their limited historical background about the specificities of each First Nations community. How can journalists improve upon their performance in the future? From outside the mainstream journalistic perspective, what can *our* writing about these issues contribute to a better understanding of how to accomplish these challenges both institutionally and personally? The matters we raise in this chapter attest to the need to hear the credible voices of participants/witnesses in a journalism that is open to the complex challenge of stitching together more than the conventional "two sides" of a story.

This chapter is not meant to be read as a dialogue among its authors, but rather as a series of parallel voices framed within a broader argument for the necessity to rethink the writing practice of Canadian journalism, as the demand for democratic inclusion becomes more vocal. The need for public mediated spaces within which First Nations peoples can speak for themselves, rather than be spoken for by others, is essential. By placing our perspectives in three columns, we are showing a fraction of the many, equally valid views emergent from the summer of 1990. We are challenging the bipolar analysis provided by "objective" mainstream media coverage, as well as leaving room for the reader to access what Raymond Williams calls the "structure of feeling"—the emergent and uneven texture of a series of events and their after-effects (Williams, 1977, pp. 128-135).

In essence, we are creating a new format for multicultural work. Our intent is to bridge a "critically distant" social scientific perspective with the "subjective reflexivity" called for in recent cultural studies, feminist work, and literatures about ethnocultural "subjects." The literary form we have chosen will complement more didactic approaches to understanding the role of mass media in the construction of crises.

Lorna Roth **Kasennahawi Marie David** **Beverly Nelson**

When I began teaching community radio techniques at the Kanehsatake Community Radio Station in January of 1990, I had no idea that these seven young Mohawk students might permanently change my perception of native/non-native relations in Canada. Nor did I anticipate as I showed Marie David the tape-recording technique for capturing live action, called "rolling tape," that 3 or 4 months later (while tiptoeing in terror through the pine forest of Kanehsatake's sacred ceremonial lands), she would record the single live-action archival tape of the July 11 *Sûreté Québec* (SQ) attack on the Mohawks. And when Susan, one of the other students, recurrently fell asleep in class because she had just tended the ceremonial fire for 72 hours at the barricades between March 11 and mid-May (when the course ended), I had no inkling what would be the implications of her commitment to defend her ancestral lands.

The circle is a very strong image in Aboriginal societies. What goes around comes around . . . everything is interconnected—life, spirituality, everything. The circle represents Mother Earth. Symbolically within that circle, the roles of elders, men, children, and of course, women are described. In particular, in the Mohawk nation (of which I am a part), the role of women is so important to the community that they are considered the custodians of the land. They hold the future of the coming generations in their hands.

Knowing this about Mohawk communities, it will then come as no surprise that women are at the forefront in educational and communications fields. During the conflict in 1990, women in Kanehsatake naturally gravitated to sections of the community where they could help the most. Many people are familiar with the soft-spoken, but firm, image of Katsi'tsakwas Ellen Gabriel, spokesperson

At two o'clock in the morning, sometime between September 1 and 26, 1990, all appeared quiet in Kanehsatake, a small Mohawk community about 40 kilometers west of Montréal, Québec (Canada). A trailer home that had been transformed into an FM radio station known as CKHQ 101.7 MOHAWK RADIO, was surrounded on all sides by soldiers of the Canadian Army. They were camped at regular intervals along the same road on which the station was situated.

The soldiers were in the area to defuse an ongoing struggle between the Mohawks of Kanehsatake and the municipal, provincial, and federal governments over a land rights issue. The confrontation erupted on July 11, when the Québec Provincial Police conducted a heavily armed raid on a group of Mohawk protesters who had erected a symbolic barricade of heaped sand across the entrance to a pine forest. The Mohawks wanted to put a stop to a proposed expansion of a golf course and the construction of a deluxe condo housing complex onto lands in the pine forest known as "The Commons." The plan

(continued)

Roth *(Continued)*

When it became apparent during the semester that the Mohawk protest might actually escalate into an armed confrontation, ethical questions arose in class about what decisions members of the class would ultimately make. Would they take the political decisions to stand behind the protest lines or would they remain professional journalists and serve their community by disseminating information by radio? Sometimes we even stopped classes and focused on these critical matters. How could they cover the issues when their own families would be among the key players? Could they maintain the critical distance that is so important in journalistic analysis? It all seemed like such a fine line to walk, so unreal.

Toward the end of the course I began to sense who would do what, who would go where. Marie, whose family has traditionally played the role of mediation in the Longhouse community, would probably stay at the station, I speculated. Marie's fam-

David *(Continued)*

for the Traditional Mohawks during that summer. Her role as spokesperson was not without its detractors. Even within the Traditional system, there is some confusion.

There are those in our community who follow the Great Law teachings of Deganawida who brought peace to the Iroquois long before the Europeans arrived. Then, there are those who follow the code of Handsome Lake.[8] Handsome Lake and his followers favor a more patriarchal arrangement as opposed to the Mother-based Great Law of Peace. The differences between the two groups of followers in the community were made perfectly clear during the time before the crisis erupted into that long, hot summer. Male negotiators, following the code of Handsome Lake, objected to the presence of their female counterparts at meetings with government officials. They kept information from them and often "forgot" to inform them of other

Nelson *(Continued)*

was approved by Jean Ouellette, mayor of Oka, a member of the existing nine-hole golf course, and his municipal councillors.

Inside the radio station, all the lights were ablaze, while two lone women were heaving and panting in their attempt to reposition some large, bulky furniture, specifically desks and tables, having just moved them from one room to another. The women were trying to move as fast as they could, keeping a watchful eye on the floors and occasionally glancing out the windows.

Suddenly, the telephone rang. Both women stopped struggling with a huge desk and ran for the phone. Station Manager Bev Nelson answered it, panting and out of breath, while Marie David, operations manager at the time, paced up and down the hall, jumping at any sudden noise or movement.

The caller was Lorna Roth, their former professor at CEGEP Jonquière. She had been involved in training Bev and Marie in investigative journalism techniques between January and June of the same year. The three women had kept in close contact around the clock throughout what has

(continued)

Roth *(Continued)*

ily are Longhouse leaders and involved in communications in one way or another. Her father often speaks publicly; her brother is a professional journalist; her sister was in the community-radio training course. I was sure who would be loyal to the objective of keeping information flowing throughout the community. Bev, already station manager, was dedicated to keeping information clear, well organized, and managed. Her skills, I thought, would be invaluable in maintaining the calm of the community. Susan would go behind the lines. In the three cases, my predictions were correct. Bev and Marie lived at the station. Susan joined the group at the Treatment Center until the very end of September. She was among those arrested and indicted, and eventually found "not guilty." There were few surprises among the other students. They either disappeared from public view by leaving town or they stayed home taking care of family and community matters. Most were

David *(Continued)*

meetings. Things came to a head when the women resigned from the negotiating team. They objected to the manipulations by their male counterparts. They objected to the men's speeches that were followed by little or no action during the negotiations period. However, because the female negotiators kept the people they represented informed, they continued to meet with federal and provincial government representatives.

Their male counterparts were no longer welcome in the circle the women represented. To some, appointing Katsi'tsakwas Ellen Gabriel as spokesperson made perfect sense. Not only could she speak fluent Mohawk, English, and French, but she was one of the aforementioned custodians of the land. She knew what that responsibility meant. It meant that she had to listen to the people for whom she was spokesperson. She had to summarize what they wanted and present it

Nelson *(Continued)*

come to be called the "Mohawk/governments' crisis of 1990," so a call at 2 a.m. was not surprising. However, Lorna was immediately alarmed by the manner in which the phone was answered—thinking something terrible had happened. Were the army or the police in the throes of some sort of maneuver against the Mohawks?

Bev's reply to Lorna's concern was unexpected. In retrospect, it was also quite humorous, though at the time more so to Lorna who wasn't there. A MOUSE had been spotted scurrying across the floor of the broadcast studio the two women had turned into a makeshift communications center/bedroom when they had become trapped at the station on September 1, 1990. Lorna's call interrupted their attempt to move higher, more protective furniture into the studio. On the surface of tables and desks, the two women could sleep safely out of reach of the mouse, while also remaining within arm's reach of the broadcast equipment. Until that night, they had been content to sleep on the floor in the studio in sleeping bags. The mice changed their comfort levels consider-

(continued)

Roth *(Continued)*

unseen by the scrutinizing eyes of the media.

The SQ raid shocked everyone, including mainstream journalists. I was not surprised that they were caught unprepared. They *would* have known the background to the SQ attack had they been doing their research, but most didn't.

Ross Perigoe is a colleague of mine at Concordia University, working out of the Journalism Program. In the September/October 1990 issue of *Content* (a critical magazine about Canadian journalism), he tells an anecdote about a television program (taped in April 1990) on the portrayal of visible minorities in the media. It is about two Kanehsatake residents who, from the audience, spoke about the golf course situation and criticized the two large English broadcasting networks, CTV and CBC, for not having paid attention to their polite requests for background media coverage, starting in March of that year.

"According to the speakers, whenever they called the local television

David *(Continued)*

to the media in a firm concise manner. As one of the negotiators, Ellen Gabriel also had to look seven generations ahead, knowing that decisions made today would have far-reaching consequences. She sought counsel from the elders before making any public statement. This is brought up to make a distinction that affects many Aboriginal communities and one that affects the role of women in particular.

The Clan System. Traditionally, when Mohawk children are born, they are born into their Mother's clan. If the mother was a Bear, then her children would be members of the Bear clan, too. Clans are really extended families, along the lines of, say, the Smiths or the Johnsons in non-native society. Under the clan system, children born Bear or Turtle, following their mother's lines, would be kin to Bears or Turtles in other Iroquois communities, and would be respectfully treated as family. In

Nelson *(Continued)*

ably, however—there could be no peace at CKHQ as long as there were mice roaming about. Bev and Marie could put up with being trapped together, away from their families, surrounded by military forces, operating a radio station on a 24-hour basis. They could even tolerate the fact that they didn't have running water. But sleeping in a p ace where the mice could roam freely was where they drew the line.

The mouse situation was just one of the problems with which we had to contend. Being recent graduates in the field of journalism, we were up against the challenge of putting our newly acquired skills to the test during a highly volatile situation. That was a difficulty in itself because events were happening in our own community, to our own people, to our own families.

Among the many other problems that we had to face was getting the community radio station recognized as a legitimate source of information and news by members of its own community, despite its having been operational since July 1987. As

(continued)

Roth *(Continued)*

news rooms to tell them about a planned protest, the question always came back, 'Will there be any guns?' The media, in other words, were saying, 'We'll only cover you if there is the possibility of violence.' In some ways one might even conclude that the media were, by inference, counselling the Mohawks that violence or the threat of violence gets attention.

"It was a poignant moment, watching these people wrestling with insensitive media that understood conflict only in terms of barricades and rifles" (Perigoe, 1990, p. 12).

Several weeks later, the barricades were up, and the situation had escalated to an armed confrontation.

With this in mind, it is easy to understand how and why the "Mohawk crisis" slipped easily into a media spectacularization process. Here were masked Indian Warriors wearing camouflage, using pseudonyms, uttering perfect sound bytes in a confrontational manner, feeling free behind disguises to

David *(Continued)*

fact, when I went to Arizona a few years ago and visited with the Hopi, I found I have family there as well. Not because they have Mohawk blood or vice versa . . . but because they also have a Bear clan.

The number of clans in the Six Nations Iroquois Confederacy[9] varies, with the Onondagas having as many as nine clans. Among the Mohawks, there are three clans: Bear, Wolf, and Turtle.

Within the Six Nations Iroquois Confederacy, of which the Mohawks are a part, women hold an important role. Like the men, they sit in clans with one woman from each clan holding special responsibilities and duties. She is the Clan Mother.

Included among her responsibilities are choosing a male candidate for Chief. This is the most important duty each clan has. The potential chief must be honest and trustworthy, among other things, and everyone within his clan must agree on

Nelson *(Continued)*

in other native communities across the country, in Kanehsatake there seems to be a lot of mistrust of mainstream media because of their history of distorted portrayal practices. Privately funded, advertisement-based media in Canada have not developed a strong record of serving First Nations' communities' interests. This factor has tainted the view of Kanehsatake Mohawks toward all media, including the output of their own community radio station, which runs on a voluntary basis and does not produce programs or news to suit either sponsors' goals or those of organizational policy makers within Kanehsatake. As a consequence, any time a newsworthy situation happens in Kanehsatake, CKHQ radio is usually the last to know about it, even though the station is within easy reach and staffed by well-trained personnel. It is always the mainstream media outlets in the big cities that get wind of a story and go after it. Being new and inexperienced, we, the journalists of CKHQ, have found it difficult to research new issues. During the summer

(continued)

Roth *(Continued)*

construct brand new personae along the flat lines of the television cartoon caricature. The Mohawks had figured out within a few months how to capture the imaginations and the attention of the Canadian public by appropriating television's own vernacular and using it to serve their political ends. Their media strategy was fairly sophisticated and worked exceptionally well throughout the summer. Not only were their symbols powerful and significant, but also the form of the confrontation fit snugly into a sensationalist media format for cowboy/Indian; the good Indian/the bad Indian; the "two sides to any given question."

As the Oka conflict took more prominence in the press, the media crisis that it precipitated, and that I spent much of my time monitoring, became more apparent. This crisis showed the public the abject neglect of mainstream media institutions for issues about First Nations. Journalists, assignment editors, and management demonstrated daily their

David *(Continued)*

the candidate before he can take on the position. Women possess the honor of choice because they raise the children and do their utmost to instill in them the characteristics necessary for community responsibility.

When the Canadian and American governments rolled their legislation across Aboriginal territories, they created Band Councils in Canada and Tribal Councils in the United States. Besides instituting a foreign form of government in Aboriginal communities, what they ultimately did was upset the balance of power and the democratic use of checks and balances. The same amount of responsibility does not exist in the Band/Tribal Council systems as is evident within the Clan system. Women's roles are not the same. The Canadian Indian Act is a patrilineal document, with an inordinate amount of power (such as it is) given to Aboriginal men.

When women were displaced from a power

Nelson *(Continued)*

of 1990, this left our local news staff angry, frustrated, and reliant on outside journalists for inside information. With persistence, eventually some local sources started to open up, which then enabled us to produce a more community-oriented perspective to the news. Talk shows were a great help also. They provided a chance for people to speak their minds while remaining anonymous.

When the story of the golf course expansion project became public in March of 1990, some of our staff took care to collect information, having a hunch that it would be a "biggie." We just didn't know how big. When outside media sources realized how important the story would be, they turned to CKHQ for background information. Later, they kept calling on us for OUR view of the events. Even media sources from around the world got in touch with us for updates. This bewildered us at the beginning, but as time wore on, we began to feel a little tired with it all—though we remained calmly amused throughout the summer as we heard,

(continued)

Roth *(Continued)*

inadequate training on native issues. The absence of native people from routine mainstream journalism became obvious by the saturation of distorted images and misrepresentations that summer. Few journalists could deal with the complexities of the story without several weeks of orientation and background research, for which they had no time.

Starting fairly early in the summer, the media became their own subject of analysis. How could reporters get better access to information? How could they produce unbiased news reports? Were the media becoming participants in the crisis itself? Were they adding fuel to the fire? How close should journalists get to the Warriors? How could journalists avoid accusations of the Stockholm Syndrome?[7] What kinds of coalitions should be established with all of the key institutional and individual participants in the crisis (the Oka, provincial, and federal governments; the SQ; the army; the Warriors;

David *(Continued)*

position, Aboriginal men adopted a more colonial viewpoint. As in non-native society, men frowned on women's opinions. They laughed when women wanted more responsibility.

In the Longhouse,[10] everyone's opinion is supposed to be respected—men's, women's, and children's, too. At least, that is the ideal. Some people who have been reared outside the Longhouse, but who have rejoined following their search for a cultural identity, sometimes have a hard time letting go of their colonialist views.

As well, the quasi-traditional teachings of Handsome Lake also espouse a rather chauvinistic attitude toward women. Still, there exists the argument that under the Indian Act, women can now be elected chiefs, but it is noteworthy that even after 20 or 30 years, the equality emergent from the Indian Act cannot be compared to the Traditional system. In the Traditional system, it is the women who can remove a Chief if he has

Nelson *(Continued)*

through other sources, of British tabloid headlines that read "SHOOT OUT AT OKA CORRAL."

The Mohawks of Kanehsatake had long contested the Municipality of Oka's claim to the pine forest and refused to accept the development of the land via the expansion of the existing nine-hole golf course and housing complex.

Beginning in March of that year, the Mohawks started occupying the forest at various checkpoints with round-the-clock patrols to keep out municipal workers. We also held marches through the town of Oka, protesting the plan and *their claim* that the forest was theirs. Eventually, a barricade of sand was erected at one entrance to the forest.

By July, the Mayor of Oka, having had enough of protests and demonstrations in the pines and through his town, called in the *Surété Québec* (SQ) to put a stop to it all. At sunrise on July 11, 1990, about 150 SQ police officers, dressed in paramilitary outfits, arrived by the truckload at the pines and stormed the barricade

(continued)

Roth *(Continued)*

the Iroquois Confeder-
acy, the Band councils,
the Mohawk community
radio employees)? How
should journalists react
to accusations of bias by
some of the parties?
How much self-censor-
ship should journalists
undertake? How much
information should be
revealed to the public
about security measures?
How much about the
lack of journalistic
preparation should be re-
vealed directly to the
public? There were con-
flicting views of journalistic norms and a range
of opinions articulated
about these issues, with
consensus on the need to
protect freedom of infor-
mation access in order to
fairly represent a bal-
anced view of what was
happening.

And then there was
censorship. As part of
the government strategy
to get the Mohawks to
leave the Treatment Cen-
ter (TC), they isolated
the journalists by remov-
ing their cellular tele-
phones, on the grounds
that if the Mohawks
couldn't get their per-
spective across to the
public via the journalists
at the TC, then they

David *(Continued)*

not conducted himself
in a responsible way for
his clan and community.

In Canada in 1869,
an Act for the gradual
enfranchisement of In-
dians was passed. This
was around the time
similar legislation was
introduced in the
United States. It was
through this Act that
the Canadian Govern-
ment first began the
plan to wipe out the
clan system affecting, in
particular, Aboriginal
women. For example,
the Act stipulated that

" . . . any Indian woman
marrying any other than
an Indian shall cease to be
an Indian within the meaning of this Act, nor shall
the children issue of such
marriage be considered as
Indians within the mean-
ing of this Act. Provided
also that any Indian
woman marrying an In-
dian of any other tribe,
band, or body, to which
she formerly belonged,
and become a member of
that tribe, band, or body,
of which her husband is a
member, and the children
issue of this marriage shall
belong to their father's
tribe only" (S.C. 1869, 31
V., c. 4, s. 15).

Nelson *(Continued)*

with tear gas and concus-
sion grenades.

Marie David, informed
of the raid, arrived on the
scene and worked along-
side the other journalists
from the commercial me-
dia outlets to cover the
story that would go on for
78 days straight. While
Marie spent most of that
day running from inter-
view to interview and putting those stories on the
air, I spent my time field-
ing reporters' calls for interviews, and connecting
Mohawk resource people
with the media in their
quest for information.

The summer wore on.
Fall arrived and the ongoing events in the commu-
nity changed dramatically,
as did the problems faced
by the news crew of
CKHQ. As the days
stretched into weeks and
then months, the news
staff of CKHQ dwindled
from four to three and finally to Marie and me—
two lone women—who be-
came trapped there when
the army, which had been
located on the perimeters
of Kanehsatake, moved in
to switch places with the
SQ, which had been sta-
tioned inside the commu-
nity. This was on Septem-
ber 1. By this time, the

(continued)

Roth *(Continued)*

would have less to lose by leaving the TC. Eventually, the isolation strategy worked, despite widespread international protest and accusations of censorship. Until this point, however, the coverage was lengthy but superficial. Journalists had never been more "on alert" in Canada. They hungered for any and all images, seeking to document new sources of information, recycling sources, old interviews, over and over again—all the while underprepared.

I remember the summer of 1990 as one in which I was there, "in the bush"—electronically present through television, radio, and telephone—almost from the start of the conflict. I spent most of my time alone at home—watching television, listening to the radio, channel switching, taping, and reading five or six English and French newspapers at a sitting. I frequently spoke with the Radio Kahnawake station manager (a former colleague). But, my telephone conversations with Bev and Marie were by far the most interest-

David *(Continued)*

Indian women were damned if they did and damned if they didn't. Also, if a woman married a Native from outside Canada, she would lose her status, even though both members of the couple were Aboriginal. Nor would their children have "status." Yet, if a non-native woman married an Indian, she gained all the rights and privileges of an Indian woman. The real brunt of the consequences of this Act are not spelled out in the law, which was meant to erode the clan system and weaken the native Traditions and laws. The Indian Act negatively affected children for many generations.

The Indian Act also imposed elections on the Aboriginal peoples, contrary to our own laws.... The Six Nations Iroquois Confederacy continued to resist imposed elections and in 1924, the Royal Canadian Mounted Police were sent into Six Nations territory near Brantford, ON. There, they physically removed the Traditional

Nelson *(Continued)*

Provincial Police had already set up roadblocks or checkpoints on all roads leading into the community. At the roadblocks, community members traveling through would be checked out and either allowed to pass, taken in and detained for questioning, arrested, or not allowed to return home. That made getting to and from the various news conferences difficult and put pressure on us to stay within the community for fear of being trapped outside, as other Kanehsatake residents had been. Those maddening experiences made us fearful, anxious, and angry. The anger was what gave us the energy to keep going instead of giving up and going home to our families. We were also encouraged to stay by our listeners, who called and told us we were doing all right and that they enjoyed listening to the way we were handling things. During this time, it was difficult and painful to watch and listen to television and radio reports describing the ways in which the police, army, and government representatives and negotiators were dealing with our own family members.

(continued)

Roth *(Continued)*

ing sources of information for me throughout the summer. We usually talked some time after midnight on a daily basis, reviewing the day's events from as many perspectives as possible. Using the telephone as an information conduit, I read them newspaper articles to satisfy their hunger for outside information from sources to which they had no access. In turn, they relayed to me what had happened each day from their perspectives. We would close our conversations with jokes and other distracting talk so as to ease the tension accumulated between phone calls. This is the way we passed the late nights of this "Indian" summer.

Bev and Marie were courageous to live at the radio station all summer and part of the fall of 1990. Feeling a community obligation to report back information about security, food, health, and movements to and from the community, as well as a need to construct a pretense of normalcy, they represented a telephone lifeline to

David *(Continued)*

Chiefs from the Longhouse and absconded with our Wampum Belts[11] and beads. At that time, a petition from Akwesasne, Kahnawake, and Kanehsatake (three of the Québec Mohawk communities) was sent to Ottawa, containing thousands of signatures opposed to the Indian Act. Majority rule was ignored.

Following the federal government crackdown on Traditional Indian governments in 1924, the Traditional people went underground. If they hadn't, their laws, traditions, and the clan system might have been lost. In 1985, after much lobbying and criticism, the Canadian federal government tried to rectify the situation by passing Bill C-31, which reinstated women and children who had lost their rights. But the previous law had been on the books since 1869 and, for many, the damage had been done. Still today, some Indian Act Band Councils resist reinstating women and children.

Nelson *(Continued)*

As the days wore on, Marie and I went a little stir-crazy. It was suggested by someone at the food bank that Marie leave the station and take short walks down the road to check on some of the elders who had refused to leave their homes. I didn't like this idea because for one thing, if either or both of us left the station, we would have to walk out in front of the soldiers who were posted all along the roadside. Second, leaving the radio station un(wo)manned might give the soldiers a chance to shut it down by locking us out. Marie became upset by my refusal to go outside and sat on the doorstep refusing to talk to me. I was already feeling isolated enough, so I finally gave in and agreed to go out.

For most of the time that we were trapped at the station, I adopted a Scarlett O'Hara attitude of "I'll think about that tomorrow, because tomorrow is another day." But the fears and anxieties that welled up inside me on that walk were hard to swallow and forget. I didn't like leaving my own home unattended, separated from my family, stay-

(continued)

Roth *(Continued)*

those trapped (in)voluntarily in Kanehsatake. They maintained social relations, called for help, stayed in touch with friends and supporters. Bev and Marie were also pivotal in interfacing between the inside and the outside and became internationally central to the dissemination of information from the perspective of insiders. Perhaps because of professional alliances and some comfort derived from camaraderie, mainstream journalists from all around the world approached *them,* despite the fact that the security officials had refused to give them formal accreditation. They became the "real" source to journalists craving to hear the "unmediated authentic native voice."

Eventually, because I had a few contacts in the media and in the local native communities, journalists discovered that I had some vague connection to the insider journalists in both Kanehsatake and Kahnawake. Subsequently, they approached me for comments on the media coverage of the crisis some-

David *(Continued)*

As noted above, the Indian Act is the form of legislation the Government of Canada uses to "govern" the Aboriginal people who reside within the boundaries that separate Canadians from Americans. What preceded the Act was another piece of legislation introduced in 1868. It was called "An Act for the Organization of the Department of the Secretary of State of Canada, and for the Management of Indian and Ordinance Lands." Right from the beginning, the legislation presumed control over our lands, by calling them "Crown Lands": Lands for the use and benefit of Native people. The Act also undermined the Traditional way of decision-making. In relation to the land, the Act states:

" . . . such release or surrender (of lands) shall be assented to by the Chief, or if there be more than one, by the majority of Chiefs of the tribe, Band or body of Indians, assembled at a meeting or a council of the Tribe, Band

Nelson *(Continued)*

ing inside a building surrounded on all sides by the army, with a constant view of a bunker outside our broadcast studio window, and I especially didn't like walking by those soldiers in their armored personnel carriers as they watched our every move, guns in hand, as we passed them by. Needless to say, we didn't go out often.

Eventually, Marie needed to talk to someone else and called the food bank to send over some clergy. That request took some time because the ministers had to be given clearance by the SQ. When that was finally accomplished a few days later, one male and one female minister were escorted over to the station with an army chaplain. That visit was somewhat futile because our fears were not alleviated. Rather, they were enhanced because we became suspicious of the chaplains' motives for being there.

To further complicate matters, CKHQ reporters were denied accreditation as acceptable journalists by the SQ, who had taken charge of such matters. In order to qualify for accreditation, journalists

(continued)

Roth *(Continued)*

time in the middle of August. What followed was much like the old snowball effect in the social sciences. One medium, CBC radio, interviewed me one week; they called back for more the next week; then, television and newspaper venues phoned. I even got a call from the provincial separatist party asking my advice on how to modify their policies on First Nations peoples to make them more progressive. Finally, CBC radio recontacted me and asked me to become one of their weekly media critics. I refused, feeling it was inappropriate in light of my other job commitments.

It was at about this time that I began to suspect that I was being surveyed by either the Canadian Security Intelligence Services (CSIS), the *Surêté Québec* (SQ), or the Royal Canadian Mounted Police (RCMP). It seemed that whenever I talked to any of my friends in Kanehsatake or Kahnawake, I heard loud crackling noises interfering with the telephone line. On several occasions our lines were even disconnected. One

David *(Continued)*

or body summoned for that purpose according to their rules and entitled under this Act to vote thereat, and held in the presence of the Secretary of State or of an officer duly authorized to attend such council by the Governor-in-Council, or by the Secretary of State, provided that no Chief or Indians shall be entitled to vote, or be present at such councils, unless he habitually resides on or near the lands in question" (Indian Act. S. 4, C.42, sc. 8).

Majority rule is a foreign concept to the people of the Six Nations Iroquois Confederacy. Within the Confederacy, the people have to agree on something totally in order for any law or agreement to pass. This is what we call "coming to one mind." As can be seen from the passage above, the government encouraged divisions by introducing majority rule.

The federal government further promoted divisions by trying to close decision-making meetings to people who habitually reside on or

Nelson *(Continued)*

were required to show media-source identification. After their credentials were checked out, they would be given specific passes allowing them access through various checkpoints covered by the police. Non-native journalists didn't have to wait very long to get their passes approved, but it was a different story for native reporters. They were made to wait for long hours in the hot sun or pouring rain for their requests to be processed. Some even had to wait days. Those with a strong will to get the story managed to bear it all, got their passes, and were permitted into the community. Because of the potential harassment, we made the decision to stay within the community and away from the police.

Many reporters turned to our station because we had been connecting journalists to various spokespeople and community members involved throughout the crisis. Some of those reporters were executive members of the Canadian Association of Journalists (CAJ). Its president came to Kanehsatake to check on how the journalists were coping

(continued)

Roth *(Continued)*

day, I discovered two RCMP officers sitting outside of my house in a car for a period of 12 hours. When I asked them what they were doing there, they explained that they were the backup car for a drug raid that other officers were mounting in the neighborhood. To me, they looked suspicious.

After this incident, I began to receive daily calls from an American stranger named Chester, who wanted to show his support for the native cause. My sense that I was being tracked by the authorities because of my public media criticism of how events were being handled led me to question Chester's motives. Was he someone put on to me by CSIS or the RCMP? Chester's calls were regular and his questions were detailed and informed. Clearly, he had followed North American Indian politics for a long time—since Wounded Knee. His claimed motive was to provide whatever support he could to further native rights. He had numerous contacts in the United States and some

David *(Continued)*

near the land in question. That mind-set is as true today as it was when the law was first introduced. But to Traditional people, if it is Mohawk land in question, then all Traditional people, as well as the nine Mohawk Chiefs,[12] the Clans, and Clan Mothers are required to attend. And they will come from each of the Mohawk Communities, not just one. During the crisis of 1990, both the media and the governments (federal and provincial) called Mohawks from Kahnawake and Akwesasne "outside instigators." Sadly, too, in 1990 I saw how deeply assimilated by the Indian Act some people are, when Mohawks from my own community objected to the presence of other Mohawks from outside communities.

Despite the odds, or perhaps because of them, Mohawk women have had to be very strong. In March 1990, the nearby non-native municipality of Oka decided to enlarge a golf course over land used

Nelson *(Continued)*

with the crisis story and also looked in on CKHQ. When he checked in on us, he tried to convince us to change our minds about passing through police checkpoints by urging us to go for our accreditation papers from the SQ. We refused, explaining that being Mohawks from the Kanehsatake community and running a Mohawk radio station would surely be used against us. We expected to be locked out of the community if we had direct contact with the police. The president of the Journalists' Association didn't think that would be the case, but he turned out to be wrong. We spoke to the accreditation officer over the phone and were informed that we could not get accreditation, given that CKHQ was not registered with the Canadian Association of Journalists (CAJ). He, being the president, indicated that that should not have been a problem, given that he could personally sponsor us. Subsequently, the police came up with other excuses, such as "neither of us had a driver's license for identification purposes." Nor did we have an address on the road on

(continued)

Roth *(Continued)*

in Canada. In time, it became apparent that he *had* contacted a lot of people on behalf of the Mohawk cause. Three years later, Chester continues to be in touch with me and is still friendly to members of the Kanehsatake Longhouse community.

The "crisis" seems to have drawn together people from all over the world focusing their energies on basic political and human rights issues. There are still hangers-on, those who don't want to give up the crisis—whose lives have been permanently changed by it, who want to recreate the excitement that was lived during the 78-day highlight of their lives. It's odd how all of these people have gotten yoked together in this small First Nations community in rural Québec. But the spirit behind the confrontation has lasted.

At the end of the confrontation, the federal government purchased what they thought was the contested land with the intention of giving it to the Mohawks. It turned out to be the

David *(Continued)*

by the Mohawks and surrounding their graveyard. Mohawk women joined the men on watch to secure the contested land against the intrusion of non-native developers. They stayed up all night when it was freezing cold and when they really wanted to be in a cozy warm bed. They kept the fire going outside even when it was raining, when the men inside a small fishing cabin let their own stove fire go out. Their commitment was strong and they soon realized how important their roles would be.

Eventually, when it became clear that things were getting serious, the women shouldered a stronger leadership role. When a spokesperson was needed, the choice of Katsi'tsakwas Ellen Gabriel was made, not because she was a woman, but because of her capabilities.

Federal and provincial negotiators were unprepared when women walked into the meeting room. Often times, they refused to

Nelson *(Continued)*

which the radio station was located, which precluded permission for us to return there.

After a while, we began to see the need to get outside stories, so we gave a neighbor, "Lorrie," who owned a car, a crash course in journalism and Charles got her accredited through the police. Lorrie was then able to travel within and outside the community to get whatever stories were available. One day, with the little practice she had, Lorrie attempted to attend a press conference being held by the army at the top of the hill in front of the golf course. She didn't make it—she was stopped by the police at the bottom of the hill after they had looked at her credentials. The CAJ president found out later that the reason she was denied access was because she was Mohawk and worked for the local radio station. For that reason alone, the police refused to let her up the hill, believing that she was there to incite a riot. It was blatantly obvious that a racist attitude was applied in that particular decision. Racist attitudes are very prevalent in this world.

(continued)

Roth *(Continued)*

wrong portion of the pines. It is 1995 and the Mohawks' land claim issue is still unsettled.

Beginning in the summer of 1991, an annual Pow-Wow has taken place in the sacred Pines on the weekend closest to July 11—in commemoration of the struggle to win land rights. The Pow-Wow organizers are the same group of people who began the land protest on March 11, 1990. Their will to attain the land is relentless and guided by the spiritual power of their ancestry.

Bev Nelson has since left the community radio station and has become a community worker. Marie David is now a broadcast journalist at CKHQ. Here are their words.

—Lorna Roth
Communication Studies
Concordia University
Montréal, Québec

David *(Continued)*

address the women directly. They also experienced culture shock during the process of negotiations. The Mohawk negotiators who attended the meetings always took suggested proposals and counterproposals back to the community for consultation. That is the Traditional way of doing things. It was and is, at times, a lengthy process because any agreements require unanimous consent of the people.

Throughout the summer, while the media focused on the men at the barricades, it was the women who outnumbered the men in the rest of the community. The women were spokespeople and negotiators. They ran the food bank, the Mohawk community radio station, and were liaisons among the Québec Provincial Police, the Canadian Army, and their community.

Don't get me wrong. Men were involved, too, in these areas, not just at the barricades. But the ratio was something like four women to every man who wasn't

Nelson *(Continued)*

Unfortunately, it is the downfall of the media that those views are reflected and not changed by most stories. We, at CKHQ, try to educate our listeners about racism by defining racist actions or remarks against a people by the so-called leaders of this country.

For the duration of the crisis, we remained at the station, rarely going out. Information was funneled to us by the phone and fax machine. We received and transmitted all the information we could get our hands on about the ongoing events on an up-to-the-minute basis. In that time also, we received reports from community members who experienced harassment at police checkpoints, so we passed on information about peoples' rights, should they be detained by the police. Over the air, we informed people of the police Code of Ethics, which had come into effect in September of that year.

We had a captive audience. Our community members, who were trapped in their homes, tuned in to us regularly, as did the people who were staying at the food bank.

(continued)

Roth *(Continued)*

David *(Continued)*

Nelson (Continued)

at the barricades. Part of the reason for this may be because in so many communities, women outnumber the men demographically. Women are also more likely to stay within the community and work for pay or on a voluntary basis. It's a social phenomenon that's not easily explained. Personally, I believe it may be because there is such a strong attachment to the geographical area, to my home. I feel the strength of my ancestors here.

The Mohawk community radio station, CKHQ, is another place where women play an important role. Programming and news and current events are produced by women who, more importantly, have volunteered their time for the past 7 years. When the crisis hit a week after finishing our last training course, it was "natural" for us

The people and journalists who were penned up at the Treatment Center (the building that the protesters occupied) listened to us as well, because we passed on personal messages from family members that we would tape live over the air then repeat at various intervals throughout the evenings. We also took into consideration the peace camps' residents outside of Oka Park and the other communities within listening range of CKHQ, thanking them for their help and encouragement. We read letters of support that were faxed to us from the people at the food bank. When we couldn't move freely anymore, we started to monitor the TV and radio reports of other stations. We then took their information as our source and gave it a Mohawk point of view before rebroadcasting what we had heard.

Throughout all of these difficulties, we tried to keep everyone's spirits up by playing "power" songs like TALKING 'BOUT A REVOLUTION by Tracy Chapman, GET UP STAND UP by Bob Marley, and requests like

(continued)

Roth *(Continued)*

David *(Continued)*

Nelson *(Continued)*

student journalists to work at the station. It was where we could help the most.

During the month of September 1990, Station Manager Bev Nelson and I kept the station on the air 24 hours daily, while surrounded by the Canadian Army and cut off from our families. It was a spur-of-the-moment decision that sometimes, in retrospect, seems a stupid one. Had we known we would be spending a month together with little to eat but hot dogs and with no running water, I don't know if the same decision would have been made. Toward the end, however, we were planning ahead. What would we do for Halloween? How could we get candy? What about Thanksgiving? I can honestly empathize with anyone who has gone through cabin fever. The army was literally a few feet away from us. We could see their tanks and their weapons on the hill across from us. The soldiers were the first thing we saw as we woke from our makeshift bedroom in our on-air studio.

KNOCK, KNOCK, KNOCK'N ON HEAVEN'S DOOR by Eric Clapton, which was sent out to Major Tremblay of the Canadian Army on September 1, 1990, and DANGEROUS TIMES by Sue Medley—a song about the Massacre at Tian'anmen Square. And when one long, long day started in on the next, we even got a little silly while on the air. At one point, we tried to play trivia games and drove some listeners crazy because they couldn't get through with the correct answers. At times, we even bickered with each other on the air. This made a lot of listeners laugh.

For Marie and me, it is the humor and silliness in our lives that gets us through a tough day, especially when faced with negative attitudes about our own race or gender. Those racist and sexist attitudes did not start in 1990 for either of us. We've lived with discrimination all of our lives. However, I don't think that I could have made any other decision than to stay at the station and be a journalist under such adverse circumstances. I did it for my people, the Mohawk

(continued)

(continued)

Roth *(Continued)*   **David** *(Continued)*   **Nelson** *(Continued)*

Their helicopters often threw spotlights on our building as we flicked our lights off and on. Sometimes, they would fly at night without any lights. We were under occupation.

The hardest part was telling members of my family on the outside of the occupation to stay there, even though I might never see them again. Or to say goodbye to my brother and friends who were prepared to die for our land. I don't know how many times I said goodbye to them.

The role Bev and I played at the radio station, however, is and was an important one for a small community under the most normal of circumstances. 1990 was anything but normal. Journalists from around the world depended on our knowledge of the situation in order to file their stories. We were also called upon to deliver crash courses in Mohawk history (usually in 5-, 15-, and 20-minute lengths) in order to provide them with the necessary background.

The question has often been asked, "Why?" Why are Mohawk women so strong? Why were they so

Nation. The experience made me more conscious of who I am and of what direction my life should take. I learned that racist attitudes are entrenched in the Canadian government through its policies (such as the Indian Act) and in its dealings with First Nations peoples. I also think that mainstream media outlets still have a lot to learn when dealing with First Nations peoples and ethnic groups. Perhaps future journalists will become more aware of institutionalized racism through their education/training and in their practice, and might handle issues more accurately and with greater sensitivity.

—Bev Nelson
Former Station Manager
CKHQ Radio Kanehsatake
Mohawk Territory

(continued)

Roth *(Continued)*   **David** *(Continued)*   **Nelson** *(Continued)*

involved in the standoff in 1990? The truth is I don't know why. It's just the way things are, or more to the point, the way we are. We, as Aboriginal women, the progenitors of our Nation, have had so many things thrown at us. The laws in non-native society, the laws the foreign governments have passed, do not favor us. If my Nation and other Nations within the Confederacy or any other Traditional peoples are going to survive, then we have to reclaim our birthright. We have to keep looking seven generations ahead and we have to remember our ancestors because they sacrificed for us to be here today.

When I was a little girl, my parents would often leave us in the care of my older sister, Linda. I always wanted to go with them, but they would say that I was too young. We missed our parents when they were away. The absences seemed to be weekly. My parents were attending Longhouse meetings. My Father is the secretary of the Longhouse in my community and very

(continued)

Roth *(Continued)*   **David** *(Continued)*   **Nelson** *(Continued)*

often they would have to
attend political meetings
of the Confederacy in the
other Iroquois communi-
ties. It hurt my parents to
be away from us so much.
My Mother would tell
Linda, since she was the
oldest and had the most
responsibilities, that
someday she would un-
derstand why they were
away from their children
so much and someday,
too, she would have to tell
her children the same
thing.

My Mother would tell
us that it wasn't enough
to be Traditional, to know
the Great Law. She told us
to learn about the Indian
Act, about Canadian and
American laws, because
we could never know
what bearing they might
have on us. Politics and
heated debates over the
breakfast table still go
hand in hand in my
house.

I come from a family
of eight kids, four men
and four women. My par-
ents treated each of us as
equals. When we were
young and being picked
on in school, they taught
us to stand up for our-
selves. In elementary
school, we would argue
with our teachers about

(continued)

the depiction of Aborigi-
nal people in our history
books . . . and we would
say, "I am not a Canadian
citizen." My parents
taught us what it is to be
Longhouse, to be Tradi-
tional, to be a fighter.
Strength goes hand in
hand with pride, knowing
and liking who and what
you are.

When the Québec Pro-
vincial Police stormed the
barricade on July 11, 1990,
my family was there (ex-
cept for three siblings who
were out of town, but re-
turned during the course
of the summer). My par-
ents could have lost sons,
daughters, and grandchil-
dren. But we always knew
that our land was worth
standing up for. I remem-
ber my Mother, a shut-in
at the time, listening to reports of the raid on a Montréal radio station. She
didn't know if we were
okay or not, but she didn't
cry . . . she was angry. My
Mother and my Father
were often sought for ad-
vice over the years and
even more so during the
summer of 1990. Their
wisdom and knowledge
about money, power, poli-
tics, and the Great Law
was a gift shared by many
who took a stand that sum-

(continued)

Roth (Continued)   **David (Continued)**   **Nelson (Continued)**

mer. My Mother has
joined the ancestors now
and I miss her always. My
Mother was the strongest
woman I have ever
known. This is for you,
*Ista tanon Rakeni.**

—*Kasennahawi Marie*
David
Broadcast Journalist
CKHQ Radio
Kanehsatake
Mohawk Territory

*Ista tanon Rakeni means
"Mother and Father" in the
Mohawk language.

Conclusion

Issues deriving from the televisual representation of cross-cultural communities in Canada are central to media analysis at the end of the 20th century. Unfortunately, the coverage of the Mohawk confrontation of three levels of government has become an exemplar of media distortions, misrepresentations, and stereotypes circulating in Canada's "multicultural" society.

In Marie David's words: "Most journalists got the spark, but they didn't see the flame." The Oka/Kanehsatake story was a complex one to research. It could not have been done on an "instant" basis. It required time and patience because of its detailed implications and long historical background. The need to tell the story itself conflicted with the journalistic imperative to enter the situation, get some quick sound bytes, and air the story. To cover the Mohawk/Oka story fairly would have required sensitive cross-cultural understanding and relational skills, trustworthy contacts within the Mohawk communities, and a formal recognition of the complexity of the issues leading up to the armed conflict. These conditions were not met by most journalists. Those non-native journalists who did have basic experience and trust within the Mohawk communities were accused of having defied the prevailing ethos of story-collecting. Two, who specifically stayed behind the barricade for longer than their media producers desired (one from the *Toronto Globe and Mail*, the other from the Canadian Broadcasting Corporation's English radio service), were accused of having the Stockholm Syndrome and were severely criticized by their colleagues and the general public. In essence, they had violated their credibility by staying longer than "objectivity" permitted (Angharad Valdivia, personal correspondence, January 27, 1994).

"Outside" journalists, consequently, failed to get the "real" story of the Mohawk/governments' conflict. Lumped together into a single homogeneous and monolithic category by the media, the Mohawk Warrior was represented as a symbol for all Mohawks who believed in the reasons for the protest in Kanehsatake. When the federal government agreed to meet with Mohawk delegates for the purpose of negotiating an agreement, they were criticized by journalists for sitting down with armed and masked enemies of the state, characterized as terrorists by Canadian military consultants.[13] When it became apparent that Ellen Gabriel was the protesters' official spokesperson, the media and the government negotiators became uncomfortable. Not accustomed to dealing with young women as authoritative representatives within a negotiations situation, the male government negotiators kept searching for the "right" person allocated to speak on behalf of the Mohawk Warriors and other protesters.[14]

> Just the fact of having a woman spokesperson seemed to surprise people, throw them off—threw the cops off. It seemed to make people uncomfortable. They were even saying that in the negotiations, male negotiators with Canada and Québec just were completely uncomfortable with the fact that they were talking to women and not men—and that the women were so strong about it (Marie David, personal communication, July 13, 1993).

Furthermore, because of consensus-based decision making within the Mohawk community, no decision would be made without a thorough community consultation. This meant that negotiations became a long and tedious process, with a back-and-forth motion to it. The incommensurability of their own cultural values with those of the Traditional Mohawks, demonstrated by the apparent lack of hierarchy and the strong and consistent leadership of women, surprised non-native people as they projected *their* (gendered and racialized) cultures' conflict resolution approach onto the crisis. The "surprise" was as true for mainstream journalists as it was for the negotiating teams of the three levels of government involved in the resolution of the conflict.

The conflict, consequently, raised important matters about public knowledge of First Nations issues and showed clearly how the media uses information fragments to construct an impression of story clarity. To fill information gaps, the media turned to governmental discourses of thuggery and terrorism and symbolically placed all Mohawks within a system of categories of violence—as exemplified in the following newspaper headlines:

- "The Mohawk Warriors: Heroes or Thugs?" (*Toronto Star*, November 2, 1990)
- "Mafia Warrior" (Aislin's political cartoon, *Montréal Gazette*, April 30, 1990)
- "The Making of a Warrior" (*Saturday Night*, April 1991)
- "The Fury of Oka: After the Showdown, Indian Leaders Promise a Violent Autumn" (*Maclean's*, September 19, 1990)
- "Canada Cannot Tolerate Violence as a Political Tool" (*Globe and Mail*, August 18, 1990)
- "Police Find 30 Guns in Kanesatake" (*Gazette*, September 28, 1990)
- "Mohawk Militancy From Wounded Knee to an Adirondack Native Commune . . . to Oka, an Idea Is Spreading" (*Ottawa Citizen*, September 15, 1990)

"Real life" coverage "out there in the pines" typically sold audiences to advertisers in ways unanticipated even by media theorists. Headliners, scoops, "live action" by masked Warriors looked good for all media services from local to international. Notwithstanding the sympathy and careful reportage of a few individual Canadian journalists, most of the international media neglected researching and publicizing the critical issues that underpinned the conflict's origin and extension. As a consequence, the international mediation of the crisis carried with it a commodification effect that made into caricature the stereotypical image of the Mohawk Warrior in full camouflage costume, including bandanna and mask. In focusing on the Warrior and ignoring the less TV-flashy ordinary person, the Mohawk traditionalist and the local citizen trying to follow her or his conscience about the land issue faded into the media background.

Media stereotyping of First Nations peoples was never more transparently framed than during the "Oka crisis." The disruption of social order was complemented by the disruption of media routines on two television channels in Canada. Twenty-four hour live coverage interrupted the smooth flow of edited media (mis)interpretations—the neatly packaged bipolar bad/good, native/non-native representations that media consumers expect. Compared with edited broadcast news, loosely stitched together by narratives of crisis, the 24-hour live coverage brought to Canadians by CBC's *Newsworld* and the French network's *Télé-Métropole* showed us raw data from the perspectives of the camerapersons located in various positions within and outside of the barricaded communities. As a lesson in media literacy, it was unprecedented in Canadian broadcasting history. Viewers sat on the edge of their seats, waiting for the next "real" episode in the conflict to take place, a simulation of the Hollywood cowboy-and-Indian film—a break in the normal media routines.

In contrast to the immediacy and flashiness of Warrior coverage in 1990 are the routine absences of native issues and journalists from present mainstream media. Few public images and analyses of native issues in Canada are native-produced, -distributed, or cross-culturally sensitive.[15] When coverage of First Nations stories is present, there is still a tendency to characterize the native community in stereotypical categories—the sidekick, the radical, the borderline psychotic, or the mystic (Hayden Taylor, 1993, Op Ed). Five years after the confrontation and the many well-intentioned First Nations sensitivity-training workshops, there have only been minor changes. There are a few more native journalists working in the mainstream press. This is mostly due to another very significant change, however. Canada has a new *Broadcasting Act* (June 4, 1991) that stipulates that aboriginal broadcasting is to become an integral part of the Canadian broadcasting system "as public funds become available" (Section 3). With current federal government cutbacks at the CBC, Canada's national broadcasting network, and the opening up of the 400-channel universe, it is likely that the potential impact of this policy legislation will be limited in scope, at least for the near future. It is, therefore, very important that mainstream journalists personally take on the responsibility to portray accurately and fairly all cultural communities, in conjunction with the legislative framework for the development of aboriginal journalism in Canada.

A legitimation crisis, such as that of 1990, is a time of fissure: a break in the tightly sealed ideological constructs that dominate our political imaginaries, material and mediated realities. The Oka/Kanehsatake/governments' conflict was one such opening in the apparently peaceful social relationship established between natives and non-native peoples and journalists in Canada.

If there is anything that we, as cultural analysts, writers, and broadcasters, have learned from the way in which mainstream media (mis)handled the

Mohawk/governments' conflict, it is that journalists need to rethink the methods by which they access specific background information and sources within cultural and racial communities about which they have been professionally taught very little. In a forthcoming paper, Valerie Alia (in press), who teaches journalism at the University of Western Ontario in London, suggests that journalists ought to learn and practice the techniques of ethnographic research to orient themselves more realistically to the specificity of cross-cultural situations and relations. We would *also* recommend that journalists open their writing or broadcasting practices to collaborative work with First Nations peoples and other formerly disenfranchised groups who, in the past, have not had direct access to public mediated forums in which to express, in their own words, *their accounts* of the world.

Notes

1. This dialogue has four participating voices: a narrator/Voice 1—Lorna Roth; Voice 2—Marie David; and Voice 3—Bev Nelson.

2. Oka is situated about 38 kilometers West of Montréal and is the non-native community immediately adjacent to the Kanehsatake settlement.

3. Québec CEGEPs are equivalent to junior colleges.

4. By *alternative* I mean complementary views that address issues not likely to have been covered by mainstream media. It is information that fills in the gaps, so to speak. By *oppositional* I refer to views that oppose the dominant ideological positions and conceptual frameworks taken up and promoted by mainstream media venues.

5. See Michèle Mattelart (1986), *Women, Media, and Crisis: Femininity and Disorder,* for further elaboration.

6. For readers interested in women's use of the telephone to establish support systems, see Lana Rakow's (1992) study in *Gender on the Line: Women, the Telephone, and Community Life.*

7. *Stockholm Syndrome* refers to the phenomenon of the hostage's overidentification with her or his hostage taker.

8. The Handsome Lake Code of the late 19th century is based on the Quaker religion but also incorporates elements of Christianity, such as confession and repentance.

9. The Five Nations (later Six) Iroquois Confederacy includes the Mohawks, Oneida, Onondaga, Seneca, and Cayuga. In the late 1890s, the Tuscarora Nation joined.

10. The term *Longhouse* is used two ways in this text. The term can refer to a traditional way of life or describe the followers of the Great Law. A Longhouse is also the place where the people gather, where meetings are conducted and ceremonies or socials are held. Each clan will sit separately. As well, the male and female members of the clan will sit on opposite sides of the building.

11. Wampum Belts are belts woven together with beads of shell and constitute records of Confederacy laws, ceremonies, and history. They were also used as a form of currency.

12. There is a total of 50 Chiefs within the entire Confederacy, 9 of whom come from the Mohawk Nation.

13. This characterization of the Mohawks as "terrorists" by the army was confirmed at a military debriefing of the media coverage of the Oka conflict that took place on November 16, 1990, in Ottawa, Canada.

14. This phenomenon suggests even more strongly than does Gaye Tuchman (1978) in *Making News: A Study in the Construction of Reality* that not only might a news organization make up a spokesperson when there isn't one, but it will look to change the one that is provided if she or he makes the organization uncomfortable.

15. At a time when native media might have added a more realistic picture of what was going on in the Mohawk communities, First Nations print journalists were just recovering from a severe (100%) cutback of their federal government subsidy and Northern Native broadcasters were adapting to their 16% reduction in funds, announced on February 23, 1990. This cutback has had widespread impact on the balance, fairness, accuracy, and context of the coverage of native issues by native journalists on a regional and national basis in Canada. With inadequate budgets for travel, few have the opportunity to do firsthand research on significant issues in communities outside of their own. During the crisis of 1990, their coverage, like that of mainstream journalists, tended to be somewhat fragmented, decontextualized, and subject to factual confusion, such as mixing up the town names and locations of Kahnawake and Kanehsatake. Their accuracy level would probably have been far better had they had the appropriate resources (financial and personnel) to invest in travel and long-distance telephone calls.

References

Alia, V. (in press). The Rashomon principle: The journalist as ethnographer. In V. Alia & B. Brennan (Eds.), *Journalistic ethics in Canada* (tentative title). Halifax, Canada: Fernwood Press.

Bakhtin, M. (1981). Discourse in the novel. In M. Holquist (Ed.), *The dialogical imagination* (pp. 259-442). Austin: University of Texas Press.

Clifford, J. (1986). Introduction: Partial truths. In J. Clifford & G. E. Marcus (Eds.), *Writing culture: The poetics and politics of ethnography* (pp. 1-26). Berkeley: University of California Press.

Fuse Magazine. (1993). [Special issue on cultural appropriation], *16*(5 & 6).

Glenn, E. N. (1992). From servitude to service work: Historical continuities in the racial division of paid reproductive labor. *Signs: Journal of Women in Culture and Society, 28*(1), 1-43.

Government of Canada. *Broadcasting Act,* 4 June 1991.

Government of Canada. *Indian Act,* S.C. 1869, 31 V., c.4, s. 15.

Government of Canada. *Indian Act,* S. 4. C. 42, sc.8.

Hayden Taylor, D. (1993, October 4). What ever happened to Billy Jack? *Globe & Mail,* Op. Ed.

hooks, b. (1992). *Black looks: Race and representation.* Toronto: Between the Lines.

Mattelart, M. (1986). *Women, media, and crisis: Femininity and disorder.* London: Comedia Publishing Group.

Minh-ha, T. T. (1989). *Woman, native, other.* Bloomington: Indiana University Press.

Perigoe, R. (1990, September/October). The media and minorities. *Content,* pp. 10-13.

Rakow, L. F. (1992). *Gender on the line: Women, the telephone, and community life.* Urbana: University of Illinois Press.

Roth, L. (1992). Media and the commodification of crisis. In M. Raboy & B. Dagenais (Eds.), *Media, crisis and democracy: Mass communication and the disruption of social order* (pp. 144-161). London: Sage.

Roth, L. (1993, Summer). Mohawk airwaves and cultural challenges: Some reflections on the politics of recognition and cultural appropriation after the summer of 1990. *Canadian Journal of Communication, 18*(3), 315-332.

Spivak, G., & Adamson, W. (1990). The problem of cultural self-representation. In S. Harasym (Ed.), *The post-colonial critic: Interviews, strategies, dialogues* (pp. 50-58). New York: Routledge.

Spivak, G., & Gunew, S. (1990). Questions of multiculturalism. In S. Harasym (Ed.), *The post-colonial critic: Interviews, strategies, dialogues* (pp. 59-66). New York: Routledge.

Tuchman, G. (1978). *Making news: A study in the construction of reality.* New York: Free Press.

Williams, R. (1977). *Marxism and literature.* New York: Oxford University Press.

4   Representing Ourselves

Films and Videos by
Asian American/Canadian Women

MARINA HEUNG

> When I left that concrete space in the margins, I kept alive
> in my heart ways of knowing reality which affirm continu-
> ally not only the primacy of resistance but the necessity of
> a resistance that is sustained by remembrance of the past,
> which includes recollections of broken tongues giving us
> ways to speak that decolonize our minds.
>
> bell hooks *(Framework, 36)*

In 1993, an unprecedented number of feature-length films by and about
Asians were released to great popular success, leading *Time* magazine critic
Richard Corliss (1993) to proclaim the arrival of "Asian chic" with a note of
foreboding that may or may not be intentional: "The Asians are coming! The
Asians have landed" (p. 68). Yet Corliss's article leaves one glaring fact un-
remarked: the absence of women-directed films among this crop of new

releases, except for the single example of Tiana Thi Tranh's *From Hollywood to Hanoi*. Even more important, the portrayal of women in these films does not depart significantly from the portrayals of Asian women already familiar from years of mainstream stereotyping. In a timely riposte to Corliss's uncritical appraisal, Jessica Hagedorn notes how, for example, in *The Joy Luck Club* (with a screenplay co-written by the novel's original author, Amy Tan), the Chinese American mothers do not escape being stereotyped as long-suffering victims. Also, beyond deflating Corliss's claims of a significant breakthrough, Hagedorn raises the key question of how entrenched stereotyping affects those who bear its brunt—Asians themselves.[1] Born and raised in the Philippines, an American colony for many years, Hagedorn uses her personal background to gain insight into the power of mass media images to conscript and appropriate individual psyches. She writes, "As I was growing up in the Philippines in the 1950s, my fertile imagination was colonized by thoroughly American fantasies" (Hagedorn, 1994, p. 74). Those of us who, like Hagedorn, grew up in colonial settings are most apt to acknowledge the cultural sway of U.S.-American popular culture as it infiltrates every aspect of lived experience in the Third World. In its most concrete manifestation, colonization consists of actual territorial conquest and occupation; however, the notion also pertains to how dominant systems of representation produce and reinforce mental structures and images to constrain, dehumanize, and disempower particular individuals and social groups in both First- and Third-World cultures. As Edward Said has shown in his classic study of Orientalism, the power of the colonizer is fundamentally constituted by the power to speak for and to represent: "*He* spoke for and represented her" (Said, 1978, p. 6; his italics). This statement further suggests how the Western Orientalizing imagination casts the East/"Orient" as female, that is, with specific connotations of sexual invitation and submission. Dual inscriptions of race and gender enforce Asian women's special visibility within Orientalist discourse as well as their vulnerability to sexist and racist projections.

Hagedorn's notion of a "colonization of the imagination" has an even more important implication for the ways in which popular images of Asian women have affected us. As Renee Tajima has noted, "Several generations of Asian women have been raised with racist and sexist celluloid images" (Tajima, 1989, p. 317). Not only does the general population accept stereotypes of Asian women as truth and then project them onto us without our consent, but we ourselves have incorporated the same images into our self-imaginings. *Internalized colonization* is the process by which stereotypes infiltrate and transform the consciousness of Asian women, with dire results for how the same women view and experience themselves. Internalized colonization, then, is one of the most insidious and destructive effects of colonialism.[2] The "traumatic character of the 'colonial experience' " has been duly noted by Stuart Hall, who recognizes how "dominant regimes of representations . . . had the power to make us see and experience ourselves as 'Other.' " Hall adds: "this kind of knowledge is internal, not external. . . . This expropriation of cultural identity cripples and deforms" (Hall, n.d., pp. 70-71). The process of "yellowface enculturation" (Tchen, 1994, p. 13) thus includes the component of internalized colonization whereby the power to represent and, by extension, to shape the consciousness of those who are the subjects of representation becomes one basic method by which racial domination operates in our culture. Accordingly, writer Gish Jen (1991) has concluded: "Over the years, Asians have been the form onto which white writers have freely projected their fears and desires. That this is a form of colonialism goes almost without saying; it can only happen when the people whose images are appropriated are in no position to object" (p. 12).

In her otherwise spirited critique of films by Asians recently released in the United States, Hagedorn ends on a note of apparent resignation:

> as females and Asians, as audiences or performers, we have learned to settle for less—to accept the fact that we are either decorative, invisible, or one-dimensional. When there are characters who look like us represented in a movie, we have also learned to view between the lines, or to add what is missing. For many of us, this way of watching has always been a necessity. We fill in the gaps. (Hagedorn, 1994, p. 79)

What would move Hagedorn beyond her quiescent stance is the realization that we need not "settle for" the self-alienating task of always "fill[ing] in the gaps." More specifically, there already exists, in Canada and the United States, a significant amount of work by women film and video artists whose objective is precisely to work in the interstices of mainstream representation and thereby to forge an aesthetic that is both resisting and self-creating. In this chapter, therefore, I will discuss films and videos produced by Asian women in the United States and Canada in which the struggle toward decolonization is front and center. As my analysis will show, this project proceeds on different fronts and assumes a variety of formal strategies and styles, but in each case the artist has simply seized on an alternative way to appropriate, revise, and re-envision the possibilities of representing herself. Above all, I will show how these significant differences are undergirded by a fundamental concern with the problem of representation, namely, the awareness that contemporary identities are the products of how others have already seen and represented us. Thus, whether these works proceed as a frontal critique of mass media or whether they explore the recesses of private memory, all of them acknowledge, directly or indirectly, the historical context in which all representations exist. By pursuing this line of inquiry, I hope to demonstrate how identities are constructed and communicated always within the historical nexus of competing and contingent representations, and that once we acknowledge this, we will understand the ways in which stories and texts speak to each other—and indeed, the reason why they speak to us.

Decolonizing the Image:
Strategies of Intervention

The first group of films and videos I will discuss performs the task of making "representational reparations" (Solomon-Godeau, 1993, p. 28) by engaging those mass media images that have historically objectified, reduced, and distorted images of Asian women. The objective is to decolonize the stereotypes that have projected Asian women as objects of sexual conquest and subjugated knowledge and, by exposing their formation through history, defuse them of their naturalness and their power. They illustrate Coco Fusco's (1993) analysis of how a decolonization of the image operates: "resistance within a colonial context is rarely direct, overt, or literal; rather it articulates itself through semantic reversals, and through the process of infusing icons, objects, and symbols with different meanings" (p. 84).

The 1988 videotape *Slaying the Dragon*[3] (directed by Deborah Gee) documents the history of the Asian woman's representation in Hollywood cinema, unraveling the permutations of her stereotyping through the figures of the dragon lady, the industrious peasant, the geisha/lotus blossom, and the recent icon of the TV anchorwoman modeled after Connie Chung. Organized chronologically from the silent period to the present, the tape interweaves its inventory of celluloid images with a critique of mass media images in general, including, for example, Singapore Airlines' exploitation of the manufactured mystique of the Asian airline flight attendant. In each instance, it carefully exposes the constructedness of stereotypes by relating their evolution to changing political agendas, global conflicts, and shifts in geopolitical power. Further, by linking Hollywood representations to the emergence of the model minority stereotype, prohibitions against miscegenation, patterns of inter-marriage, intra-ethnic sexual relations, and inter-ethnic politics, the video-tape delineates the injuries inflicted on the professional and personal lives of Asian women. Although it regrettably uses a male voice-over in its narrative and features a predominantly male roster of "experts," it nevertheless surveys a panoply of Asian women—actresses, producers, journalists, students— whose images and voices counteract the one-dimensional celluloid stereo-types with which they are juxtaposed. For instance, veteran actress Nobu McCarthy describes how she walked out of an audition in which she was asked to play a "dragon lady," and another actress, Kim Miyori, recalls the process by which she rejected delivering the stereotype of the exotic Asian woman "with long hair and skirts slit up the sides." In an extended anecdote, anchor-woman Emerald Yeh recalls her painful experience of being groomed by CNN-News to be a Connie Chung look-alike. Having initially tried to con-form, she now describes her efforts to counter the stereotype of passivity that Connie Chung has represented to her.

In *Slaying the Dragon*, TV producer Yeh Tung remembers with horror how a film crew challenged her authority, and she concludes that "being Asian and being female . . . it's very hard to separate the two." The tape demonstrates that for Asian women, race and gender are indeed inextricably fused and textually produced. Gee's tape, however, also goes beyond simply exposing the history of an oppressive representational system and its production of colo-nized subjectivities. As Gwendolyn Henderson (1991, p. 30) suggests in rela-tion to black women writers, the task of resistance is interventionist as well as intertextual and revisionist. In other words, any project seeking to resist the colonizing effects of mass media must proceed from the knowledge of and the will to subvert, interrupt, and revise established representational conventions. In this vein, the women in *Slaying the Dragon* articulate an actively interven-tionist stance toward their dilemma. For instance, Jiyoung Kim, a student, protests, "I'm not like that! I don't go around, you know, learning these weird sexual techniques. . . . I'm not this subservient person. . . . Asians, especially Asian women are brought up very strict. . . . That really strongly contrasts with this stereotype that these women are just fireballs inside." Also, a ribbon of laughter runs through many of the women's narratives, expressing the shock of recognition, indignation, and a mocking irreverence. Humor and outrage turn out to be effective antidotes to the naturalizing effect of the images under critique and form modes of nonverbal intervention. For instance, Amy Hill simply laughs off the advice to be more demure and quiet, saying with a chuckle, "But I can't . . . it's too late—I'm too old for that now!" Sara Ishikawa, a professor of architecture, recalls how she would be greeted as "Suzie Wong!" on the streets of New York; she ends her anecdote with a laugh, and adds conspiratorially, "Right?"

Yellow Tale Blues: Two American Families[4] (co-directed by Christine Choy and Renee Tajima in 1991) likewise adopts an interventionist and intertextual strategy, juxtaposing numerous clips from Hollywood movies with documentary scenes from the lives of the videomakers' families. Both a saga of generational change and a corrective narrative of national identity, the videotape undercuts the vitriolic racist content of mainstream cinema by featuring scenes of a Korean American grandmother being sworn in as a naturalized American citizen and of the Tajima family paying a visit to the Statue of Liberty. Early in the tape, movie clips capturing the essence of Orientalist fantasy are seamlessly blended with black-and-white home movie clips of the two families; here, the incongruous juxtaposition drives home the mismatch between two conflicting conceptualizations of cultural identity and nationhood. In particular, overlapping dialogue opposes mass-media enforced ideology to the lived experiences of actual Asian Americans. Thus, when the Tajimas are visiting the Statue of Liberty, a shot of the monument is briefly overlapped with the dialogue from a World War II war film in which the male hero bombastically conjures up the threat of an imminent invasion by a horde (of Asians?) who will "blacken your skies, and burn your cities, and make you get down on your knees and beg for mercy." Elsewhere, the speaking voices of family members are used to diffuse the racist and sexist content of Hollywood images. For instance, the voice of Marsha Tajima is heard over clips from Vietnam-era films, dismissing the images as "patronizing." In interviews, the videomakers' family members speak of how their self-image and attitudes have been shaped by movies. One of the women talks about wishing that her eyes were "larger, rounder . . . that I had double eyelids," while Mark Tajima acknowledges that his image of an ideal woman was modeled after the Hollywood bombshell, Bo Derek. Finally, the tape highlights the daily routine of Cathy Choy, videomaker Choy's sister, who works a double shift as a restaurant cashier and a postal worker in order to support her three children and mother. In one instance, she shows the videomakers the sleeping quarters that she shares with her family, and the sequence is intercut with a scene from the Hollywood movie *The World of Suzie Wong* in which the male lead strolls through an open market in Hong Kong where women sell their wares. Here, the tape underscores the disparity between two kinds of looks: the engaged "insider" camera-eye of Choy and Tajima and the touristic gaze of the Western male. Despite its rich allusions to Hollywood cinema, *Yellow Tale Blues* substitutes for Hollywood narrative a different account of lives based on generational continuity and change, suggesting that the process of acculturation may have another kind of "happy ending." When Eddie, Cathy Choy's son, goes off to college, he expresses his pleasure at attending a college where there are not many Asians, although he himself grew up in an Asian-dominant environment, and his remark suggests the optimistic possibility that his generation has outgrown the burden of monolithic racial affiliations. Similarly, Mark Tajima marvels that his young son doesn't know pejorative racial terms (like *Jap*) that he has been so familiar with, the implication being that the boy has managed to escape the racial baiting that his father suffered when he was young.

Abjuring the documentary approach of *Slaying the Dragon* and *Yellow Tale Blues,* Valerie Soe's *Picturing Oriental Girls*[5] (1992) carries the technique of quotation to an extreme. This 12-minute collage compiles quick movie clips and written text from a variety of sources, including mail-order-bride catalogues, men's magazines, and the novel *The World of Suzie Wong.* Subtitled *A (Re)Educational Tape,* this work turns racist and sexist ideologies against themselves through the simple techniques of citation, attribution, cross-referencing, and ironic juxtaposition. Often, a written quotation scrolls up over a movie clip, straightforwardly reinforcing the image's content. Then, a series of dots leads our eyes downwards across the screen and delays the attribution of the quotation, so that when the citation is finally given, it has the effect of a punch line or an in-joke. For example, over a clip from *Teahouse of the August Moon,* a geisha in a kimono plays a samisen while the title starts to scroll: "Asian women are renowned for their beauty, femininity, traditional values, and loving dispositions. . . . They are sincere . . . faithful . . . devoted . . . and believe in a lasting marriage." These words are strung out singly or in groups over additional shots of a geisha kneeling and bowing, a woman embracing a white man and lighting his cigarette, a Japanese bride with an android. The tape momentarily allows—perhaps even encourages—us to take this information "straight," but following a string of vertically arranged dots and a series of black-out frames, the source of the quotation is finally revealed as the *Sunshine International Catalog,* an Asian mail-order-bride catalog.

Sometimes the tape finds a particularly sly way of subverting and revising the meaning of the texts it cites. For instance, immediately after the sequence just described a title comes up to say: "Just occasionally she does go off the rails. She becomes a Madame Mao or a Mrs. Marcos." Then follows a series of gun-toting, brick- and dish-throwing Asian women, accompanied by the title: "Overnight, the waif has metamorphosed into a dragon lady." Here, a quotation followed by an attribution (to *GQ Magazine*) fulfills a double purpose: Even though the sequence introduces the worn stereotype of the karate-chopping dragon lady, it comes right on the heels of an array of submissive Asian women, so that this abrupt explosion of female rage and violence can be read also as a cathartic and appropriate rejection of imposed servility. At such moments, *Picturing Oriental Girls* transcends the one-dimensional narrative logic of pure quotation to ignite a scenario of parody and subversion, lending justification to Fusco's analogy between guerilla warfare and the media arts, both of which take "elements of an established or imposed culture and [throw] them back with a different set of meanings [by utilizing] the tactics of reversal, recycling, and subversive montage" (Fusco, 1993, p. 83).

The three video works discussed in this section amply show how the social existence and psychic reality of Asian women are enmeshed within multilayered intersections of images, texts, and prejudices. Obviously, it is not possible to speak about being female and Asian without taking into account how these terms are to a large extent defined for us by others who wish to create us in their image. In each of these three tapes, the strategic use of montage and collage—whereby documentary sequences are interwoven with quotations and media clips—speaks to how the identities and self-images of Asian women are products of not only individual histories, but also of how these histories have already been narrated by others. Yet, as these works suggest, appropriation need not be a one-way process. Another recent film, Christine Chang's *Be Good My Children* (1993), interweaves a narrative about a Korean American family, told in straightforward documentary style, with parodic episodes in which the daughter becomes "Mae East." Judy's impersonation of the Hollywood star's irreverent humor, self-mocking swagger, and exhibitionistic excess turns ethnic stereotyping upside down. At the same time, her incorporation of a hyper-"American" icon within an immigrant narrative reverses the typical pattern by which the "exotic other" is typically appropriated and produced for Western consumption.

Body Politics

Literally, colonization operates by taking over land and bodies. On a symbolic level, it works on bodies because physical anatomies become the canvas onto which cultural meanings are projected. Although it is apparent that Asians, like people of color in general, are marginalized and rendered invisible in the mass media, Asian women are, through representation, "embodied" in a distinctive and at times literalized way. As enforced through media representations, the bodies of Asian women are idealized and judged according to Western standards of exotic beauty, in conformity to the edicts of what Renee Tajima has termed "aesthetic imperialism" (Tajima, 1989, p. 314). Whether portrayed as objects of sexual conquest and seduction, casualties of war, and mail-order items for sale, or reduced to exotic but interchangeable elements of the decorative landscape (Tajima, 1989, p. 314), the bodies of Asian women are palpably present in the mass media in the most physicalized and sexualized terms. The history of the representation of Asian women illustrates the proposition that bodies are "shot through with meaning, riddled with definitions and qualities not of our own choosing" (Kennedy, 1992, p. 111) and governed by "mediations enacted on the body by the body politic" (Smith, 1993, p. 140). For Asian women especially, ideologies of gender, race, ethnicity, and sexuality place their bodies under the burden of erasure while also marking them as receptacles of projected cultural meanings. In this vein, Trinh T. Minh-ha notes: "The Body, the most visible difference between men and women, the only one to offer a secure ground for those who seek the permanent, the feminine 'nature' and 'essence,' remains thereby the safest basis for racist and sexist ideologies" (Trinh, 1987, p. 18). Literalizing Elspeth Probyn's remark that "societal discourses come to be written almost exclusively on female bodies or those considered 'other' " (Probyn, 1992, p. 86), the opening sequence in *Picturing Oriental Girls*—a collage of clips in which they are painted, sketched, tattooed, and used as surfaces for elaborate artistic designs—shows how the bodies of Asian women are used as actual writing surfaces.

In this section of the chapter, I will discuss works that treat the theme of the body as the site of "cultural betrayal" (Smith, 1993, p. 143). In Pam Tom's *Two Lies*[6] (1989) and Helen Lee's *Sally's Beauty Spot*[7] (1990), the body of the Asian woman has been appropriated by cultural prescriptions that distort female conceptions of bodies and identities; in each case, her body is subjected to denial and mutilation. In *Two Lies,* a daughter's insight into aesthetic imperialism arises from her rejection of the mutilated maternal body. In *Sally's Beauty Spot*, a young woman's identification with a screen image causes her to view her own body with alternating obsessiveness, ambivalence, and revulsion.

According to its director, *Two Lies* was made "to challenge our traditional notions of beauty and culture [and] to focus on social and psychological pressures faced by women and to dramaticize [sic] the many contradictions and complexities of being Asian and female in America" (director's note, unpublished film synopsis). As the film opens, two daughters greet their mother, Doris, returning home from having eyelid surgery to make her eyes rounder (more Caucasian). A single mother, Doris wants to get a new grip on life. Her consent to physical mutilation, however, also comes from her submission to gender- and racially inflected cultural codes. For one thing, Doris wants to attract Caucasian men. Her first suitor is a Caucasian man who calls her "fortune cookie" and "lotus bun." Later, resting at a motel on the way to visit an Indian pueblo with her daughters, she lies pool-side flirting with a man who is fascinated by her ethnicity.

Shot on contrasty black-and-white film stock to convey an almost Gothic sense of subjectivity and grotesquerie, *Two Lies* offers a critical perspective on a mother's psychic betrayal of her older daughter, Mei-ling. While the younger daughter, Esther, seems simply curious about her mother's surgery, Doris's actions are seen primarily through Mei's eyes. Constructed around the motifs of eyes and (in)sight, the film thematically connects the mother's surgery and her daughter's dawning rejection of her. The first shot of the film shows a close-up of the younger daughter's eyes as she looks through a mock-up of an Indian pueblo that she is building for a class project. When Doris comes home, we see the two sisters through the filmy gauze of her eye-bandages in a subjective camera shot. As the film progresses, the power to see—and therefore to know—is transferred from Doris to Mei. At the motel, Doris's flirtation with a man is seen from Mei's point of view as she watches from across the pool. Later, at the pueblo site, Doris stops flirting with the tour guide (who suggestively asks, "Did you know that lipstick was invented in China?") only when she feels her daughters staring at her. Later, Mei finally rejects her mother's protestation ("There's nothing wrong with wanting to look and feel better") by confronting her: "I was telling you what they call it in school: two eyes—two lies."

Significantly, the last time we see through Doris's eyes is when she goes looking for Mei inside the darkened pueblo after their quarrel. Her disorientation and partial blindness are emphasized through the jumpy editing and erratic movements of the handheld camera. Finally collapsing in exhaustion, she begs her younger daughter, "I can't see so well—help me." As the three drive away, the film's last shot is again that of a pair of eyes—this time of Mei's—reflected in the car's rearview mirror. This image unites the motifs of eyes and mirror. Earlier, we have seen Doris's obsession with mirrors, indicating not only her vanity but also the distorted modeling that she represents for her daughters. At the end, Mei rejects identification with her mother; appropriately, therefore, the tilted rearview mirror is angled to reflect her eyes, not her mother's. As in *Yellow Tale Blues*, *Two Lies* acknowledges the psychic damage that results when judgments of physical attractiveness and self-worth are internalized from culturally imposed expectations. Despite the darker tone in *Two Lies*, however, both films suggest that generational change can bring progressive emancipation and agency.

In *Two Lies*, while their mother is applying makeup in the bathroom, Mei and Esther look through a medical text on cosmetic surgery. As Mei flips through pages of photographs of women (interestingly, with a TV image of Connie Chung playing in the background), she enumerates aloud different parts of the female anatomy—"eyes, buttocks, breasts, chin, ears"—that, apparently, are susceptible to alteration and "improvement." This scene highlights the way in which the female anatomy has been subjected to inventory, fragmentation, objectification, and medicalization. The visual structure of Helen Lee's *Sally's Beauty Spot* provides correlatives of such violations by presenting the female body in terms of parts: ear, eye, hair, skin, mouth, and breast. Adopting an analytic approach, the film "anatomizes" the Asian female body into its components, creating an effect that duplicates the fragmented subjectivities these physical parts construct. As the title suggests, Sally is obsessed with a mole on her chest. She tries to remove it by scrubbing away at it, and she tries to hide it by covering it up with makeup. At one point, a female voice asks: "Have you considered a surgical method of removal?" Later, a montage of photographs shows us a series of women with facial moles, but their studied poses remind us that such markings are also considered beautiful in other contexts. Alternatively a source of attractiveness or repulsion, Sally's "beauty spot" is an elastic signifier, with meanings that are subjectively and culturally constructed. However, with the repeated shots of Sally looking in the mirror, brushing her hair, or scrubbing at her mole, we infer that her preoccupation arises from an internalized sense of how her body should conform to imposed ideals of physical beauty. For Sally, her mole has come to symbolize her sense of her physical difference; more specifically, because it is a black mark on white skin, it also signifies her discomfort with racial difference. In the same way, Sally's other physical attributes are "colored" by their association with racial identity and difference. Over shots of Sally brushing her hair, we hear her describe her boyfriend's reaction to her new haircut: "He liked it . . . still shiny and black . . . I guess I looked different," a statement that is then queried by another female voice: "Different from what?"

Sally's bodily preoccupations are linked to her sexual and racial identity, as suggested in Sally's statements, "It's the first thing I see when I look in the mirror," and "It's always been there when I was a girl." These lines ostensibly refer to the mole, but because they are overlapped with clips from the movie *The World of Suzie Wong,* the "it" can also be read as referring to this movie that has functioned as an object of fascination and a source of ambivalent identification for Sally and many Asian women. If Suzie Wong is offered as a privileged text for the formation of Asian female subjectivity, its conflation with the mole suggests that Sally's ambivalence derives in part from the self-image she has absorbed from this master-text of Orientalism. As in *Two Lies,* the recurring interplay between eyes, mirror, and body in this film suggests how identity and self-image are products of our identification with external objects as well as internalization of imposed meanings.

The first clip from *Suzie Wong* shows Suzie (played by Nancy Kwan) dressed up in a ridiculously tawdry floral outfit as she caresses her body and looks coyly at the camera. Her gesture mimics Sally's compulsive scrubbing and grooming and also suggests how a woman can be complicit in her own fetishization. Other clips from the movie show the white male hero (William Holden) painting her portrait, angrily stripping her down to her underwear, or reverently kneeling down and kissing her while she is dressed in an elaborate Chinese costume. When, in the first clip, we hear the William Holden character berate Suzie for dressing up as a "cheap European street walker," the moment illuminates how the Western gaze insists on maintaining categories based on distinct racial differences. According to her white lover, Suzie Wong must conform to his expectations of what a "real" Chinese woman looks like, so her putting on "Western" dress immediately earns her his abuse and rejection. Following the same logic, it is only when Suzie puts on a "traditional" Chinese costume that she wins her lover's respect and approval (Marchetti, 1991, pp. 45-48).

Sally's Beauty Spot also focuses on *Suzie Wong's* glamorized treatment of interracial romance, which has become an essential part of its legacy to Asian women and Western audiences alike.[8] In the first part of Lee's film, there are repeated shots of Sally leaning forward in close-up to kiss a Caucasian man; this shot is then match-cut with another shot of the male hero in *Suzie Wong* kissing Suzie, so that both pairs of lovers echo each other's positioning within the frame. Near the end, there is yet another parallel shot of Sally kissing a black man, also composed in the same way. These recombinant interracial pairings invoke a binary logic based on assumptions of essentialized racial differences, an effect reinforced by the fact that the film systematically plays on visual oppositions between black and white throughout. Not only is it shot on black and white stock, but there are also patterned contrasts between a black mole on white skin, a white robe and black hair, white makeup applied on a black mole, black letters (literally the word *b-l-a-c-k*) being typed on white paper, a black male hand grasping a white female hand, and finally, the occasional fading out of shots into either black-out or white-out screens. However, this apparent binarism in fact masks an elaborate conceit—centered on Sally—exposing the instability of representational systems and signs. As an Asian woman, Sally is, racially speaking, neither black nor white, yet the use of literally black-and-white film stock makes the rendering of her ethnicity a slippery matter: when seen with a white man, she is read as "nonwhite," but when she kisses a black man, his blackness and the black-and-white film stock code her as "white." And of course, underlying all this, it is Sally's "true" skin color—neither black nor white—that is left unrepresented. This play on color coding casts Sally's skin color—and by extension, her racial identity—as a mobile signifier whose meaning is defined by its immediate context, and, of course, the materiality of the film medium itself. Thus, the radical project of *Sally's Beauty Spot* implies that all racial meanings and symbols are provisional because they are based on a representational system communicating in terms of arbitrarily encoded signs and contextually determined meanings.

Two Lies and *Sally's Beauty Spot* expose the cultural conditioning, textual productions, and internalized distortions that put women at war with their own bodies. What these two films portray, in particular, is the complicated nexus between women—Mei and her mother; Sally and Suzie—around which the tasks of resistance and self-definition revolve and evolve. In each instance, the ambivalent oscillations between self and other and between affinity and disindentification suggest all too clearly how precarious and porous are the physical and psychic boundaries of the self.

Disappeared Bodies/Erased Histories

The history of marginalized peoples can be interpreted as one in which bodies are disappeared and erased from history. In the final group of films and videos I will discuss, the artists' attempts to recover a personal past is played out in terms of a desire to retrieve the life stories of significant figures whose stories have been left unwritten or forgotten in the annals of official history. These "primal figures" that figure so prominently in women's autobiographies (Portuges, 1988, p. 340) are in most cases close family members. In *Family Gathering*[9] (codirected by Lise Yasui and Ann Tegnell, 1988), Yasui sets out to excavate her memories of her grandfather, who was interned during the Second World War as a Japanese spy. Two other works attempt to trace mother-daughter linkages. In *History and Memory: For Akiko and Takashige*[10] (1991), Rea Tajiri is haunted by a recurring image of her mother at an internment camp, and Janice Tanaka's *Memories From the Department of Amnesia*[11] (1991) is an elegiac meditation on her mother's life and death.

Family Gathering and *History and Memory* are instances of the "desire to create an intergenerational testimonial for the benefit of parents or children and to recount a story formerly repressed, silenced, or distorted" (Portuges, 1988, pp. 242-243). Both artists set out on personal journeys (involving physical travel as well as a return to the past) to recover their connection with a familial other. Both works are autobiographical, yet because they define identity as intersubjective and intergenerational, they challenge the traditional autobiography's assumptions about a unitary and autonomous self in a tactic typical of autobiographies by women and racial minorities (Smith, 1993, pp. 5-20; Sommer, 1989). The autobiographical projects in *Family Gathering* and *History and Memory* demonstrate the continuity between the personal and the familial; however, these two vectors of experience are in turn shown to be shaped by the larger forces of social history, so that subjective memory provides entry to shared racial identity and a collective past. Yet even when they explore the intermeshings of the subjective and the communal, both works ultimately reveal history itself to be a textual construct and therefore idiosyncratic and incomplete. In *Family Gathering* and *History and Memory*, the past is rendered through the unspooling of multiple visual and written texts—archival footage and still photographs, home movies and snapshots, government documents and memorabilia—that have survived accidents of time and dislocation. The revelation is that personal memory, familial storytelling, collective memory, and public history exist on a continuum of uneven erasure and recall and are subject to the contingencies inherent in all forms of representation and narration.

Family Gathering begins by invoking the specter of a disappeared person, when the filmmaker narrates in voice-over: "On December 12, 1941, five days after the Japanese attacked Pearl Harbor, my grandfather was arrested by the FBI. When my grandmother asked where they were taking him, the agents refused to answer. And when they drove away, no one knew how long he'd be gone." The filmmaker is a third-generation Japanese American woman who sets off to recover her family history, especially the story of her grandfather. She takes her camera from the East Coast to Hood River, OR, where her grandfather, Masuo Yasui, settled as a first-generation immigrant. Yasui's personal journey is also framed as an excursion into her own childhood memories, kept alive on the screen and in her memory by the preserved home movies of family reunions. These images have a privileged status for Yasui, for she says: "My understanding of family history came from the movies we watched every Sunday night." At the same time, her repeated references to "movies" elicits inevitable association with Hollywood films, but only to suggest how these "different" movies provide an indirect antidote to Hollywood's demeaning and dehumanizing images of Asians. But from the start, even the tangible visual presence of her grandfather in the home movies reveals the traps of unreliable memory. Initially Yasui uses the images to promote her memory of her grandparents' first visit to her family when she was a child, and she recalls how her grandfather told her stories into the night. Yet she immediately admits that this story is "one I made up," because her grandfather died before she was born, so the visit could not have occurred.

Yasui's film probes the mystery and silence surrounding her grandfather's life and death. Aware that her own memory is unreliable, she turns to her father, only to run up against his silence. In interviews with her father and her aunt, she finds her father reluctant to remember and to speak, while her aunt engages in a roundabout form of denial, insisting: "Well, Dad had such a meaningful life, I don't know that I'd be terribly concerned about how Dad died or when he died. I think the significant thing is that he lived!" It is not until later in the film that Yasui discovers the truth about her grandfather's death. After 28 years of silence, her father finally reveals that her grandfather was deeply affected by his wartime internment and committed suicide at age 71.

Utilizing the framework of the personal documentary, Yasui attempts to reassemble the pieces of history surrounding her grandfather's life and death by interweaving archival footage, family photographs, letters, newspaper headlines, and government documents. But this incomplete record only deepens the piercing emptiness at the center of her narrative—her grandfather's absence—and the provisional character of any attempt to reconstruct his life fully. Surprisingly, Yasui finds that her grandfather comes most convincingly to life when his letters to his sons are read aloud. Although this reading is clearly done by an actor, for Yasui this is "the closest [she's] come to the voice of [her] memory." At the same time, the voice of the filmmaker herself and those of her aunt, uncle, and father are overlapped with archival images, forming a bridge between the localized memories of these witnesses and the documents of public history, or what Richard Chalfen (1989) has termed "dominant memory" (p. 529). This seamless strategy informs the film's overriding rhetorical strategy, in which both individual memory and personal identity are shown to exist at the crossroads between autobiography and biography, the personal and the historical, the private and the public, the individual and the communal.

In *Family Gathering*, identity is seen to be at once intersubjective, intergenerational, intertextual, and actively constructed. Using an array of texts and sources, the film exemplifies the project of "pry[ing] open the process of subject formation" (Sommer, 1989, p. 109). In this way, Yasui

offers her viewers many opportunities to consider an array of related matters—how people get remembered, who controls information, how individual biographies and family histories get recorded and passed from generation to generation, who acts as "gatekeepers" of information and knowledge, and how different communication media can and often do offer alternative things to say about people, events and lives. (Chalfen, 1989, p. 526)

Throughout the film, the appearance of sprocket holes and black-out frames reminds us that Yasui's account of her journey is itself an artifact constructed for our viewing. Most important, the historian's and (auto)biographer's reliance on witnessing yields to the realization that both self and history are filtered through documents or testimonials whose adherence to "truth" is very much in doubt. *Family Gathering* suggests, then, that identity is constructed partly through family legend and partly through an active and willful self-invention. So, in the end, although Yasui knows that her memory of her grandfather's visit is only imaginary, she concludes by saying: "And although my grandfather died before I had a chance to meet him, I'll always remember that one evening I stayed up late, listening to him talk through the night."

In Rea Tajiri's *History and Memory*, a daughter tries to recover her mother's memories about her wartime internment.[12] Because of the gaps in her mother's recollections, the artist has grown up feeling that "things have been left out" of her family history; she feels "lost, ungrounded, somewhat like a ghost floating above a terrain, witnessing others living their lives, and yet not having one of its own." Although she was not with her mother during her internment, she is haunted by a memory of her mother at the camp in Poston, AZ. This image, repeated throughout the tape, shows a woman against the dusty background of a desert holding out a canteen to be filled. Tajiri acknowledges in voice-over: "I had never been there, yet I had a memory of it." When she arrives in Poston to retrace her mother's past, she uses her intuition to project herself into her mother's experience: Walking through the camp, she is able to locate the exact spot where her mother was housed by using an "internal divining rod." By following a subjective mental image, Tajiri discovers the larger story behind that image, and she is finally able to connect her mother's experiences to the collective history of Japanese Americans. At the end, she says: "I could forgive my mother her loss of memory and could make this image for her." In this crucial statement, the wish to recreate the "truth" of history yields to the videomaker's active intervention in, and deliberate construction of, the past, which in turn allow her to bridge her mother's past and her own need to know.

History and Memory ends with one final shot of Tajiri's mother with the canteen splashing herself with water; by this time, we view this poignant image with the full knowledge of its status as a fabrication. Before this point, Tajiri has already recognized how her own subjectivity was infiltrated by manufactured images from the mass media. Acknowledging "how the movies [have] influenced our lives," Tajiri uses Alan Parker's *Come See the Paradise,* a recent film about the Japanese American internment, to illustrate Hollywood's tendency to portray the experiences of Japanese Americans through the perspective of a white hero. Despite her suspicions about how Hollywood co-opts history for its own purposes, Tajiri nevertheless succeeds in appropriating Hollywood for her own story. In the second half of the tape, she interweaves clips from John Sturges's 1955 *Bad Day at Black Rock* with her account of her visit to the internment camp in Poston, Arizona. In *Bad Day,* Spencer Tracy arrives in a Western town to investigate the disappearance of a Japanese American man called Komoko. Tajiri parallels Tracy's search with her own. Like

Tracy, she arrives in a dusty desert town to remind the townspeople of a history they wish to forget. In *Bad Day*, the missing Japanese American is never seen. Yet, Tajiri says, Komoko's "absence is his presence": His disappearance from the film speaks to how Japanese Americans have been systematically erased from history.

Although *History and Memory* is about family history, Tajiri's family members, like Komoko, are only elusive. While the tape is densely layered with footage from numerous sources and time periods, the family members are rarely shown in person. Instead, they are presented obliquely: Their voices are heard in voice-overs, conversations, or quotations from letters, and their imprint on history is alluded to by old photographs, artifacts, and superimposed titles. These indirect ways of evoking their presence remind us of the difficulty of writing an all-inclusive history and prevent us from engaging with this history as mere consumers of facts and images.

Finally, Tajiri asks: What about those events that have escaped memory and history because no camera was present to record them, or no one was around to witness them? While trying to recover her mother's memories of internment, for example, Tajiri learns that cameras were forbidden in the camps. And because her mother does not remember much of what happened, will her past remain beyond the reach of recall? In part, the complex narrative structure of *History and Memory*—produced by the multilayered interweaving of newsreels, documentary footage, archival materials (such as photographs and documents), and numerous clips from Hollywood films—supplies the answer to Tajiri's question. This technique of "overlay and overlap" enacts the process of postcolonial identity construction that consists of fabricating a hybrid subjectivity out of the "different layers of an elusive and mercurial identity" (Solomon-Godeau, 1993, p. 57). In its use of written texts, Tajiri's videotape illustrates Solomon-Godeau's observation that among subordinate identities, "race, gender, and ethnicity are entities produced and reproduced within language" (p. 31). This view of a textually constructed, multivocal identity takes for granted that some images may have entered history and memory only through accident or secondhand re-creation, while other essential components of the past are forever lost. So, Tajiri says: "There are things in the world which have happened while there were cameras watching—things we have images for. There are other things which have happened while there were no cameras watching, which we re-stage in front of cameras to have images of." In other words, some events exist in the historical record because a camera just happened to be there to record them;

where no such evidence exists, our collective psyche is populated by images
from the media. As Fusco (n.d.) contends:

> one of the effects of diaspora, it seems, is that a sense of history, and of popular
> memory, have to be pieced together with fragments, with remnants and with
> documents that we did not always produce. We are not drawing on unified
> traditions, but partial objects and partial truths. (p. 14)

Using the task of remembering as an interventionist tool for rewriting
history and coming to terms with family memories, *Family Gathering* and
History and Memory are nevertheless unstintingly honest about the impossi-
bility of perfect recall. Yet in each work the failure to achieve an unmediated
and unadulterated encounter with the past itself provides impetus toward
revelation and insight. Along with Janice Tanaka's *Memories From the Department of Amnesia*, these works elaborate the "entwined themes of loss, mourning, and reparation" typical of women's autobiographical filmmaking,
expressing the "desire to make restitution for pain inflicted, real or imagined,"
and to undertake "a quest for reparation and reconciliation with lost family
and national identity" (Portuges, 1988, pp. 343, 350).

Memories From the Department of Amnesia is an experimental videotape
about loss and mourning whose emotional power far exceeds its short length
of $12\frac{1}{2}$ minutes. The first part of the tape consists of a series of intensely
subjective images built around repeated shots of a bicyclist riding around and
around the interior of a diner. The second half employs a minimalist collage
combined with the use of a split screen to enumerate the biographical facts
forming the life of Tanaka's mother, Yuriko Yamate. At screen right appears a
succession of candid photographs (mostly of Yuriko), showing her change
from a young woman to a mother and leading up to her death. The left side
of the screen repeatedly shows a hand entering the frame holding a series of
small snapshots (presumably family photos); each time, the hand "peels away"
the photograph to leave its photo-negative imprint on the screen. Meanwhile,
about 36 titles are superimposed on the left side of the screen, tersely encap-
sulating the key events in Yuriko's life, including her early abandonment by
her mother and molestation by her father, her marriage and motherhood, her
internment during the war, her divorce from her husband who is declared
insane, her numerous relocations and loss of friends, her declining health and
nervous breakdown, and the refusal of her mother to acknowledge her when
they are reunited in Japan.

As in *History and Memory, Memories* is both a meditation on the problem of representing an individual life and a project of reconstructive memory. The use of dissolves and the repeated transitions between positive and negative images enact the subjective experience of memory as a process of successive advance and retreat, as does the technique of fading in or out from a blank white screen. Thus, the first photograph of Tanaka's mother fades in from a dead-white screen to show her in close-up as a young woman. This same photograph is also the last image we see in the tape: It fades in from a blank whiteness, is held momentarily, and then dissolves into another white screen. Then, a final superimposed title appears to say: "Dies May 23, 1988."

Because it so effectively evokes the mute tragedy and hidden violence of Yuriko's life with a total avoidance of exaggeration or melodrama, it would be easy to read *Memories* simply as a work of reparation and mourning for a life heroic for its unspoken pain. The tape operates more intricately than this, however, if only because we have to reconcile the apparent discrepancy between the personal tragedies inventoried in the subtitles and the numerous images of a radiant, beautiful, and smiling woman. But above all, as in *Family Gathering* and *History and Memory,* the soundtrack of *Memories* introduces a counterpoint to the visuals. Accompanying the collage of photographs, two female voices, which we quickly infer are those of Tanaka and her daughter, reminisce about Yuriko. This lighthearted and casual conversation runs counter to the mood and content of the subtitles, as the two women laugh and giggle through their memories of Yuriko as a woman with a "warped sense of humor," a "hot rod" who drove a Mustang, dated a lot of men, encouraged her family to eat arsenic-laced prune pits, and stored her wild outfits in a cedar trunk.

Conclusion

In surveying the history of independent Asian American media, Renee Tajima has noted that there are "few directly feminist films by Asian American women" (Tajima, 1991, p. 24). This conclusion is unexpected, given a virtual explosion in the numbers of Asian women producing work in the United States and Canada in recent years. Yet Tajima's remark is defensible if "feminist" media is defined strictly in the terms of direct struggle within social and institutional arenas. As the films and videos surveyed in this chapter suggest, however, the existing body of work is based on an emergent aesthetics and ethos drawing strength not so much from group action and an agenda of social change, as from an individualized politics grounded in the body, lived experience, family relations, and immersion in culture. And so, regardless of the point of departure—the subversion of media images, a negotiation of body politics, or the reclaiming of family history—the imperative of decolonization insists that there is no aspect of social or personal experience that has not already been worked over, territorialized, and already written about in the language of dominant culture. In this sense, then, all representation is political: Whether the camera lens is turned inward at the self or out toward the world, all that matters is that it reflect images of our own making.

Notes

1. In this chapter, the term *Asian* is used to refer to women of Asian descent living in the United States and Canada. This has been done to circumvent the awkwardness of using the more accurate term, *Asian Canadian and Asian American women.* I also acknowledge problems with the term *Asian American,* in that *America* properly refers to the continent of America (North and South), and not only to the United States.

2. The process of how mass media images operate as a tool of colonization for black people (and black women in particular) has been persuasively articulated by bell hooks in her 1992 book, *Black Looks: Race and Representation;* see especially pp. 1-7, 21-39, 61-77.

3. *Slaying the Dragon* quoted by permission of Women Make Movies.

4. *Yellow Tale Blues: Two American Families* quoted by permission of Filmakers Library.

5. *Picturing Oriental Girls* quoted by permission of Valerie Soe.

6. *Two Lies* quoted by permission of Women Make Movies.

7. *Sally's Beauty Spot* quoted by permission of Women Make Movies.

8. See also Marchetti's 1993 book-length analysis of Hollywood's treatment of miscegenation and interracial romance, *Romance and the "Yellow Peril": Race, Sex, and Discursive Strategies in Hollywood Fiction.*

9. *Family Gathering* quoted by permission of Lise Yasui.

10. *History and Memory: For Akiko and Takashige* quoted by permission of Women Make Movies.

11. *Memories From the Department of Amnesia* quoted by permission of Janice Tanaka.

12. I have previously written about this work in a review published in *New Directions for Women* (see Heung, 1991).

References

Chalfen, R. (1989). Family gathering. *American Anthropologist, 91*(2), 525-527.

Corliss, R. (1993, September 13). Pacific overtures. *Time,* pp. 68-69.

Fusco, C. (1993). Passionate irreverence: The cultural politics of identity. In *1993 biennial* (pp. 74-85). New York: Whitney Museum of American Art.

Fusco, C. (n.d.). About locating ourselves and our representations. *Framework, 36,* 7-14.

Hagedorn, J. (1994, January/February). Asian women in film: No joy, no luck. *Ms.,* pp. 74-79.

Hall, S. (n.d.). Cultural identity and cinematic representation. *Framework, 36,* 68-81.

Henderson, M. G. (1991). Speaking in tongues: Dialogics, dialectics, and the black woman writer's literary tradition. In C. A. Wall (Ed.), *Changing our own words: Essays on criticism, theory, and writing by black women* (pp. 16-37). New Brunswick, NJ: Rutgers University Press.

Heung, M. (1991, November/December). Documentary recovers memories of wartime internment. *New Directions for Women,* pp. 12-13.

hooks, b. (n.d.). Choosing the margin as a space of radical openness. *Framework, 36,* 15-23.

hooks, b. (1992). *Black looks: Race and representation.* Boston: South End.

Jen, G. (1991, August 11). Challenging the Asian illusion. *New York Times,* Sec. 2, pp. 1, 12-13.

Kennedy, L. (1992). The body in question. In G. Dent (Ed.), *Black popular culture* (pp. 106-111). Seattle: Bay Press.

Marchetti, G. (1991). White knights in Hong Kong: Race, gender, and the exotic in *Love is a many-splendored thing* and *The world of Suzie Wong. Post Script, 10*(2), 36-49.

Marchetti, G. (1993). *Romance and the "yellow peril": Race, sex, and discursive strategies in Hollywood fiction.* Berkeley: University of California Press.

Portuges, C. (1988). Seeing subjects: Women directors and cinematic autobiography. In B. Brodzki & C. Schenck (Eds.), *Life/lines: Theorizing women's autobiography* (pp. 338-350). Ithaca, NY: Cornell University Press.

Probyn, E. (1992). Theorizing through the body. In L. F. Rakow (Ed.), *Women making meaning: New feminist directions in communication* (pp. 83-99). New York: Routledge.

Said, E. W. (1978). *Orientalism.* New York: Vintage.

Smith, S. (1993). *Subjectivity, identity, and the body: Women's autobiographical practices in the twentieth century.* Bloomington: Indiana University Press.

Solomon-Godeau, A. (1993). *Mistaken identities.* Santa Barbara, CA: University Art Museum.

Sommer, D. (1989). "Not just a personal story": Women's *testimonios* and the plural self. In B. Brodzki & C. Schenck (Eds.), *Life/lines: Theorizing women's autobiography* (pp. 107-130). Ithaca, NY: Cornell University Press.

Tajima, R. (1989). Lotus blossoms don't bleed: Images of Asian women. In Asian Women United (Ed.), *Making waves: An anthology of writings by and about Asian American women* (pp. 308-317). Boston: Beacon.

Tajima, R. (1991). Moving the image: Asian American independent filmmaking 1970-1990. In R. Leong (Ed.), *Moving the image: Independent Asian Pacific American media arts* (pp. 10-33). Los Angeles: UCLA Asian American Center and Visual Communications.

Tchen, J. K. W. (1994). Believing is seeing: Transforming Orientalism and the Occidental gaze. In *Asia/America: Identities in contemporary Asian American art* (pp. 12-25). New York: Asia Society and New Press.

Trinh, T. M. (1987). Difference: "A special Third World women issue." *Feminist Review, 25,* 5-22.

Suggested Readings

Fung, R. (1994). Seeing yellow: Asian identities in film and video. In K. Aguilar-San Juan (Ed.), *The state of Asian America: Activism and resistance in the 1990s* (pp. 161-172). Boston: South End.

Higashi, S. (1993, October). Review of *History and memory, Memories from the department of amnesia, Who's going to pay for these donuts anyway?*, and *Days of waiting. American Historical Review*, pp. 1181-1184.

Hulser, K. (1991, October). Review of *History and memory. American Historical Review*, pp. 1142-1143.

Hwang, D. (1985, August 11). Are movies ready for real Orientals? *New York Times*, Sec. 2, pp. 1, 21.

Juhasz, A. (1994). Our auto-bodies, ourselves: Representing real women in feminist video. *Afterimage, 21*(7), 10-14.

Appendix 1
Film and Video Distributors

Be Good My Children (Christine Chang, United States, 1992; 16 mm./video, 47 minutes). Source: Women Make Movies.

Family Gathering (Lise Yasui & Ann Tegnell, United States, 1988; 16mm./video, 30 minutes). Source: New Day Films.

History and Memory: For Akiko and Takashige (Rea Tajiri, United States, 1991; video, 32 minutes). Source: Women Make Movies.

Memories From the Department of Amnesia (Janice Tanaka, United States, 1991; video, 12$\frac{1}{2}$ minutes). Source: CrossCurrent Media.

Picturing Oriental Girls: A (Re)Educational Tape (Valerie Soe, United States, 1992; video, 12 minutes). Source: CrossCurrent Media.

Sally's Beauty Spot (Helen Lee, Canada, 1989; 16 mm./video, 12 minutes). Source: Women Make Movies.

Slaying the Dragon (Deborah Gee, United States, 1988; video, 60 minutes). Source: CrossCurrent Media; Women Make Movies.

Two Lies (Pam Tom, United States, 1989; 16 mm./video; 25 minutes). Source: Women Make Movies.

Yellow Tale Blues: Two American Families (Christine Choy & Renee Tajima, United States, 1990; video, 28 minutes). Source: Filmmakers Library.

CONTACT:

CrossCurrent Media
National Asian American Telecommunications Association
346 Ninth Street, 2nd Floor
San Francisco, CA 94103; ph. (415) 552-9550

Filmmakers Library
124 East 40th Street, Suite 901
New York, NY 10016; ph. (212) 808-4980

New Day Films
22D Hollywood Avenue
Hohokus, NJ 07423; ph. (201) 652-6590

Women Make Movies
462 Broadway, Suite 500
New York, NY 10013; ph. (212) 925-0606

5 News, Consciousness, and Social Participation

The Role of Women's Feature Service in World News

CAROLYN M. BYERLY

Some 20 years ago (1975-1985), women began to take an active, organized interest in altering their relationship to the male-owned and -oriented global media industries. *The World Plan of Action,* passed by delegates at the first U.N. Decade for Women conference, in México City in 1975, and later the subsequent *Forward Looking Strategies* report, provided an essential framework for both new academic research on women and the media and for interventionist strategies to increase women's access to media channels. Although we have a significant body of research documenting women's systematic exclusion from media messages and their production from this period, we know

AUTHOR'S NOTE: The author appreciates assistance from Joy Morrison, H. Leslie Steeves, Susan J. Kaufman, Anita Anand, Rebecca Foster, and Angharad Valdivia in the preparation of this chapter.

less about what happened after the mid-1970s as a result of women's intervention in media systems. Nor do we have an adequate assessment of what feminism has contributed to the making of new public policy on the media or on the creation of alternative media industries (Steeves & Arbogast, 1993).

This chapter responds to the need for such a line of inquiry. Underlying my discussion is the question, "How has organized feminist effort, utilizing both mainstream and independent structures, expanded women's voices in world news?" My particular concern is with feminist efforts in developing nations, where women's material well-being and social status has been consistently lower, and where much of the U.N.-funded communication and development work of the past three decades had overlooked women's needs, interests, and meaningful participation (Anand, 1992; Boulding, 1992; Buvenic & Yudelman, 1989; Steeves & Arbogast, 1993).

The U.N.-sponsored women's feature service project, and its most significant descendant, the New Delhi-based Women's Feature Service (WFS), offers an important case study to assess feminist impact on global news in general, and development news in particular. The original project was a strategic intervention to expand women's voice in international news, which in the 1970s carried less than 2% about women (Gallagher, 1981). Today, WFS is both the longest lived and largest women-controlled global news agency (Byerly, 1990b). The agency's stories are distinguished by several characteristics. They have an intentional gender orientation, focusing on development events and processes from a "progressive women's perspective." They also give prominence to women's contributions in local and national public affairs and they analyze structural barriers to women's fuller social participation (Women's Feature Service, 1993). WFS also has a unique history of self-determination, beginning as a mainstream (male)-sponsored program, based in Europe, and evolving to its present independent status with headquarters in the Third World. The agency has followed a path of potential use to other feminist news projects, and it demonstrates how a global women's news agency can serve as an informational bridge between women of developed and developing nations.

Theoretical and Philosophical Issues

There was not yet a fully developed feminist media critique when delegates met together in 1975 in México City for the first U.N. Decade for Women conference. There were, instead, some emerging criticisms and an array of early studies that focused on three particular problems: (a) women's underrepresentation in the content of news and serious programming, (b) trivialization and sex-role stereotyping in content, and (c) underrepresentation in decision-making (gatekeeper) positions.

Feminists from varied philosophical and theoretical positions approached their analysis of women's problems and solutions with the media sharing at least two goals. The first was to explain whether and how the media helped to perpetuate women's secondary status in societies. The second was to explore how the media might be used as a vehicle to advance their ideas, status, and political power. But feminists diverged in their approaches for accomplishing these. Liberal feminists, who were generally reformist in strategy, were more likely to see solutions to women's underrepresentation in terms of increasing the numbers of women in both entry-level and decision-making (gatekeeping) positions and in reforming media programming to include more women in content (Steeves, 1987). Socialist feminists, concerned about structural aspects of social and economic relations and the role of both male- and capitalist-dominant ideologies disseminated through the media, questioned whether placing women within existing media structures would necessarily alter messages and representations of women. Socialist feminists also criticized advertising and other media for seducing women into consumerism and for limiting women's creative influence on media content (Mattelart, 1986; Steeves, 1987).

Many of the concerns and analyses defined by socialist feminists make use of Gramsci's (1971) concept of *hegemony,* the process by which a ruling class secures the conditions for its own domination with the consent of the subordinated population (Steeves & Arbogast, 1993). In the feminist application, the ruling class is composed of *male elites,* and the dominated class, *females.* The news media, thus, are believed to take on the role of agency, reinforcing not just economic class relations, but *gendered relations* in society. Extending Marx and Engels's theory from *The German Ideology* (Marx & Engels, 1986), that those who own the means of production also determine the ideas to be produced, Gramsci (1971) emphasized that hegemonic (dominant) forces were typically both *ordinary* and *routine.* News thus might serve as the means by which a dominant class, such as white male elites, could condition a population of subordinate classes (women, minorities, and those at lower economic levels) to adopt prevailing values and behaviors, thereby perpetuating an inherently unequal system of power (see O'Connor, 1990).

Radical feminists were similarly concerned about the media's role in the "construction" of consciousness and gender identities. An analysis of male dominance in the media and other social institutions was, in fact, central to radical feminism, which identified the need for women to separate themselves from male-controlled systems and create their own organizations and structures (Donovan, 1985). Radical feminism, perhaps more than any other form of feminism, has been responsible for generating a plethora of women's publishing houses and periodicals around the world these past 20 years.

By the mid-1970s, women in former colonial states of Asia and Africa had also become strongly identified with indigenous liberation movements, many of them successful in expelling foreign ruling governments.[1] Third World feminism merged themes associated with national self-determination (i.e., self-rule and economic independence) with those more specifically addressed to women's position in their societies. The U.N. Decade for Women, whose theme was "Women, Development and Peace," reveals that postcolonial feminism strongly influenced the direction of this decade-long event. Women in Development (WID), who examine women's lives using variables of gender, race, ethnicity, culture, and economic relations among nations, were critical of development communication projects in the 1950s and 1960s, which had ignored women as both participants and beneficiaries. They stressed that communication technology should be used to disseminate new ideas about women and society and to increase women's participation in their nations' development (Anand, 1992; Buvenic & Yudelman, 1989; Charlton, 1984; Steeves & Arbogast, 1993). Like feminists from other philosophical positions, WID saw news, information, and other forms of media as essential vehicles to reorganize and advance new goals for women.

News and Women

News, in all of its various forms, has historically underrepresented and misrepresented women. Through the late 1970s, world news routinely ignored women's problems and accomplishments as subjects for serious coverage in most countries. Even as women's rights movements in the 1960s and 1970s helped to expand women's roles in the public spheres of paid workforces and politics, news coverage ignored or trivialized their gains. One content analysis of international wire services in the late 1970s revealed that only 1.5% of major wire service news was about women (Gallagher, 1981).

Development news, which has been defined as news concerned with economic, political, and social change and with historical and other factors bringing those about (Giffard, Byerly, & Van Horn, 1991; Shah, 1990), has also ignored women through the years (Anand, 1992; Giffard et al., 1991). Development news (or journalism) has been practiced primarily in developing nations of the Third World, where it has been believed that traditional Western news, with its focus on singular events and oddities, is less useful than news that can forge a coherent picture of a particular nation and its relations to other nations. The informational needs of the news audience, emphasis on self-reliant development, and advances in socioeconomic structures (such as land reform and new educational programs) are major themes of development news (Giffard, 1984).

Some recent research has shown that through the years, there has been little improvement in either the quantity or quality of news and other information about women in the world's media. Mohanty's (1991) cross-cultural survey found that prevailing news values still define most women and their problems as un-newsworthy and, when women are included, their portrayals are predictably sexual or confined to the private sphere of home. Rakow and Kranich (1991) suggest that news is essentially "a masculine narrative in which women function not as speaking subjects but as signs" (p. 9). The authors add that, "Any improvement in women's treatment in news will require not simply more coverage of women or more women journalists . . . but a fundamental change in news as a narrative form" (Rakow & Kranich, 1991, p. 9). Similarly, Bird and Dardenne (1988) conclude that the journalist-storyteller is "indeed using culturally embedded story values," but they believe it is also within the journalist's power to "actively reshape" patterns in news and thereby to "repair the paradigm" (p. 81). Their stress on individual influence differs from Rakow and Kranich's (1991) narrative structural approach.

Critical scholars like Tuchman (1978), Hall (1980), Gitlin (1980), and Herman and Chomsky (1988) have been more concerned with structural influences on news content, such as those posed by the filters of news organizations' corporate goals and values, the journalistic routines of newsmaking, and the knowledge and philosophies that individual journalists have acquired through hegemonic educational systems steeped in elite values. Through structural influences, news stories are *framed*, or given perspective and interpretation.

Like other marginalized groups, women have not been able simply to ignore the import of news. There is evidence that for marginalized groups to gain greater power, they must have greater visibility and public voice—they must be able to frame their own issues and then communicate them, not just through interpersonal channels or their own specialized media, but also through mainstream news and other media channels that reach larger audiences. Kielbowicz and Scherer (1986) have shown that the press has long been essential to Western social movements, both in the early stages to mobilize public interest and membership, and in the later stages to maintain momentum. Socialist feminists have been particularly vocal in their insistence that the media can be one site of struggle between dominant and oppressed classes (Steeves & Arbogast, 1993). O'Connor (1990) has pointed out that the active use of the mass communications media by marginalized groups can help in the formation of their own identities and cultural agendas. An active effort to co-opt media channels represents, in fact, an intervention in the status quo. For example, Anand (1983), a development specialist, maintains that information is useless to women unless it helps

> to raise their consciousness about the oppressive structures that keep them in positions of powerlessness.... [What a woman] craves is knowledge of why she must bear so many children, work endless hours without respite, be beaten and raped, have an alcoholic husband, and go hungry. (p. 7)

Female journalists have been in a potentially central position to contribute to gender advancements by including women's perspectives and achievements in news stories. For example, Kate Abbam, editor of the women's magazine *Obaa Sima* (*Ideal Woman*) in Ghana, found that "Women in media professions are at the forefront of bringing about women's emancipation in Ghana" (in *Media Report to Women*, August 1, 1975).

This interventionist philosophy permeated the *World Plan of Action*, passed by 1,000 female and male delegates attending the U.N. Decade for Women conference in México City in June 1975. The plan named the mass media as the central mechanism through which women's roles would be changed, their social participation accelerated, and discrimination against them ended: "the mass communication media . . . could exercise a significant influence in helping to remove prejudices and stereotypes, accelerating the acceptance of women's new roles in society and promoting their integration into the development process as equal partners (*Decade for Women: World Plan of Action*, 1975, paragraphs 161-162).

But the plan went on to note the inadequacy of the media to carry out the task: "At the present time, the media tend to reinforce traditional attitudes, often portraying an image of women that is degrading and humiliating and fail to reflect the changing role of the sexes" (*Decade for Women: World Plan of Action,* 1975, paragraph 162). As such the Women's Feature Service was designed to address this gap between potential and reality.

Intervention Through
Women's Feature Services

The present-day Women's Feature Service, headquartered in New Delhi, has its roots in the "women's feature service project," which was envisioned by its creators to be a partial solution to these problems. The original umbrella project—which operated between 1978 and 1983 under the direction of the U.N. Educational, Scientific, and Cultural Organization (UNESCO), with funds from the U.N. Fund for Population Agency (UNFPA)—was proposed by journalists and feminist leaders attending a special media workshop after the México City conferences. The project contained elements of several feminist philosophies. On the one hand, the project aimed to interrupt or intervene in hegemonic news systems, where women and their concerns had been marginalized, underrepresented, and misrepresented, by making a place for female journalists and news about women in "the existing information networks and systems that might operate in promoting a regular service of news, information, and background on women's issues" (*UNFPA Project Request,* July 1, 1976).

Although it might be argued that this was a liberal reformist strategy, there also are clear signs of intent to create a space for oppositional (feminist) personnel and ideas in a previously closed male system. Moreover, the project was designed to guarantee feminist control of both the individual feature service programs (see below) and the content of the stories they produced. In other words, the individual programs maintained a strong degree of autonomy and separation from their sponsor agencies. There was, in addition, a stated mission of independence in the UNESCO program. Women's feature service project administrator Yvette Abrahamson made it clear from the outset that U.N. funds would end in 1983 and that individual programs needed to work toward self-sufficiency from their respective beginnings (Byerly, 1990b). Women's informational needs, lives, views, achievements, and creative control were top priorities for both the umbrella project and its five individual programs. Male sponsorship was approached as a necessary but temporary measure in the programs' self-determination.

Those five services and their sponsors included: (a) the *Oficina Informativa de la Mujer* (OIM), sponsored by the Inter Press Service, in San José, Costa Rica, to serve the Latin American region; (b) the *Caribbean Women's Feature Syndicate,* sponsored by the Caribbean News Agency, in Barbados, to serve the Caribbean region; (c) the *Depthnews Women's Service,* sponsored by Press Foundation of Asia, in Manila, the Philippines, to serve Southeast Asia; (d) the *African Women's Feature Service,* sponsored by Inter Press Service, in Nairobi, Kenya, to serve both Anglophone and Francophone Africa; and (e) the *Arab States Women's Feature Service,* sponsored by the Federation of Arab News Agencies, in Beirut, to serve the Middle Eastern region. UNFPA's start-up and operation funds, which ranged in annual amounts from $5,000 (for the Caribbean Women's Feature Service) to $30,000 (for IPS's administration of the OIM and African Women's Feature Service) were set to end in 1983, when sponsoring agencies were to have found other financing to continue their operations.

UNESCO's women's feature service project personnel also approached the major international news services—based in North America and Europe—to be sponsors, but found them uninterested. Gallagher (1981) reported that these agencies

> had their own established networks of correspondents (mainly male), a primarily Western orientation in coverage, and an emphasis on "spot" news rather than feature or background information, [so] there was no real perception for the need for the kind of material called for by the [WFS] project. (p. 146)

Gallagher suggests that these agencies' refusal to participate signified a fundamental incompatibility between the project's goals of increasing women's access and self-determination and the news industries' vested interest in keeping their structures and policies intact.

The project had emerged in the context of the globally turbulent 1970s, during which gendered struggles coincided with newly defined international political and economic struggles. Third World nations' proposals for both a New World Information and Communication Order (NWICO) and a New International Economic Order (NIEO), which UNESCO supported, were seen by Western governments and news enterprises as fundamentally anti-

Western, anti-free press, and anticapitalist. The WFS project's goals to intervene in the order of things, with women in developing nations being the primary benefactors and UNESCO again the advocate, provided yet another occasion for a clash between developed Western and Third World nations. Roach (1990) notes the essential irony in this conflict in her assessment of why the NWICO and NIEO failed: Women had had little relationship to either of these, because they had been denied a voice in both formulating and debating the NWICO and NIEO proposals. Had women been allowed participation by Third World male elites, the proposals would have had a broader base of support, Roach insists. Instead, women's concerns about both development and communication were relegated to a separate international public arena in the form of U.N. Decade for Women events.

The women's feature service project met with mixed success in its 5 years of operation. The project generated an estimated 100 or more new female journalists in developing nations over a 5-year period. The project also strengthened the visibility of issues related to women and to both community and national development processes. Using the development news format, these stories revealed not just women's problems but the historical circumstances out of which problems grew, as well as how women were addressing them. Exemplary was one story filed in Cotonou, Benin, for the African Women's Feature Service in 1980, explaining why women in rural Benin could not get loans to finance farming cooperatives: "In most cases rural women take part in the production process, but [they] do not own what [they] produce. A woman has no right to own property and she is considered, once married, as an asset for her husband's personal belongings" (Gisele, 1980).[2] The story went on to report on a new program being set up in all six counties of Benin to teach literacy to and initiate community development projects for women. Some groups of men and women would teach new information about the role of women in rural development (Gisele, 1980).

Overall, the project increased the number of stories about women in news by about 1,200 during its 5-year operation. This increase was seen most strongly in Latin America and Southeast Asia, where the respective women's feature service programs had been most productive and well received (Byerly, 1990b; Rush & Ogan, 1989). Higher literacy rates, a longer tradition of women's participation in public affairs, and the established credibility of Inter Press Service (OIM's sponsor agency) in Latin America are possible reasons that OIM showed particular success in this region (Byerly, 1990b). The Caribbean area produced fewer stories and encountered less enthusiasm among male editors, who preferred to run stories reflecting women's traditional roles and problems (Gordon, 1981; Rush & Ogan, 1989).

Sexist attitudes in news selection by male gatekeepers had also been a problem in Africa, where the media were so reluctant to use stories about women that UNESCO's Yvette Abrahamson organized a series of meetings with African leaders and media representatives to confront the problem. Similarly, in the Middle Eastern region, the Arab States Women's Feature Service had trouble producing its required number of stories, in part because male journalists in some nations had blocked the work of Arab Women's Feature Service correspondents (Abrahamson, 1982; Byerly, 1990a). Technical and logistical difficulties prevented timely distribution of stories in some areas of Africa and the Middle East, which still relied on mail for delivery. And unforeseen political difficulties, such as the bombing of the Federation of Arab News Agencies (and its Arab Women's Feature Service) headquarters in Beirut had interrupted news production (Abrahamson, 1982).

When UNESCO sponsorship of the women's feature service project ended in 1983, only the Rome-based Inter Press Service and the Press Foundation of Asia, in Manila, had succeeded in finding the means to continue their programs. Of these, Inter Press Service (IPS), with media, government, and other subscribers in 80 nations, adopted a long-range plan to support a global news service for women. In 1986, IPS Director Roberto Savio hired development specialist Anita Anand to head the "Women, Communication and Development" project, with Anand's primary duties being to merge the flagging remains of the Latin American and African women's feature services and then to expand these services' operations around the world (Byerly, 1990a). The original project, the product of global feminism, had laid the foundation for a new generation of women-defined and women-controlled news.

Strengthening Organizational
and News Directions

By 1986, women's feature programs under IPS sponsorship had been through two developmental stages—an original organizational and experimental stage, with U.N. funding, and a transitional stage, with IPS funding. IPS's women's news component entered its third phase in 1986, one characterized by a consolidated identity as Women's Feature Service (WFS) and by mobilization aimed at independence. Between 1986 and 1989, under Anand's direction, WFS established a global administrative structure, strengthened its regional journalistic personnel, and secured funds for independent operation. WFS also identified its new headquarters as New Delhi, an important symbolic step that would, in 1990, move it from Europe to the developing world it primarily served (Anand, 1983).

This was a period of rapid change in many respects; however, WFS remained fairly constant in several ways. The agency continued to circulate its stories both in English and Spanish, with IPS as its distributor. Many stories continued to be translated into local languages at regional IPS offices around the globe. In addition, WFS maintained its commitment to the feminization of development news, with particular emphasis on the development news feature story. This commitment to include feminist perspectives within the development news format, refined by nearly a decade's practice, represented (and continues to represent) a substantial contribution to world news.

Recent research continues to show that, on the whole, women remain marginalized in most news from and about the developing nations, in terms of the number of women writers and female subjects in news content (Giffard et al., 1991; Rush & Ogan, 1989). Statistical findings derived from counting the number of women in bylines, story themes, attribution, and photos are useful in revealing the work yet to be done, but they should not overshadow the significant efforts of agencies to expand the amount of news about women as well as to reframe news using women's views and daily experiences. Although more difficult to measure, the aspect of framing holds perhaps the greatest potential for assessing how feminism has influenced world and local news. In their study of the news from the Caribbean News Agency (CANA), Rush and Ogan (1989) demonstrate one way of assessing news frames within a more traditional quantitative analysis. The authors identified stories within their sample that might have included a woman's perspective (or angle) and did not. More familiar treatment of news frame analysis by Tuchman (1978) and Gitlin (1980) provides additional models, though both are concerned with U.S. news.

Byerly's (1990b) analysis of WFS stories utilized both statistical and qualitative methods to reveal that WFS stories make a particular effort to frame their content using "a progressive woman's perspective" (*Women's Feature Service,* 1992b). Issues like politics, economics, war, peace, environmental destruction, religion, social customs, families, health, and all other topics related to Third World culture and development become the stuff of WFS news features. However, issues are developed within the context of women's daily lives, questions, and social participation. One 1988 story from Bihar, India, for example, concerned police brutality, a common problem in industrial and Third World nations alike. But this story, which focused on the long-standing practice of police rape of village women, was framed by a feminist analysis of rape. Village women were allowed to speak of their outrage in the article, as well as to outline their efforts to have policemen who assaulted women fired from their state-paid jobs (Dasgupta, 1988). The story foregrounded women's right to fight back and to interrupt the patriarchal practices of using violence against women as a means of control. This story was also typical in providing a history of police rape of Indian women and a status report on women's efforts to respond through organized resistance and local services for victims.

Byerly's analysis also revealed that WFS stories expanded the numbers of women at all levels of the socioeconomic scale to be heard. In a sample of 105 stories, from 1986 through 1989, the author found that 78% of all primary sources were female, and, of those, 56% were nonelite women, whose occupations ranged from mothers to agricultural and unskilled workers (Byerly, 1990b). The aforementioned study suggests that individual journalists have more power to reshape news codes (Bird & Dardenne, 1988) in favor of marginalized groups when they operate in structures controlled by those groups (Rakow & Kranich, 1991). WFS stories illustrate the ways in which women journalists, using a progressive perspective, have been able to embed new cultural codes favorable to women in their news features.

It is important to grasp the contribution that this new kind of news agency structure and the news stories it produces has already made to world news. As production of stories increased, WFS stories found favorable reception among their largely mainstream subscribers. One analysis of publication rates revealed that 60% of the approximately 500 stories disseminated for the months March, April, and May between 1986 and 1989 were published at least once and as many as eight times. Publication rates continued to be highest in Latin America, particularly in Venezuela, México, and Bolivia. Demand also has grown steadily in Europe, where 23 Finnish and 8 Dutch publications printed WFS stories on a regular basis in the years surveyed (Byerly, 1990b).

WFS presently centralizes the final editing and distribution of features and manages its overall financial and administrative affairs from its new headquarters. The agency receives and recirculates news features regularly among nations in Latin America, Africa, South Asia, the Philippines, the United States, and Japan, with intermittent service from Southeast Asia, the Pacific, the Middle East, and Europe. News features are written by paid part-time correspondents, many of whom are employed as full-time journalists at mainstream media organizations. The service was extended to Japan in 1992. Located in Tokyo, this operation has become the first in the WFS network to meet its own expenses (Women's Feature Service, 1993).

Since 1990, WFS has produced about 500 stories annually (from all regions), with major languages still English and Spanish; translations to other languages are still performed at regional levels. The service reports that 70% of its stories are published or broadcast annually, indicating stable and reasonably high demand for its materials. Since WFS relocated to New Delhi, the publication rate in India has increased 100% in the mainstream media, with all major dailies now carrying the women's features (Women's Feature Service, 1993).

All this is accomplished on an annual budget of well under $1 million. Major sources of income include grants from U.N. agencies such as UNIFEM, Dutch and Swiss development cooperation agencies, both large and small nongovernmental organizations, and subscriber fees. There are also a number of minor sources of revenue, such as UNICEF, which provide funds according to the number of features produced. Fundraising is a major part of the director's work (Anand, 1993; Rebecca Foster, personal communication, July 1993).

The agency ended its arrangement with IPS for telex distribution in 1992 and has since established its own multichanneled dissemination. This has made distribution more versatile but not entirely adequate to reach the broad IPS audience in the 80 nations of earlier years. In the United States, for instance, where WFS has expanded its marketing push, clients can access news features through regular mail, fax, or through subscription to the WFS *Bulletin,* and through the Internet (PeaceNet News, Institute for Global Communication). In addition, the agency tries to provide commissioned stories, on request (Margaret Bald, personal communication, July 1993). Still, financial constraints, together with long-standing difficulties finding markets for products in some areas, have meant some streamlining of services. After years of unsuccessful attempts both to produce and market the stories in the Caribbean region, WFS closed its Caribbean operation in Jamaica in 1992 (Women's Feature Service, 1992a).

On the other hand, WFS has continued to cover major world meetings, such as the U.N. Conference on Environment and Development in Rio de Janeiro in 1992 and the U.N. Conference on Human Rights in Vienna in 1993.

WFS staff are working with Asian women's groups to develop a regional media strategy for news coverage of the next U.N. Decade for Women follow-up meeting, to be held in Beijing in 1995 (Women's Feature Service, 1993). In an effort to reach nonreading publics, WFS has begun to experiment with news feature videos. One 25-minute segment on literacy campaigns for women in India was distributed in India in 1993, for instance (Rebecca Foster, personal communication, July 1993).

Conclusion

Status quo social practices must be interrupted if new ones are to be introduced and eventually to replace them. Such interruptions, or interventions, stand the best chance of succeeding when they are institutionalized, either through existing structures or new ones. The original women's feature service project—and its descendant, the New Delhi WFS—was the first intentionally organized effort to interrupt global news practices that had historically ignored and marginalized women's concerns and achievements. Under UNESCO funding and administration, the original five services took an important symbolic step to assert greater control over the creation of messages and representations in news. The project had limited success, in terms of the numbers of stories it produced over its 5-year life and in the degree to which mainstream print media used them.

But first steps are not necessarily final steps. In this project's case, two of the feature services have continued on, still serving both specialized and mainstream media and nonmedia organizations throughout the world. This could signal the coming of a new era, one in which woman-controlled news agencies can become viable in the competitive world of global newsmaking.

Still primarily concerned with women's participation in development processes, WFS challenges traditional definitions of not only Western (event-oriented) news, but development (process-oriented) news as well. WFS news features make gender central as they foreground the daily experiences, views, activities, and analyses of their female subjects and sources. News features make no particular effort to "balance" these with more traditional (male-oriented) interests. In this way, WFS stories may recognize that women in developed and developing nations are divided by material differences in their daily lives, as well as cultural and political histories, while at the same time sharing important elements in their paths toward self-determination.

Other issues related to women's suffering and progress cross national boundaries: new diasporas of refugees escaping war, persecution, and economic hardship—many of these women with children seeking asylum in industrial Western nations; the dramatic spread of AIDS, first among heterosexual African women and, more recently, heterosexual female populations in North America and Europe; the persistence of men's rape and battering of women in nations at war, like Bosnia, as well as in other nations ostensibly at peace; and, of course, women's unflagging determination to address these situations.

Any woman's news service would be challenged to tackle the enormity of what remains to be done in bringing women more soundly into world journalism and, by extension, women's problems, efforts, interpretations of events, and accomplishments into public consciousness. And yet there is a compelling case to be made for efforts in this direction, not just by the Women's Feature Service—which provides an obvious prototype—but for other organizations that might spring from need and opportunity. But where to begin?

The difficulties that first the parent WFS project and, more recently, the successor Women's Feature Service of New Delhi, had in reaching literate publics with information about women in the Arab, African, and Caribbean regions would give pause to the most determined of leaders. But neither cultural inhibitors, such as predominantly oral traditions in many African states and the Caribbean, nor persistent lower literacy rates should represent permanent barriers to future initiatives to reach large, diverse populations with new ideas about women's roles in society. As women's movements gain momentum in these areas, there may be a wider opening for renewed efforts to bring these regions (particularly the Caribbean) into WFS activities, or for other women's news systems to emerge and carry out the task.

Arab women's forceful entrance onto the world stage in recent years suggests new possibilities for informational linkage among women-owned networks. Such invitation seems implied in statements like this one by Syrian academic Bouthaina Shaaban (1993), who was reflecting on a long (but relatively unknown) tradition of Arab feminist journals when she wrote:

A stream of articles that appeared in a number of these journals established an interesting link between the emergence of political movements for national independence and the awakening of a feminist consciousness in the Arab world, arguing that no country can be truly free so long as its women remain shackled. (p. 76)[3]

Shaaban articulates the quintessential case for informational mechanisms committed to helping women's voices to be heard, both among each other and in the general population. News production under the control of and in the service of women assures the best guarantee of achieving this task, as ample stores of data demonstrate.

Notes

1. Many Latin American women after 1970 also identified with these liberation movements, even though their nations had achieved political independence beginning more than a century earlier. This identification is due, at least in part, to many Latin American nations' continued economic reliance on (and exploitation by) economically stronger industrial nations. For a fuller discussion, see Flora (1984).

2. From Inter Press Services African Women's Feature Service wire story. Reprinted by permission of IPS-Women's Feature Service.

3. Reprinted by permission of *Ms.* Magazine © 1993.

References

Abrahamson, Y. (1982). Minutes of Women, Development and Communication Meeting, Libre-ville, Gabon, February 1982. (*UNESCO Archives, Registry No. 307:392:2-055.2,* Paris.)

Anand, A. (1983). Rethinking women and development. In Isis International Information and Communication Service (Ed.), *Women in development: A resource guide for organization and action* (pp. 5-11). Geneva: ISIS.

Anand, A. (1992). Introduction. In Women's Feature Service (Ed.), *The power to change: Women in the Third World redefine their environment* (pp. 1-21). New Delhi: Kali Press for Women.

Anand, A. (1993). The clothesline goes up at the Human Rights Conference. *WFS Bulletin, 3*(3), 2.

Bird, S. E., & Dardenne, R. W. (1988). Myth, chronicle, and story: Exploring the narrative qualities of news. In J. W. Carey (Ed.), *Media, myths, and narratives: Television and the press* (pp. 67-86). Newbury Park, CA: Sage.

Boulding, E. (1992). *The underside of history: A view of women through time.* Newbury Park, CA: Sage.

Buvenic, M., & Yudelman, S. W. (1989). *Women, poverty, and progress in the Third World* (Headline Series No. 289). New York: Foreign Policy Association.

Byerly, C. M. (1990a). Taking a stronger hand: The Women's Feature Services and the making of world news. *Development, 2,* 79-85.

Byerly, C. M. (1990b). *The Women's Feature Services and the making of world news.* Unpublished doctoral dissertation, University of Washington.

Charlton, S. E. M. (1984). *Women in Third World development.* Boulder, CO: Westview.

Dasgupta, R. (1988, Fall). *India: Abusing the uniform* (wire story). Parraria, Bihar, India: Inter Press Service.

Donovan, J. (1985). *Feminist theory: The intellectual traditions of American feminism.* New York: Continuum Publishing.

Decade for women: World plan of action. (1975). Washington, DC: Women's Equity Action League Educational and Legal Defense Fund (WEAL Fund). (Condensed version of the World Plan of Action and Related Resolutions adopted at México City in July 1975 by the United Nations World Conference of the International Women's Year.)

Gallagher, M. (1981). *Unequal opportunities: The case of women and the media.* Paris: UNESCO.

Giffard, C. A. (1984, Autumn). Inter Press Service: News from the Third World. *Journal of Communication, 34*(4), 41-59.

Giffard, C. A., Byerly, C. M., & Van Horn, C. (1991). *The world of Inter Press Service.* Unpublished report prepared for the International Association for Mass Communications Research (IAMCR), The Hague, the Netherlands.

Gisele, A. (1980, September 7). *Benin: Toward improving rural women's lives* (wire story). Inter Press Service-African Women's Feature Service.

Gitlin, T. (1980). *The whole world is watching: The making and unmaking of the New Left.* Berkeley: University of California Press.

Gordon, L. (1981). The portrayal and participation of women in the Caribbean mass media: A socio-economic perspective. In M. Cuthbert (Ed.), *Women and media decision-making in the Caribbean.* Kingston, Jamaica: CARIMAC.

Gramsci, A. (1971). *Selections from the prison notebooks.* New York: International Publishers.

Hall, S. (1980). Encoding/decoding. In S. Hall et al. (Eds.), *Culture, media, language: Working papers in cultural studies* (pp. 128-132). London: Hutchinson.

Herman, E., & Chomsky, N. (1988). *Manufacturing consent: The political economy of the mass media.* New York: Pantheon.

Kielbowicz, R., & Scherer, H. (1986). The role of the press in the dynamics of social movements. *Research in Social Movements, Conflict and Change, 9,* 71-96.

Marx, K., & Engels, F. (1986). *The German ideology* (Part I). New York: International Publishers.

Mattelart, M. (1986). *Media, women, and crisis: Femininity and disorder.* London: Comedia Publishing.

Mohanty, C. T. (1991). Introduction: Cartographies of struggle: Third World women and the politics of feminism. In C. T. Mohanty, A. Russo, & L. Torres (Eds.), *Third World women and the politics of feminism* (pp. 1-47). Bloomington: Indiana University Press.

O'Connor, A. (1990). Culture and communication. In J. Downing, A. Mohammadi, & A. Sreberny-Mohammadi (Eds.), *Questioning the media* (pp. 27-41). Newbury Park, CA: Sage.

Rakow, L., & Kranich, K. (1991). Woman as sign in television news. *Journal of Communication, 41*(1), 8-23.

Roach, C. (1990). The movement for a New World Information and Communication Order: A second wave? *Media, Culture and Society, 12*(3), 283-307.

Rush, R. R., & Ogan, C. L. (1989). Communication and development: The female connection. In R. R. Rush & D. Allen (Eds.), *Communication at the crossroads* (pp. 265-278). Norwood, NJ: Ablex.

Shaaban, B. (1993, May-June). The hidden history of Arab feminism: Women's networks and journalism have flourished since 1892. *Ms.,* pp. 76-77.

Steeves, H. L. (1987). Feminist theories and media studies. *Critical Studies in Mass Communication, 4*(2), 95-135.

Steeves, H. L., & Arbogast, R. (1993). Feminism and communication in development: Ideology, law, ethics, practice. In B. Dervin & U. Hariharan (Eds.), *Progress in communication sciences 11* (pp. 229-277). Norwood, NJ: Ablex.

Tuchman, G. (1978). *Making news: A study in the construction of reality.* New York: Free Press.

UNFPA Project Request. (1976, July 1). Paris: UNESCO.

Women's Feature Service. (1992a). *Annual report 1992.* New Delhi: Women's Feature Service.

Women's Feature Service. (1992b). *The power to change: Women in the Third World redefine their environment.* New Delhi: Kali Press for Women.

Women's Feature Service. (1993). *Women's Feature Service: Reporting on change* (core proposal for the period January 1993-December 1995). [Available from: Women's Feature Service, 49 Golf Link, New Delhi, 110 003, India]

PART II

(Con)Textual Analyses

A favorite methodology in media studies is textual analysis. Scholars closely examine popular culture texts for manifest and subtextual meanings. Whether this is done in a quantitative or qualitative manner, textual analysis is usually the beginning point in many a media scholar's career. After all, the ubiquitousness of media products is both seductive and deceiving, as anyone who has tried to get a representative sample will tell you. The deceit stems not only from the difficulty of providing a sample, however, but from the leaps of logic often taken when linking textual analyses with social and cultural influences and outcomes—thus the title of this section: (Con)Textual Analyses. From a feminist multiculturalist perspective, we cannot consider texts outside of their sociocultural context. Historically and theoretically grounded analyses should illuminate some of the many dark spots on our nocturnal map. Though we are not saying that texts reflect culture or vice versa, we find that, especially in a situation of absence or symbolic annihilation, we need to explore relevant conditions and other texts. The five chapters in this section employ a textual method of analysis that includes examination of issues of gender, race, class, sexuality, and global origin.

In Chapter 6, Marguerite Moritz explores the phenomenon known as "lesbian chic." Here is a classic case of media blitz: Lesbians in the limelight. A cursory analysis would suggest that recent press coverage signals the end of symbolic annihilation for lesbians. Moritz's chapter reveals, however, that the construction of lesbian celebrity is problematic in many ways. First, the whole phenomenon smacks of "star persona" characteristics—that is, famous out lesbians and/or sympathizers are highlighted with the implication that being lesbian is the height of fashion. Not only does this approach efface most lesbians by virtue of their lack of celebrity status, but the construction of lesbian chic also contains major race and class components that symbolically annihilate lesbian women of color and working-class women.

Lisa M. Cuklanz expands on the themes presented by Moritz—namely that a few from a marginalized group are highlighted at the expense of other members of that group. In Chapter 7, Cuklanz demonstrates how women gain a voice through the use of a feminist analysis of rape in the case of the Big Dan rape trial, but this is conducted at the expense of the local Luso American community. This is done despite both groups' attempts to reject that setup. In addition, class functions as a marginalizing variable as the working-class status of much of the Luso American community becomes a major reason for their lack of credibility and the hostility directed at them. Again, what might first be seen as a victory for feminist positions on rape and violence is much more problematic when we consider ethnic and class issues.

In Chapter 8, Jasmine Paul and Bette J. Kauffman focus exclusively on the issue of class and women in Hollywood film. Not surprisingly, they find very few instances of working-class portrayals. The few they find are quite problematic. In a decade-by-decade analysis, they are able to suggest some of the sociohistorical components that may have influenced the production of Hollywood film in general and the portrayal of working-class women in particular. They also find that even when a popular film about working-class women is discussed in the press, as was the case with *Thelma & Louise,* the fact that these women were working class and that this plays a major function in the narrative appears to escape the attention of mainstream and feminist critics. In a capitalist society, wherein popular culture is produced for profit, the explicit examination of class remains a taboo subject.

Although there is an abundance of work about women and advertising, Katherine Toland Frith's Chapter 9 provides a somewhat different approach. Rather than analyzing women per se, Frith analyzes the construction of gender in advertisements that use nature for their background. Through the examination of a purposeful sample, Frith explores one of the basic feminist themes—namely the binary characterization of nature versus culture. The former is gendered feminine and the latter masculine. These "nature" ads position nature as ripe for the taking and culture, especially technology in the form of automobiles and computers, as masculine, active, dominant, and unstoppable. Sexual connotations pervade this imagery. Technology can always improve on nature. Furthermore, culture and consumerism are linked, completing a modernist approach that has proven to be quite harmful to the environment. Thus Frith links these advertisements to the debate over ecology and the return to goddess religions, wherein nature was revered and protected.

Completing the global sweep of textual analyses is Rashmi Luthra's Chapter 10. Beginning with an analysis of the world population control debate, one might conclude that, finally, Third-World women are at the center of global policy and attention. As all of the chapters in this section show, however, a closer analysis that takes into account context and the source of the voices, reveals that Third-World women continue to be silenced. Even though the entire debate is carried on in the name of Third-World women, we seldom hear their voices nor are their positions represented in the debate. In fact, major geopolitical players invoke the name of Third-World women to accomplish their own agenda—quite often at the expense of the very women they claim to represent.

Textual analysis remains an extremely useful tool in a feminist multiculturalist strategy. Though it is true that some kind of presence is better than a total lack of it, we must not be complacent with mere frequency of appearance. First, that frequency applies only to some women, mostly white, middle-class, heterosexual Western women. Second, frequency can contain stereotypes or representations that exclude the input of the very group(s) being represented. Third, sadly, the increased frequency appears to be accomplished at the expense of other members within a particular marginalized group or of other marginalized groups. Multiculturalism thus is accomplished as a zero-sum game. Someone must pay for the increased and/or improved representation of a previously marginalized group or segment of a group. Finally, representation is not necessarily enduring. For whatever reasons, and this is why it is so important to consider context, there are moments when certain marginalized groups are highlighted or manage to gain access to the media limelight. *Moments* is the key word here, however, for the attention is short-lived. Furthermore, the selection of these moments is not necessarily motivated by the needs and goals of the marginalized groups, though these moments can be useful openings for feminist multiculturalist interventions.

6   Lesbian Chic

Our Fifteen Minutes of Celebrity?

MARGUERITE MORITZ

When, within a matter of months, lesbians appear on the covers of *Newsweek, New York Magazine,* and *Vanity Fair,* when the family-hour drama *Picket Fences* has two teenage girls exploring their mutual attraction, and when *Roseanne* successfully convinces ABC to air her infamous kiss with Mariel Hemingway, one might wonder whether a revolution has taken place in the nation's most influential media circles. Indeed, the attention lesbians are receiving today in the mass media is long overdue and in some senses gratifying, but despite "Lesbian Chic," "The Power and the Pride," and other such encouraging headlines, media practices—in particular news media practices—continue to be deeply implicated in the perpetuation of a sexist, heterosexist, homophobic, and class-driven culture and in the privileging of elite white, conservative male voices.

Not surprisingly, it is precisely this bias that informs the mass media mini-blitz on lesbians. Taking the articles in *New York Magazine, Newsweek,* and *Vanity Fair* as a starting point, I will argue that all three offer "cover stories" in more than the literal sense of the term because, by and large, these reports mask what is not articulated in the text. The very term *chic,* to take the most obvious example, suggests a level of elitism, classism, and sexism that is in fact covered up or naturalized in the process of accepted news practice.

More than two decades ago, in their groundbreaking work on women and media depictions, Tuchman, Kaplan-Daniels, and Benet (1978) used the term *symbolic annihilation* to describe the ways in which media operate as a gendered discourse that denies a voice to women. Representations of women that do exist in Hollywood cinema, mainstream advertising, and prime-time television, to take the most obvious examples, are typically sexist and therefore oppressive. Cirksena and Cuklanz (1992) have shown how these idealized representations have functioned to establish standards of beauty in the culture:

> images of the ideal female body reproduced in advertising, film, television and other texts served to create a conception of the female body against which real people measured themselves and others . . . [So we can see that the body is] linguistically or symbolically constructed, and thus that people's understandings of their own and others' bodies were actually constrained and defined by linguistic and imagistic repetition of ideals and non-ideals. (p. 35).

It is my argument here that contemporary depictions of lesbians in mass media still function symbolically not only to deny lesbians a real voice in the culture but also to construct them in the same sexualized and sexist ways that women in general have been formulated. Media thus create lesbians whose personas and lifestyles convey an idealized and unattainable version of appearance, beauty, and style. Lesbians who cannot meet this standard are marginalized or made invisible altogether.

Although Tuchman et al.'s (1978) original analysis focused on gender, their theory of symbolic annihilation later was applied to issues of race, class, and sexual orientation. I hope to demonstrate how contemporary media depictions of lesbians are oppressive not only because of their essential sexism and heterosexism but also because they ignore crucial issues of race and class differences and reduce the lesbian experience to that of the privileged, educated, professional women. In this construction, white lesbians are shown to be the norm and lesbians of color remain largely invisible. Houston (1992) uses the phrase *interlocking identities* to describe the impact of race and class on women and the phrase *interlocking oppressions* to describe how these differences operate in the culture. When we begin to unmask mass media constructions of lesbians, we begin to see that they cover up rather than expose the interdependencies of sexism and homophobia, of racism and classism. Thus the chic lesbian shown in the slick mass market magazine is a creation that succeeds as a commodity but fails utterly as an explanation of who lesbians in all their diversity are and what they experience in this culture.

Approach to the Study

Just as it is problematic to write about women and indeed about lesbians as one undifferentiated group, so too is it misleading to write about media as a monolithic enterprise in which all products are seen as having essentially the same content. We know that there is a great deal of difference in the definition of women's issues and in the framing of these topics in *Ms., U.S. News & World Report*, and *Cosmopolitan*, for example, even though all three are mass circulation magazines produced in the United States. Television products have important differences from print products; cinema is not the same as advertising, even though both may be done on film and may have many other points of similarity.

Nonetheless, there are instances when it is useful to speak of mass media in a general way. For example, depictions of women in the 1950s in all mass media are not the same, at least not in terms of surface content, as today's media depictions. News media practices, both in print and in electronic media, are also evolving. We can see major differences in all news media products, for example, in terms of coverage of lesbians and gays, when we compare the 1960s and the 1990s. My point here is that mass communication research cannot be ahistorical and that when writing about different time periods it can be inappropriate to generalize about media industries.

In this study, I am attempting to examine contemporary media accounts of lesbians. I approach this study knowing that I am writing about a particular historical moment; that current professional practices are not uniform; that media content is not the same across industries; and that what I have chosen to examine is a select set of media products. I attempt to distinguish in this chapter between current media practices and products and those that existed and emerged from earlier historical moments. By placing this analysis in a historical framework I hope to illustrate the ways in which professional practices change and the ways in which they remain relatively constant over time.

To be more specific about my selection of media products, I began with a reading of three articles in major mainstream magazines, all of which appeared in 1993 and all of which featured lesbians on their covers. This seemed a logical starting point precisely because these articles appeared as historical firsts and because they in turn generated media attention as well as public debate. For example, in the issue following its cover story on lesbians, *Newsweek* reported having received hundreds of phone calls and letters to the editor commenting on the article. In seeking to establish how these three accounts fit into the larger media picture, my selection process is more random than systematic. I am writing about examples I have encountered in a variety of ways, sometimes as a media consumer, sometimes as a mass communication researcher, sometimes as a political activist, sometimes as a lesbian reader.

My method of analysis is qualitative and largely informed by feminist theories on film and television. One important approach, for example, is to distinguish between surface features of media products and underlying structural content. This is what feminist film theorists did when they critiqued the so called New Women's films of the 1970s, revealing how these films structurally position women as dependent on and subservient to men, even though the surface features of these female characters showed them as seemingly autonomous individuals by virtue of being lawyers or doctors. One of my points of inquiry has been to look for ways in which lesbians are structurally positioned as deviant from the normative straight world and as subordinate to the more visible gay male world.

Feminist film theorists such as Kuhn (1982) have long claimed that the work of cultural products is to mask inequities in our social system and that the work of feminist critics is to make visible that which is invisible. Toward that goal, it is useful to examine what is not in the text, for it can be as revealing as what is. Tuchman et al.'s (1978) notion of the symbolic annihilation of women in media is just such an approach and is easily applicable to lesbians. Houston's (1992) analysis of race and class provides another instance of looking for that which is absent, and her work provides an important background to my reading of these texts.

My own earlier work on celebrities and media also proved useful here. I have argued elsewhere (Moritz, 1992) that in an increasingly competitive marketplace, mass media journalism has successfully developed a cult of celebrity that both creates and exploits high visibility personalities. In film theory, this is the star persona analysis. By promoting celebrities, media narratives imply that celebrity lives represent or reflect the experiences of others in the group they supposedly represent. Kurt Cobain thus becomes the fallen symbol of his twentysomething generation in much the same way as Janis Joplin was mythologized two decades earlier. In 1980, when the Billie Jean King galimony story broke, newspapers, magazines, and television news all had a feeding frenzy. Five years later the media showed a similar appetite for the Rock Hudson-AIDS story and indeed AIDS did become an ongoing story in the press. Except for those notable cases, however, the ordinary lives and issues of gays, lesbians, and bisexuals remained largely off limits in the mass media throughout the 1980s. Coverage that did exist was often framed in a negative way; in addition, these stories were typically focused on white, affluent gay men. In the process of promoting celebrity, the everyday lives of ordinary group members remain obscured or completely invisible. In the case of lesbians, this becomes especially problematic because there are so few arenas within the culture in which they are given any significant voice.

Despite my earlier disclaimers, I do attempt throughout this chapter to draw some general conclusions about media practices; it is the work of the careful reader to evaluate the accuracy and validity of those conclusions.

History of News Depictions

Despite journalists' claims that they don't make the news, they just report it, news organizations have a well-documented history of being selective, and biased, in their choice of news topics. "The works of Epstein, Gans, Tuchman and others have made it axiomatic that what mainstream journalism offers as 'news' is a highly selective text and that what it portrays as reality is highly constructed" (Moritz, 1992, p. 152). News organizations, print and broadcast, never have been prohibited from writing and reporting on gays and lesbians. But unwritten news codes—those generally accepted definitions of what constitutes a story—for decades provided a powerful barrier to coverage of many minority groups, including gays and lesbians. Far from being independent, news codes flow out of the larger culture and reflect the attitudes and socioeconomic hierarchies in society at large. Given that system, it is hardly surprising that gays and lesbians were not considered worthy of coverage well into the 1980s. In 1987, to cite one notorious case, both *Time* and

Newsweek ignored the gay rights march in Washington, D.C., the largest civil rights demonstration in the capitol since 1969 (Freiberg, 1993).

What coverage the incipient gay rights movement did get was often problematic. Before 1973, when the American Psychiatric Association removed homosexuality from its list of mental illnesses, the occasional news accounts that did exist often framed gayness as psychological sickness. Stories on gays and lesbians have a long history of being cast as "morality tales, with the homosexual being the negative reference point in a discourse that reaffirmed society's sense of what is normal" (Fejes & Petrich, 1993, p. 402).[1] In the 1980s, media attention focused on the emergence of AIDS and re-framed gays around their

> "promiscuous and abnormal" sexual behavior and lifestyle. . . . A common media frame was to distinguish between the "innocent" victims of AIDS, those who did not acquire the virus from gay sexual contact, and, implicitly, the "guilty" victims of AIDS, those who did. (pp. 403-404)

As AIDS became the gay story of the eighties, gayness became equated with deadly disease. Yet at the same time, the networks could point to their coverage of AIDS as satisfying gay advocates' demands for visibility; even in this instance, the coverage of the emerging epidemic was limited until the story of Rock Hudson's death from AIDS in 1985 sparked the first significant media response to reporting on the disease.

Ironically, the subtext of the Rock Hudson story was that AIDS might be infiltrating the straight world. "Now fears are growing that the AIDS epidemic may spread beyond gays and other high risk groups to threaten the population at large," *Newsweek* reported (Clark, 1985).[2] *Time* offered a similar narrative: "For years it has been dismissed as the 'gay plague,' somebody else's problem. Now, as the number of cases in the U.S. surpasses 12,000 and the fatal disease begins to strike the famous and the familiar, concern is growing that AIDS is a threat to everyone" ("The Frightening AIDS Epidemic," 1985, p. 1).

Lesbians, meanwhile, remained almost as invisible as ever. Yet, because the media had consistently used the word *gay* to refer to both men and women, lesbians were implicated in the AIDS crisis even though they are among the lowest risk subgroup for the disease, a fact that rarely is reported.

Although coverage of AIDS no doubt has had its negative implications, in some real ways the epidemic also gave gays and (by implication and association) lesbians increased public visibility. In a lengthy account of gays and the media, the gay and lesbian newspaper *Washington Blade* contended that "it was not until the AIDS crisis that stories about individual gay men and lesbians—and the issues that concerned them—began to appear with regularity" (Freiberg, 1993, p. 55).[3]

In 1990, the American Society of Newspaper Editors (ASNE) decided for the first time to examine the coverage of gays and lesbians as well as the working conditions for gay and lesbian newsroom personnel. Its national survey gave the nation's newspapers "a grade of mediocre" on the issue of coverage and said that anti-gay attitudes remain "the last acceptable basis for discrimination among so-called acceptable Americans, including editors." Although the study found newsrooms "largely hospitable" to gay and lesbian employees, it also noted "a palpable undercurrent of bias" (American Society of Newspaper Editors [ASNE], 1990, p. 9). The newly organized National Gay and Lesbian Journalists Association (NGLJA) is dedicated to improving news coverage of gay and lesbian issues and to encouraging gay and lesbian staff members to become more visible on the job. By 1995, NGLJA had attracted 1,000 members in 14 chapters around the country. Among their goals is increased visibility in newsrooms and in news content (Freiberg, 1993). Despite the emergence of this group and the vast improvements in news coverage of gay and lesbian issues, heterosexism remains a prevailing norm.

In news coverage, for example, contemporary news accounts increasingly are focused on issues of gay rights. But even as demands for equal protection are viewed as legitimate news, Fejes and Petrich (1993) point out that "the legitimacy" of those demands is still viewed as "questionable" (p. 402). The ongoing media debate over the appropriateness of outing offers another example. Outing, after all, rests on the homophobic assumption that being identified as gay or lesbian is still a stigma. If it were not, then it would not be problematic to reveal any person's sexual orientation (Fejes & Petrich, 1993). News headlines in local papers still refer to "openly gay" individuals (Knopper, 1993).

As recently as July 1993, well after the media flurry around gays in the military, the *Chicago Sun-Times,* a major metropolitan paper, felt the need to define "coming out" in an article about a gay newscaster (see Williams, 1993). And, although many newspapers have editorialized about lifting the ban on gays in the military, Fejes and Petrich (1993) note that "they are often quick to point out that such support does not mean they endorse the gay lifestyle" (p. 405).

The creation and selection of images to represent gays and lesbians represents another level of concern. In terms of mass media images, gay men have

been limited to a few very stereotyped portrayals: hairdressers, floral design-
ers, houseboys, men in black leather, men in baths, men in bars—often
faceless, shown from the back or from an angle designed to obscure their faces,
men in doctors' offices, in hospital beds, men with AIDS.

Lesbian images are far more rare on television and in print—just as images
of women in general are far more rare than images of men in the media. The
few lesbian images that have been featured over the years have relied on
stereotypes that have included sadistic prison wardens, blood-sucking vam-
pires, murderers, or, at the other extreme, asexual spinsters. Even today our
collective imagery does not include visual vocabulary that defines gay or
lesbian.

In news, both still photos in print and moving images on television have
been a point of contention. In their early attempts to depict gays and lesbians,
journalists often utilized the bizarre to illustrate the homosexual look. News
editors showing gay pride parades, for example, typically selected 20 seconds
of footage that featured whips, chains, and bare breasts. Gay watchdog groups
in cities around the country pressured television newsrooms to change. The
Gay & Lesbian Alliance Against Defamation (GLAAD) still instructs media
personnel on the issue. "Do not show or describe only the most unconven-
tional members of our community. There is nothing wrong with unconven-
tionality—many in our community quite properly celebrate it—but it is
nevertheless unfair to reinforce misperceptions that all lesbians and gay men
are into, say, leather or drag" (*Media Guide*, 1990, Sec. 2, pt. 1, p. 31).[4]

Television news practices did begin to change and images that reflected a
more mainstream look became more common. But that technique has now
led conservative critics to complain that the liberal media is sanitizing the issue
in an effort to be politically correct. In essence, the religious right is arguing
for a reframing of lesbian and gay images precisely so that they will illustrate
perversion.

While the framing of images and stories about lesbians and gays remains
highly contested, there is no question that in the 1990s media interest in these
issues has accelerated. The *Washington Blade* has described this phenomenon
as an explosion of interest, a "radical departure" from news practices of even
the late 1980s, a "sea change," like being on "a different planet" (Freiberg, 1993,
p. 55). Even the formerly distant *New York Times* has done an about-face,
increasing its coverage of gay and lesbian communities by "65% from 1990 to
1991 and the paper began using the word 'gay' instead of 'homosexual' " (Fejes
& Petrich, 1993, p. 405). Because of its impact as the national paper of record,

this change created "what many activists and media watchdogs assert is a 'ripple effect' on other media" (Freiberg, 1993, p. 55).

Lesbian Chic

The lesbian cover stories may be part of the ripple effect, but in terms of media practices I am arguing that they should not be viewed as a wave or a tidal wave, much less a sea change. Instead of underscoring the ways in which these accounts are different from past practices, I would like to focus on the ways in which they are very much the same.

As a starting point, I'd like to take up the term *lesbian chic*. Lesbian chic is a play on the 1970s term *radical chic*, a reference to well-off liberals who adopted some of the postures that coalesced around Free Speech, Sexual Liberation, and other antiestablishment movements. I'm not certain where and when the term lesbian chic first emerged in the mass media, but after it was used as the headline for a *New York Magazine* cover story in the May 10, 1993 issue (see Kasindorf, 1993), it popped up repeatedly in popular discourse, to say nothing of lesbian discourse.

Geraldo, for example, offered a program titled "Lesbian Chic" that featured a panel of lesbians in the entertainment field. The National Gay and Lesbian Journalists Association held a panel, "Lesbian Chic, Hip or Hype?", at its annual convention in fall 1993. (By way of contrast, in 1992 NGLJA had a panel titled "Lesbian Invisibility and How to Deal With It.") Even a small-town, family newspaper like the *Boulder Daily Camera* (Martin, 1993) in the conservative state of Colorado used the term in a headline.

Not only did the phrase gain wide currency, but the notion of lesbians as cover story material also took off. One month after the *New York* piece (Kasindorf, 1993) appeared, *Newsweek* offered its unprecedented look at "Lesbians Coming Out Strong" in an article (see Salholz, 1993) that asked on its cover, "What Are the Limits of Tolerance?" By August 1993, *Vanity Fair* was on the scene with a cover story profile of k. d. lang (Bennetts, 1993), complete with its not-soon-to-be-forgotten (or matched) centerfold of k. d. and model Cindy Crawford.

The media attention to lesbians in those few months was so striking and so unusual that even the gay *San Francisco Bay Times* got into the act, issuing a copy-cat cover called Dykeweek (1993) that featured a smiling, wholesome opposite-sex couple on the cover. The headline over that picture read,

"HETEROSEXUALS . . . WHAT ARE THE LIMITS OF TOLERANCE?" Continuing the send-up, the piece offered a glossary that defined heterosexual terminology such as *wife* ("Traditionally the 'feminine' partner; responsible for domestic tasks and child care'"); *husband* ("Wears suit or other 'manly gear.' Watches sports on TV. Performs heavy lifting, household repairs and yard work"); and *marriage* ("Ancient quaint custom in which males and females pair up, supposedly for life. 50 percent failure rate").[5] These definitions presented a foil for *Newsweek's* glossary (see Salholz, 1993) of lesbian vocabulary that included *femme* ("Traditionally the 'feminine' partner; young women are now redefining the role as less submissive"); *butch* ("Wears suit, motorcycle jacket or other 'manly' gear"); and *vanilla* ("Likes kissing, holding hands, no rough stuff").[6]

Of course, Dykeweek was a successful dig precisely because, in the words of Modleski (1991), "heterosexual presumption and power asymmetry is still intact" (p. 6). Just as mass media articles on women frequently "assume and promote a liberal notion of the formal equality of men and women" (p. 6), mass media representations similarly mask the ways in which lesbians are systematically oppressed by both sexism and homophobia.

The most recent spate of lesbian press remains largely true to the star persona model, the attention being either to celebrity or to white, upper middle-class, professional, fashionable, affluent urbanites who can be constructed as chic. The text of *New York's* cover story on "Lesbian Chic" (Kasindorf, 1993) focuses almost entirely on celebrities who are either self-identified as lesbian or who have some lesbian connection such as playing a lesbian character or publicly asserting a lesbian sensibility. Thus Paragraph 1 is on Madonna. Paragraph 2 is on NOW president Patricia Ireland, Madonna (again), and actress Sandra Bernhard. Paragraph 3 refers to actress Sharon Stone, Bernhard (again), and Roseanne. The fourth paragraph names k. d. lang, who is pictured on the cover.

Where is Martina? In Paragraph 10, after references to Dee Mosbacher, best-selling author Dorothy Allison, Clinton appointee Roberta Achtenberg, and political activist Torie Osborn. Before it's all over we also hear about author Rita Mae Brown and comics Lea DeLaria and Kate Clinton.

The *Newsweek* article (see Salholz, 1993) is remarkably similar in its focus on celebrity. The very first person named is k. d. lang. Then comes Sandra Bernhard, Roseanne, actress Morgan Fairchild, comic Suzanne Westenhoefer, then, Roberta Achtenberg, Kate Clinton, Lea DeLaria, Dorothy Allison, and so on.

The lesbian couple appearing on the cover—presumably put there as representative of today's young lesbians—is not mentioned until the fifth page of the article. And then the women are covered in the following two sentences: "Growing up in a small, Southern town, Ashley Herrin (who appears on *Newsweek's* cover [Salholz, 1993] with her partner Catherine Angiel) turned to alcohol to deaden her feelings of sexual difference. Today she's sober and is studying to become a therapist for homosexuals" (p. 58).

When the focus is not on celebrity lesbians, who are by definition chic, it typically shifts to lesbians with money, style, and sexual cachet. Writes *Newsweek* of supposedly typical lesbian life: "There is a vital, sex-positive scene with nightly dancing at places like the Clit Club in New York and San Francisco's twice-a-month sex clubs" (Salholz, 1993, p. 59). The *New York Magazine* piece offers an even more telling account of everyday life among chic lesbians, describing

> a sexy, young, tawny skinned woman . . . thick, dark, curly hair flowing into her eyes . . . talking to her pretty blonde lover. . . . Over by the pool table, there's a woman in an Armani suit. [There's] a gorgeous brunette with a movie-star face . . . and a Boycott Colorado T-shirt. (Kasindorf, 1993, p. 33)[7]

As a Coloradan and a lesbian I might suggest that that may be as close to this state as these women ever get. Even though that is partly facetious, it is also the central point: these cover stories—while they do move the idea of lesbian into the arena of public discourse and they do promote lesbian success stories—also suggest a kind of essentialism in which every lesbian is living in New York, Los Angeles, or San Francisco where nightly dancing in fashionable clubs is a possibility. Every lesbian is white and relatively wealthy. Every lesbian is riding the crest of this wave of popularity. In this way, lesbians who are removed from the "sex-positive" bar scene are also made invisible. Descriptions of a "gorgeous brunette with a movie-star face" similarly serve to insist that lesbians worthy of attention conform to conventional Hollywood standards of beauty. In addition, these media narratives typically take "the concerns of the middle-class, articulate white woman as the norm" and ignore "the hierarchical structuring of the relations between black and white women" (Modleski, 1991, p. 134). As one lesbian said of the *Newsweek* article, "I loved it because my mother liked it, but I also hated it because my mother liked it" (Salholz, 1993). Constructed as they are, these articles not only impose a sexist notion of what makes a woman desirable, but they also deny a voice to lesbians of color, working-class lesbians, older lesbians, Birkenstock lesbians, cowboy lesbians, and ordinary lesbians whose daily lives are not the stuff of which mainstream magazine articles are made. Rakow (1992) has suggested that the very subject matter taken up as important excludes the talk of those not in positions of power. It is precisely in this sense that it becomes a concern that lesbians who are not celebrities, and not powerful or privileged (read *chic*) do not get a voice in these cover stories.

The gender-bending spectacle created by *Vanity Fair* (Bennetts, 1993) may be camp and trendy but it is also market driven. Lesbian celebrity in this sense is packaged to sell as sexuality. Glossy magazine photographs of chic, sexy lesbians are voyeuristic and fetishistic in much the same way that Alloula described the colonial postcard, obsessed with veiled Eastern women; the camera's gaze is the colonial gaze of domination. Similarly, the camera's gaze at lesbian women constructed as objects of sexual pleasure illustrates how "photography and spectatorship continue to be complicit technologies and machineries of domination and subordination" (Ganguly, 1992, p. 74). Thus we see the media holding up lesbian specimens, the forbidden oddities, for examination and closer inspection.

Still Locked Out

Despite lesbian chic, I think it is politically imperative for us to acknowledge that most lesbians and indeed most women do not fit this idealized model of femininity and fashion. And certainly lesbians are still largely invisible in mainstream media. Critic Laura Flanders (1993), writing about coverage of the 1993 March on Washington, termed this ongoing phenomenon "Lesbian Lock-Out":

> Just what do lesbians have to do to get a photo on the front page of the *Washington Post?* . . . Even when the Lesbian Avengers mobilized thousands of women—some bare-breasted, some on motorcycles—to demonstrate in front of the White House, the *Post* still went with a picture of gay men. (p. 16)[8]

Of course, Lesbian Lock-Out is just another term that describes the invisibility and marginalization that have worked against numerous groups, including women, racial and ethnic minorities, and the economically disadvantaged. Historically, invisibility and marginalization have been the hallmarks of media coverage, or more accurately noncoverage, of gay issues in general and lesbian issues in particular. This still exists and functions in many of the same ways it has for decades. Most significantly, lesbians are often still invisible. Hollywood offered just such an example in 1992 by not naming or showing the lesbian relationship in *Fried Green Tomatoes*. In his *New Republic* review, critic Kauffmann (1992) complained about this, calling it evidence of "the script's implicit cowardice" (p. 28). And of course there were no lesbian ballplayers in *A League of Their Own*, which was also released in that year.

In 1994, when Hollywood's first AIDS film, *Philadelphia*, became a box office smash, *Time* asked if the movie industry could "still shun gay themes" (Corliss, 1994, p. 62). Its lengthy feature article on the film indicated that the answer was at least a qualified no. Indeed, it listed four films (*The Normal Heart, Angels in America, And the Band Played On*, and *Good Days*) already in the offing. All feature gay men, thus leaving Hollywood versions of lesbians still locked in what Russo (1981) termed the "celluloid closet."

Television remains similarly hesitant. There were no lesbian mothers in the *Murphy Brown* family values episode aimed at Dan Quayle, even though the point of the entire episode was to demonstrate the large variety of family models that exist. ABC demonstrated this drive to keep lesbians invisible when it initially refused to air the same-sex kiss episode of *Roseanne*, despite the fact that countless television shows feature women being raped, assaulted, and otherwise brutalized as a matter of course.

Media reappropriation is another form of lock-out. The April 4, 1994 issue of *Time*, for example, carried a lengthy feature story on mass murderers that discusses the thousands of people—mostly women—who have a fascination with killers and, for example, correspond with them (see "Crime," 1994). Reappropriating the term lesbian chic, *Time's* index refers sardonically to the article as "Serial Killer Chic." *Cosmopolitan* offered an even more damaging reframing in its "21 Page Special Update on Feminism in the 90s." After some Catharine MacKinnon and Andrea Dworkin-bashing, the article says:

> Another strident voice in the feminist movement—and one that's made most of us equally uncomfortable—has been that of militant lesbians. For a time they got in there and pretty much tried to take over. Feminism became an arena to give them recognition, status, ways of fighting homophobia. While the majority of us—straight or gay—were definitely for every conceivable gain all women could make, we didn't have much rapport with that acutely hostile crowd. (Baroni, 1994, p. 197)[9]

Even positive stories about gays and lesbians often undercut lesbian visibility by focusing on white, gay men. An *Adweek* article from July 1993 titled "The Way Out . . . After Years of Silence, Gays in Advertising Are Starting to Be Heard" (Sharkey, 1993) is a case in point. In its conceptualization this piece might be considered a breakthrough because it suggests that gay men and lesbians are coming out of the closet in an industry that has not always been hospitable. In its execution, however, it follows a familiar and sexist prototype, featuring the stories of eight gay men (all with prominent photos) and one lesbian. Perhaps that should not be surprising in an industry where women are still very much underpaid in comparison to their male counterparts and underrepresented in virtually every realm except that of display where women are, of course, very much the center of attention.

Redbook offered a similar white, male focus in its piece on college life entitled "Gays on Campus" (Mansfield, 1993). The headline sets the tone for the entire piece by using the word *gay* as an umbrella term to cover both gay men and lesbians, a fairly common media practice. The opening page of the article features four separate photos showing a total of six gay men and no lesbians. The next page of the piece features nine separate photos, three of lesbians, six of gay men. Similarly, the text uses *gay* as the encompassing term; the word *lesbian* doesn't even appear until the ninth paragraph and then only in a reference to the formal title of a campus event called Gay and Lesbian Awareness Week. In another especially noteworthy example of lesbian erasure, a newspaper headline used the word *gay* ("TV's Good at Putting up 'Fences' on Gay Themes," Rosenberg, 1993) for an article about an episode of *Picket Fences* in which two high school girls explore their mutual sexual interest. Not only does the headline use the word *gay,* but never in the piece itself does the word *lesbian* appear, even though lesbian sexuality is what is under consideration (Knopper, 1993, p. 4).

By subsuming the term *lesbian* under the heading of *gay,* journalistic practices tend to erase the specific experiences of lesbians who are impacted by the culture's pervasive sexism in ways that gay men are not. White gay men, after all, still benefit from white male privilege in some instances even though they may suffer from homophobia in others. In her essay on "Compulsory Heterosexuality and Lesbian Existence," Rich (1980) argues that the lesbian experience is indeed profoundly different from that of the gay man:

> In defining and describing lesbian existence I would hope to move toward a dissociation of lesbian from male homosexual values and allegiances. I perceive

the lesbian experience as being, like motherhood, a profoundly female experience with particular oppressions, meanings and potentialities we cannot com-
prehend as long as we simply bracket it with other sexually stigmatized
existences. (p. 650)

Just as the experience of lesbians is quite distinct from the experience of
gay men, so too is there a crucial difference between white lesbians and
lesbians of color, between those who are economically privileged and those
who are not. These differences also are erased, however, by media practices
that naturalize elite white subjects and make theirs not only the normative
experience but seemingly the only experience. And this erasure, as Houston
(1992) suggests in her analysis of women generally, obscures crucial differences.

Race and class differences among women are not simply variations in "surface"
features, such as skin color or hair texture; they are not merely interesting, but
innocuous, variations in ethnic cultural practices, or economic "survival skills."
These things are no more the primary social differences between white women
and women of color or middle-class women and working-class women than
female genitalia, high-pitched voices, and "nurturing skills" are the primary
social differences between women and men. The primary race and class difference among women, like the gender difference, is power; more specifically, it is
the unequal distribution of and access to social and economic power and
privilege. (pp. 46-47)

As lesbians, we are all too aware that this is a culture that remains racist as
well as both sexist and homophobic. On some level lesbian chic articles permit
mass culture to acknowledge political struggles and at the same time reconstruct the very notion of lesbian by emphasizing mainstream definitions of
beauty and fashion. The result is a media formulation of lesbian that leaves
out race and class considerations. Even if we set those aside and attempt to
look at media coverage of gays and lesbians as one undifferentiated group, the
picture is still highly problematic.

Conclusion

Clearly the place of homosexuality in the culture is one of the central
debates of the decade, and consequently media representations will continue

to be a contested terrain for some time to come. Lesbian stories in some cases may advance the debate, increase visibility, or at least put the issue on the table.

"You can't know the impact of all those *Newsweek's* having been delivered to all those homes ensconced in homophobia, where Dad had to pick it up off the coffee table and see the L-word. And for all of those terrified teenagers who are gay—think of the boost," Torrie Osborn, executive director of the National Gay and Lesbian Task Force, was quoted as saying (Martin, 1993, p. 4).[10] Nonetheless, Osborn is quick to add that recent media attention should not be over-estimated. "We're the flavor of the month . . . I don't think we should pretend it's something it's not. Being a fickle press' temporary subject is not a substitute for political power" (quoted in Martin, 1993, p. 4). Meantime, lesbian chic articles that focus on celebrity status and upward mobility may have a negative impact by obscuring more serious issues that remain largely out of bounds in the media, including lesbians in the military, adoption, artificial insemination, medical benefits, health issues, and spousal rights. In addition, as lesbian columnist Deb Schwartz remarked, these cover stories remake lesbians into more sellable commodities. "The recent hetero media googlyness over lesbians isn't about documentation—showing the realities of lesbian lives—it's about creation: building a better lesbian, one palatable enough for mainstream consumption. . . . In order to show off the new and improved qualities of these lovely ladies, a line is drawn between the fab lesbians of today and those cruddy old dykes of yore" (quoted in Martin, 1993, p. 4). Ultimately, what we have in these media stories are carefully crafted constructions that not only sell us but also sell us short.

Notes

1. Quotations from "Invisibility, Homophobia and Heterosexism: Lesbians, Gays and the Media," by F. Fejes and K. Petrich, *Critical Studies in Mass Communication, 10*(4), 1993, pp. 396-442. Used by permission of the Speech Communication Association.

2. M. Clark, "AIDS: Special Report," *Newsweek* (August 12, 1985). From *Newsweek*, August 12, 1985. © 1985, Newsweek, Inc. All rights reserved. Reprinted by permission.

3. Quotations from "Gays and the Media," by P. Freiberg, *Washington Blade*" (April 23, 1993) are reprinted by permission of the *Washington Blade*.

4. From *Media Guide to the Lesbian and Gay Community,* 1990. Reprinted by permission of GLAAD/SFBA.

5. From "Dykeweek," *San Francisco Bay Times* (July 1, 1993).

6. E. Salholz, "Lesbians Coming Out Strong: The Power and the Pride," *Newsweek* (June 21, 1993). From *Newsweek*, June 21, 1993. © Newsweek, Inc. All rights reserved. Reprinted by permission.

7. J. Kasindorf, "Lesbian Chic: The Bold, Brave New World of Gay Women," *New York Magazine* (May 10, 1993). Copyright © 1993 K-III Magazine Corporation. All rights reserved. Reprinted with the permission of *New York Magazine*.

8. L. Flanders, "Lesbian Lock-Out," *Extra!* (June 1993).

9. D. Baroni, " 'Feminist' . . . What Is It About That Word?" *Cosmopolitan* (May 1994).

10. L. Martin, "Lesbians Have Mixed Feelings About Being Mainstream Chic," *Boulder Daily Camera* (August 29, 1993). Quotations reprinted by permission.

References

American Society of Newspaper Editors Human Resources Committee. (1990). *Alternatives: Gays and lesbians in the newsroom.* Unpublished report.

Baroni, D. (1994, May). "Feminist" . . . What is it about that word? *Cosmopolitan,* pp. 195-215.

Bennetts, L. (1993, August). k. d. lang cuts it close. *Vanity Fair,* pp. 94-98, 142-146.

Cirksena, C., & Cuklanz, L. (1992). Male is to female as ___ is to ___: A guided tour of five feminist frameworks for communication studies. In L. Rakow (Ed.), *Women making meaning: New feminist directions in communication* (pp. 18-44). New York: Routledge.

Clark, M. (1985, August 12). AIDS: Special report. *Newsweek,* pp. 20-29.

Corliss, R. (1994, February 7). The gay gauntlet. *Time,* pp. 62-64.

Crime: Serial killer chic sweeps the country. (1994, April 4). *Time,* p. 3.

Dykeweek. (1993, July 1). *San Francisco Bay Times,* p. 1.

Fejes, F., & Petrich, K. (1993). Invisibility, homophobia, and heterosexism: Lesbians, gays, and the media. *Critical Studies in Mass Communication, 10*(4), 396-422.

Flanders, L. (1993, June). Lesbian lock-out. *EXTRA!,* p. 16.

Freiberg, P. (1993, April 23). Gays and the media. *Washington Blade,* pp. 53-57.

Ganguly, K. (1992). Accounting for others: Feminism and representation. In L. Rakow (Ed.), *Women making meaning: New feminist directions in communication* (pp. 60-82). New York: Routledge.

Houston, M. (1992). The politics of difference: Race, class, and women's communication. In L. Rakow (Ed.), *Women making meaning: New feminist directions in communication* (pp. 45-59). New York: Routledge.

Kasindorf, J. (1993, May 10). Lesbian chic: The bold, brave new world of gay women. *New York Magazine,* pp. 31-37.

Kauffmann, S. (1992, February 3). Alabama and elsewhere. *New Republic,* p. 28.

Knopper, S. (1993, November 12). Openly gay flirtations mix goofy fun with stirring solemnity. *Boulder Sunday Camera,* p. 4.

Kuhn, A. (1982). *Women's pictures: Feminism and cinema.* London: Routledge & Kegan Paul.

Mansfield, S. (1993, May). Gays on campus. *Redbook,* pp. 124-127, 140-142.

Martin, L. (1993, August 29). Lesbians have mixed feelings about being mainstream chic. *Boulder Daily Camera,* p. 4.

Media guide to the lesbian and gay community. (1990). New York: Gay & Lesbian Alliance Against Defamation.

Modleski, T. (1991). *Feminism without women: Culture and criticism in a "postfeminist" age.* New York: Routledge.

Moritz, M. (1992). How U.S. media represent sexual minorities. In P. Dahlgren & C. Sparks (Eds.), *Journalism and popular culture* (pp. 154-170). London: Sage.

Rakow, L. (1992). The field reconsidered. In L. Rakow (Ed.), *Women making meaning: New feminist directions in communication* (pp. 3-17). New York: Routledge.

Rich, A. (1980). Compulsory heterosexuality and lesbian existence. *Signs: Journal of Women in Culture and Society, 5*(4), 631-660.

Rosenberg, H. (1993, April 29). TV's good at putting up "fences" on gay themes. *Boulder Daily Camera,* p. B5.

Russo, V. (1981). *The celluloid closet: Homosexuality in the movies.* New York: Harper & Row.

Salholz, E. (1993, June 21). Lesbians coming out strong: The power and the pride. *Newsweek,* pp. 54-60.

Sharkey, B. (1993, July 19). The way out . . . After years of silence, gays in advertising are starting to be heard. *Adweek,* pp. 22-31.

The frightening AIDS epidemic comes out of the closet. (1985, August 12). *Time,* pp. 40-47.

Tuchman, G., Kaplan-Daniels, A., & Benet, J. (Eds.). (1978). *Hearth and home: Images of women in the mass media.* New York: Oxford University Press.

Williams, S. (1993, July 27). Going out in public. *Chicago Sun-Times,* p. B1.

7 News Coverage of Ethnic and Gender Issues in the Big Dan's Rape Case

LISA M. CUKLANZ

One of the most highly publicized rape trials in recent U.S. history involved the six men accused in what became known as the Big Dan's case. On a March night in 1983, a young woman was raped in Big Dan's Tavern by two men, with the assistance of other bar patrons. The story made national headlines immediately, purportedly, as news stories claimed, because the rape had been unusually brutal and the behavior of the bar patrons unusually callous. Onlookers in the bar were said to have cheered the event as if it were a ball game (Starr, 1984). Although initial reports claimed that up to 15 men had participated in the rape, only 6 were brought to trial and only 4 were convicted. The case brought together complex issues of gender, ethnicity, and class on the difficult and historically problematic topic of rape. The case reached national attention at a time when rape law reformers had been working for 10 years to alter public perceptions of rape, its victims, and perpetrators. However, it also raised questions of ethnic marginalization. The rape took place in New Bedford, MA, a community composed primarily of Portuguese immigrants and Portuguese Americans, and this fact quickly became one of the most highly publicized aspects of the case.[1] Although the district attorney and the victim were of Portuguese descent, it was the Luso American identity of the defendants that received the most attention from mainstream news media. All 6 defendants were working-class Portuguese immigrants. This chapter examines national circulation mainstream news coverage of the Big Dan's case in an attempt to answer questions about how mainstream news handles complex intersections of gender, ethnicity, and class in coverage of contemporary issues. This analysis is based on news and editorial coverage from mainstream sources with national circulation, including the *New York Times,* news magazines such as *Time, Newsweek,* and *People,* and broadcast coverage on CBS, NBC, and ABC.

Issues in News Coverage of Ethnicity and Gender

Since the Kerner report of 1968, studies of race, ethnicity, and racism in mainstream news have proliferated. Most treat issues relevant to African American concerns and most focus on issues of representation, topic selection, and the definition of news (Daniel & Allen, 1988; Entman, 1990, 1992; Mazingo, 1988; Thomas, 1984; van Dijk, 1991). Many of these works, however, draw broad conclusions that can be applied to news coverage of other ethnic groups and issues. Van Dijk's (1991) book *Racism and the Press* concludes that "during the last decades the coverage of ethnic and racial affairs in the Press, on both sides of the Atlantic, has gradually become less blatantly racist, but . . . stereotypes and the definition of minorities as a 'problem' or even as a 'threat' is still prevalent" (p. 245). Because this chapter focuses on one specific case dealing with a little-known and seldom-reported group, the more relevant question is whether this same phenomenon occurs in some way in the absence of widely dispersed and easily recognizable stereotypes. No readily definable "Portuguese" stereotype, or in Entman's (1990) terms "old-fashioned stereotype," for Portuguese Americans exists in mainstream U.S. culture. However, drawing an analogy between race and Portuguese ethnicity, previous findings suggest that ethnicity will be treated as difference or separateness and that this difference will be treated as problematic.

Similarly, studies of gender and mainstream news have focused primarily on the visibility of women as news anchors or sources (see Foote, 1992; Kahn, 1991), or on the function of news as a mechanism of social control and perpetuator of gender stereotypes (Robinson, 1978; Tuchman, 1978). Several studies have combined analyses of race/ethnicity and gender into a unified analysis (see Stone, 1988; Ziegler & White, 1990), although these studies also focus primarily on *visibility* of group members across texts rather than on the specific techniques or strategies employed by mainstream news sources in covering intersecting issues of relevance to women and ethnic or racial groups. In their important essay on the signification of women in mainstream news, however, Rakow and Kranich (1991) discuss uses of dual identity sources in mainstream news. They note that when a woman is used as a news source because of her identity as "woman," she is almost always white, whereas when a nonwhite source is cited, that person is almost always a man. News writers fail to treat women members of ethnic and racial groups as persons able to speak *both* for women as a group and for the ethnic or racial community as a group. This finding can be applied usefully to the treatment of women as news *subjects*. It is likely that news subjects who are both women and members of ethnic or racial groups will be treated in mainstream news as one or the other (either as women or as ethnic/racial group members) in most coverage, because mainstream news has not previously recognized multiple identities of news sources except in very limited situations. Rakow and Kranich's work suggests an inability of mainstream news to recognize openly complex issues of multiple identity and politics, and points to a tendency to focus instead on conflicts among and within marginal groups. Individuals within such groups are treated as having only a single interest rather than as complex persons with multiple, sometimes conflicting affiliations and beliefs. This chapter explicates the techniques or methods used by mainstream news to avoid outright, or to direct attention away from, such complexities.

Case Background

From the outset, citizens of New Bedford, MA, where the rape took place, protested the irresponsible media coverage of the case. New Bedford citizens claimed that the case received quicker and more detailed attention than it would have if the defendants had not been Portuguese (Rangel, 1984a). They further asserted that mainstream news coverage was especially lurid and sexually charged, and that biased phrasing was used to describe the testimony of the defendants and the victim-witness, suggesting the guilt of the defendants (Charles Kuralt, *CBS News*, April 1, 1984). In addition, court documents filed at the Bristol County Courthouse for this case reflect a genuine and well-articulated concern on the part of the defense attorneys that news coverage created a significant obstacle to the possibility of a fair trial ("Memorandum in Support," 1984). Defense attorneys noted that news stories had created a hostile environment for the trial, and it was moved to a nearby town. Although this move did acknowledge the legitimacy of claims of media bias, it did not affect the inclusion of such bias in future coverage of the trial and verdicts. Attorneys also claimed that the police had treated the defendants unfairly during their arrest and questioning. All of these claims were related to the ethnic identity of the defendants and the feeling of Portuguese Americans that they had been consistently treated as second-class citizens in their own town and, after the case became public, in the nationally circulated news.

Certainly, both ethnic and gender issues were central to the Big Dan's case. Because it took place in the context of a 10-year struggle by rape law reformers for fairer treatment of victims (in both the justice system and in the news), this case was significant as a ground on which reformed and traditional ideas about rape could be adjudicated publicly. Rape law reformers had been working for a decade to improve the media and court treatment of victims during rape trials. The traditional trial, often labeled a "second rape," featured the victim as lead witness under attack by defense attorneys. This "second rape," detailing all the faults of the victim as well as the specifics of the crime, was sometimes replayed in news accounts of the trial (Benedict, 1992), which focused on dramatic, personal, and emotional elements to provide exciting news (Cuklanz, 1993). Reformers successfully argued for a limit on the types of evidence (such as sexual history evidence) that could be allowed at trial and argued persuasively that women who are not of spotless moral character might also be victims of rape. Reform and traditional views have also clashed on the question of who a rapist might be, with reformers arguing against the traditional view that strangers and members of racial minorities were more likely to be perpetrators of rape. Reformers have emphasized racist sentencing practices and lingering elements of lynch ideology that mistakenly lead to the conclusion that marginalized men are particularly likely to commit rape.[2]

This chapter investigates the question of how mainstream news coverage handled the complex issues of race and gender involved in the case, and argues that these sources largely ignored complex issues in favor of the more familiar themes of confrontation and morality. In an interview with Helen Benedict after the trial, Manuel Ferreira of the *Portuguese Times* asserted that, contrary to the fact that the United States is the most violent society in the world, mainstream media coverage of the case suggested that the extreme violence of the incident was due to the culture of the defendants and not related to the larger culture of the United States (Benedict, 1992, p. 101). Mainstream news coverage perpetuated this belief in three ways. First, it presented a biased account of the case, siding implicitly with the victim and focusing somewhat critically on defense strategy. Mainstream news failed to cover issues related to whether "greenhorns"[3] could obtain justice given the cultural and media climate that had been created surrounding the case, continuing to perpetuate the problems over which complaints had already been registered. Second, mainstream news tended to suggest that the rape and community support for the defendants were a direct result of the attitudes of a traditional and perhaps outmoded working-class community not in touch with contemporary U.S. thought on the subject of rape. Third, mainstream sources discursively pitted feminists and Portuguese citizens against each other, failing to articulate the arguments of either side in their criticism of news and trial practices.

News Bias:
Implicit and Overt Support for the Victim

In mainstream coverage of this case, the reformed view of rape was defined in a very limited way, with relation to the issues of consent only. Significantly, mainstream news coverage of this case suggested widespread agreement with the reform idea that women do not enjoy or "ask for" violent rape. Most mainstream news accounts avoided even the suggestion that this might have been the case. Although support for other reform tenets was less forthcoming, public discussion of the case could be said to represent progress on this one issue of victim responsibility. Other aspects of the coverage, however, were more positive: Women's groups organized a protest in New Bedford to call attention to the history and prevalence of violence against women and were treated with some respect by news sources covering the protest. Since Tuchman's (1978) observations about the hostile coverage of the women's movement, some progress has been made. News accounts were generally supportive of the victim. This may have been due in part to the fact that significant corroborating testimony was available in this case, including a reluctant eyewitness to the rape and a "handprint" of bruises on the victim's thigh. It may also have been due in part to her identity as a mother of two young children. Unfortunately, support for the victim was achieved in mainstream news in part by vilifying the defendants and their community.

There were indications during the Big Dan's trial that the victim had lied, cheated on welfare, and brought a previous complaint of rape, yet these facts seldom made the headlines. The victim in this case was almost exclusively referred to as a "21-year-old mother of two" in national-level media stories. More than 15 *New York Times* articles used this phrasing. An article in *People* reported that she had refused sleeping medication since the incident because she might not be able to hear her children if they needed her (Vespa, 1984, p. 81). In subtle and more direct ways, mainstream news coverage supported the position of the victim. Lurid and detailed descriptions of the alleged crime created emotional sympathy for her, and other elements of coverage tipped the balance against the defendants. Coverage of the victim's character, though present in virtually all stories of the trial, frequently took the form of a summary of trial evidence rather than direct quotation, thereby lending it less credibility, as in the following example:

> The woman . . . denied under cross-examination by Mr. Vieira's attorney, David H. Waxler, that she had told another woman in Big Dan's that she was seeing a psychiatrist and having problems with her live-in boyfriend, Michael Lagasse, the father of her children. ("Reports to Police Questioned," 1984, p. A18)[4]

A second *New York Times* story was typical in its emphasis on the prosecution tactics including stares, shouting, and gestures. The story noted that the prosecution was trying to damage the woman's credibility by depicting her as a liar and committer of welfare fraud, among other things. Although some evidence of this type was included in many stories, damaging evidence concerning the victim's character was usually limited to one or two sentences in stories that did not focus on her cross-examination testimony, and some broadcast stories emphasized the defense strategy and the fact that there were two trials and six defense attorneys. These carried trial footage demonstrating defense tactics, and in one story Tom Brokaw (*NBC Nightly News*, May 17, 1984) noted that it did seem as if the victim were on trial rather than the defendants. Damaging testimony was summarized rather than directly quoted, and defense strategy was highlighted as much as the results of that strategy. When the victim was mentioned in passing, it was usually in a favorable light: "The nearby city of New Bedford, the old whaling port, was stunned and embittered last March when six men were charged with raping the mother of two children on a pool table in Big Dan's bar" (Rangel, 1984b,

p. A6).[5] One report seemed to take her side, noting that the fact that she had to testify at two trials created an unusually difficult task for her (Starr, 1984).

Overt support for this aspect of the victim's perspective was so strong that some media accounts of the trial actually denounced the defense for attempting a consent strategy (the argument that the woman had consented to whatever sexual activity had occurred) in this case. After quoting defense attorney Judith Lindahl's statement that humiliation during cross-examination can only happen to witnesses who lie during a rape trial, *New York Times* commentator Sydney Schanberg (1984) asserted that Lindahl was wrong in both this assertion and in her suggestion that the victim could have been at fault.

Many other observers expressed opinions favorable to rape law reform and to the verdict in this case. Cautioning that it may have been imprudent for the victim to go to Big Dan's by herself at night, *The National Review* concluded that the victim was fully within her legal rights to do so ("Big Dan's Tavern," 1984, p. 20). This in turn could be connected to the valiant efforts of victims who did press charges in spite of the treatment they could expect in court. Indeed, a consciousness of some of the goals of rape law reform pervaded discussions of the New Bedford case, helping to solidify a clear-cut, right-and-wrong attitude toward the case and toward this one aspect of rape law reform.

Feminists were occasionally quoted in explanation of the rape shield law (used to eliminate sexual history evidence from this case). In one *CBS Morning News* story, a Pennsylvania judge was interviewed on this subject. Diane Sawyer (*CBS Morning News*, March 22, 1984) asked specifically how it could be fair that the defense was disallowed from introducing evidence that could have benefited the defendants. Judge Richette responded that the evidence that the woman had had two children out of wedlock and that she had cheated on welfare was disallowed because it had no direct relevance to the question of whether or not she had been assaulted. In another report, the victim's attorney explained the difficulty with sexual history testimony as evidence of "character," noting that the questions put to the victim served to highlight the problems with traditional rape trials that always delved into a victim's past (Rangel, 1984a). District Attorney Kane asserted on *CBS Morning News* that the trial might function as a deterrent for other victims who might fear the type of treatment witnessed in the televised trial (Kurtis, *CBS Morning News*, March 23, 1984).

News Bias:
Unnecessary and Lurid Details

This acceptance of the victim's perspective on the issue of consent and gang rape was accomplished at the expense of other important elements of the reformed perspective on rape. A second prevalent myth, that rapists are members of marginal ethnic groups, was implicitly reinforced in news coverage of the Big Dan's case. The victim, though also of Portuguese descent, was treated in most news accounts as a representative of women rape victims, not as a female member of the Portuguese American community. Much news coverage framed acceptance of the victim's perspective as warranted by the excessive brutality of the case. In turn, this brutality was linked to both the "stranger" element of the case and to a racist equation of gang rape with the Portuguese community in which the rape had taken place. Perhaps most significant, news stories seldom discussed gang rape as a common or deplorable social problem: Rather, only *this* gang rape was discussed, and it was frequently linked to "Portuguese" attitudes about gender and rape. By focusing on the Portuguese community, news coverage managed to avoid discussion of the incidence or cause of gang rape in terms of gender within the larger culture.

One of the primary claims of bias made by some representatives of the Luso American community in New Bedford was that news coverage included unusually detailed descriptions of the crime, often focusing on violent and/or sexual elements. Throughout trial coverage, mainstream sources did include arguably unnecessary details, further implying that there were clearly right and wrong positions on this case. Descriptions of the crime often exaggerated sensational elements and offered moralistic commentary, and many stories quoted the police report's estimate that there were up to 15 men cheering and encouraging the rapists. One story reported that the woman was raped so many times she lost count (Hurschfeld, 1983). Pretrial reports such as this one exaggerated details to add to the dramatic effect of the story. As the trial progressed, reports reduced the total number of cheering men to fewer than 10. However, even later coverage dramatized the crime in its descriptions. A *Newsweek* summary reported that the men in the bar cheered as if they were at a baseball game and that one of the men threw the woman on the floor (Starr, 1984). A month later, an Associated Press story characterized the rape as an explosion of violence ("Reports to Police," 1984). Coverage of the crime became even more dramatic during the trial when the victim's testimony was quoted: "a 22-year-old woman told a jury today that she had been pinned down and raped on a pool table in Big Dan's Tavern while several people ignored her screams. 'I was screaming—I was begging for help,' the woman said . . . 'I could hear people laughing and cheering, yelling,' she said" ("Court in New Bedford Rape, Hears Woman's Testimony," 1984).[6] In connection with overt links between the Luso American community and a laissez-faire attitude about rape, these biased descriptions of the defendants implied their guilt.

Blaming the Portuguese

In addition to descriptions of the crime emphasizing excessive brutality on the part of the defendants, mainstream news linked a "blaming the victim" attitude rejected by newswriters themselves, with the Portuguese community in general. This association of traditional ideas about gender and rape within the Portuguese community was most frequently accomplished through an oversimplified or even misrepresented reporting of Portuguese protests about the way the case was handled. The initial furor was over the airing and publishing of extremely negative and racist comments about Luso Americans in New Bedford. In a compiled list of quotations from the local and national press, the district attorney included a range of harmful and violent opinions about Luso Americans. According to a motion filed by the defense, the *Fall River Herald* printed the suggestion that New Bedford would benefit if its Portuguese citizens were sent back to Portugal ("Memorandum in Support," p. 6). *CBS News* re-aired a call-in statement from a local station asserting that Portuguese immigrants did not even try to understand the United States and that they contributed nothing (C. Kuralt, *CBS News*, April 1, 1984). Perhaps more to the point, another caller observed that Portuguese immigrants did not understand U.S. laws and norms because they did not try to take part in the larger community. By airing call-in comments from prejudiced and hostile callers, mainstream news raised questions about the legitimacy of Luso American claims to justice and equal treatment while at the same time bolstering the connection between the six defendants and the larger community of which they were a part.

Substantial arguments were made by the defense attorneys to the effect that their clients were treated unfairly by the police at several stages of the investigation: The ethnic and noncitizen identities of the defendants contributed to a climate in which, defense attorneys asserted, they could not obtain a fair trial. One defense attorney questioned the procedures used to detain and question the defendants in light of his defendant's trusting nature and beliefs about authority:

> Joseph Vieira had no English background, left school in the Azores at age eleven, did not understand even the basic premises of trial and arrest within the criminal justice system, and had an abiding trust and belief in the police department's duty to act in a manner consistent with his best interests. He had a similar belief that police actions were not subject to his objection. ("Reply Memorandum," p. 2)

In summarizing the complaint of unreasonable seizure, the argument was that "perhaps most significantly, the arrest was accomplished in open court with the eyes of the court looking on, a silent approval of the procedure in the eyes of person like Vieira" ("Reply Memorandum," p. 4). In conclusion, the defense argued that the police were "lying in wait" for Vieira, wanting "another shot at obtaining incriminating statements" (p. 7). This defense argument referred to Vieira's disadvantage in the legal process, both because of his class and his ethnicity. Because he was poor and had no attorney or advisor present, he was vulnerable to perceived pressures or expectations of the police at the time of his arrest. Because Vieira had no knowledge of the system in which he was operating and did not speak fluent English, defense attorneys argued that he could not adequately defend himself, and no attorney had been present on his behalf. Significant questions of how adequate justice can be achieved for such a person (an uneducated, non-English-speaking immigrant) were raised in this case, but were not discussed in any detail in news coverage. In the absence of direct discussion of the problems of rendering justice to greenhorns, the comments about their lack of understanding of community knowledge implied that there was little surprise that those who didn't know the "law of the land" had found themselves in trouble.

This biased coverage of the case helped eliminate discussion of rape and law reform from news coverage, as implicit blame for the rape was placed on "uniquely" Luso American attitudes toward women and rape. While such coverage subtly diverted blame from the larger patriarchal culture, it also reinforced the racist myth that only members of marginalized groups are rapists. Victim-hating quotations were attributed to Luso Americans as if the community was responsible for the attitudes that made the rape possible, as in a *Newsweek* report that quoted an elderly woman shouting that the woman/ victim should have been home rather than out in a bar ruining men's lives (Beck & Zabarsky, 1984).[7]

Through the direct or subtle connection between the Luso American community and attitudes toward rape implicitly no longer held by mainstream culture, news created an opportunity for moralistic commentary on the progress of rape law reform, the absence of racism in this case, and the undeniable fairness of the judicial system:

> The demonstrators are wrong. What attracted attention were the circumstances of the rape, not its perpetrators. Nor did the victim embarrass her community. As Judge William Young observed, to have reduced the penalties because she visited a bar would "virtually outlaw an entire gender for the style of their dress, the length of their skirts or their choice to enter a place of public refreshment." Nor does the rape shame the victim. The idea that sexual assault dishonors the victim is a cruel, archaic reading of the crime. The jury had no difficulty distinguishing between the trials of the victim and her assailants. May the crowd learn to do the same. ("The Shame in New Bedford and Dallas," 1984, p. A26)[8]

The Luso American community was linked with the rape through quotes and direct commentary by journalists. The rape was implicitly explained as the outcome of a certain community-related attitude, whereas discussions of gang rapes, rape law reform, and rape trials were virtually absent. Rather than being caused by a set of social or political relations identified and coherently described by feminists (gang rape as the natural result of a culture that dehumanizes and objectifies women while encouraging men to be tough and uncaring and to think of women as under their control) or by Portuguese community leaders (this gang rape as a crime that attracted so much lurid attention because it was committed by Portuguese and Luso American men), the crime was explained as part of an attitude held by a particular U.S. subculture. No self-conscious discussion of ethnic or class bias in the news, or in law or justice, was included. Analysis of systems of law, racial oppression, or gender were virtually absent from news coverage, which instead focused on testimony and on comments of protesters during rallies for Portuguese American people or for rape victims. News coverage reinforced the traditional myth of the minority stranger rapist while pointing out "progress" in one area. Although this progress of public support for the victim is significant, the fact that it was partly achieved through a reinforcement of racist and classist ideology cannot be overlooked.

Mainstream news stories deflected attention away from other substantive issues in the case and back toward a comparison between progressive and allegedly Portuguese American attitudes toward rape. After the verdicts were announced, one report noted that shrieking and sobbing filled the courtroom at news of the convictions and that the courtroom was filled with the sounds of disappointment and sadness of the defendants' supporters. The brief article concluded with a quote of Prosecutor Raymond Veary's plea that the jury leave the victim's humanity intact, at the very least (Goldman, Fuller, & Burgower, 1984, p. 39). This article openly discussed "the myth," the idea that women desire and ask for violent rape. The article was subtitled "Rejecting the Myth," and it argued against the traditional belief. News reports supplied a ready-made morality for the case, with the correct view siding with the victim in general against the wrong-headed notion that women "ask for" violent rape. This latter position was in turn equated with the "traditional" Portuguese community.

Conflict Between Feminists
and the "Portuguese Community"

Additional drama was garnered for news reports of this case through emphasis on the protests of both Portuguese supporters of the defendants and feminist supporters of the victim. Benedict's analysis suggests that local coverage helped to solidify public sentiment against the victim by playing up the "she deserved it" mentality of community members and by seeming to pit the victim against her own community (Benedict, 1992, chap. 4). Although *both* groups criticized media coverage, these criticisms were often diverted into a drama of conflict between two opposing sides: The story that emerged was one of feminists against local Portuguese citizens. Numerous stories covered the protests at length, and some of these made little mention of the trial or the specifics of the case.

Typical of this transformation or diversion of complaints of bias was a CBS version that asserted that the case pitted the Portuguese community against supporters of women's lib (*CBS Evening News*, February 24, 1984). In their actual statements, neither the representative of the *Portuguese Times* nor the woman from the New Bedford Woman's Center asserted that the other group was in any way at fault. In fact, both were implicitly criticizing media coverage. The preview, however, framed their comments as being "pitted against" each other. In general, although both feminists and Portuguese American groups protested and were sometimes supporting opposing positions on the case, the point most frequently emphasized by representatives of the Portuguese American community was that media coverage was biased. Asked to give an example, Mrs. Castro of the *Portuguese Times* noted that there had been clapping in the courtroom when the prosecution finished its closing arguments and that testimony was labeled differently in news accounts depending on who was testifying. While most testimony was simply called "testimony," the defendants were said to "give their tales," thus suggesting that they were lying (*CBS Morning News*, March 19, 1984). Unwilling to focus on the allegations against the press or the point being made, Diane Sawyer noted that the prosecutor was also of Portuguese descent and switched back to the question of how these problems could affect the way in which justice was served during the trial. In general, media discussions of the case demonstrated an inability to be self-critical, deflecting direct criticism of media coverage into a criticism of any "public outcry" and feminist critique.

The following *New York Times* story illustrates the approach of depicting the arguments of feminist and Portuguese protesters as antagonistic to each other:

> "I'm annoyed at what's happened to the defendants and to the Portuguese community," Mr. Pina [District Attorney on the case] said, standing in the Victoria graystone courthouse . . . "It's been vicious."
>
> "People call it a Portuguese rape trial," he added. "When was the last time you heard of an Irish rapist? It's just a rape case."
>
> His feelings were echoed by Alda Melo, one of the organizers of the Committee for Justice, a group that helped raise bail for the defendants.
>
> Although women's groups were particularly outraged, Miss Melo says they were too emotional. "I believe in women's liberation," she said, "but what I'm doing is defending the right of an immigrant to live in this country without being judged guilty." (Butterfield, 1984)[9]

Similarly, a second *New York Times* story framed the issue as one of the Committee for Justice versus feminist groups whose tactics had influenced the public reaction to the case. The quotes used, however, noted only that the case had attracted attention largely because of the Portuguese identities of the accused and that the coalition was upset about rape in general, but that the media had picked up on this particular case and feminists had followed their lead. No direct criticism of feminist groups was quoted on the part of the Portuguese representatives, and no anti-Portuguese sentiments were quoted from feminist organizers (Rangel, 1984a).

In each example, the assertions of contrast made by the reporter are not directly supported by the quotes of Miss Melo, and in each example the structure and implication of the article suggests antagonism although no evidence is cited to illustrate this antagonism. The writers imply that the criticism was of the feminist protesters and organizers, though the actual quotes indicate that the central criticisms were of the justice system and the media. Again, although some antagonism did exist, none of these reports were able to describe accurately the source or cause of this antagonism other than by the vague implication that some people supported the defendants while others supported the victim. This oversimplified contrast enabled the interpretation that each group's main complaint was against the other. The article structure and reporter framing deflected attention away from the substance of the quotes. Finally, by bifurcating the two groups and presenting them as opposed to each other rather than as dual oppositions to systems of justice and media, these articles precluded the possibility of Portuguese feminist voices. Indeed, no such voice emerged in mainstream news coverage of the case. Mainstream sources pitted feminists (concerned for rape victims) against Portuguese Americans from New Bedford (concerned for the rights of equal protection and due process for the defendants). This news frame deflected attention away from criticism of the quality of news coverage by *both* groups and allowed reporters to appear to adjudicate among the "competing" claims for equal treatment. Rakow and Kranich (1991) have observed that mainstream news seldom cites feminists as sources. In this case, when feminists were cited it was often as a counterpoint to the misconstrued claims of Luso Americans. Although there was some antagonism between feminists and Portuguese Americans, the primary complaint of both was about media handling of the case. Outside these mainstream constructions of the "two sides," both feminists and Luso Americans are likely to agree that mainstream news coverage of this case failed to point out that gang rapes are not the product of particular subcultures, but rather are a frequently occurring symptom of the larger culture of violence in the United States.

Conclusion

The failure of mainstream news sources to deal with substantive concerns of both feminists and members of the Portuguese community in this case limited coverage to a few primary themes that were reiterated in story after story. Mainstream media expressed support for an important element of the victim's perspective on the reality of rape: Gang rape was not something that women desired or asked for, and no kind of personal history could change that fact. In supporting the guilty verdicts in this case, news coverage took on a pro-law-reform position, although this position was limited to one sub-issue, the question of whether women provoke rape through reputation, behavior, dress, or other means. Rape reform reasoning was seldom discussed beyond the simple assertion that placing the victim "on trial" was wrong; discussion of the overall problems faced by rape victims was minimal. Mainstream news coverage for the most part also supported the specific victim in this case, in part for her courage in enduring the defense questioning, which followed the normal strategy of attempting to discredit her testimony. This expression of support was given at the expense of other issues of concern to rape law reformers, and the traditional stranger rapist myth was actually reinforced in news coverage of the Big Dan's case. Links between Portuguese Americans and the traditional idea that victims provoke rape were the only explanations for the crime, implicit or explicit: The causes of rape and gang rape were not explored in news coverage beyond these loose connections.

Likewise, through descriptions of feminist and Portuguese concerns as antagonistic to each other, news sources avoided meaningful discussions of how the press might improve coverage of a similar case in the future. In addition, no space was created for the articulation of a dual or multiple identity position on the issues. No Portuguese feminist voice was heard, because the frame of conflict between the two groups precluded this as a logical possibility. Mainstream news sources did not consciously recognize the complexity of intersections between issues of gender, ethnicity, and class. Portuguese Americans were certainly treated as "different" from mainstream America, and this difference was often construed as problematic and directly related to the violent crime that had been committed. Little difference of opinion among Luso Americans was documented. Indeed, by describing feminist and Portuguese claims as mutually exclusive and directly opposed to one another, stories eliminated the rational possibility that such a voice could exist. Nationally circulated U.S. news employed the primary themes of antagonism and morality in this case, in accordance with previous findings on coverage of issues involving ethnicity, race, and gender, with the result that multiple identities and complex beliefs were eliminated from public discourse.

Notes

1. The prominence in mainstream news of the fact that the rape took place within a Portuguese American community was noted with dismay and anger by many within the community. Some of these reactions are discussed and quoted later in this chapter. Although mainstream news did not successfully eliminate habitual references to the Portuguese American community in stories about the case, it did attempt to compensate for this practice with a number of articles about the whaling trade and the tradition of hard work within the community.

2. Rape reformers have consistently argued that convicted black rapists receive much higher sentences than whites. Susan Brownmiller (1975, p. 216) noted black rapists of white victims received average sentences of 15.4 years whereas white rapists of black victims received average sentences of 4.6 years. Sentences were even lower for intraracial rapes.

3. This label for the defendants was used by the victim in her statement to the police, and was picked up by some mainstream news reports. Because the defendants were not U.S. citizens and were not fluent in English, the defense argument that they may have given self-incriminating statements without fully understanding what they were doing was reasonable.

4. "Reports to Police Questioned," *New York Times* (March 22, 1984). Copyright © 1984 by The New York Times Company. Reprinted by permission.

5. J. Rangel, "Rape Trial Keeps Massachusetts Area on an Emotional Edge," *New York Times* (Mar. 4, 1984). Copyright © 1984 by The New York Times Company. Reprinted by permission.

6. "Court in New Bedford Rape, Hears Woman's Testimony," *New York Times* (February 25, 1984). Copyright © 1984 by The New York Times Company. Reprinted by permission.

7. This was yet another way in which the Luso American community was linked with outmoded mainstream attitudes toward rape. More up-to-date mainstream observers defended the victim's right to enter the traditionally male space of the bar, while Luso Americans apparently would deny her this right on the basis of gender alone.

8. "The Shame in New Bedford and Dallas," *New York Times* (March 28, 1984). Copyright © 1984 by The New York Times Company. Reprinted by permission.

9. F. Butterfield, "Trial of Six Starts Today in Pool Table Rape in Massachusetts," *New York Times* (February 6, 1984). Copyright © 1984 by The New York Times Company. Reprinted by permission.

References

Beck, M., & Zabarsky, M. (1984, April 2). Rape trial: Justice crucified? *Newsweek*, p. 39.

Benedict, H. (1992). *Virgin or vamp: How the press covers sex crimes*. New York: Oxford University Press.

Big Dan's tavern. (1984, April 20). *National Review,* p. 20.

Brownmiller, S. (1975). *Against our will: Men, women, and rape.* New York: Simon & Schuster.

Butterfield, F. (1984, February 6). Trial of six starts today in pool table rape in Massachusetts. *New York Times,* p. A6.

Court in New Bedford rape, hears woman's testimony. (1984, February 25). *New York Times,* p. 12A.

Cuklanz, L. (1993). Truth in transition: Discursive constructions of character in the Rideout rape in marriage case. *Women's Studies in Communication, 16*(3), pp. 74-101.

Daniel, J., & Allen, A. (1988). Newsmagazines, public policy, and the black agenda. In T. A. van Dijk & T. Smitherman-Donaldson (Eds.), *Discourse and discrimination* (pp. 23-45). Detroit: Wayne State University Press.

Entman, R. (1990). Modern racism and the images of blacks in local television news. *Critical Studies in Mass Communication, 7,* 332-345.

Entman, R. (1992). Blacks in the news: Television, modern racism, and cultural change. *Journalism Quarterly, 69*(Summer), 341-361.

Foote, J. (1992). Women correspondent visibility on the network evening news. *Mass Communication Review, 19*(1), 36-40.

Goldman, P., Fuller, T., & Burgower, B. (1984, March 26). New Bedford rape: Rejecting the myth. *Newsweek,* p. 39.

Hurschfeld, N. (1983, June 26). The shame of New Bedford. *New York Daily News,* p. A17

Kahn, K. (1991). Women candidates in the news: An examination of gender differences in U.S. Senate campaign coverage. *Public Opinion Quarterly, 55*(Summer), 180-199.

Mazingo, S. (1988). Minorities and social control in the newsroom: Thirty years after Breed. In T. A. van Dijk & T. Smitherman-Donaldson (Eds.), *Discourse and discrimination* (pp. 93-130). Detroit: Wayne State University Press.

Memorandum in Support. In Bristol County Superior Court (No. 12265).

Rakow, L., & Kranich, K. (1991). Woman as sign in television news. *Journal of Communication, 41*(1), 8-23.

Rangel, J. (1984a, March 9). Rape trial is monitored by a women's coalition. *New York Times,* p. A10.

Rangel, J. (1984b, March 4). Rape trial keeps Massachusetts area on an emotional edge. *New York Times,* p. A6.

Reply Memorandum of Joseph Vieira. In Bristol County Superior Court (No. 12265).

Reports to police questioned. (1984, March 22). *New York Times,* p. 3.

Robinson, G. J. (1978). Women, media access, and social control. In L. Epstein (Ed.), *Women and the news* (pp. 87-108). New York: Hastings House.

Schanberg, S. H. (1984, March 27). The rape trial. *New York Times,* p. A31.

The shame in New Bedford and Dallas: It's not the victim who should be tried. (1984, March 28). *New York Times,* p. A26.

Starr, M. (1984, March 12). Gang rape: The legal attack. *Newsweek,* p. 38.

Stone, V. (1988). Trends in the status of minorities and women in broadcast news. *Journalism Quarterly, 65*(Summer), 288-293.

Thomas, E. K. (1984). The other America: Race-related news coverage. *Journal of Ethnic Studies, 11*(Winter), 124-126.

Tuchman, G. (1978). *Making news: A study in the construction of reality.* New York: Free Press.

van Dijk, T. (1991). *Racism and the press.* Hillsdale, NJ: Lawrence Erlbaum.

Vespa, M. (1984). No town without pity, a divided New Bedford seeks justice in a brutal case of gang rape. *People Weekly*, p. 77-81.

Ziegler, D., & White, A. (1990). Women and minorities on network television news: An examination of correspondents and newsmakers. *Journal of Broadcasting and Electronic Media, 34*, 215-223.

8   Missing Persons

*Working-Class Women
and the Movies, 1940–1990*

JASMINE PAUL
BETTE J. KAUFFMAN

The 1991 release of *Thelma & Louise* generated much controversy among film critics and other observers of popular culture. Most of the debate was over the gender politics of the film: Was it a feminist film? An anti-feminist film? A male-bashing film? Little attention was paid to the fact that Thelma and Louise were members of a tiny sorority: working-class women in the movies, particularly working-class women in heroic roles.

This chapter chronicles the visibility—more precisely, the invisibility—of working-class women's experience in Hollywood cinema. Beginning with the 1940s and 1950s, we identify economic, political, and social forces that shaped movies and thus structured not only representations of but the presence and absence of working-class women.

Using Barbara Ehrenreich's (1989) definition, we distinguish throughout between working women characters and working-class women characters:

Not only industrial workers in hard-hats, but all those people who are not professionals; who work for wages rather than salaries; and who spend their working hours variously lifting, bending, driving, monitoring, keyboarding, cleaning, providing physical care for others, loading, unloading, cooking, serving. (p. 22)[1]

As Ehrenreich notes, the working class so defined constitutes a 60%-70% majority of the population of the United States, albeit a silenced and invisible one.

1940s and 1950s:
The Rise and Fall of Rosie the Riveter

During World War II, millions of women took up blue-collar work as cab drivers, dock workers, welders, machinists, and more (French, 1978, p. xvi). By 1943 women were more than 36% of the labor force, with "more than four million . . . employed in munitions work alone" and an additional 15 million "doing such formerly 'masculine' jobs as coal mining, operating machines, and firing and cleaning anti-aircraft guns" (Rosen, 1973, p. 24).

These wartime conditions produced two types of cinematic working woman: women in combat and the "working girls" of "woman's films" who were among Rosie the Riveter's primary entertainments (Rosen, 1979, p. 24). The first type—military women and other front-line professionals—made their appearance in the mainstream of World War II movies. Typically strong characters, they "idealized female bravery and participation" (p. 24), holding their own against war and opposite major male stars. "Lana Turner matched nerves and deadliness with Clark Gable as a war correspondent in *Somewhere I'll Find You* (1942)" (Rosen, 1973, p. 191). Patricia Neal matched courage and crustiness with John Wayne as a combat nurse in *Operation Pacific* (1951).

Woman's Films

"Woman's films" were produced by Hollywood from the late 1930s to the early 1950s with a primarily female audience in mind. They achieved prominence during a time when women workers had become the backbone of U.S. wartime production. The working women featured were typically "spunky professional heroines"; common themes pitted women's relational and private lives against their work and public lives: *Lady in the Dark* (1944) urged women to relinquish a career for love, *Little Women* (1933, 1949) urged the opposite (Walsh, 1984, pp. 25-26).

Rosie the Riveter herself appeared in a handful of films. These, however, were more "tributes to patriotism" (Rosen, 1973, p. 190) than stories of women's struggles and accomplishments in factory and shipyard. Indeed their work was backdrop rather than focus of the drama, with "actual scenes inside munitions factories or on assembly lines . . . kept to a minimum" (p. 191). Nevertheless, the films were certainly relevant to the experiences of millions of women, and spirited heroines cheerfully answering the call to duty became inspirational models for women learning to manage life without men (Rosen, 1973).

Not surprisingly, many of these silver-screen Rosies were clearly not working-class women at all but middle- to upper-class women taking blue-collar jobs "for the duration." Lucille Ball is a movie star who "puts aside her minks to serve in a defense plant" in *Meet the People* (1944) (Rosen, 1973, p. 191). Ann Sothern in *Swing Shift Maisie* (1943) is really a showgirl, her stint as an aircraft worker in this film just one of a series of Maisie's "adventures." In *Since You Went Away* (1944), Claudette Colbert first must "sacrifice" her comfortable "fireside and chintz" existence to the war by taking in a boarder; eventually she becomes a welder (Rosen, 1973, p. 191).

Although middle- to upper middle-class women did indeed take blue-collar jobs during the war, documentaries like *The Life and Times of Rosie the Riveter* (1980) clarify that many were working-class women (of all racial identities); many were single parents; and many worked before, during, and after the war out of economic necessity. The major difference the war made to them was that they earned good wages for a short period of time. But their often dramatic stories of struggle over child care and household arrangements, of pride in acquiring valuable skills, of prejudice and solidarity in the workplace, did not make it to the wide screen.

The tendency of Rosie-the-Riveter films to focus on middle- to upper-class wartime hardships was in fact consistent with the class and gender perspectives of woman's films in general. The 1940s female stars such as Claudette Colbert, Joan Crawford, Bette Davis, Katherine Hepburn, and Myrna Loy were themselves mature, successful working women whose autonomy on the set had been won in serious battle with Hollywood heavies. These star personas and the career women they portrayed helped to further an ideology central to the woman's film: "middle-classness, not just as an economic status, but as a state of mind and a relatively valid moral code" (Haskell, 1987, p. 159). Not only were the careers portrayed middle to upper middle class—reporters, lawyers, actresses, homemakers—but the ambiance of the films was middle class: "neat, ordered and quite comfortable" (Walsh, 1984, p. 28). Many, like *His Girl Friday* (1940), were light in tone, veering dramatically away from factory reality. Thus, with the exception of a handful of talented black women like Hattie McDaniel, Louise Beavers, and Butterfly McQueen, who played maids, servants, and mammies, working-class women remained largely invisible on screen.

Nevertheless, the majority of woman's films are constructed around precisely those concerns and issues that women of our culture are socialized to structure their lives around, namely "dilemmas of moral choice focusing on themes of interpersonal connection and the fear of separation from loved ones" (Walsh, 1984, p. 42). Popular films of the 1940s thus not only spoke to the needs and desires of many women, but in some way bonded working women together, not only through portrayals but in contributing to the construction of female spectatorship. This distinctive albeit limited feminine presence both on and in front of the screen was to suffer a severe setback, however, for when World War II ended, an army of men returned to the United States and the film industry rushed to meet them with open arms.

Domesticating Rosie

If World War II brought women new recognition as workers and cinematic subjects and audiences, the postwar era saw a regression to an earlier status quo. Polls taken of women early in their wartime working career indicated that 95% expected to leave their positions in peacetime. By 1944, however, more than 75% had changed their minds and wished to continue their employment after the war ended (Walsh, 1984, p. 74).

The years 1945 to 1950 saw profound struggle over gender definitions and relationships. Thousands of men, already psychologically exhausted by war, returned "to discover that 'home' had not survived their absence; that their marriage no longer existed, in emotion or in reality" (Bell-Metereau, 1985, p. 50). Women who were no longer dependent appeared to have lost their femininity. Industry hummed along quite nicely without the returning men. The United States had the highest industrial production of any nation in 1945, but it also had "the highest divorce rate in the world" (Bell-Metereau, 1985, p. 50).

In the face of such disruption and loss, pressure on women to restore and reaffirm traditional roles was extraordinary. Political, religious, and industrial leaders who had so recently recruited women workers with appeals to their devotion to family and country, now shamelessly reversed themselves. Said Frederick C. Crawford, Chairman of the Board of the National Association of Manufacturers: "From a humanitarian point of view, too many women should not stay in the labor force. The home is the basic American unit" (Rosen, 1973, p. 202). More than two million now technically skilled women were forced from lucrative positions (French, 1978). Women who did stay in the workforce suffered a sharp deterioration in economic and legal status. Their wages declined to two thirds of what men earned, and old discriminatory laws based on notions of women's physical frailty were resuscitated (Rosen, 1973).

Films of the late 1940s and early 1950s portraying "the readjustment of the returning soldier" gave scant consideration to the "parallel problems" of Rosie and her sisters (Rosen, 1973, p. 205). The new working women launched by the 1940s were out in the cold, if not back at the comfortable, middle-class hearth. The working-class woman with her newly low-paying, pink-collar job struggled as invisibly as before. As for African American women, as late as 1959 U.S. Americans were "still rewarding the mammy image," which fit well with the decade's renewed emphasis on the sanctity of the female-centered domestic sphere (Nesteby, 1982, p. 200).

One of Hollywood's contributions to the postwar tendency to "hold women responsible for society's ills" was film noir, a genre that portrayed women in positions of power as "ambitious, craven monsters, emotionless killers who seduce men into their evil services" (French, 1978, p. xviii)[2] while glorifying women in traditional roles as nurturing madonnas whereby men could transcend cynicism and despair. The only truly working-class woman in film noir was the "B girl" who entertained men in bars for the price of a drink. As a sexually compromised and low-status woman, she was an ideal sacrifice to the mise-en-scène. Thus in films like *The Big Heat* (1953), her death by violence early in the film lends pathos and sexual intrigue to the narrative disruption without "stealing the show," so to speak.[3]

The Kinsey report on women, released in August 1953 to "the most massive press reception ever accorded a scientific treatise" (Dyer, 1986, p. 27), contributed also to the sexual upheaval of the 1950s. According to Kinsey, of the 8,000 women interviewed, "28% acknowledged having had erotic responses to other women, 13% had experienced orgasm with another woman, and 19% had experienced some sexual contact with another woman by the age of 40" (Blumefield, 1988, p. 79). Women, it must have seemed, were rejecting men even sexually, and the culture responded with portrayals of women as solely (hetero)sexual beings. In other words, good-bye Rosie, hello Marilyn.

The "glamour girl" was a mass-produced ideal of sexualized femininity for both women and men. At the same time, the Hollywood Production Code forbade overt sex, so filmmakers were limited to lots of tantalizing visuals: breasts straining against halter bodices, billowing skirts, and the like. Woman's sexuality was made further "safe" by often being situated in comedy; her sexual innocence contrasted humorously with her sexual power appealed to male viewers and supported as well the anti-Rosie social and political climate (Dyer, 1986). Barbara Stanwyck, star of the 1952 film *Clash by Night*, recalled that the "gentlemen of the press" were not interested in her; rather, they sought out Marilyn Monroe: "We want to talk to the girl with the big tits" (p. 23).

Where did the films of the 1950s leave working-class women? Despite a few good-hearted attempts like *Marty* (1955) and *On the Waterfront* (1954) "to bring the working class and its world back into focus," Hollywood remained centered around middle- and upper middle-class concerns and perspectives (Quart & Auster, 1991, p. 63). The narrative disruptions presented by popular films of the decade, like *Come Back Little Sheba* (1953), *The Man With the Golden Arm* (1956), and *Rebel Without a Cause* (1956), included "alcoholism, labor union corruption, drug addiction, and juvenile delinquency," all constructed as "basically family problems [that could] be solved only by a return to traditional family values and structure" (Byars, 1991, p. 114).

The venomous anticommunism spawned by Joseph McCarthy and the House Un-American Activities Committee (HUAC) also impeded working-class representation, for the merest hint of working-class solidarity, indeed any challenge to the dominant definition of the United States as a classless society, was typically equated with communism and viewed as undermining belief in the self-sufficient nuclear family unit. HUAC and its powerful blacklist drove many actors, writers, and directors underground or out of the country (Quart & Auster, 1991). Social problem films declined markedly and in their place Hollywood "assembled . . . a fictional world in which all tensions" arose out of family and community (Stead, 1989, p. 170).

In sum, when Rosie the Riveter appeared in government propaganda, she became the target audience for and occasional subject of woman's films that portrayed working women's lives and dilemmas within a middle-class ambiance. When Rosie was no longer considered an asset to government or business, the image of the working woman warped, with the aid of film noir, into that of an aggressively independent, castrating dominatrix pitted against not only men but the madonna of home and hearth. And hand in hand with women leaving the workforce (or forced into low-status, low-pay jobs such as clerk, waitress, and cook), Hollywood foregrounded woman's sexual roles. She was the perky, wholesome marriage-prospect-next-door, epitomized by Debbie Reynolds and Doris Day, or the sexily innocent object of desire, epitomized by Marilyn Monroe. Ultimately, traditional roles in patriarchal family structures defined normalcy for women in the 1950s.

1960s and 1970s: The Film Front

In a decade animated by civil rights and antiwar activism, women's lives and concerns were generally not considered social problems. From the dominant sociological perspective, "men were considered to exist in two spheres—the public or social, and the private or domestic—[but] women were conceived of only in terms of the domestic" and their problems remained nameless (Byars, 1991, p. 116).

Working-class female characters were as voiceless in 1960s Hollywood as they were in their working lives. Social problems were expressed cinematically either through male characters or "as those of male characters" (Byars, 1991, p. 116). In fact, late 1960s and early 1970s Hollywood produced a plethora of male working-class spokespersons in a "rediscovery of the working class world" that film theorists have often connected to "a crisis of masculinity in the professional middle class" (Traube, 1992, p. 106). Unfortunately, *class* was not defined in terms of work or economics "but as a lifestyle: tailfin cars and juke boxes, half-sentences and four-letter words" (Garafola, 1980, p. 14).[4] Class conflict was thus muted; films like *Meanstreets* (1973), *Taxi Driver* (1976), *Rocky* (1976), *Blue Collar* (1978), *F.I.S.T.* (1978), *Saturday Night Fever* (1978), and *The Deer Hunter* (1978) linked class with a nostalgic, romanticized ethnicity instead of social inequity (Garafola, 1980), and constructed the intersection of class, gender, and ethnicity in the ultra-masculine ethnic hero as "a locus of defiant masculinity" (Traube, 1992, p. 106) by which middle-class white men might transcend their own constrained existence (Garafola, 1980).

With the exception of *Norma Rae,* in which Sally Field plays a union organizer, most women in these male-dominated working-class films serve primarily as outlets for abuse. Stereotypes of women abound, as they fit hand in glove with stereotypes of the abusive working-class male. In *Rocky,* Talia Shire works in a pet shop, but she labors continually under the gaze of her brother and later Stallone. In *Saturday Night Fever,* "Annette is gang-banged by Tony's Bay Bridge pals. . . . Connie, in *The Godfather,* is beaten black and blue by her husband, and Francine . . . is pummeled by Robert DeNiro in Scorcese's *New York, New York*" (Garafola, 1980, p. 10). The working-class woman is not only dependent financially upon the males in her community, but "is transformed into a symbol of the ghetto itself" (p. 10).

Desperately Seeking Rosie

At the same time, between 1969 and 1975, 17 autonomous women's unions were formed, primarily on the West Coast and in the Midwest and Northeast (Hansen, 1990). The unions formulated goals later embraced by feminist organizations: reproductive rights, "twenty-four-hour free quality day care" in the workplace, and equal pay for equal work (Hansen, 1990, p. 216). These goals were actually goals of the relatively privileged daughters of the middle class, however, for the unionizers "were generally not members of the con-stituency they hoped to organize—Third World women, working class women, and so on" (Hansen, 1990, p. 220). Rather, their memberships were composed primarily of white, middle-class women between college and pro-fessional careers who had been politicized by campus civil rights and antiwar movements (Hansen, 1990). In short, the women's unions suffered from the same limitation that has hobbled the contemporary women's movement, namely an inability to locate the "true" working class. Guilt-laden discussions at union meetings struggled with the problem of definition: "Were working class women those whose fathers had working class jobs while the women were growing up? Or, were they women who currently worked in pink- or blue-collar jobs regardless of their family background?" (p. 220).

Concurrent with the unionizing by labor organizations outside academia, feminist scholars and filmmakers within it were addressing women and cinema from many angles. The "first generation of feminist documentaries" appeared in 1971, followed by women's film festivals (New York in 1972, Washington in 1973, Chicago in 1974), women's film journals (*Women and*

Film, 1972; *Jump Cut,* 1974), and books about women on all sides of the camera (Doane, Mellencamp, & Williams, 1984, pp. 3-4). Had this growing feminist inquiry into woman's image in film and potential filmmaking voice within the academy come together with the unionization of women in industrial areas, a major influx of women into film and other media industries might have, and should have, occurred. But when scholarship and production did mesh, it remained within independent filmmaking for theoretically trained audiences—outside of Hollywood and still removed from working-class women. Not coincidentally, both feminist academic and feminist union movements were led by white, middle-class women.

The immediate consequence of this well-intended liberal feminism was "second-guessing the primary issues for working class women" while the constituency itself "remained elusive" (Hansen, 1990, p. 221). Looking for the "other" and working on behalf of the "other" is ineffectual when the more powerful group has little clue as to who the "others" are, what their concerns are, and what strategies they would deem appropriate for achieving their goals. Worse, when those more powerful groups assume the role of spokesperson anyway, the spoken-for constituency not only remains unknown but becomes alienated from those who would be its allies.

(Re)Containing Rosie

In a context of greater freedom afforded by a newly revamped production code[5] and increasing scrutiny from a growing women's movement, Hollywood in the early 1970s offered a bleak picture of women's lives and roles. Early successful films of the decade, including *A Clockwork Orange* (1971) and *Straw Dogs* (1972), were highly reactionary. In them, "women were more likely to be raped . . . than adored, as in previous films" (McCreadie, 1990, p. 146). Portrayals of women who worked were rare, and when they occurred the situation was emotionally, financially, or psychologically costly to the woman character. Many films involved the familiar "no win" theme: Women can have or be preoccupied with love or with career, but not both. In *Carnal Knowledge* (1971), Candice Bergen portrays a character who sets aside her ambition to become a lawyer in order "to be liked by Art Garfunkel and Jack Nicholson" (McCreadie, 1990, p. 146). In both *The Turning Point* (1977) and *An Unmarried Woman* (1978), women characters desire careers but are narrowly drawn, emotionless, often isolated. The message emanating from Hollywood by the late 1970s was thus mixed: Careers are for women, even a necessity for middle-class women (McCreadie, 1990), but the price is high.

Working-class characters, on the other hand, offered Hollywood a way to show working women without seriously threatening class and gender hierarchies. Thus in *Five Easy Pieces* (1970), Karen Black plays Rayette, a waitress. Waitressing is safe, for it is a job most men do not want and it does not suggest upward mobility. Likewise, Jodie Foster in *Taxi Driver* (1976) plays a prostitute, the veritable bottom rung of the "employment" ladder. Her youth is a tantalizing enhancement of her economic status, for she is too young in appearance and her cynicism is too cute to threaten an audience, as the bitterness or hardness of an older prostitute might have.

The success of a film like *Klute* (1971), in which Jane Fonda played a prostitute, can be understood in similar terms.[6] Giddis (1973) attributes the palatability of the film to how Fonda's character is constructed: "[Bree] is not self-consciously liberated, or even struggling with self-definition. If anything she is going in the opposite direction: from a brittle but genuine independence to love and dependence on a man" (p. 57). Essentially, Bree is an individual: She is not situated within a larger context of female struggle. Although she can be read as an independent woman, her independence is equated with what is—especially for women in a culture that socializes them to be specialists in relationship—a form of personality disorder: the inability to feel or to love or trust another human being.

This individualization of working-class women is both valuable and limiting. Its value is in challenging the categorical treatment of a social group long assumed to be homogeneous in thought and behavior. But individualization also isolates and separates the person from socioeconomic contexts that shape and constrain thought and behavior, thereby locating responsibility for outcomes solely on The Individual and rendering larger ideological institutions blameless. *Lady Sings the Blues* (1972), with Diana Ross as Billie Holiday, earns just such a mixed review. Clearly, in representing the life of an accomplished African American woman, the movie offered extraordinary opportunities for identification, stereotype revision, or new cultural awareness to its various audiences. Yet it individualized Holiday and her accomplishments in ways that generally declined to implicate the society's racial practices in the problems and tragedies of her life. An individual woman whose "personal problems" result from her very success is certainly less threatening a figure than one whose "success" is circumscribed by gender, race, and class strain.[7]

According to Robin Wood (1986), the two Hollywood films most often "singled out to represent Hollywood feminism" (p. 206) are Paul Mazursky's *An Unmarried Woman* (1978) and Martin Scorsese's *Alice Doesn't Live Here Anymore* (1974). Wood has outlined a half-dozen commonalties in the life situations of the women in the two films, one of which is relevant to examination of the portrayal of working-class women. As Wood (1986) observes, after various trials and tribulations the female protagonists find new jobs. But while still adjusting to their newly acquired independence, each meets "a non-oppressive male whom she can relate to on equal terms and with whom she develops a satisfying, if troubled, relationship" (p. 204). Apparently the working-class woman's long, hard struggle toward independence and job security ends in the arms of a man.[8] Such scenarios placate audiences, assuring them that even though women can be strong and independent, the status quo in gender relations will be maintained.

Norma Rae (1979) portrays a successful textile-worker's strike, but focuses less on labor issues than on the title character's development and self-actualization (Quart & Auster, 1991). Thus, even though this film about a working-class woman did not end with the heroine in the arms of a newly acquired liberal man, Hollywood's devotion to individualized heroes and heroines again persisted.

Glorification of The Individual has consequences, particularly for groups engaged in struggle for social change. Valorizing individual working-class women incorporates them into a cultural story about the past that is dominated by white middle- to upper-class men and their accomplishments, and into a way of doing history that fails to situate persons and actions within social contexts and forces. History marches on; the "exceptional" woman and working-class person so incorporated satisfies popular demand for representation without invoking class and gender struggles that might seriously undermine the veneer of male-female and management-labor relationships.

In sum, films containing class themes arose around both World War II and the Vietnam War, and both postwar periods produced backlashes against working-class and working women characters, with working-class women of all colors except white singled out, on their rare appearances, for particular brutality or infantilization. Thus, sadly, although the seventies appeared primed for broad media recognition of working-class women, Hollywood remained closed to women filmmakers while it successfully promulgated troubling concepts of class, gender, ethnicity, and the relationships among them.

The 1980s, Into the 1990s:
Reagan, Rainbows, and Invisibility

From their brief heyday in the 1970s, depictions of working-class life fell by the wayside as economic and political climates hardened toward the working class in the 1980s and 1990s. Yet the fewer working-class films of these decades offer greater diversity in the social roles afforded working-class people.

In these decades, people worked harder, employers made greater demands, and media validated materialism more than before. Juliet Schor (1992) argues that this was especially true for the working class and the corporate executive. Accelerated economic demands placed the greatest responsibility on those groups at each end of the economic spectrum. The working class, according to Schor, responded to serious competition from the Japanese workforce with a higher investment of energy; the corporate worker, faced with a new and growing economy of takeovers, mergers, and European investment, also responded in kind.

In the 1980s, the manufacturing sector increased by more than one million jobs while "overtime hours rose by 50 per year"; by the early 1990s, "time squeeze" was the focus of national media attention (Schor, 1992, pp. 39, 17). Workers on permanent layoff saw former co-workers climb to a higher standard of living. Many went into debt for materialistic goals, only to find their overtime cut a year later as American companies faltered in the face of foreign takeover and product superiority. The influence of Reaganomics was manifold: Deficit spending for defense hurt the working class most; simultaneously, corporations and upper-class families gained tax loopholes and economic privileges.

In the 1990s, women (exceeding 53 million) constituted 45.4% of U.S. civilian labor (National Committee on Pay Equity [NCPE], 1992, p. 129), but the presence of women in the workforce failed to elicit much sympathetic attention from Hollywood. For this time period, we offer five categories of films that address class issues: (a) understated class themes, (b) class as history/biography, (c) working mother/social victim, (d) class fantasies, and (e) working teen angst films.

Understated Class Themes

Four films depict class struggle, but in an understated way: *Thelma & Louise* (1991), *Silence of the Lambs* (1991), *Poetic Justice* (1993), and *Dirty Dancing*

(1987). These narratives focus on romance and conflicts somehow separated or detracting from economic issues. The problem lies not in the fact that class is not the center of attention; rather, it is that class aspects are muted by various cinematic conventions, and class as a driving force is lost to the narrative.

Thelma & Louise (1991) wreaked havoc with audiences and critics alike. In the hullabaloo over its gender politics, issues concerning the class aspects of the film were ignored. Thelma was stranded in her home without a vehicle because it fed her husband's pride that she didn't have to work and could cater to his needs. Thelma was, in a sense, her husband's luxury item. Louise's car was an important economic asset and key to her, later their, survival.

But all is overshadowed by the loss of innocence, the trading of the power of the victim for the power of defiance, when Louise kills a potential rapist. While herself praising Thelma and Louise for "modeling power, not lingerie," Laura Shapiro notes that the press in general has concluded that the characters "committed too much social and moral damage to qualify as proper heroines" (Shapiro, Murr, & Springen, 1991, p. 63).[9] To say that "*Thelma & Louise* leave their humdrum lives behind and . . . find themselves," not only understates the claustrophobic nature of their working-class existence, but the conditions under which "finding themselves" occurred (Billson, 1991, p. 33). In short, social class is not merely overlooked but often invisible to middle-class commentators and audiences.

In *Silence of the Lambs* (1991), Jodie Foster's FBI-agent-in-training from a working-class background has "made good" due to talent and a strong work ethic. But her efforts to "pass" for the class identity to which she aspires are detectable by the psychopathic killer (Anthony Hopkins):

> You know what you look like to me, with your good bag and your cheap shoes . . . (drawling in a Southern accent) . . . a rube. Good nutrition has given you some length of bone. You're just a generation away from poor white trash. And that accent you tried so desperately to shed, pure West Virginia . . . What was your father? A coal miner?

As she is shamed for having grown up in a working-class environment, we are invited to understand social class, linked with nature more than nurture, least of all with social and economic inequity, as an inescapable stigma.

Poetic Justice (1993) draws viewers into a community of predominantly working-class African Americans. Though class is not openly discussed, it drives most of the narrative. People are shown working to survive and to be something better in order to escape the ghetto environment. The narrative demonstrates how relationships within a certain economic class take on a different meaning due to economic struggle. Much as in *Thelma & Louise*, people hesitate to get emotionally involved due to the financial risk the pooling of resources poses. Both films represent economic independence as hard won and important to mental health.

The film's ending is hard for defenders of working-class culture to swallow, for it mimics middle- and upper middle-class values: the beautiful home, the successful entrepreneur, the controlling patriarch, the quiet and emotional matriarch, the smiling child. Working-class reality and the options of working-class people become invalid and understated, for it is the reality of the upper classes that is glorified.

Dirty Dancing (1987) deserves more credit than has been its due. Strictly speaking, the film does not understate its class theme. Indeed class is one of its main focuses, and there are moments when class analysis shines through. Several of Johnny's monologues concerning his past and his fear of ending up a failed dancer and factory worker are telling. Penny's botched abortion and struggle for money evoke empathy. However, several features serve to undermine the class theme for viewers so disposed. For one, the point of view of the film is Baby's, and she is an upper-class girl with a passion for social work and political do-gooding. We see her concerns above all: her first love, her father worship, her "class struggle." It is only when she stumbles into unpleasant circumstances that we see working-class "truth," as it were. We never see the working-class kids talk among themselves. We never see social distance from *their* point of view.

Another problem with the film is the typecasting of the characters. Johnny is incredibly moral, sweet, and lovable, but his intellectual capacity is questionable and his stunted emotional range encompasses, basically, tenderness and rage. Penny is the stereotypically tough working girl with a heart of gold. In sum, the working-class characters are as good as bread and as clear as spring water. They are clannish, talented, and well aware of their place in the world. The upper-class characters are quite the opposite: ignorant, rude, unaware, and immoral. Perhaps most significantly, the economic ideology of the narrative is classic bourgeois capitalism: With hard work and honesty, success will be yours. A film's class analysis is understated when viewers are left with no questions and none of the gritty taste of struggle and conflict between working and upper classes.

Class as History/Biography

Films centered on the historical/biographical experiences of working-class women can also be animated by the notion that success comes to individuals through hard work, determination, and honesty. They include: *The Dollmaker* (1983), *Silkwood* (1983), *The Accused* (1988), *What's Love Got to Do With It?* (1993), and *The Color Purple* (1991).

The Dollmaker is historical fiction; Gertie (Jane Fonda) experiences what many women of rural background did in the 1940s. She travels from a farm in the South to Detroit, where her husband has gotten a job in an automotive plant and has already gone into debt on factory credit. Gertie struggles to keep the family together and save money to buy a farm of their own in the South. A Detroit grade school teacher discovers her "whittling" and helps her sell it through a gallery, though she rejects his calling her an "artist." A value of the film is that it shows a working-class woman coping with familial and societal pressures and it rewards the hard-working, talented individual, yet it eschews a classic fantasy ending. Rather, the family returns to the South with materially less than they had in the beginning. As a "period piece," however, its relevance to contemporary class struggle is left tenuous.

Silkwood—like *The Accused* and *What's Love Got to Do With It?*—documents the life of a working-class woman encountering harsh circumstances. Karen Silkwood worked in a nuclear plant and discovered physically harmful and unlawful activities. She was found dead in her car while carrying incriminating documents that were never recovered.

Silkwood was exceptional in showing multiple dimensions of working-class life. There was camaraderie among the plant workers; they depended on each other in a familial fashion. Yet conflicts erupted when Silkwood (Meryl Streep) joined the union and brought corporate pressure upon them. Corruption within the union is shown along with Karen's emotional trauma at the loss of her co-workers' support.

These films tend to portray working-class women in oppressive and physically threatening situations as lacking social supports. In *The Accused*, Jodie Foster plays Sarah, a waitress who has been gang-raped and decides to take it to court, generally against the advice and wishes of everyone. In *What's Love*, Tina Turner's physical and mental abuse for years causes her to withdraw into herself; battered women tend to do this as a symptom of their abuse. But all three films valorize the individualism of the women more than they politicize the isolation of women in trouble. Similarly, in the film *The Color Purple*, the main character, Celie, is isolated and alone much like Turner, whereas in Alice Walker's novel she has a significant social network. Hollywood is among those dominant cultural and political institutions that valorize the Horatio Alger type and perceive solidarity among oppressed groups as threats to "democracy" and the moral order. The tribute these historical and biographical films pay to working-class women is important, but it is problematic that the women featured gained notoriety by virtue of their isolation.

Working Mother/Social Victim

Hollywood's partiality for women characters as victims was especially evident in 1988, when "all but one of the women nominated for the Academy Award's Best Actress played a victim" (Faludi, 1991, p. 138). The working-class mother as social victim is a subset that encompasses four films: *Stella* (1983), *Mystic Pizza* (1988), *Gas, Food & Lodging* (1991), and *Little Man Tate* (1991).

By asking who suffers and who benefits, patterns emerge in how victimization manifests itself in these films. First, children are generally included when filmmakers depict working women, and the children benefit in varying degrees as the mother undermines her own mental health in order to provide for them. Second, the personal relationships of the mother outside of the family either fail or are virtually nonexistent.

Gas, Food & Lodging, Mystic Pizza, Little Man Tate, and *Stella* (to an extent) provide examples of working-class mothers who are social victims in that they are poor, without partners, and with little outside contact. Like the two thirds of the adult female population in this country who work outside the home, averaging weekly "over 80 hours of housework, child care, and employment" (Schor, 1992, pp. 20-21), these characters work double shifts and are intensely involved with their children. Nevertheless, they seek to transcend the oppressive aspects of their situations. They express humor, love, and perseverance— without turning into poor-but-happy caricatures.

Stella is a remake of the 1940s film, *Stella Dallas*. In both films, the working-class mothers (Bette Midler and Barbara Stanwyck, respectively) are intelligent, diligent, loving, and humorous. And in both they abandon their talents and jobs, and relinquish their daughters to wealthy fathers. Apparently the intervening 40 years of women's movement and women entering the workforce did not temper the cinematic glorification of a mother's sacrifice of herself and her daughter.

In both films, lower-classness is an inborn stigmatizing force. Thus, as in *Silence of the Lambs*, it is inescapable and visible to others in a negative way. Though both *Stellas* are industrious and talented, they are stripped of these characteristics. Bereft of their original, individual style, both end up daughter-less, alone, and unable to succeed financially—but, we are asked to believe, as a consequence of having made a necessary sacrifice. The credibility and value of a strong mother-daughter relationship early in the films is undermined by the out-of-character sacrifice.

In *Little Man Tate*, Jodie Foster also plays a working-class mother compelled to sacrifice her son to a higher good. Unlike the *Stellas*, she does not lose him permanently. Indeed, she is rewarded by her son's return in better condition than when he left. These movies propose that working-class mothers cannot provide their children with acceptable value systems and lifestyles.

In *Gas, Food & Lodging* and *Mystic Pizza*, working mothers do not sacrifice their children to some outside force. Instead, the children must depend—not on their emotionally distant mothers—but solely on each other. The values of these films are: (a) they show the stress that working mothers face, (b) they depict the effect economic hardship has on relationships, and (c) they convey the importance of networking and community among women of the working class.

The problem with the four films in this category is that there are not enough of them in mainstream media. The invisibility of the working-class mother's experience serves to aggravate the binary oppositions that we are presented with—working mother succeeds/working mother fails. It becomes important to realize that personal success is judged through the accomplishments of the mother's children. The importance of a film like *Alice Doesn't* increases after the barrage of other films because *Alice* shows that a mother does not necessarily succeed or fail—she exists, she has a life outside of her mothering, her children exist, and her children respect her person.

Class Fantasies

Class fantasy films offer an especially ambiguous viewing experience. On the one hand, they take working-class women's experiences seriously, that is, as fitting cinematic subject. On the other, they provide easy gratification by glossing over those experiences. Beautiful pictures and happy endings do indeed respond to audience desires. Moreover, it would be harsh and unfair to demand depressing topics and ambiguous endings from films involving working-class women. Nevertheless, these fantasies too readily feed U.S. American myths that class distinctions are superficial, things of the past, and/or easily overcome. The films include *Swing Shift* (1990), *9 to 5* (1980), *Pretty Woman* (1992), *Flashdance* (1983), and *Working Girl* (1988).

Swing Shift takes place in the 1940s. Goldie Hawn plays a homemaker who becomes somewhat liberated when her husband goes to war and she obtains a lucrative factory position. Like *A League of Their Own,* the film explores an intense and historically meaningful time for working-class women. But neither film provides a sense of the pressures of government and media propaganda; or of the extreme working conditions the women faced, including blatant on-the-job sexism and racism; or of the difficulty of arranging child care and, often, managing extended families; or, finally, of the extreme pain for many at the loss of these jobs and the difficulty of returning to the home.

9 to 5 is another fantasy film that delivers a big payoff without examining the conditions of working-class women. Indeed, the film proved cathartic for many viewers—this is important. But might not a film be cathartic for viewers while still taking seriously the social context of the characters' lives? *Pretty Woman* inspires the same question. Whereas in *9 to 5* the former secretaries successfully (if fantastically) undermine their boss and transform their work environment into a veritable haven, Julia Roberts in *Pretty Woman* transcends her life as a prostitute only to be captured again by Prince Charming. Were we the only viewers who wished desperately that the film had ended with her moment of triumph in taking the money and heading back to school, rather than with her recontainment in the arms and sports car of her wealthy "john"? In these films the male protagonist (*Pretty Woman*) and antagonist (*9 to 5*) are unlikely representatives of what working-class women are likely to encounter on the job.

Flashdance deserves credit for its gritty cinematic quality. The main character, played by Jennifer Beales, is a welder, and her environment is shown as particularly harsh and dangerous. The ending, though relatively upbeat, is not particularly problematic because throughout the film the main character has asserted herself as an independent working woman. Driven by talent and passion, she is tough, works incessantly toward her goal, and resists the attentions of her enamored boss in order to succeed on her own.

In *Working Girl* this same passion and talent can be seen in the character of Tess, played by Melanie Griffith. Tess is not only smart and ethical, but emotionally secure enough to dump her long-time beau after catching him in bed with another woman. Moreover, Tess does not abandon her community of secretary-pool friends after her success; in the final scene she calls them from her new office, and she treats her own newly acquired secretary with respect and diplomacy. The ending is particularly valuable for its ambiguity. After Tess "succeeds," a long zoom backs viewers out her office window to show that hers is just one among hundreds of indistinguishable cubes with a window. She has indeed achieved a personal goal, but in the larger scheme of things she is still a worker, a small cog in the machine of big business. It is a shame that Tess's foil had to be another female, a hard-bitten, dishonest, unhappy, loveless, and desperate career woman. The foil does, however, draw attention to class differences among women.

Working Teen Angst

That economic topics infiltrated films aimed at youth is symptomatic of the larger cultural climate. In 1990, 53.7% of teenagers were part of the labor force; half worked more than 20 hours a week, motivated perhaps by a growing consumerism in that age group (Schor, 1992, p. 26). In this context, films like *The Breakfast Club* (1985), *Pretty in Pink* (1986), *Say Anything* (1989), *Can't Buy Me Love* (1987), *Sixteen Candles* (1984), and *River's Edge* (1987) were quite popular.

With the exception of *River's Edge,* these films establish a pattern: Poor female/male falls in love with wealthy male/female. The bulk of the action takes place in high schools that, not surprisingly, feature the same class divisions and conflicting work ethics and value systems of the larger society. If anything, class boundaries in high schools are more rigidly enforced; there is little mobility between class cliques.

In both *Pretty in Pink* and *Sixteen Candles,* a lower-class girl falls for an upper-class boy. *Sixteen Candles* is less politically charged; though it ridicules upper-class values and middle-class aspirations, the "class struggle" is mostly family conflict. On the other hand, *Pretty in Pink's* Molly Ringwald character (she stars in both films) asserts her class identity in the face of disparagement from higher status classmates, cares that her relationship with a rich boy might threaten class solidarity among her friends, and turns a need-based skill—sewing—into cultural capital. Both female characters get the boy of their dreams through patient effort and quite a bit of luck. Both endings are stunningly romantic; the new generation, it seems, can and will transcend class boundaries.[10]

Say Anything and *Can't Buy Me Love* are veritable mirror images of the above movies: Here working-class boys desire the attentions of upper-class girls. In contrast to the female characters in *Pretty in Pink* and *Sixteen Candles,* however, male protagonists are quite the self-sufficient entrepreneurs and show more aggressiveness when it comes to making money. In *Sixteen Candles,* the main female character doesn't even have a job; in *Pretty in Pink,* she works to compensate for her nonworking father, but her job as a clerk in a record shop is important to who she is only to the extent that it enables her to buy the inexpensive items she assembles into fantastic outfits.

The Breakfast Club comments on class through the dialogue and changing relationships among five high school kids from different backgrounds. Although the characters at first appear stereotypical (a jock, punk, priss, nutcase, and nerd), as they survive 8 hours of Saturday detention in the library, ambiguity and nuance of character emerge; they confront and deal with stresses due to class backgrounds and how they view each other.

What we most value about this film is how the ending differs from the previous four films. Instead of "happily-ever-after," *The Breakfast Club* suggests that even though these kids have connected for the moment, today's camaraderie is unlikely to effect change among them when classes resume on Monday. Class boundaries also survive; we are invited to see school as an institution also bent on the maintenance of such boundaries.

Perhaps the finest film dealing with class relationships among youth in the 1980s and 1990s is *River's Edge.* Loosely based on an actual case in which a high school boy murdered his girlfriend, and his friends helped him hide this from authorities, the film's characters are imbued with the sense of emptiness many working-class kids have about themselves and the outside world. The film shows how class oppression contributes to estrangement between lower working-class parents and their children, and to drug and alcohol abuse and a skewed concept and valuation of community among disenfranchised youth.

One theorist writes that in the 1980s "more than ever before American films were prepared to admit that there were class differences" (Stead, 1989, p. 248). We concede the point, but must add that however visible in the films of the past and present decade, class issues are nevertheless generally treated as solvable within a romance or an individual's perseverance. There are too few films like *Gas, Food & Lodging, The Breakfast Club,* and *River's Edge* that succinctly examine working-class existence and the lives of working-class women.

Notes

1. From B. Ehrenreich, "The Silenced Majority," *Zeta Magazine* (September 1989). Reprinted by permission.

2. The "evil woman" syndrome had begun to a small degree even in the very early 1940s. For example, when Ginger Rogers's character in *Lady in the Dark* (1941) "takes her private demons to a shrink," he diagnoses the problem: "You've had to prove you were superior to all men; you had to dominate them." "What's the answer?" she begs. "Perhaps some man who'll dominate you" (Rosen, 1973, p. 25).

3. See E. Ann Kaplan's (1980) anthology for excellent analyses of the various women's roles in film noir.

4. L. Garafola, "Hollywood and the Myth of the Working Class," *Radical America* (January-February 1980). Quotations reprinted by permission.

5. Two major factors had brought about another revamping of the motion picture production code: (a) competition from increasingly popular foreign films, and (b) the predominance of television, which enabled Hollywood to demand the freedoms that other vehicles for entertainment enjoyed on the grounds that it was no longer solely responsible for audience morality (Parish, 1992, p. xx). Thus began the ratings system in 1968; henceforth any film could be made, but it would receive one of four labels: "G = general audiences, all ages admitted; M = suggested for mature audiences . . . ; R = restricted, children under 16 required an accompanying parent or adult; [and] X = no one under 16 admitted" (Parish, 1992, p. xx). Until late 1977, only minor changes were made in this system.

6. As Parish (1992, p. 235) reports, the film grossed $8,000,000 in domestic rentals, the screenplay was nominated for an Academy Award, and Jane Fonda won Best Actress.

7. In related fashion, Cicely Tyson's portrayal of a "watchful, proud, and loving mother in *Sounder* (1972)" might be read by different audiences as a heroic black woman facing odds alone or as a stereotype-affirming devoted black woman/servant (Rosen, 1979, p. 29). In general, culture critiques do well to avoid the "good media/bad media" pitfall and instead consider the limits and values of various media products for various audiences.

8. Classifying *An Unmarried Woman's* heroine as working class is a bit problematic. Her ambiguously defined job early in the film appears to be clerical or secretarial, but its setting is the elite world of New York art dealerships and her husband's work has clearly afforded them a middle-class lifestyle. Again, though financial hardships due to the divorce are alluded to, her romantic liaison by the end of the film is with a clearly wealthy artist.

9. L. Shapiro, A. Murr., and K. Springen, "Women Who Kill Too Much," *Newsweek* (June 17, 1991). From *Newsweek*, June 17, 1991. © Newsweek, Inc. All rights reserved. Reprinted by permission.

10. Some theorists view this trend in filmmaking as "the excuse the Reagan era offered as a cover for a systematic demobilization of a large number of especially young working class and underclass people into low-wage service sectors and 'temporary' employment" (Ryan & Kellner,

1988, p. 120). The stress on *temporary* is important, for it alludes to the often lengthy time children of the working class actually spend in these positions.

References

Bell-Metereau, R. (1985). *Hollywood androgyny.* New York: Columbia University Press.

Billson, A. (1991, July 12). Women drivers. *The New Statesman and Society, 4*(159), p. 33.

Blumefield, W. J. (1988). *Looking at lesbian and gay life.* Boston: Beacon.

Byars, J. (1991). *All that Hollywood allows.* Chapel Hill: University of North Carolina Press.

Doane, M. A., Mellencamp, P., & Williams, L. (1984). *Re-vision.* Frederick, MD: University Press of America.

Dyer, R. (1986). *Heavenly bodies.* New York: St. Martin's.

Ehrenreich, B. (1989, September). The silenced majority. *Zeta Magazine, 2*(9), 22-23.

Faludi, S. (1991). *Backlash: The undeclared war against American women.* Garden City, NY: Doubleday/Dell.

French, B. (1978). *On the verge of revolt.* New York: Frederick Ungar.

Garafola, L. (1980, January-February). Hollywood and the myth of the working class. *Radical America, 14*(1), 7-15.

Giddis, D. (1973). The divided woman. *Women and Film, 1*(3 & 4), 57-61.

Hansen, K. (1990). Women's unions and the search for a political identity. In K. Hansen & I. Philipson (Eds.), *Women, class, and the feminist imagination.* Philadelphia: Temple University Press.

Haskell, M. (1987). *From reverence to rape: The treatment of women in the movies* (2nd ed.). Chicago: University of Chicago Press.

Kaplan, E. A. (1980). *Women in film noir* (rev. ed.). London: BFI Publishing.

McCreadie, M. (1990). *The casting couch and other front row seats.* New York: Praeger.

National Committee on Pay Equity (NCPE). (1992). The wage gap: Myths and facts. In P. S. Rothenberg (Eds.), *Race, class, and gender in the United States* (2nd ed.). New York: St. Martin's.

Nesteby, J. R. (1982). *Black images in American films.* Washington, DC: University Press of America.

Parish, J. R. (1992). *Prostitution in Hollywood films.* Jefferson, NC: McFarland.

Quart, L., & Auster, A. (1991). *American film and society since 1945.* New York: Praeger.

Rosen, M. (1973). *Popcorn Venus: Women, movies, and the American dream.* New York: Coward, McCann, & Geoghegan.

Rosen, M. (1979). Popcorn Venus or how the movies have made women smaller than life. In P. Erens (Ed.), *Sexual stratagems* (pp. 19-30). New York: Horizon Press.

Ryan, M., & Kellner, D. (1988). *Camera politica.* Bloomington: Indiana University Press.

Schor, J. B. (1992). *The overworked American.* New York: Basic Books.

Shapiro, L., Murr, A., & Springen, K. (1991, June 17). Women who kill too much. *Newsweek,* p. 63.

Stead, P. (1989). *Film and the working class.* New York: Routledge.

Traube, E. G. (1992). *Dreaming identities.* Boulder, CO: Westview.

Walsh, A. (1984). *Women's film and female experience.* New York: Praeger Special Studies.

Wood, R. (1986). *Hollywood from Vietnam to Reagan.* New York: Columbia University Press.

9   Advertising and Mother Nature

KATHERINE TOLAND FRITH

An advertisement is both a marketing tool and a cultural artifact. In order to understand the social and cultural aspects of advertising, however, we must begin to move beyond the surface message of products and services for sale to explore the deeper underlying meanings. We must search out the cultural stories and mythologies that form the body of knowledge from which advertising's creative people draw as they solve advertising and marketing problems. By using critical methods like deconstruction we can begin to undress advertising and to see the role ideology plays in shaping advertising messages. As Goldman (1992) points out:

> Advertising is a form of social practice insofar as corporate profitability and control over markets relies on the existence of a built environment which presupposes commodified relations, such that the world depicted in advertisements comes to be thought of as the only possible world. (p. 34)

Within the world of advertisements, nature and the environment are valued only insofar as they can improve the profitability of the advertiser. Marlboro, for example, uses beautiful shots of mountains, rivers, sunsets, and other aspects of nature as backdrops for their cigarette ads. However, these pictures of nature are meant symbolically to connect the product, cigarettes, with what Williamson (1978) calls a "referent system." By using nature as a referent system, advertisers are able to connect something that is valued and desirable within society (nature) to something that is purchasable (cigarettes).

This chapter uses critical methods like deconstruction and textual analysis to begin to "isolate and detail the ideological codes that animate ads" (Goldman, 1992, p. 2). In particular, this chapter will examine some feminist themes related to the way in which both women and nature are undervalued in a patriarchal society, while those things that are gendered male—science and technology, for example— are highly esteemed even when they are destructive to the environment. We shall trace the growth of these cultural values through an historical analysis of goddess and nature worship and begin to understand how the demise of the Goddess and the demise of the environment might be connected.

In order to begin to understand the environmental problems our planet faces, we must begin to consider nature within the context of multicultural and feminist studies. In particular, we must trace our sources for understanding the environment back beyond our Judeo-Christian, European-centered roots and begin to see how the favoring of certain Western ideals, such as technology and development, may actually run counter to environmental awareness. As feminist Vandana Shiva (1989) notes, in the introduction to her book on women, ecology, and development:

> Industrialism created a limitless appetite for resource exploitation, and modern science provided the ethical and cognitive license to make such exploitation possible, acceptable and desirable. The new relationship of man's domination and mastery over nature was thus also associated with new patterns of domination and mastery over women, and their exclusion from participation as partners in both science and development. (p. xiv)

The links between the treatment of women and the treatment of the environment are readily accessible through examination of mass media artifacts like advertisements.

Critically Analyzing Advertisements

The vast majority of mainstream advertising research published in the United States tends to focus primarily on the "effects" of advertising on consumer sales. Articles of a philosophical or critical nature dealing with the impact of advertising on culture, language, value systems, or morality are generally left to the "critical" researchers. Into the hodgepodge called critical researchers fall ethicists, anarchists, feminists, neo-Marxists, multiculturalists, and semioticians.

The "effects" researchers see the mass media as having an objective and measurable impact on the target audience. The social and historical context within which the communication act takes place is simply overlooked or ignored. Advertising research, as a form of "effects" research, has generally conformed to the dominant paradigm and continues to favor positivist, economic methodologies. This bias has been exacerbated by advertising's close relationship to marketing—a trade influenced by the particularly narrow positivist worldview held by economic theorists whose methodologies are structurally incapable of dealing with social and cultural values. In the economic tradition, cultural and environmental variables have remained unchallenged assumptions or been discarded as "externalities."

Critical research, by contrast, is a problem-posing activity that attempts to discover the ideological basis for the communication. Hall (1986) defines ideology as:

> The mental frameworks—the languages, the concepts, categories, imagery of thought, and the systems of representation—which different classes and social groups deploy in order to make sense of, define, figure out and render intelligible the way society works. (p. 29)

Critical researchers see advertisements as reflecting the dominant ideologies of the society that produces them. In order to analyze advertisements critically we must look at the entire ad—visual as well as copy—because, as Shields (1990) notes, "The production of visual texts takes place within dominant ideological structures" (p. 25). The entire text, therefore, has the ability to reflect dominant cultural discourses about such things as gender, race, ethnicity, and class.

In many advertisements, representations of nature are prominent. By analyzing the meaning of these representations we begin to see how contemporary representations of nature, as well as those of science and technology, are gendered. I have chosen a series of ads that contain both representations of nature and of science and technology for contrast. These ads were taken from issues of popular magazines, including *Vogue, Time, L'Official,* and *Sports Illustrated.* These ads, though supporting my basic thesis, are not unique. I chose these advertisements because they are representative examples of the advertising categories that I am discussing in this chapter: power over nature, women, and animals, and over others.

The Historical Demise of the Goddess

Any discussion of the modern representations of women and nature in advertising must be preceded by some historical and theoretical background. The connection between women and nature has persisted in the ancient mythologies of both East and West. The Great Mother, Mother Earth, or Gaia—as the Greeks called her—existed in many forms in ancient civilizations. The Egyptians called the Goddess Isis, the Babylonians called her Tiamat, to the Hindus she is known as Kali. To various ancient peoples she was known as Nana, Ninhursag, and Mami (Murdock, 1990). She was the creatrix principle—the Mother Earth. Whether the Goddess was envisioned as a personified Being or as the energy that occurs within and between women, her image was revered for centuries as the source of life and creativity.

> She was thought to exhale the breath of life, which nourished living organisms on her surface . . . fluids flowed within her and the water came out of her springs like blood. Within her body there were veins, some of which contained liquids and other solidified fluids. . . . She bore stones within her womb and nurtured them as they grew, like embryos, within her, ripening at their own slow pace. (Sheldrake, 1991, p. 15)

Goddess worship continues to this day in India and the Far East, but it was gradually displaced in Europe and the Near East between 4,000 and 3,500 B.C. by invaders whose warrior gods "dethroned the old goddesses, demoting them to wives, daughters and consorts of the new male-dominated pantheons" (Sheldrake, 1991, p. 18). Patriarchy eventually replaced goddess worship, and as the values of patriarchy took hold, the concept of the earth as sacred was gradually displaced, as well.

The final blow to the sacredness of Mother Nature was dealt during the 16th and 17th centuries when philosophers like Francis Bacon and René Descartes conceptualized nature as nothing more than a machine.

> The universe of Descartes was a vast mathematical system of matter in motion. Matter filled all space. . . . Everything in the material universe worked according

to mathematical necessities. His intellectual ambition was boundless; he applied this new mechanical way of thinking to everything, even plants, animals and man. (Sheldrake, 1991, p. 49)

Within Descartes's newly emerging scientific paradigm "Mother Nature was no more than dead matter, moving in unfailing obedience to God-given mathematical laws" (Sheldrake, 1991, p. 49). This scientific view of the universe, coupled with the first few chapters of Genesis, gave the patriarchy rights over women, animals, and the land. Mother Nature, once considered sacred by the ancients, could now be dominated and desecrated in the name of science, technology, and development.

Power Over Nature

"The earth-based spirituality that was inherent in ancient societies that valued the Goddess conceived of power as "power-from-within" (Starhawk, 1987). Unlike the "power-over" values that were practiced in later patriarchal societies, power-from-within was thought to arise from and be connected to the earth. It stressed the value and interconnectedness of all aspects of nature and the immanent worth of all life forms.

"If we call the world non-living, we will surely kill her. But when we name the world alive, we begin to bring her back to life" (Starhawk, 1987, p. 8). In her book *Truth or Dare,* feminist author Starhawk describes the rise of power-over cultures as the "story of the literal dismemberment of the world" (p. 14). Feeding upon dreams of conquest and warfare (dreams fueled by a particular deployment of science and technology) the culture of power-over has grown until most of the world today lives within the power-over value system. In the power-over worldview, human beings have no inherent value but acquire or are granted value through systems of rank. Power-over cultures are based on domination, hierarchy, and authority. The language of power-over cultures is the "language of hierarchical law and rules" (p. 18).

Modern technological societies that require a constant supply of natural resources demonstrate a power-over attitude toward nature. Power-over consciousness of the environment is considered to be an essential element in maintaining economic growth. Within this value system of exploitation, no place is sacred. This attitude is exacerbated by advertising that promotes wasteful consumption in the name of modernity.

In the religions of earlier societies, many places on the planet were called sacred. Mountains, for example, were considered holy places. Moses spoke to God on Mount Horeb, Mohammed first heard the voice of the angel Gabriel in a cave on Mount Hira near Mecca. The Native Americans consider Mount Rainier in the Pacific Northwest and California's Mount Shasta to be sacred. In the earliest mythologies, mountains were symbols of the Goddess (Campbell, 1988, p. 171). Today, however, as one author notes:

> If a mountain stands in the way of convenient travel between two points, slice off the top of the mountain or tunnel through it. To most North Americans the expression to "move a mountain" is not a metaphor symbolizing the impossible but rather an optimistic challenge based on past experience. (Ferraro, 1991, p. 104)

The Army/ROTC expresses this sentiment explicitly in their ad that features a magnificent mountain with the headline, "Move It." Because most members of the Armed Forces are male, we can assume that the implied reader for this ad is male. The imperative mood of the language reflects the hierarchical, power-over value system of the patriarchy with phrases that remind the young man to develop "leadership skills, for success . . . in the world beyond." The copy uses words like *potential, confidence, initiative,* and *self-discipline* to remind the male reader that it is "his" move and that the Army/ROTC is the smartest "course" he can take.

Another example of the mountain symbol used in an advertisement is the photograph in the advertisement for the Evian bottling company. Here we see a photograph of the "pristine" French Alps. The headline, however, notes that the unspoiled, virgin Alps are, in fact, "Our Factory." The concept that virgin territory, the natural unspoiled aspects of the earth, can be "had" or taken over and developed by an industry is a theme that appears and reappears in different forms in Western advertising. Regardless of whether or not the picture shows an Evian bottling plant, we must assume that to get the pure water from the French Alps, the Evian company had to venture into this "unspoiled" area to bottle the water. We are told in the last sentence that: "We do indeed have a factory. But we don't run it, nature does." The irony here is that a factory is a factory and that it is not run by nature, it is run by people; people who are exploiting one of nature's resources—pure water. As Vandana Shiva (1989) points out, in her book on women, ecology, and development:

The scientific revolution in Europe transformed nature from "terra mater" (earth mother) into a machine and a source of raw material; with this transformation it removed all ethical and cognitive constraints against its violation and exploitation. (p. xvii)

The unchallenged assumption expressed in this ad is that nature is a coconspirator in this process of exploitation. By stating that Evian is not exploiting nature—"we don't run the factory, nature does"—the destruction of nature appears to be a normal event that occurs in the name of modernity and development.

Nature and the Machine

Nowhere are themes of power-over nature more prevalent than in automobile advertising. Car advertising frequently refers to nature as an "obstacle" that can be overcome with a sturdy automobile. In one Nissan ad the headline reads: "What to do when nature calls." The subtle disdain for nature is evidenced here by the play on words in this headline. In car advertising, nature is never considered sacred: It is something to be conquered, dominated, used, and abused in an air-conditioned vehicle. The copy in this ad assures the reader that plant life, represented in this case by the logs and twigs that lie along the road, can be overcome or surmounted in a Nissan 4×4. The text explains that branches are no problem for the "automatic-locking hubs and gargantuan steel-belted radials" on this vehicle. Domination, rather than preservation and co-existence, is the theme in this ad.

Animals are objectified and distanced from human nature in the Nissan ad. The copy reads: "The Pathfinder has a large glass area. Fun for things like looking at wildlife." The irony, of course, is that few animals would stand frozen in their places to be "observed" by humans and that, in general, the only humans who are especially interested in "spotting" animals are hunters who are bent on destroying them. Automobiles allow for a power-over/distance-from nature. The copy in this ad is full of references to power-over the environment. For example, one sentence reminds the reader that this car has power-steering, power-brakes, and "It is the best combination of power, comfort and durability of any vehicle on the road." In reality, driving over nature in a 4×4 implies pollution and disruption of nature whether there is hunting or not.

Automobile ads often demonstrate a patriarchal disdain for the feminine, which is equated with nature. One such ad from the Ford Motor Company features the following: "for families who refuse to let Mother Nature rule the roost"—this sentence reflects the dominance of male control within most families. The ad's headline notes that this car "Handles the road as easily as it handles Mother Nature"—in effect, Mother Nature, or the environment, is easily subjugated and no match for man's technology.

In another similar ad for a Nissan 4×4, the visual shows a four-wheel-drive vehicle splattering through a stream during a heavy rainfall. The headline on this ad states: "The Nissan 4×4. Because Nature can be a Mother." The term *Mother* is used here in a negative way, connoting *bitch*. The inference being that the environment is dangerous and harmful and that the automobile, the man-made machine, is needed to protect the driver from the wrath of nature.

In yet another ad, such as the one for Toyota, we are once again reminded of man's incredible achievement, the automobile. The power-over theme is again repeated. In the headline we are told that "Darwin was Right," and the copy reminds us that man is indeed the most powerful (power-over) being on earth. It states that for more than "forty years the Toyota Land Cruiser has roamed the earth as a dominant species." Need we say more?

Animals in Advertisements

Whenever evolution of human intelligence is depicted in advertisements, it is with a depiction of an ape evolving into "a modern man." This depiction is both specie-ist and sexist and again suggests a power-over mentality. In an ad for Toshiba computers, we are shown the ever-familiar picture of an ape evolving into a modern man. Here, man is represented as the culmination of evolution while the machine, the computer, appears to represent mankind's greatest achievement: Man giving birth to artificial intelligence. Again, we see evidence of a relationship between machines and power-over. The visual depicts a man evolving over the supposedly "lower" life forms while the copy states, " . . . these are the times people can really use the power of computing."

In contrast, when women are represented with or as animals, the inferences are quite different. Whereas man, and his scientific accomplishments, are represented as the technological zenith (higher than animals), women are often represented as being equal to animals. In her book *The Sexual Politics of Meat: A Feminist-Vegetarian Critical Theory,* Carol Adams asserts that in patriarchal cultures a hierarchy exists in which men are at the top and women and animals are similarly positioned as inferior. This relationship between women and animals has been naturalized in the language of our culture. Mary Daly suggests "raiding *Playboy's* playground to let out the bunnies, the bitches, the beavers, the squirrels, the chicks, the pussycats, the cows, the nags, the foxy ladies, the old bats and biddies so that they can at last begin naming themselves" (Daly, 1978, p. 7). In one Maidenform ad the reader is reminded of this positioning of women as inferior in our culture. The ad shows a chick, a doll, a tomato, and a fox, and the headline reads: "A helpful guide for those who confuse women with various unrelated objects."

Women as Prey

An extension of the concept of power-over is demonstrated in the relationship between predator and prey in our society. Although the oppression of women and animals is experienced in vastly different ways, the concept of man-as-hunter and woman-as-prey is a dominant theme that is frequently expressed in the culture. As Collard and Contrucci (1989) note:

> Hunting is the modus operandi of patriarchal societies on all levels of life—to support one level is to support them all. However innocuous the language may sound—we hunt everything from houses to jobs to heads. It reveals a cultural mentality so accustomed to predation that it horrifies only when it threatens to kill us all, as in the case of nuclear weapons. Underlying all this hunting is a mechanism that identifies/names the prey, stalks it, competes for it, and is intent on getting the first shot at it. This is blatantly done when the prey is named woman, animal or land. (p. 46)

In advertisements it is considered quite normal to see depictions of women as animals. In an ad for Coco Chanel, a woman is depicted as a bird with a leash around her foot. Another woman wears the mask of a kitten for Adrienne Vittadini, and yet another has been painted with tiger stripes for the Animale perfume ad.

Collard and Contrucci assert that within power-over patriarchal societies women and animals have both been included in the ranks of rightful prey. They point out that in fur industry ads, the woman and the animals become fused. These ads, they say, encourage women to "take the bait" (the fur coat). Collard and Contrucci note that the man who has bought the fur coat has taken on the role of the hunter. His success in this role is reflected in the kill. They say that in reality the woman and the animal, one alive and the other dead, are the prey that has been brought down.

This depiction of woman as prey becomes most evident when live women are featured with dead animals in advertisements. Women are shown lying on bearskin rugs, draped in animal skins, covered in feathers, or dressed in tight-fitting leather clothing. Adams reminds us that women in patriarchal cultures are, in fact, meat. Though the woman-as-meat depiction is more obvious in pornography than in advertising, this theme can occasionally be seen in advertisements. In one ad from Hebrew National, a slim woman in a bathing suit is featured with the headline: "There's more fat on her than on our salami."

Polluting the Sacred

If nature can be both sacred and gendered feminine, then pollution is the act of desecrating the virgin (see Merchant, 1980). Once the virgin has been desecrated she is no longer respectable. In fact, she becomes suspect. In advertising, nature and the environment are often depicted as suspect. The environment is often described in advertising as passive, polluted, dangerous, or toxic, and a variety of products are sold to help consumers protect themselves from the now-suspect environment. Sunlight, for example, is described in cosmetics advertising as something you must protect yourself against on a daily basis. One advertisement for Lazarus cosmetics advises women who have been exposed to the elements to "Detoxify" themselves. The ad points out that "intelligent" skin care combats the environmental influences of air pollution, smoke, alcohol, and UV rays. Food, which was once the pure and wholesome fruit of Mother Earth, has also become suspect in postindustrial 20th-century society. The American Cancer Society ran an ad that featured an empty plate with a fork resting on it and the headline: "You're looking at a lethal weapon." Man-made products, on the other hand, are often touted as being superior to their natural counterparts. One ad for Skittles candy features the headline: "No Pits. No Peels. No Seeds." In this case a processed, artificially colored, artificially flavored candy is presented to the reader as being "better" than natural fruit.

Conclusions

An advertisement is both a marketing/sales tool and a cultural artifact. As cultural artifacts, advertisements shape human consciousness and reflect the values and mores of a society. Critical analysis from a feminist, multiculturalist perspective allows us to begin to undress the symbols used in advertisements and to expose the underlying value system.

Twentieth-century American culture has evolved along hierarchical, individualistic, competitive, paternalistic, and capitalistic lines. These structures and the social realities that they produce are not necessarily right, true, moral, or universal. These structures of thought do, however, create the dominant paradigm within which we—both male and female—must live and construct our sense of reality.

In a power-over, patriarchal system, the values expressed in advertising mirror the dominant ideological themes. In this chapter I have looked at the history of goddess worship and examined how the death of the Goddess has resulted to some extent in the demise of the environment. We have traced a variety of feminist themes and examined how these themes are expressed in modern advertising.

The argument here is not so much that advertising creates environmental problems, but that the oppression of women and the oppression of the environment are linked and that this link can be seen in advertising. In this culture, science and technology are by and large gendered male and dominant and therefore more important than nature, which is gendered female and undervalued. This has implications not just in terms of environmental issues but also in terms of global issues altogether, as the Western industrialized nations make their global claims based partly on their technological superiority over the Third World.

Finally, and just as important, because advertising encourages consumption, it effaces the processes of production that are themselves very demanding and destructive of the environment and Mother Nature. As certain critics have pointed out (Shasser, 1989), advertising is antithetical to environmentalism because it promotes wasteful consumption, yet it glamorizes this consumption to avoid making people feel uncomfortable or self-conscious about being wasteful.

By circulating and recirculating negative images and myths about women and nature, advertising supports the dominant ideological themes that undermine environmental consciousness and that allow not just a gender—but a global region and a particular vision of life—to remain dominant.

In this chapter I have tried to point out the importance of critically deconstructing the images in advertisements in order to better understand the dominant ideological themes that undermine a true environmental consciousness. In fact, as has been noted, it is not just women who are under siege: All aspects of the ecosystem—animals, vegetables, and minerals—are affected by attitudes and views that undervalue the feminine.

References

Adams, C. J. (1991). *The sexual politics of meat: A feminist-vegetarian critical theory.* New York: Continuum.

Campbell, J. (1988). *The power of myth.* Garden City, NY: Doubleday.

Collard, A., & Contrucci, J. (1989). *The rape of the wild: Man's violence against animals and the Earth.* Bloomington: Indiana University Press.

Daly, M. (1978). *Gyn:Ecology: The metaethics of radical feminism.* Boston: Beacon.

Ferraro, G. P. (1991). *The cultural dimension of international business.* Englewood Cliffs, NJ: Prentice Hall.

Goldman, R. (1992). *Reading ads socially.* New York: Routledge.

Hall, S. (1986). The problem of ideology: Marxism without guarantees. *Journal of Communication Inquiry, 10*(2), 28-44.

Merchant, C. (1980). *The death of nature: Women, ecology, and the scientific revolution.* San Francisco: Harper & Row.

Murdock, M. (1990). *The heroine's journey.* Boston: Shambala.

Shasser, S. (1989). *Satisfaction guaranteed.* New York: Pantheon.

Sheldrake, R. (1991). *The rebirth of nature: The greening of science and God.* New York: Bantam Books.

Shields, V. R. (1990). Advertising and visual images. *Journal of Communication Inquiry, 14*(2), 25-39.

Shiva, V. (1989). *Staying alive: Women, ecology and development.* London: Zed Books.

Starhawk. (1987). *Truth or dare: Encounters with power, authority, and mystery.* San Francisco: Harper & Row.

Williamson, J. (1978). *Decoding advertisments: Ideology and meaning in advertising.* London: Marion Boyars.

10 The "Abortion Clause" in U.S. Foreign Population Policy

*The Debate Viewed Through
a Postcolonial Feminist Lens*

RASHMI LUTHRA

It is no accident that the term *Third World* conjures images of poverty, desperation, chaos, and excessive breeding. It is also no coincidence that *Third World woman* conjures up images of the veil, the harem, the sati, the illiterate, the victim, unable to control her own destiny. Historically the "Third World" has been represented in the West as the untamed land, the land of darkness, and the woman in this land as mysterious, inaccessible, oppressed. This representation has served important purposes for the colonial powers and continues to serve the current nexus of neocolonial power.

This chapter shows how postcolonial peoples, particularly postcolonial women, are used symbolically and physically as the grounds for foreign intervention in the international population arena. Intensive analysis of a debate in international population funding policy reveals how depictions of human suffering in the postcolonial world are manipulated at the discursive level to legitimize the agendas of powerful lobbies in the United States. Postcolonial people's, and especially postcolonial women's, own concerns and needs are lost in the tug-of-war among various powerful interests, including the international population establishment, Neo-Right economists, and the "pro-life" lobby. Each of these lobbies in turn poses as a defender and protector of postcolonial women, only to enhance their own positions of power.

The case of U.S. international population policy analyzed here is the "abortion clause" introduced by the Reagan administration in 1984. My interest in this case stems from the opportunity it provides to understand the place of discourse in the "practice of ruling" (Mohanty, 1991a, p. 21) by a neocolonial power. This particular policy battle is waged among powerful U.S. lobbies, and yet it is waged on the discursive terrain of the "Third World," and "Third World women." It is a clear instance of "a conversation of 'us' with 'us' about 'them,' of the white man with the white man about primitive-native man" and the primitive-native woman (Trinh, 1989, pp. 64-65). This conversation is replete with the "binary logic" characteristic of colonial (and neocolonial) discourse (Ganguly, 1992, pp. 71-72), a logic defining the "Third World" as dark, chaotic, irrational, deviant, and more, in the very same moment that it defines the "First World" as orderly, rational, just, and so on. Within international development policy (and international population policy as a subset) this logic extends to the location of the backwardness of postcolonial states to internal constraints rather than colonial legacy or the world economic system (Melkote, 1991, p. 110). This in turn justifies a host of attempts to "modernize" postcolonial nations through technological and economic solutions devised by the West. The analysis of a particular debate within the policy arena reminds us of the political interests underlying, and served by, neocolonial discourse. The immediate interest served by such discourse is the justification of economic and political intervention. And yet, as Mohanty points out, the binary logic of colonial discourse serves a related and perhaps more fundamental purpose. She says, "only insofar as 'Woman/ Women' and 'the East' are defined as *Others,* or as peripheral, that (Western) Man/Humanism can represent him/itself as the center" (Mohanty, 1984/ 1991b, p. 73). This is a crucial aspect of the logic of domination.

The analysis of this particular debate also allows us to see the complicity of the press in the neocolonial project. By supporting and replicating the binary logic of neocolonial discourse, the press contributes to the silencing of postcolonial women—and postcolonial people more generally. Rather than questioning prevailing dichotomies and constrictive definitions, the press participates in the construction of "Third World" and "Third World Women" as Other.

Background to the Policy Debate

In 1984, the Reagan administration took two new initiatives in the area of international population policy. The first was the tightening of restraints on the use of population assistance. Although in 1973 the Helms Amendment to the Foreign Assistance Act prohibited the use of U.S. funds to support abortion overseas, the Reagan administration proposed to increase restrictions in the following three ways: (a) where U.S. funds are contributed to nations that support abortion with other funds, the U.S. contribution was to be placed into segregated accounts that could not be used for abortion; (b) the United States was no longer to contribute to nongovernmental organizations that perform or actively promote abortion as a method of family planning in other nations, regardless of the source of funds for the abortion activities;[1] and (c) The United Nations Fund for Population Activities (UNFPA) would have to provide concrete assurances that it did not provide funding for abortion or coercive family planning programs before the United States contributed funds to it. The second major initiative was the public communication of a new stance with regard to the "population crisis." Whereas in the late 1960s and early 1970s the United States had spearheaded the move for establishing population programs in the Third World on the basis of a perceived "population crisis," now the Reagan administration denied the existence of a population crisis and insisted that the promotion of "free market" economies was the key to development and to balancing population and environment.

Both of these areas were hotly debated after their introduction a few months before the International Conference on Population in México City in August 1984. There were varied reactions to a policy statement prepared for the conference by the Reagan administration incorporating both new stances. Although the "free market" declaration was rejected by the conference, the "abortion" stance was accepted in a modified version. The abortion controversy as related to U.S. foreign funding extended into 1985 and 1986 and beyond as the administration enforced its policy and as various attempts were made to challenge the policy, both in Congress and in the Courts.

Although the "México City policy" was ultimately reversed by President Clinton on January 22, 1993 (Toner, 1993, p. 1), the analysis of the debate surrounding the initial imposition of the policy remains the focus here, and the lessons drawn from the debate remain valid as an instance of the use of policy discourse to intervene in the postcolonial world. The analysis is important in feminist terms because it enables an understanding of the ways in which internal U.S. politics influence the lives of postcolonial women and of the role of public discourses in this hegemonic process. Indeed, the outcome of this debate had potentially serious consequences for postcolonial women, determining their degree of access to safe abortion and abortion counseling and to other family planning methods.

Method

I have identified the major discourses in the debate and have attempted to identify the major ideological bases that shape these discourses.[2] This ideological analysis includes the question, "What are the meaning-structures about the postcolonial, about First World and postcolonial relations, and about postcolonial women, that underlie the discourses/rhetoric?"[3] A related set of questions has to do with the rhetorical strategies used by the various lobbies in the debate and the impact of these rhetorical strategies on the process of making foreign policy.

The *New York Times Index* was used to locate articles from 1984 and 1985 pertaining to the new policy initiatives; it yielded 60 articles for this period. Relevant articles in the *National Right to Life News* and some literature by Planned Parenthood Federation of America and International Planned Parenthood Federation, were also included in the analysis. All material in the *Congressional Record* pertaining to the policy initiatives from May 1984 to June 1985 was used in the analysis, including 36 newspaper articles and editorials referenced by legislators in support of their arguments. The articles appeared in various newspapers, including the *Washington Post,* the *Philadelphia Inquirer,* the *Chicago Sun Times,* the *Star-Ledger,* the *Washington Times,* the *Journal of Commerce,* the *Minneapolis Star and Tribune,* the *Tulsa World,* the *Chicago Tribune,* the *Boston Globe,* the *Wall Street Journal,* and the *Christian Science Monitor.*[4]

Textual analysis was used to access the various discourses and meaning structures in the debate. This analysis operated at various levels of denotation and connotation, weaving in and out of manifest and latent levels of content to access both the rhetorical process and the cultural assumptions on which the process is based.

The Major Discourses in the Debate

According to newspaper reports, the two major forces that propelled the new policy initiatives of the Reagan administration in the area of international population policy were the "pro-life" lobby and a New Right economists' lobby.[5] On the other side of the debate were population control and family planning organizations (including groups dedicated to advocacy, such as the Population Crisis Committee). Other voices, heard infrequently, were heads of particular governments. Congressmen (and they *were* mostly men) of the United States actively joined the debate, but their voices generally reflected the other major factions, the population control lobby, the "pro-life" lobby, and sometimes the New Right economists. Although the major lobbies used rhetoric emanating from fairly well-defined, self-contained discourses of their own, they drew on other identifiable discourses, such as the "pro-choice" discourse of feminist activists in the United States and an "anti-imperialist" discourse. Postcolonial voices, particularly postcolonial women's voices, were barely audible in this debate.[6] Postcolonial women were spoken about, but they never spoke. As we shall see, this is because the debate was neither about nor initiated by them, but about national security, economic prosperity, the world economic order, and U.S. domestic politics. They were merely part of the terrain on which the debate was waged, the "ground" for the contestation of conflicting political views, to borrow a term from Lata Mani.[7]

The population control discourse was heard the most frequently and also was given the most media space and prominence in this debate, particularly in 1984.[8] This discourse was positioned both against the Neo-Right economist (Cornucopian) discourse, and against "pro-life" discourse. In general, but especially in the press, the population control lobby was cast as the defender of reproductive rights, as it battled the extreme positions of the New Right economists and the "pro-lifers."[9] In most of the articles, and especially the editorials, the population control (and the milder family planning) position was articulated with such frequency and poignancy that it appeared to defend not only the population establishment, but also the ideological position of the press itself. It is as if a major religious tenet of the press were being attacked in questioning the existence of the population crisis, requiring a strong dose of population control rhetoric to restore normalcy.[10]

In defending the existence of a population crisis, *New York Times* articles, as well as articles from various newspapers cited on the floor of Congress (and printed in the *Congressional Record*), most often quoted Robert McNamara and often quoted the World Bank's *World Development Report 1984*. They referred frequently to passages from an article by McNamara in *Foreign Affairs*. This article exemplifies the approach taken by the population control lobby in this debate in many ways, as well as the ideological nexus on which the population lobby's platform is based. The entire tone is neo-Malthusian. The article features population projections of mind-boggling numbers of people, such as in the following passage:

> India will more than double in the next 45 years, becoming almost 40 percent larger than China is today. Bangladesh in the same time will have nearly tripled and will have 259 million people jammed into an area, alternately swept by flood and drought, the size of the state of Wisconsin. (McNamara, 1984, p. 1115)

In this ideological structure, political instability is predicted as one of the main negative outcomes of the "population explosion," and political instability is expected to lead, in turn, to the establishment of authoritarian governments.

> Rapid population growth, in sum, translates into rising numbers of labor force entrants, faster-expanding urban populations, pressure on food supplies, ecological degradation, and increasing numbers of "absolute poor." All are rightly viewed by governments as threats to social stability and orderly change. (McNamara, 1984, p. 1119)

Following Malthusian logic, the passage implies that the solution lies in decreasing the numbers of the absolute poor, rather than addressing the structural underpinnings of poverty itself. McNamara rounds out the argument by asserting that if reasoned action is not taken today to persuade larger numbers of people to exercise family planning, governments and families will be forced to take drastic measures, such as higher levels of abortion, particularly of female fetuses, and higher rates of female infanticide, when the explosion becomes unmanageable. He cites China as a perfect example of this dynamic. Lastly, McNamara points out that not only national stability of the developing countries, but world stability is at stake. *New York Times* articles frequently quoted members of the Population Crisis Committee, the International Planned Parenthood Federation (IPPF), and the United Nations Fund for Population Activities as saying that the possible withholding of funds will cost the programs such-and-such dollar amounts and inflict hardships on programs funded by the major population agencies. Emile Elias of IPPF was quoted as saying, "If you cut this money off, there will be untold dangers to programs that have been built up for years with United States money" (Engelberg, 1984, p. 1).[11] This remark is typical of this lobby. Several of the articles pointed out the motives behind the policy initiatives, in order to discredit the content of the new policies. Motives mentioned in the articles were (a) the need to pander to "pro-life" groups that were an important constituency for Reagan, especially in light of the then upcoming Republican Convention (held 1 week after the México conference); (b) the need to assert control over the population control lobby; (c) the need to distance Reagan administration policy from the pessimistic outlook of the Global 2000 report brought out during the Carter administration; and (d) the need to emphasize the Reagan administration's free market and "Big Government off our backs" approach both domestically and on the foreign policy front. All of these motives were related to the fact that 1984 was an election year and therefore an important time to build support among constituencies and to establish a distinct platform for the Reagan-Bush team.

In its defense against the "pro-life" aspect of the new Reagan policy, population control rhetoric focused on bringing out the irony of the situation by asserting that withdrawing money from particular population agencies would actually lead to a greater number of abortions by restricting choices available to postcolonial populations, particularly postcolonial women, thereby defeating one of the Reagan administration's own purposes—minimizing the number of abortions on a world scale. This argument is illustrated by the following quote: "And when people understand the economic and social value of small families, and use family planning effectively, they have less need to resort to drastic measures such as abortion" (Salas, 1984, p. 1).[12]

The "pro-life" lobby itself was heard infrequently in the mainstream press and in Congress during 1984, with the administration's statement at the conference as one of the few articulations:

The United States will continue its longstanding commitment to development and family planning assistance in other countries. By exercising greater care in determining how those contributions are used, the United States expects to increase the effectiveness of its economic assistance while insuring that its family planning funds are used in ways consistent with human dignity and family values.

The United Nations Declaration of the Rights of the Child (1959) recognizes the right of children to protection before birth as well as after. ("Statement by U.S. Delegate," 1984, p. 1)[13]

Implying that abortion contradicts human dignity and family values and inflicts harm on children before birth (and, therefore, these children require protection), the administration's rhetoric was consistent with "pro-life" rhetoric in general. In addition, by referring to children before and after birth in the same breath, this rhetoric paralleled the successful efforts of the "pro-life" lobby in establishing the substantiality of the fetus as a human being, as "life."[14] In fact, by quoting a United Nations Declaration, the administration was not only seeking to make the "pro-life" stance acceptable to the United Nations audience but was also adding global legitimacy to the "pro-life" stance itself. Nevertheless, the statement reflected compromise. It was restrained in its reference to abortion, never directly calling it violence or murder. Moreover, the administration found it necessary in the first sentence to reassure the population control lobby and the United Nations audience that it will continue its (financial) commitment to family planning. Although initially the administration was deliberating cutting family planning funds by about $100 million in response to "pro-life" pressure, the vocal opposition in the press and in Congress led the administration to continue the level of assistance, redirecting funds to agencies that were not tainted by abortion.

Also in 1984, Senator Jesse Helms introduced an amendment to an amendment, which would have blocked the administration's new antiabortion policy, that read as follows:

it is the sense of Congress that the President is to be commended for his outstanding leadership in condemning abortion at home and abroad as a grave injustice against unborn human beings and that, consistent with law, the President should be encouraged to continue to modify the domestic and foreign policies of the United States Government to protect unborn human beings from the violence of abortion. (*Congressional Record: Senate*, 1984, p. S9934)

Once again, the direct reference to violence and the use of hyperbole ("grave injustice") matched "pro-life" rhetoric in general.

By 1985, the "pro-life" rhetoric in this foreign policy debate came into form. The lobby made its voice heard mainly in Congress, in an attempt to block money from going to the UNFPA. Unlike with IPPF, the administration had vacillated with regard to funding for UNFPA. Since Steven Mosher's exposé in 1983 of coerced abortions and forced sterilizations in China under the one-child policy, the "pro-life" lobby had put pressure on the Reagan administration to withdraw funding from UNFPA, which contributed to population activities in China. In the face of the administration's vacillation and renewed reports in the press on abuses of the one-child policy in China, the "pro-life" lobby stepped up its persuasive efforts. The resulting rhetoric was replete with detailed descriptions of coercion and intrusion into women's lives, as well as frequent references to the violence inflicted on fetuses, particularly late-term fetuses. The following two quotations are typical (both passages refer to China):

> Expectant mothers, including many in their last trimester, were trussed, hand-cuffed, herded into hog cages and delivered by the truckload to the operating tables of rural clinics, according to eyewitness accounts. . . .
> After inducing labor . . . doctors routinely smash the baby's skull with forceps as it emerges from the womb. . . . In some cases, he added, newborns are killed by injecting formaldehyde into the soft spot of the head. (*Congressional Record:* Weisskopf, 1985, p. H1432[15])

The metaphors suggestive of animal slaughter in the first passage and the imagery of violence in the second add emotional force to the description of coerced abortion. Mr. Smith of New Jersey introduced the account of coerced abortions by saying, "Mr. Weisskopf's sobering insights should shock even the most committed proabortion member of this body" (*Congressional Record:* Weisskopf, p. H1431). This framing implicitly links coercive practices to abortion policies, generalizing the horror of coerced abortion to an abhorrence of abortion per se.

The details on abortion were also framed by frequent references to China as a "totalitarian state," to "intrusion by the state into the most intimate of human affairs" (*Congressional Record:* Weisskopf, p. H1432); "Communist China" (*Congressional Record: Senate,* 1985, p. S4133); and the "forces of tyranny" (*Congressional Record: Senate,* 1985, p. S7776). The following quote from Weisskopf's article in the *Washington Post* is typical:

But it is not mere sentimentalism that produces a response of outrage to what is going on in China. A totalitarian state is using its immense resources to intervene crudely, often violently, in the most delicate personal choices of millions of human beings. (*Congressional Record:* Weisskopf, p. H1434)

The "pro-life" discourse in Congress and the press reports on the Chinese one-child policy served to reinforce notions about the evils of totalitarianism and communism in general. Framed in this way, the reports of coercive practices confirmed what the U.S. populace had been told all along: Communism is evil and, justifiably, "the enemy." For the mainstream press, the narrative of coercive practices was readily usable because of its shock value. Furthermore, it was congruent with the general Cold War framework of relations between East and West and superpower conflict within which most stories about the postcolonial world were reported, from the 1960s into the 1980s.[16] Finally, the narrative of coercion was also congruent with the Human Rights framework commonly used by the press in the 1980s.[17] This was too good a story to pass up, even if it did play directly into the hands of the "pro-life" lobby.

Both the population control lobby and the "pro-life" lobby included anti-imperialist discourse within their arguments, although this was a minuscule part of the mass of rhetoric. They mainly used this discourse to make the opposition look bad or to put it on the spot. Each of the lobbies accused the other of "cultural elitism." In addition, the population lobby accused the "pro-life" lobby of ignoring the "sovereign rights" of developing countries and "imposing their morality" on these countries. The defense of the population lobby is instructive:

They [pro-life lobby] allege that the United States was trying to force its views on others, that U.S. population policies are "culturally elitist." But some would impose a rigid set of economic policies on the international population efforts, and use U.S. assistance as leverage on the abortion policies of other nations. (*Congressional Record: House,* 1984, p. H7429)

The irony is that the accusations of both sides ring true. Even within the rhetoric itself, it becomes apparent that both sides are using narratives about postcolonial people's misery and postcolonial women's misery to justify intervention, whether population control intervention, economic intervention, or moral intervention of the United States in the postcolonial world. This becomes obvious because the few references to postcolonial sovereignty are drowned out by the mass of rhetoric portraying the postcolonial countries as going "out of control," as impoverished, famine-struck, or as authoritarian and politically unstable, their populations ignorant, fatalistic, and generally in need of help. Within this overarching ethnocentric framework, the defense of postcolonial nations' sovereign rights is ironic, to say the least. Similarly, each side's defense of postcolonial women is ironic. The next section elaborates on this.

Postcolonial Peoples in the Major Discourses

As previously noted, the postcolonial world was mentioned often in the major discourses, but people from the postcolonial world rarely spoke. The same applies to postcolonial women. Their voices were never heard; rather, the major lobbies spoke in their behalf or their defense.

In the 250 pages analyzed for this chapter, there were 32 instances of postcolonial leaders quoted directly. They almost always spoke in an official capacity and represented the postcolonial elite, who are part of the international population establishment.[18] (The only exceptions were three quotes from local officials in China describing resistance to the one-child policy.) For example, Rafael M. Salas, Executive Director of UNFPA, was quoted in the *New York Times* as saying that UNFPA does not fund abortion programs but rather responds to requests by countries to aid in implementing voluntary family planning programs. Salas echoed the population control lobby's argument that the Reagan policy will actually create the conditions for a greater number of abortions. In the rest of the article, he defended the existence of the "population crisis," directly echoing the general population control rhetoric. This is not surprising, given that UNFPA has played a key role in cultivating a "consensus" on the importance of population control on a global scale (Hartmann, 1987, pp. 106-110).

Four other articles referred to Chinese reaction to the U.S. policy. One was a letter from Chinese Ambassador Zhang Wenjin to Secretary of State Schultz, printed in the *Congressional Record*, saying the abuses are not part of Chinese population policy, nor are they condoned by the Chinese government. The Chinese provided the single strongest statement about sovereignty, and about a woman's right to have an abortion, in the entire debate:

The [unnamed] official said that abortion in China was only provided at the request of the woman after contraceptive failure or for health reasons. "This is the legitimate right of a woman, which therefore should be fully respected," he said.

"We hold consistently that the population strategy and policy of each country should be formulated by its own government according to its own conditions, and that this should be respected by other countries," he said. "This is a matter of the sovereign rights of every country." (Burns, 1985, p. 3)[19]

The Chinese government representatives also said that "not a single U.S. dollar" (Burns, 1985, p. 3) has gone toward abortion in China and that the Chinese government is investigating abuses with a view to stopping them. The Chinese officials also blamed the U.S. policy on the "distorted reports in the American press" ("Around the World: China Regrets U.S. Curb," 1985, p. A5).[20]

Although few of the sources were postcolonial leaders and none were ordinary people from the postcolonial world, all the major discourses were replete with references to the poor men and women of the postcolonial world. In the population control discourse, postcolonial people serve three rhetorical purposes. First, they are used symbolically to convey the reality and the dangers of the population explosion, as in the following passages:

In countries like México, when the children were kids in a rural hut, they were a private family matter. Today, those children are masses of young adults, roaming jobless, restless, impressionable and sometimes violence-prone as they seek something out of life. Now they are a public matter in the Méxicos of the world. . . .[21]

Countries undergoing rapid population growth are susceptible to famine, uncontrolled migration and environmental deterioration, which in turn can result in widespread death, disease, civil disorder and degradation of human life. (*Congressional Record: Senate*, 1985, p. S5447, citing testimony for the record by W. Fornos)

Second, postcolonial peoples are also used symbolically by the population control establishment to position themselves as defenders of the postcolonial world, especially postcolonial women. The following quotes exemplify the symbolic manipulation of postcolonial women:

Effective family planning reduces abortion because fewer unwanted pregnancies occur. If the availability of methods of contraception plummets, pregnancies follow. . . . Some women inevitably will resort to abortion, with all of the dangers of back-street abortionists. (*Congressional Record: House*, 1984, p. H7430).

Women living in developing countries need access to safe and effective methods of family planning if they are to exercise their right to make decisions about family size. (*Congressional Record: Senate*, 1984, p. S9935)

Third, population control rhetoric emphasizes "personal choice," which defuses critiques of population programs both from feminists in the United States and from various postcolonial countries. The AID (Agency for International Development) position paper for the México conference states, "Our goal is to enhance personal choice" (*Congressional Record: Senate*, 1984, p. S7444).

The frequent references to choice are ironic in view of the fact that there is never any mention of a woman's right to an abortion. In fact, the presentation of family planning as "the best antidote to abortion" ("World Population Bomb Must Be Defused Now," *Philadelphia Inquirer*, July 23, 1984, as quoted in the *Congressional Record: House*, July 25, 1984, p. E3301) implies that abortion is to be minimized at all costs—which feeds into the negative aura surrounding abortion and thereby delegitimates women's struggle in various postcolonial countries to legalize abortion (Akhter, van Berkel, & Ahmed, 1991; Hartmann, 1987). This may, however, be a necessary rhetorical strategy for the population control lobby within the present debate. Because Congress had already prohibited the use of U.S. funds for abortion overseas in 1973, and the present effort is geared toward preventing further restrictions, direct support of abortions as a "right" could have been counterproductive. In any case, most of the rhetoric on postcolonial women refers to them as numbers of illegal abortions, as mothers, and as maternal mortality figures rather than as human beings who can be expected to exercise "choice." The following statement is telling in this regard: "Illegal abortion is now a leading cause of death for women in many developing nations, leaving millions of children motherless (*Congressional Record: Senate*, August 8, 1984, p. S9935).

Just as in "pro-life" discourse, women are construed as wombs and mothers, not as sentient human beings with their own volition and demands. In general, the population lobby's rhetorical defense of postcolonial women belies any real concern for them, juxtaposed as it is with fears of the growing numbers of the poor and with the fervor surrounding the need for a strong push in population control. Rather, it is clear that postcolonial women are being used as the grounds for population control intervention.

A similar dynamic is apparent in the "pro-life" discourse. In addition to the already quoted account of women being "trussed" and subjected to coerced abortion, there are about 50 pages of such "atrocities against Chinese women and children" (*Congressional Record: House,* 1985, p. H1431) in the *Congressional Record* in 1985. Chinese population policy is frequently attacked as opposing "family values," as "an all-out government siege against ancient family traditions" (*Congressional Record:* Weisskopf, p. H1431). Moreover, the whole discourse is framed by an opposition to abortion, whether coerced or voluntary, as a crime against the "unborn child" (*Congressional Record: Senate,* 1984, p. S9936). There are frequent parallels with forced abortions in Nazi concentration camps (*Congressional Record: House,* 1985, p. H1434), references to "abortuaries" (*Congressional Record: Senate,* 1985, p. S4133), and many grizzly details about the killing of late-term fetuses. The use of hyperbole and pathos in this way, and the litany about coerced abortions, takes away from the "pro-life's" defense of Chinese women. Their overall discourse completely ignores postcolonial women's struggle in various countries to legalize abortion and to make safe abortions available to women (Akhter et al., 1991; Hartmann, 1987) and contributes to the general stigma and guilt attached to abortion. All of this suggests that postcolonial women are merely being used as the grounds for establishing an "international pro-life standard" (*Congressional Record: Senate,* 1985, p. S4133).

The symbolic manipulation of postcolonial women becomes especially clear when particular aspects of "suffering" are put into the rhetorical service of both the "pro-life" and population control discourses, as with the use of female infanticide in China. The "pro-life" lobby blames female infanticide on strict enforcement of the one-child policy and uses this connection morally to censure coercion in China as well as abortion in general. The population control lobby warns that female infanticide will become a fact of life for most postcolonial countries if population growth is not curbed immediately and uses this connection to justify intensified population control measures.

There is very little space devoted in the debate to New Right economists' discourse, other than in the Reagan policy statement itself. But even in this limited space, the New Right economists manage to pose as defenders of postcolonial peoples. Of the *World Development Report 1984* and its projections of the dangers of excessive population growth, they say:

> This grim picture portrays human beings as engines of poverty and obstacles to material progress and leads to the deceptive conclusion that population control is the key to economic growth. Such a negative view does little to enhance the reputation of development economists, and it does much to present the Chinese practice of female infanticide as a respectable antipoverty program. (P. C. Roberts, "Overpopulation Is Not the World's Worst Threat," as cited in the *Congressional Record,* August 2, 1984, p. E3441)

Once again, the fact of female infanticide in China is being used to further a particular agenda; in this case, the Reagan administration's need to assert control over the international population establishment and the New Right Economists' need to propagate their own worldview.

Conclusions and Discussion

The major parties in the population funding debate—the population control lobby and the "pro-life" lobby—although taking opposing stands, share certain ideological underpinnings. Neither is fundamentally opposed to U.S. intervention in the affairs of postcolonial countries, and both are fundamentally opposed to radical structural change. Moreover, both use the postcolonial world and postcolonial women as grounds for their justification of intervention.

"Pro-life" discourse is mainly concerned with the "injustice" inflicted upon unborn fetuses. These tales of injustice graphically depict the plight of "Third World women" only because they happen to be the carriers of the fetuses. On the other hand, the population control discourse has a neo-Malthusian thrust and is replete with assumptions that accompany a neocolonial world order— assumptions about the rightness and inevitability of marked economic inequalities, even economic exploitation, on a world scale. The fear that growing numbers of the poor in developing countries will eventually have "ripple effects" on the rich and on the "world community" stems precisely from the need to maintain the status quo in which the superpowers determine the terms of economic exchange for the poorer nations and in which the populations of a few rich nations consume a disproportionate amount of world resources. In this discourse, "Third World women" are depicted as deprived of choice and birth control resources, but only so that the population control establishment can retain its hold internationally.

The policy-making process utilizes the assumptions of domestic lobbies, assumptions derived from a neocolonial framework that takes the current world power configuration for granted when making policy. This framework, utilized by all major parties in the debate, largely excludes postcolonial arguments about their sovereign rights and completely excludes postcolonial women's own views on population and abortion. Two of the statements from the "Declaration of Comilla," emerging from the FINRRAGE-UBINIG (Feminist International Network of Resistance to Reproductive and Genetic Engineering-Unnayan Bikalper Niti Nirdharoni Gobeshona) International Conference in 1989 (see Akhter et al., 1991), give some clue as to a whole set of feminist discourses missing from the policy-making process. The statements read as follows:

> We support the recovery by women of knowledge, skill and power that gives childbirth, fertility and all women's health care back into the hands of women. We demand recognition, support and facilitation of the work of midwives and reestablishment of midwifery services under the control of women.
>
> We demand the United Nations and the governments of the respective countries stop population control policies as preconditions for developmental aid.
>
> We support the exclusive rights of all women to decide whether or not to bear children without coercion from any man, medical practitioner, government or religion. We demand that women shall not be criminalized for choosing and performing abortion.[22]

It is clear from these statements that none of the discourses dominating the policy-making process at the international level intersect postcolonial women's concerns. The women activists at the FINRRAGE-UBINIG conference reject the motives and logic represented by the population control lobby, the "pro-life" lobby, and the Chinese government. In rejecting any form of coercion, and in asking for deep structural change that would address patriarchy as well as poverty at its roots, they make clear the limits of the population controllers, the "pro-lifers," and the New Right economists.

The limiting of international population discourse to a narrow ideological domain has damaging implications for the policy-making process. As Hartmann (1987) reminds us, both the New Right economists and the Malthusians "dodge the real issues of power and inequality" (p. 29), and, "The population control and antiabortion philosophies, although diametrically opposed, share one thing in common: They are both antichoice" (Hartmann, 1987, "Introduction"). The press contributes directly to the narrowing of the ideological domain by repeating the stances of the major power-holders in the debate rather than questioning the assumptions of the major parties, breaking out of prevailing dichotomies, and presenting buried discourses such as those voiced by postcolonial women. This is not surprising given the role of the Western press as an objective purveyor of "facts." To do otherwise, to expose the very ideological basis of the debate, would necessitate the press's exposure of its own cloak of objectivity (Altschull, 1984), a highly unlikely occurrence given the current press system.

Limiting the international debate on population to a few prominent lobbies means limiting the frameworks of interpretation available to the general public and to Congressmen whose constituencies are composed of sections of the general public and special interests.[23] This in turn limits policy outcomes in the long run. A sense of future possibilities is rooted in the ideologies underpinning particular discourses, and when the ideologies themselves lie within a narrow domain, policies fail to challenge current arrangements of power. In the guise of protecting and enfranchising the poor in the postcolonial world, especially poor women, these policies ultimately contribute to their continued disenfranchisement.

Notes

1. This part of the statement is directed mainly at the International Planned Parenthood Federation, which (it becomes clear through speeches in Congress) has been a major target of "pro-life" groups for its vocal support for the expansion of the availability of safe abortion.

2. The terms *voices* and *discourses* are used almost interchangeably here. The major voices in the debate were identified by locating institutions represented by those speaking in the debate, and institutions referred to by those speaking in the debate, both in news articles and through representatives on the floor of Congress. The discourses, then, were the embodiment at the symbolic and rhetorical level of these institutions as embedded in the debate, which itself was instrumental in dictating policy outcomes.

3. The term *discourse* has been used variously in different traditions. Perhaps the closest meaning for my use of the term is "an identifiable 'set' within language used in news, and other

written and spoken content, consisting of certain rules and regularities defining the boundaries of this type of content." Here I have borrowed elements of the definition from Jo Ellen Fair's "Are We Really the World? Coverage of U.S. Food Aid in Africa, 1980-1989" (an unpublished paper), who in turn has borrowed from Stuart Hall's (1975) use of the term. For the terms *rhetoric* and *ideology* I quote definitions given in Celeste Michelle Condit's book, *Decoding Abortion Rhetoric: Communicating Social Change.* Rhetoric is defined as "the use of language to persuade; the persuasive dimensions of a communicative act . . . persuasive discourse." Ideology is defined as "the set of beliefs, values, and ways of communicating of a social group; always more or less partial and preferring" (see Condit, 1990, pp. 227-229).

4. The majority of the articles referenced by legislators were from the *Washington Post*, with one or two each from the other newspapers. The articles do not in any way provide a comprehensive picture of newspaper coverage of the issue in the press, because they are selected by particular Congressmen according to their purpose and their ideological standpoint. They were included here to broaden the scope of the analysis a little bit, rather than limiting it to the *New York Times*, and because they were an integral part of the debate in Congress on international population assistance and thus an integral part of the policy-making process in this area.

5. In *Reproductive Rights and Wrongs: The Global Politics of Population Control and Contraceptive Choice*, Hartmann (1987, pp. 28-29) explains that the New Right economists heavily influenced the drafting of the policy statement for the México City conference. She calls the New Right economists the "conservative Cornucopians" because of their "unrepentant optimism" and their belief in the ability of free enterprise and nuclear energy to overcome any problems created by resource shortages. Government interference, and not excessive population growth, is seen as the culprit in the Cornucopians' scenario. Julian Simon and Herman Kahn, authors of *The Resourceful Earth*, are two key Cornucopians.

6. I will elaborate on the articulations of "Third World women" and the "Third World" in this debate in a later section of the chapter.

7. Mani (1989) argues that the debate on the abolition of sati (widow immolation) in 19th-century India was cast within a distinctly "colonial" discourse that used women as the ground for the rearticulation of "tradition." She defines *colonial* discourse as "a mode of understanding Indian society that emerged alongside colonial rule." I see definite parallels in the abortion clause debate, in that it uses women as the grounds for a rearticulation of world economic and population policy within a "neocolonial" discourse. By a *neocolonial* discourse I mean a mode of understanding the Third World that emerged alongside the neocolonial world order, involving economic domination (with political and military domination playing a supportive role) of the south by the north.

8. In fact, in 1984, the "pro-life" discourse is articulated only through the administration's policy paper for the México conference, Buckley's public statement of the administration policy at the conference, and occasional statements by a few conservative Republican Congressmen on the Senate and House floor. "Pro-life" discourse is almost absent from the *New York Times* at this stage.

9. Hartmann (1987) echoes this finding. She points out the irony of the fact that the population control lobby is cast in the role of the defender of reproductive rights. She also says that the debate served both to legitimize the position of the population establishment and to open up a space to contest and modify new-Malthusianist thinking as embedded in the population establishment.

10. In *Manufacturing Consent*, Herman and Chomsky (1988) say that anticommunism has become the "dominant religion" in the United States. It can also be said that population control ideology has attained the status of religion in the United States when it pertains to the poorer nations. Olasky (1988) shows, through a historical analysis of press coverage of abortion, how

the press had become "a lap dog for the abortion lobby" by the 1970s, partly through concerted public relations efforts by organizations like Planned Parenthood. It appears a parallel influence has occurred over the past two decades in the area of population control. Hartmann (1987) describes the process by which a consensus was created among world leaders on the need for population control. She alludes to the role of the press in creating such a consensus in the United States.

11. S. Engelberg, "Conservatives Hope to Link Abortion With Overseas Aid," *New York Times* (June 24, 1984). Copyright © 1984 by The New York Times Company. Reprinted by permission.

12. R. M. Salas, "Poisoning population assistance," *New York Times* (June 28, 1984). Copyright © 1984 by The New York Times Company. Reprinted by permission.

13. "Statement by U.S. Delegate to the Conference on Population in México City," *New York Times* (August 9, 1984). Copyright © 1984 by The New York Times Company. Reprinted by permission.

14. Condit (1990) shows how the "pro-life" lobby has made effective use, particularly of visual imagery, to establish the substantiality of the fetus, so much so that both supporters and opponents of abortion have had to reckon with this "truth." Condit argues that this particular success has been partly responsible for a compromise in the U.S. response to abortion—with the Courts defending the legality of abortion and Congress restricting funding for it.

15. *Congressional Record: House,* March 25, 1985, pp. H1431-H1434, citing M. Weisskopf, "Abortion Policy Tears at China's Society," in the *Washington Post,* January 7, 1985. Cited hereafter as *Congressional Record:* Weisskopf.

16. Hallin (1986) shows convincingly in "Cartography, Community and the Cold War" how the Cold War paradigm dominated news coverage in the mainstream U.S. press from the 1960s to the 1980s. In *Manufacturing Consent,* Herman and Chomsky (1988) identify anticommunism as a major "filter" and "control mechanism" in the press, determining both the inclusion of stories and the framework of interpretation.

17. Hallin (1986) says that in the 1980s, the Human Rights framework sometimes competed with the Cold War framework in the interpretation of stories.

18. Hartmann (1987) aptly reminds us of the "great social barriers of class and caste in many countries, which are often stronger than bonds of nationality" (p. 31), and that the international population control "consensus" is really a consensus among a select few in the world's privileged elite.

19. J. F. Burns, "China Assails U.S. on Population Funds," *New York Times* (February 10, 1985). Copyright © 1985 by The New York Times Company. Reprinted by permission.

20. "China Regrets U.S. Curb on Population Funds," *New York Times,* (April 4, 1985). Copyright © 1985 by The New York Times Company. Reprinted by permission.

21. G. A. Geyer, "Ignorance Abounds in Population Position," *Chicago Sun Times,* June 26, 1984, as quoted in the *Congressional Record: House,* July 27, 1984, p. E3345.

22. These are Items 14, 17, and 18 of the "Declaration of Comilla" (Akhter et al., 1991).

23. News coverage of the debate had an important place in the policy-making process. Congressmen often read newspaper articles into the *Congressional Record* in support of their arguments.

References

Akhter, F., van Berkel, W., & Ahmed, N. (Eds.). (1991). *Declaration of Comilla. In Proceedings of FINRRAGE-UBINIG International Conference 1989.* Bangladesh: UBINIG.

Altschull, J. H. (1984). *Agents of power: The role of the news media in human affairs.* New York: Longman.

Burns, J. F. (1985, February 10). China assails U.S. on population funds. *New York Times,* p. 3.

China regrets U.S. curb on population funds. (1985, April 4). *New York Times,* p. A5.

Condit, C. M. (1990). *Decoding abortion rhetoric: Communicating social change.* Urbana & Chicago: University of Illinois Press.

Engelberg, S. (1984, June 24). Conservatives hope to link abortion with overseas aid. *New York Times,* Sec. 4, p. E3.

Ganguly, K. (1992). Accounting for others: Feminism and representation. In L. F. Rakow (Ed.), *Women making meaning: New feminist directions in communication* (pp. 60-79). New York: Routledge.

Hall, S. (1975). Encoding and decoding in the television discourse. In *Education and culture* (Vol. 6). Strasbourg: Council of Europe.

Hallin, D. C. (1986). Cartography, community and the cold war. In D. K. Manoff & M. Schudson (Eds.), *Reading the news: A Pantheon guide to popular culture* (pp. 109-145). New York: Pantheon.

Hartmann, B. (1987). *Reproductive rights and wrongs: The global politics of population control and contraceptive choice.* New York: Harper & Row.

Herman, E. S., & Chomsky, N. (1988). *Manufacturing consent: The political economy of the mass media.* New York: Pantheon.

Mani, L. (1989). Contentious traditions: The debate on Sati in colonial India. In L. Sangari & S. Vaid (Eds.), *Recasting women: Essays in Indian colonial history* (pp. 88-126). New Delhi: Kali Press for Women.

McNamara, R. S. (1984). Time bomb or myth: The population problem. *Foreign Affairs, 62,* 1107-1120.

Melkote, S. R. (1991). *Communication for development in the Third World: Theory and practice.* New Delhi: Sage.

Mohanty, C. T. (1991a). Introduction. In C. T. Mohanty, A. Russo, & L. Torres (Eds.), *Third World women and the politics of feminism* (pp. 1-47). Bloomington: Indiana University Press.

Mohanty, C. T. (1991b). Under western eyes: Feminist scholarship and colonial discourses. In C. T. Mohanty, A. Russo, & L. Torres (Eds.), *Third World women and the politics of feminism* (pp. 51-80). Bloomington: Indiana University Press. (Original work published 1984).

Olasky, M. (1988). *The press and abortion, 1838-1988.* Hillsdale, NJ: Lawrence Erlbaum.

Roberts, P. C. (1984, August 2). Overpopulation is not the world's worst threat. *Congressional Record,* p. E3441.

Salas, R. M. (1984, June 28). Poisoning population assistance. *New York Times,* p. 1.

Simon, J. L., & Kahn, H. (1984). *The resourceful earth.* Oxford: Basil Blackwell.

Statement by U.S. delegate to the Conference on Population in México City. (1984, August 9). *New York Times,* p. 1.

Toner, R. (1993, January 23). A flurry of edicts: Clinics free to advise—Anniversary of ruling marked by protest. *New York Times,* pp. 1, 10.

Trinh, T. Minh-ha. (1989). *Women, native, other.* Bloomington: Indiana University Press.

PART III

Combining Methodologies
and Narratives

The third section of this book includes three chapters that use a combination of methodologies to study feminist multiculturalist issues. Actually, all of the chapters in this book used more than one approach and methodology. As the introductory chapter notes, when studying multiculturalist issues one must combine theoretical and methodological strands. Previous binary approaches are inadequate to the study of spectrums, constant change, cultural struggle, and fluidity. The three chapters in this section, however, demonstrate some of the possibilities and indeed the necessity of a multipronged methodological approach. Judging from anecdotal experiences shared by multiculturalist scholars, these attempts are met with great resistance by the established academic community. Essays are rejected by journals for "methodological confusion" or the even more scathing "lack of methodology altogether." Thus a major component of the nascent area of feminist multiculturalist studies must be the refinement of previous methods and the development of new methods to study our heterogeneous reality.

In Chapter 11, Susan Kray tackles the difficult task of finding the Jewish woman in U.S. television programming. Her quest takes her into the research areas of production, audience, and textual analyses. Here we have a case in which the usual visual markers, one of the mainstays of television textual analyses, are not helpful. As well, narrative markers and oral cues do not add much more to our search for the missing Jewish woman. Kray has to expand her analysis into production issues and questions. This is a significant issue, given the high incidence of Jewish individuals' input in Hollywood production. Finally, who among the audience picks up on the very subtle cues that signal female Jewishness and how? All of these are questions that Kray seeks to answer. As such, her chapter is an implicit criticism of our reliance on visual cues, despite our protests that race and ethnicity are not biological constructs. We could use her analysis as a springboard for the analysis of a number of other "invisible" oppressed groups, such as lesbian women or Latina women.

Whereas Kray navigated the different types of media studies areas when focusing on her quest for the missing Jewish woman, in Chapter 12, Frances Negrón-Muntaner connects a variety of cultural products and authors/producers in exploring the boundaries of Black and lesbian narratives. This chapter also combines production with textual and audience analysis, especially the possibility of interpellation. As well, this chapter considers gender, race, and sexuality issues at once, thus reiterating many of the issues brought up in previous sections and chapters. For example, some of the narrative and thematic components of the video *Tongues Untied* appear to draw on yet not attribute debt to lesbian texts and authors. Negrón-Muntaner carries this analysis within an integrated framework of identity politics, exploring the overlapping discourses and subjectivities that contribute to the formation and identification of an oppressed community, or indeed any community. As she takes us on a mediated tour of a number of interrelated texts, she demonstrates how too often identity politics and empowerment struggles are carried on at the expense of other marginalized groups. Her chapter is an elegant warning not to reify "identity at the expense of other possibilities."

In Chapter 13, Kyra D. Gaunt explores Black women's production and reception of hip-hop music. Indeed she asks, Why is it that many question whether this is music or not? Gaunt draws on a diverse combination of theoretical and conceptual perspectives, including speech acquisition and early childhood play theories. Of course she uses feminist textual analysis and the work of Lisa Lewis on female address in music video. As video scholars have noted, this particular cultural form is difficult to study because we are unsure whether it is music, television, both, neither, or something beyond. Issues of pleasure, on the part of producers and audiences, are considered against a backdrop of mainstream dismissal based on gender, race, and class variables. Gaunt also includes original poetry and weaves in Black rhymes to demonstrate the continuity between hip-hop and previous cultural forms.

The three chapters in this section provide us with a glimpse of the possibilities of feminist multiculturalist research. WARNING: This is a difficult task. WARNING: One must be conversant with many literatures and methodologies as well as in touch with current popular culture and sociohistorical context. WARNING: If we do not engage in such an undertaking, we will not know or understand what is going on.

11 Orientalization of an "Almost White" Woman

A Multidisciplinary Approach to the Interlocking Effects of Race, Class, Gender, and Ethnicity in American Mass Media: The Case of the Missing Jewish Woman

SUSAN KRAY

Nearly all continuing major protagonists in episodic prime-time television within the past 3 years (viewing seasons 1990-1991, 1991-1992, and 1992-1993) are physically perfect, white, American[1]-born Christians of North European extraction. The images and voices of Jewish women are largely absent, even where the narrative seems to have made space for them. Jewish male characters do appear, but they pair with Gentile female characters.

AUTHOR'S NOTE: Research on which this chapter is based was supported by the American Association of University Women, through a Beckman Fellowship.

Not only are Jewish female characters largely missing, but none of the other characters comment on their absence. In fact, there has been amazingly little comment from audiences, industry personnel, critics, or scholars.[2]

When a Jewish woman does appear, it is almost always in a secondary part, with almost no identifiably Jewish characteristics, no interest (unlike the males) in her ethnic/religious heritage, and (again, unlike nearly all the males and unlike many Gentile females) no stable love life. Again, this situation has received almost no comment, scholarly or otherwise. An exception is an article (see Weiner, 1993) in *Forward,* a secular Jewish weekly newspaper[3] published in New York since 1897, complaining that the Jewish population of prime-time heroes consists of males, who find their fulfillment with Gentile females: "Although the negative image of the Jewish woman has receded, it has been replaced by nothing" (Weiner, 1993, p. 1).

Theoretical Framework

Feminists have for good reason called women "the canaries in the mine," those whose condition signals systemic problems in a given community. One signal of systemic problems in America is that even in eras of civil rights strivings and multicultural consciousness, minority women are subjected, by women as well as men, to the interlocking effects of race, class, gender, and ethnic discrimination. Another signal is that this situation goes largely unremarked, although some have complained that minority women suffer "double discrimination," as women and as minority members.

Recent studies have, however, shown "the inadequacy of additive models ... [treating] white women ... solely in terms of gender, while women of color are thought to be 'doubly' subordinated by the cumulative effects of gender plus race ... [failing to capture] the interlocking, interactive nature of these systems" (Glenn, 1992, p. 1). That is, we tend to arrive at separate understandings of the ways in which society deals with one's gender, race, and ethnicity, and then to add them up, but only for nonwhite women.

Glenn's (1992) alternative model draws our attention to some ways in which "white women" often secure their own status by sacrificing that of "women of color," who either work for them directly as household menials or are confined to low-level dead-end job classifications, such as nurses' aide, within a given field. These low-level categories both highlight and guarantee the relatively higher status of positions mainly reserved for white women, such as that of RN.

The white woman uses the "woman of color" to distract attention from the conflict between white men and women and displace it to the conflict between women of different colors. She thereby distracts herself from the insecurity and marginality of her own status.

Glenn's (1992) model is a great advance over those that try to address the racial dimensions of nonwhite women's experience but leave out the racial dimension of white women's experience. As Glenn points out, it carries us from a simple "additive" model—minority women are doubly oppressed by the white majority, once for being female and once for being minority members—to an "interlocking effects" model. Moreover, it addresses explicitly the conflicts among different groups of women, undercutting once and for all the illusion—if anyone still retains it—that all women are sisters with common experience and common goals. This is an important advance.

Glenn's "interlocking effects" model, however, still cuts rather broadly. First, it contrasts all "white" women with all "women of color," losing important ethnic and class distinctions among various "white women" on the one hand and also between various nonwhite women on the other. Glenn's model does not at all address the situation of some "ethnics" whose "whiteness" is uncertain. If Jews are sometimes treated as "white" in current debates, that whiteness is nevertheless relatively recent and insecure.[4] Nor does this whiteness stand up to scrutiny, because many of the world's Jews are Arabs, Africans, and members of other races. Even some American Jews descended from East European communities may be darker in skin and hair color than many Americans whose "African-ness" or "Hispanic-ness" are unquestioned. The majority of American Jews are perhaps best categorized as "almost white." About the almost white or the sometimes white, Glenn's model is silent.

Second, we need a model that will address the ways in which pressure from outside the group leads to conflict within the group. Just as "white women" deflect pain from themselves by inflicting it on minority women, minority communities do the same to "their women."[5]

Discrimination against "almost white" women may be subtle and largely unremarked. Jewish women of the generations since World War II, for example, are not generally relegated to menial jobs. They are, however, subjected to the same prejudices as are Jewish men, with the addition of two even more prevalent, stigmatizing stereotypes: "Jewish mother" and "Jewish princess."

Some Jewish feminists, moreover, have recently pointed out that the Jewish community itself discriminates in severely hurtful ways against Jewish women. Some complain of feeling excluded from Judaism (Pogrebin, 1991), "peripheralized" within it (Adler, 1983), deprived of accurate historical memory and access to spiritual resources (Plaskow, 1990), taught that "Jew" means "man" ("My own Synagogue is the only place in the world where I am not named Jew" [Ozick, 1983, p. 125]), and made to feel that men have the "right to grant or withhold, to moderate or mediate, women's access to *Torah* [religious teachings] [and] to God" (Magnus, 1992).

Additional complaints are that Jewish communal institutions exclude women from the higher levels; that men batter women and the community does not want to hear about it (Scarf, 1983); and that men level at women a vicious brand of public humor (E. T. Beck, lecture at University of Illinois, Urbana-Champaign, 1990), augmenting Gentiles' anti-Semitic stereotypes with contributions of their own, including ugly racist/sexist slurs against the "Jewish mother" and the "Jewish princess." Perhaps because of this perceived pattern, the author of the *Forward* article assumes that Jewish men are behind the misrepresentation of Jewish women in the media: "Jewish men . . . sluff [off false anti-Semitic labels such as pushy or materialistic] by . . . applying them to Jewish women. [But t]he displacement of a burden does not make it disappear; it only shifts its weight" (Weiner, 1993, p. 10). Accurate or not, such a perception by Jewish women can only add to their sense of isolation and stigma within their own community as well as in society as a whole—another sign of systemic problems.

Such systemic problems acknowledged by the entire community include the twin issues of assimilation and intermarriage. A frequently quoted figure is that of all American Jews who marry, half marry non-Jews. In some regions of the country (with smaller Jewish populations) the figure is much higher. A related issue is the degree to which intermarrying Jews dissociate from each other in order to dissociate from unpleasant stereotypes (Cowan & Perel, 1992, p. 61), that is, to flee the stigma of belonging to the Jewish minority. This is undoubtedly much of what Philip Roth's character means by "the original Jewish [man's] dream of escape . . . with the beloved shiksa" (i.e., Gentile woman) (Roth, 1986, p. 125).

Mass Communication

Theory

At the most public interface between a marginal (or minority) group and the larger society, Gitlin (1980) has observed that media personnel appoint as newsmakers individuals they feel to be representative of marginal groups. Other individuals become invisible. We can readily translate his insight from the context of news to that of entertainment. The media have appointed certain relatively presentable or amusing male Jewish characters as fictional representations of Jews. Although some Jews—males—are elevated to the status of spokesperson or representative, others—females—are "symbolically annihilated."

Even members of the minority group in question may, perhaps inadvertently, collaborate with the process by suppressing alternative voices within the group. Patai (1991) has proposed that stigmatizing a minority group leads to the phenomenon of "surplus visibility," the feeling among minority members and others that whatever members of that group say or do, it is too much, and, moreover, they are being too conspicuous about it (p. A52).

The group then tends to work hard to avoid drawing attention to itself. Members, in fact, police each other's visibility. Accusations of "surplus visibility" lead minority members to try for invisibility. Hence, even when programs have Jewish producers or writers, they may not push for changes—like the inclusion of more Jewish female characters—that result in higher visibility for their minority.

In the Jewish case, furthermore, the drive to avoid surplus visibility is reinforced by centuries of practice because of the millennia-long "Christian obsession with Jews" (Eckardt, 1989), which has historically resulted in "super-scrutiny" of Jewish populations.[6] Avoiding "surplus visibility" is a long-standing Jewish survival strategy.

In fact, a society under stress often acts out its anxieties by increasing its control over women (Sanday, 1981), and—I might add—women's images (following Douglas, 1966). Because male media managers and creative workers use their control over program material or personnel to express their own fears and fantasies (Faludi, 1991), the agenda of a male Jewish producer or writer might be expected to mesh well with that of Gentile producers, writers, network executives, or advertising authorities whose practice it is to obscure most minority females.[7]

Author (and co-founder of *Ms.*) Letty Cottin Pogrebin (1991)—writing from her experience in a women's black-Jewish support group (moderated by Donna Shalala, currently U.S. Secretary of Health)—concluded that minority men tend to react to "defamatory or discriminatory treatment not solely" in racial or ethnic terms but as an attack on their manhood, which they can then redeem by "lord[ing] it over [*their*] perceived inferiors, [their] women" or by

"reject[ing] them [as mates] in favor of women of the dominant majority"
(p. 280). This is much the same mechanism described by Glenn (1992) as
enabling white women to secure their status by "ladying it," so to speak, over
women of color. In any event, as Farquhar (1992) points out, no matter what
its origin, once a set of negative images takes hold (even in a scholarly
tradition, let alone a media industry) about a woman (or a group of women),
it "act[s] like computer viruses, infecting [all] subsequent [representations]"
(p. 12).

We see just why, whether or not Jews may be among the "gatekeepers"
(White, 1950) of specific programs, Jewish women, like other minority
women (except some blacks) do not get through the gates. When the "virus"
of excluding and stigmatizing Jewish women is perpetuated by Jews as well as
non-Jews, even by feminists (see Pogrebin, 1982), and saddest of all, by Jewish
women, we see a kind of "spiral of invisibility" (compare Noelle-Neuman's
[1973] "spiral of silence").

Those with whom I have discussed this issue commonly object that the
near-total absence of Jewish women is justified by "the demographics." Indeed, Jews constitute only about 2.4% of the U.S. population, compared to
about 12.1% for blacks. Demographics alone, however, do not explain everything. They do not explain why male Jews, representing 1.2% (i.e., half of
2.4%) of the American population, outnumber, as major characters on prime
time, Hispanics of both sexes, who constitute 9% of the U.S. population. It
seems clear that audience demographics may influence but do not determine
representation on prime time. But it is not the proportion of people in the
general population that makes a difference—or we would have advertisers
clamoring to address the unemployed, the underemployed, and the impris-
oned. Nor does representation on screen depend directly on how many people
of a group have discretionary income, because Hispanics do constitute a large
market in this country. On the other hand, blacks living in households with
incomes of more than $35,000 a year—surely a desirable audience—outnum-
ber the entire American Jewish population by 3 to 2, and interesting and
likable black characters on television are both more numerous and more
diverse than the Jewish characters.

The relevant variables are several and complexly interrelated. Briefly, to
appear as important protagonists on prime time a group must have discretionary income *and* it must be seen by advertisers and producers as having
discretionary income *and* the way must be cleared by a tradition of depicting
that group as strong and interesting. In this confusing situation it is natural

that there will be more blacks than Jews on prime time. More blacks than Jews have incomes above the $35,000 mark, the advertising world generally is aware of black buying power, and television has a tradition several decades old of depicting a variety of heroic black characters.[8]

What the demographics do not explain, however, is why male Jews so vastly outnumber female Jews on prime time. Nobody is claiming that the real-life American Jewish population contains 7 or 8 times as many men as women, or that every last male Jew is married to or dating a Gentile (or, in one case, a non-American Jew), as are major Jewish characters on prime time. The agenda has been set (McCombs & Shaw, 1972), and Jewish women are mostly not on it. Years after it first appeared, the "virus" is working, not necessarily at the level of ideology or creative strategy, but at a more mechanical level, that of occupational routines (Whitney, 1978) for selecting (in this case, dramatic) elements from those available. Having little else to draw on, when creators of characters attempt to eschew negative stereotypes, they may replace them, as Weiner points out, with nothing.

In a sense, too, we may view female American Jews as being treated according to Said's (1978) model of "orientalization." Just as the middle-class male European constructs himself as a civilized Christian by distancing and "exoticising" the non-European Other, so American society, including Jewish men, constructs itself as objective, rational, and civilized partly by its "orientalization" of minority women, including Jewish women. Minority women may of course collude with this process, distancing themselves, for example, from other black women who are poorer or blacker or other Jewish women who are more ethnic and/or religious.[9]

We may consider, as well, Alloula's (1986) model of the "harem"—that is, the Westerner's concept of the exotic, deficient, isolated, and specifically female foreigner in "the Other's" culture, a female whose distorted humanity is depicted through the lens of a distorted sexuality. In the Jewish case, this sexuality is distorted by the observer into several contradictory directions.

The Jewish woman is sensuous and frigid, motherly and destructively over-maternal, clever and stupid, nurturing and materialistic, self-sacrificing but also hyper-feminine: over-made-up, overdressed, overwrought, shrill, shallow, and self-absorbed. She is, in a sense, the female counterpart of the traditional European and American anti-Semitic stereotype of the Jew—greedy, materialistic, ostentatious, pushy, conniving, shallow, unmanly, ungentlemanly. Jewish women have thus fallen heir to a feminized version of anti-Semitic imagery no longer considered acceptable when applied to men.

The American Jew is, for historical reasons, one might say, "almost a white man or woman." Until after the Holocaust, Americans considered Jews a race—and not a desirable one. Jews have been accused over the years of comprising "half the criminals in New York City" (Fried, 1980, p. 57[10]); of funding the international Communist conspiracy; of the evils of capitalism; of being, at the start of the century, too poor, filthy, lazy, and ignorant, and now, at the end of it, too middle class; of having too much power in the media; and of being, in general, not good enough, not American enough, not "white" enough, and "not our sort" (Dershowitz, 1991)[11] and "not one of us." Manhood was at stake here, too. The Jewish man was said to be weak, physically inept, and incapable of sports or hard labor; neither a "gentleman," therefore, nor a "a real man." Now it is the Jewish woman who is not good enough, not one of us, weak, and inept; neither a "lady" nor a "real woman."

Technology

A continuing theme in American life has been the worry by the "traditional cultural elite" (Sklar, 1975, p. 134) that scary new technologies, like movies, supposedly controlled "not in spots only . . . but entirely" (Ford, 1921, p. 8, as cited by Gabler, 1988, p. 277) by "foreign" elements, "recent citizens" (Sklar, 1975, p. 249), or to put it simply, Jews (Gabler, 1988, p. 2), might be poisoning the wells of our nation's intellectual, artistic, political, and moral life (Gabler, 1988, p. 2; Sklar, 1975, p. 249). American mass communication research, in fact, evolved largely through studies (such as the Payne Fund Studies of the 1920s) on the "effects" of movies on audiences.

These "effects" studies were first prompted by Nativist concerns that, as one author wrote, it "is the genius of that race to create problems of a moral character" (Ford, 1921, p. 8, as cited by Gabler, 1988, p. 277). Anti-Semitic imagery was intertwined early and often with apprehensions about the media, with quantum leaps in reasoning to claims about Jews' supposed power through the media over the American people and even the government.

In September 1941, Charles Lindbergh charged that Jews, the British, and the Roosevelt administration were "pressing this country toward war," the Jews being "the most dangerous because of their large ownership and influence in our motion pictures, our press, our radio and our government" (Friedman, 1987, p. 45). U.S. Senator Gerald P. Nye, who late in 1941 told Americans that "if anti-Semitism exists in America, Jews have themselves to blame" (Friedman, 1987, p. 45), complained during World War II that American moviemakers should not be trusted with any share in the war effort because they were "insufficiently American in origin, intellect and character" (Sklar, 1975, p. 249).

Clearly, anti-Semitism has involved issues of class, gender, and race. It has also been interwoven with the fear of new communication technologies. Jews in the media are felt to endanger both private morality and the common weal. Some who no longer worry that Jews are in league with the Devil are not so sure about whether they are safe from Jews who, they fear, control "the media."[12]

Method

A word on method is appropriate because of the peculiar nature of the problem of dealing with missing television representations. The truth is, that the "Jewishness" of female characters is often so well suppressed that the scholar, even a Jewish scholar, can find herself puzzling over "who is" and "who isn't."

It is, of course, true that in "real life" Jews can often not tell who other Jews are. The task is made more complicated by assimilation and intermarriage; last names—which many use as clues to ethnicity—descend, after all, through the male line (and are adopted by wives), whereas Jewish identity, according to Jewish tradition, descends through the female line (or is conveyed through formal conversion by appropriate authorities). Jewish "looks," moreover, may not be readily distinguishable from Italian or other "looks." The accents some identify as "Jewish" are usually nothing more or less than New York City regional speech.

The situation is, however, even more subtle and complex on television. After all, in "real life," you can ask, if you want. Watching television, you can only stay alert for any clues that may happen to come your way.

Sometimes it is simple. Producers may obviously intend a character to be Jewish, giving him or her a "Jewish" name and designing some explicit Jewish references, as in the cases of Miles Silverberg (*Murphy Brown*) and Joel Fleischman (*Northern Exposure*), who refer regularly and explicitly to their Jewishness. This pattern obtains, however, only for a few male characters and not for female ones.

Most often, producers seem to intend a character to be Jewish—but not too Jewish. This is true of some male characters and all the female characters.

In order to ferret out female Jewish identity, one must usually be an experienced viewer of the program. Furthermore, Jewish female characters are played by Gentiles more often than are Jewish male characters.

Jewish men play Jewish characters more often than Jewish women play Jewish characters. Conversely, male Jewish characters are played more often by Jewish actors than are Jewish females played by Jewish actresses. Because the tendency is to let the "Gentile-ness" (if any) of a performer or character prevail over any Jewishness, the net result is that Jewish identity is suppressed more in the case of female characters and actresses than in the case of males.

The female character's Jewishness is largely obliterated and is conveyed only by subtle or infrequent cues. Producers may strew a few subtle hints among a year or more of programs. For example, in two or three episodes of *The Commish* (ABC) and another two or three of *Reasonable Doubts* (NBC), a character confirmed the Jewish status that the names "Rachel Scali" and "Tess Kaufman" only suggest by explicitly saying, "She's Jewish." Other clues are Tess's grandmother's candlesticks (*Reasonable Doubts*) and Rachel's Jewish-seeming brother (*The Commish*).

Sometimes, producers seem ambivalent. Occasionally, they seem to make up their minds as they go along. Viewers who watched *L.A. Law* since its inception in 1987 may have been puzzled in 1991-1992 to see, when Roxanne Melman (played by Susan Ruttan) went shopping for a headstone for her father's grave, that the scene opened on a shot of a Hebrew engraving. Before his death, Mr. Melman, played by Vincent Gardenia, had been celebrating Christmas with roommate Benny Stolowitz, with no mention of his (or Roxanne's) being Jewish. Did the stonemason handle both Gentile and Jewish business?

On a recent show, however, Roxanne announced, "I'm a Jewish girl."[13] One suspects that she *became* a Jewish girl late in the show's history, as one of many changes in the cast and characters.

So clues can help; but clues can fool us, too. On one episode of *thirtysomething*, Ellyn Warren sings a Jewish children's song that "my grandmother taught me." On another episode, however, we meet her Christian parents and hear about her childhood Christmases. Did the producers change their minds, or maybe just lose track of their character?

So clues are not enough. And, of course, one may watch many episodes before happening on a clue. The clues, moreover, are often in code—a song, a Yiddish word, a religious artifact.[14] In addition to watching for clues—which means viewing multiple episodes—one scrutinizes the credits. For example, I surmise that Frankie's business partner (on *Sisters*) is supposed to be Jewish when I see that the credits list a character named Barry Gold, played by an actor named Ron Fassler. I see, however, many fewer Jewish women's names than men's, whether because men may be more openly Jewish, or because there are more Jewish men in the industry. Male Jews, moreover, are more often easily identified on the screen by virtue of the characters' and actors' names and through conventional signals involving speech patterns and comic routines, not to mention their greater likelihood of referring explicitly and frequently to their Jewishness.

Six years' acquaintance with anyone in "real life" would certainly more than suffice to clear up any ambiguities one wanted to clear up. Six years of watching *L.A. Law* introduced ambiguities, rather than resolving them. I have therefore supplemented these methods by reference to Jewish and other periodicals. The difficulty of determining which characters (and which actresses) fall into the category under discussion underscores the very problem this chapter addresses, namely the suppression of Jewish identity in female television characters, far beyond any such suppression for male characters, and far more effectively than mere assimilation or confusion normally suppress the Jewishness of "real life" people.

Programming

Shticklessness

Additional sources of confusion arise because traditional Jewish-marked roles and performances handed down from early movies are used on prime time more by male than by female performers (partly, perhaps, because more of the male Jewish characters are played by Jewish performers). There is a traditional comic *shtick* for Jewish males that may go back to the early days of film when, in the relentless stereotyping of all races and ethnicities, it fell to Jews (usually male Jews) to be frequently depicted as "gullible, silly Jews . . . butts of the comic action . . . buffoons" (Friedman, 1987, p. 30), characterizations based partly on the real-life helplessness and bewilderment of a largely immigrant population. Jewish male performers have fallen heir to a persona, made famous by Woody Allen, that one might characterize as the nervous, frantic, overreacting little Jew who is never quite at home in what other people consider ordinary surroundings.

Thus, Miles Silverberg, played by Grant Shaud on *Murphy Brown* (CBS), is in a constant state of panic, in contrast both to Murphy and to Audrey Cohen, his British girlfriend; Paul Reiser's nervous character on *Mad About You* (NBC) contrasts with the relative calm of his Gentile wife; Rob Morrow's nervous character on *Northern Exposure* (CBS), an urban Jew in the wilderness, contrasts with the calm of his Gentile romantic interest, Maggie O'Connell, who calls him (during the 1991-1992 season) "an emotional car-wreck"; and Jay Thomas's nervous, compulsive character on *Love and War* (CBS) contrasts with the relative calm and more stubborn compulsiveness of Gentile girlfriend Wally.[15]

There is no corresponding shtick for Jewish female comic characters, for no comic Jewish female character exists in a lead role.[16] Where they do appear, female Jewish characters tend to be quiet, supportive, relatively colorless characters, like Rachel Scali (played by Theresa Saldana), the Gentile hero's Jewish wife in *The Commish* (ABC, 1991-1992, 1992-1993), whose job it is to offset the humor and liveliness of her husband by being sweetly supportive and, as of this writing, extremely pregnant. Female Jews as supporting characters (both dramatically and sociologically speaking) also include the somewhat stilted women in *Brooklyn Bridge* (CBS, 1991-1992, Fall 1992), some played by Gentile actresses.

Although Tess Kaufman (Marlee Matlin, *Reasonable Doubts,* 1991-1992, Fall 1992) is by no means repressed or colorless, it is nevertheless worth noting that the character, like the actress, is deaf, and so speaks almost entirely through sign language and (male) interpreters. It is almost as if, in a sense, we "pay" for seeing a Jewish heroine's image by not getting to hear a Jewish heroine's voice. Thus the "less than white" woman is muted.

Most commonly, the speech of Jewish female characters (unlike that of many black female characters) is stripped of any peculiarly "ethnic" energies or intonations. Not only style, but content, too, is watered down (again, with the exception of Tess Kaufman of *Reasonable Doubts*[17]). If an accent does appear, it is an unidentifiable generic accent,[18] like that of the grandmother on *Brooklyn Bridge,* played by an apparently Gentile actress, and is coupled with a vaguely Anglo-Saxon demeanor, achieving only a kind of stilted, vague, generic "differentness."

One effect of so frequently casting Gentiles in female Jewish roles is to deprive Jewish actresses of work, or at least certain kinds of work, and the chance to develop their own expressive style as Jews (an opportunity accorded a certain number of Jewish males). A corollary effect is to erase the Jewishness of female characters. Speech patterns and other items in Jewish culture's (or, one should say, Jewish cultures') behavioral repertoire(s) tend to disappear. The particulars of Yiddish culture vanish, depriving females, though not males, of their culture's traditional irony, emotional range, facial expressions, gestures, and humor.

Although female Jewish characters are emptied of cultural style and content, the energies of Jewish actresses are given to other kinds of ethnic portrayals.[19] Theresa Saldana plays subdued, supportive Jewish wife Rachel, but actress Rhea Perlmann of *Cheers* turns in a lively, colorful characterization as Carla, a (presumably Catholic) Italian (for in television-land, all Italians and Irish are Catholic), and Miriam Margolyes plays the Italian title role on *Frannie's Turn* (CBS, fall 1992). Ashlee Levitch plays the Protestant family's daughter, Francie, on *I'll Fly Away* (PBS); Jordana Shapiro played the Gentile Westons' daughter on *thirtysomething* (McNeil, 1991). Roseanne Arnold, who says she is half-Jewish, plays energetic, emotional, humorous white-Protestant Roseanne Connor. On *Mad About You*, the Jewish husband's ex-girlfriend, played by an actress with a Jewish name, Lisa Edelstein, turns up in one episode with a Jewish-looking face but with Anglo-Saxon speech and demeanor and the name Lynn Stoddard.

The unacceptability of Jewish women encompasses performers as well as characters. Even *TV Guide*—a part of the broadcasting industry in its own way—singles out Jewish women as negative examples, even where a Jewish man is a positive example. The "Best-Dressed, Worst-Dressed" issue (October 17-23, 1992) names three Jewish performers: One best-dressed Jewish man, Jerry Seinfeld ("indisputable flair"), and two worst-dressed Jewish women: Mayim Bialik (*Blossom*, NBC)—"frightening fiasco . . . freaky"—and Miriam Margolyes (*Frannie's Turn*, CBS)—"secondhand horror."

Distance

The female Jewish character is distanced from the Jewish actress and the Jewish audience as well as from Jewish male characters. For when a Jewish character or Jewish actress does appear, the portrayal is rendered as little "Jewish" and as little informed by "Jewish" style as possible. Every effort is exerted to mitigate whatever danger the few female Jewish characters might pose to the equilibrium of flight-poised, escape-minded, Gentile-seeking Jewish males.

Perhaps the simplest distancing tactic is geographical. *Northern Exposure* (CBS, 1991-1992; fall 1992) ensures the distance of the Jewish hero from Jewish women by placing him in a tiny Alaskan settlement (where he is working off his medical school financing). The only Jewish woman he encounters is the ex-girlfriend who briefly visits from New York.

Living in the wilderness, Joel Fleischman embodies two superimposed archetypes: the Jew with his Gentile woman and the classic American lone-hero archetype. Over both are then superimposed the frantically neurotic Jewish comic male shtick.

To review briefly: The classic hero, always an American-born Protestant white male (Huckleberry Finn and his grown-up counterparts, including numerous heroes of the classic Western movie), embodies two worlds—civilization and savagery (Cawelti, 1975; Fiedler, 1966). In perpetual flight from civilization and white women, like John Wayne's Western character who tells his fiancee, "Margaret, you're a nuisance. Let's call it off, Margaret; I have country to put behind me" (*Angel and the Badman,* 1947), a man is constructed as a Western hero precisely through this flight.

Joel Fleischman reproduces this hero in comic, mutated form as an urban Jew in the Alaskan wilderness, distrusting trees, animals, and guns, gradually reconstructing himself as a healthier, more vigorous person (more of "a real man") through his flight from Jews. As with Jewish characters since movies began (Friedman, 1982), his Jewish past and his religious/ethnic ties hold no promise of growth, no lure of return. They must be transcended before the character can grow.

Thus, informed of his uncle's death, he sets out to round up 10 Jews—10 male Jews (because his uncle was traditional, although Joel is not)—for a *minyan,* the quorum necessary for saying the *Kaddish.* Joel spends a whole show searching, not to find his Jewish roots, but to fulfill a religious obligation for which he has no real feeling and that is not even his obligation—because he is not the son of the deceased. And no sooner has he rounded up an assortment of 10 diverse Jewish strangers from all over Alaska, than he dismisses them. They are not his community. "You are my community," he tells his Gentile friends.

Similarly, it is not his Jewish ex-girlfriend Elaine visiting from New York, but bush pilot Maggie O'Connell, his Gentile girlfriend, who excites, intrigues, and engages him. She challenges him to grow out of his Jewish neurosis. His fascination with her leads to his emotional and spiritual growth.

His relation to the wilderness is a comic inversion of the white lone hero's relation to it. To the mutated Jewish hero, the Christian white woman represents, not a barrier to salvation in the pure, unfettered wilderness (Cawelti, 1975; Fiedler, 1966), but the hope of escaping the neurotic fetters of his Jewish background. She will award him the magical cure for his Jewishness: escape with a "beloved shiksa."

Geographic distancing, with the resulting archetype of ethnic independence, is one tactic. Another distancing tactic is the joke. In *Murphy Brown,* Miles Silverberg aims humorous barbs at offstage Jewish female characters as part of his "neurotic Jewish male" shtick, thereby reaffirming his spiritual and social distance from them. For example, he draws on the "desperate, shrill" stereotype of the socially unacceptable Jewish woman, likening someone's "desperate bid for attention" to his aunt's attempt to impress a new rabbi by wearing provocative clothing (*Murphy Brown, CBS, September 21, 1992*).

Similarly, Corky Sherwood Forest, a Gentile character, bases a joke on the unacceptability of Jewish women as women, claiming that the Max Factor company started in Russia with a "family full of amazingly unattractive women" (*Murphy Brown, CBS, November 11, 1991*).

When Miles refers to his mother, the context is invariably comic and stereotypical; Murphy has both comic and serious references to her mother, with obvious efforts to break stereotypes. When Jewish mothers are taken seriously and accorded dignity, they most often remain offstage. For example, Frankie, on *Sisters* (NBC, October 17, 1992), quotes a Yiddish proverb to the effect that man proposes and God disposes (the actual Yiddish, not quoted in the show, is *"man tracht un Gott lacht"—man thinks but God laughs*) that she heard from her Jewish mother-in-law.

Seinfeld's parents appear in some episodes as rather stock Jewish-parent characters. Miles Silverberg's (*Murphy Brown*) parents turn up in one episode (playing against the stereotype, as sixties activists who ruined his childhood with their idealism). Other Jewish characters hardly seem to have mothers. Jewish female characters are distanced from Jewish relatives even as secondary characters.

On one Saturday night (October 10, 1992), an incidental character on *Empty Nest* (ABC), Arthur (played by Jerry Orbach, who also played the Jewish father in *Dirty Dancing*), marries his Gentile woman in the main protagonist's living room, without any Jewish relatives present. On *Sisters* (ABC), Frankie, who is married to a Jew, Mitch Margolis (played by Ed Molinaro), meets his relatives only when she accompanies him to New York (that quintessentially stereotypical Jewish location) for his nephew's Bar Mitzvah.

On *The Commish* (ABC), the distance of Commissioner Tony Scali's Jewish wife Rachel from Jewish males is emphasized by the absence to date (October 1992) of any Jewish relatives except a snoopy, free-loading brother who has now been sent on to mooch off other relatives. The distance is even more powerfully highlighted by the presence in this household of a rather Gentile Jew, son David (played by Kaj-Erik Eriksen), whom they are raising as a Jew,[20] and who is somehow the Nordic blond child of a brown-haired Italian character played by an actor with a Greek name (Michael Chiklis) and a dark-haired Jewish character played by an actress with a Catholic Hispanic name (Theresa Saldana). The distance is preserved.

If two continuing prime-time Jews somehow manage to evade the norms and mate with each other, an odd exogamy code dictates that at least one will not be American. Hence Miles Silverberg's girlfriend Audrey Cohen (on *Murphy Brown*) is British and Tess Kaufman's temporary lover Asher Roth (*Reasonable Doubts*) is Israeli.

Flickering Past

Some characters hardly do or say anything. We only glimpsed—at the Sabbath dinner table—the quiet, supportive, unmemorable wife of Rosie's boss, Ben Meyer (played by Ron Rifkin, on *Trials of Rosie O'Neill* [CBS, 1991-1992] starring Sharon Gless). His wife had to be Jewish, because he was Orthodox; but she was kept offstage. A Jewish mother or two flickers past even faster. Tess Kaufman's ex-mother-in-law turns up briefly on a *Reasonable Doubts* episode; her own mother appears even more briefly on another.

Miles Silverberg's (*Murphy Brown*) radical activist parents visit him in one episode. Michael's mother (*thirtysomething*, currently in syndication on Lifetime Channel; played by Barbara Barrie, who also played Barney Miller's ex-wife, 1975-1976) visits when his son Leo is born. But she plays so effectively against the stereotype that she hardly says a word; her gentleman friend Ben does most of the talking and emotional relating. Ben, rather than Michael's mother, convinces Michael to have the new baby circumcised, for the sake of Jewish continuity.

The program hardly touches on the fact that in the absence of a Jewish mother (Michael's wife Hope, the baby's mother, is Gentile), tradition does not recognize "Jewish continuity." The *mohel* (official who circumcises a Jewish baby) has to be tricked into performing the ceremony, part of which is a sin, being a "blessing said in vain" (because it erroneously implies that the baby is Jewish). In television-land, Jewish women are so superfluous that one can proceed as though they existed whether they do or not, then ignore the ethical implications of the deception.

Female Jewish characters, although to a much lesser extent than black or Asian women, also appear occasionally as victims of crime. *Law & Order* and *Reasonable Doubts,* in one episode each (1991-1992), showed us a quiet young widow of a murdered Hasidic Jew, surrounded by her children. An elderly woman, marked as Jewish by her celebration of a Sabbath eve dinner, appeared on one *Commish* episode (1991-1992) as a victim of blackmail.

Jewish women, like other minority women, although (it is my impression) to a lesser extent than they, also appear in the small, transient "judge" roles that "cop," lawyer, and district attorney shows so often need.[21] In addition, the first 2 years of *Night Court* had two older Jewish women as bailiffs.[22]

Occasionally a female Jewish character is allowed a love life, but only a short one. We glimpse a few as transient romantic characters destined to leave male protagonists' lives immediately, if not sooner.

A Jewish girl appeared on a couple of episodes of *I'll Fly Away* (1991-1992), but her parents, after catching continuing character Nathan Bedford in her bed, shipped her off to boarding school, whence she has not been heard from since (as of the show's cancellation and this writing, June 1993). Joel Fleischman's Jewish ex-girlfriend Elaine Shulman (*Northern Exposure*) arrived in town (1991-1992), agreed they had grown past each other, and disappeared back into the void, all in one episode.[23] Jerry Seinfeld (*Seinfeld,* NBC) tells his parents about his breakup with his friend (also a Jewish woman named Elaine): "We decided we don't work as a couple" (1992).[24]

Love does not linger much longer even for a main character. Israeli secret agent Asher Roth appears in Tess Kaufman's life (*Reasonable Doubts*) on December 1, 1992; by early January he has gone, pursuing his secret-agent destiny.[25] Jewish women, it seems, have no romantic future.[26]

Evolutionary Dead Ends

They also seem to have no reproductive future. Not only are Jewish women ignored, unchosen, outgrown, or left offstage; even birth produces almost no new ones. Female Jews, it seems, rarely form families. When they do, they produce sons, as have *The Commish's* Jewish wife Rachel and Frasier's wife Lilith (played by Bebe Neuwirth on *Cheers*). Tess Kaufman (*Reasonable Doubts*) has no husband and no children. Neither does Melissa Steadman (*thirtysomething*). Only Rachel Scali, on the November 21, 1992 episode of *The Commish*, gives birth to a daughter, Sarah—the one Jewish girl-child born on any of these programs.[27]

Important Jewish male protagonists do not produce daughters, either,[28] even the non-Jewish ones that would spring from a non-Jewish mother.[29] Murphy Brown's Jewish lover fathered a son, Avery Brown (born at the end of 1991-1992 season); Frankie's child Thomas George Margolis (*Sisters*; born on the November 14, 1992 episode), fathered by her Jewish husband Mitch Margolis and carried surrogate-fashion by her sister Georgie, is a (non-Jewish[30]) son, to whose Bar Mitzvah—a traditionally male celebration— Frankie is already looking forward long before his birth. Hope, Gentile wife of Jewish husband Michael Steadman of *thirtysomething*, bears a (non-Jewish) son, Leo, in an episode centering around the baby's *brit*—ritual circumcision. The children on *Brooklyn Bridge* are boys.

Adoption, too, brings only sons, as with Jewish husband Stuart Markowitz and Gentile wife Ann Kelsey (on *L.A. Law*; played by a real life Jewish husband/Gentile wife—Michael Tucker/Jill Eikenberry; 1991-1992). The absence of Jewish females, or even Jewish-engendered females, is preserved.

Conclusion

Where, then, are the Jewish women? They are there, if one may venture an obscure formulation, mainly not by being there—that is, by reference and through absence. Except for the occasional tamed, quiet housewife, they are mostly offstage images representing deficits. They are not full, developing characters, but symbols of the undesired aspects of ethnicity.

Whether by plan or by the invisible workings of taken-for-granted assumptions about marketable casting and performances, the design of Jewish female characters works to affirm, precisely through absences or character deficits, the dignity of Jewish male characters. They function as a semiotic resource to nourish, through continual contrast, male characters' connections with a Jewish heritage and their viability in American society. The images of Jewish female characters and their human dignity is, in effect, offered up as the sacrifice with which Jewish male characters seek to ransom themselves.

Only an analysis of the interlocking effects of class, race, gender, and ethnicity on women "not quite white" can reveal the tortuous form taken by this particular brand of narrative oppression. Studying the highly accessible case of Jewish women and the media may help us to recognize other representations that suppress women's, but not men's, ethnic or racial characteristics.[31]

Notes

1. There are varying reactions to the use of the terms *America* and *American,* which will be discussed elsewhere.

2. Even studies of theatrical motion pictures, a subject about which there has been nearly a century in which to accumulate information, comment little on the depictions or relative absence of Jewish women, compared to those of Jewish men. Writing about Jews and theatrical motion pictures, neither Gabler (1988) nor Friedman (1982, 1987) has an index entry for *women,* although Friedman (1982)—but not Pogrebin or Gabler—does comment briefly on the repeated male Jew/female Gentile pairings in film. The male-female imbalance continues unnoted. This is true even when observers (such as Pearl & Pearl, 1993) comment on the almost 100% Jewish intermarriage rate on prime time but ignore the paucity of Jewish women.

3. *The Jewish Press*—roughly a religious counterpart of the *Forward*—that I have been reading during the same period, mid-1992 to the present, has given no attention to this issue as of this writing (summer 1993).

4. Jews, who constitute many racial and ethnic groups with, in fact, a cluster of religions (which some scholars call "Judaisms" (Neusner, Green, & Frerichs, 1987), with a variety of Jewish languages—Yiddish, Hebrew, Judaeo-Spanish, Judaeo-Arabic, and others—have in this country been treated largely as one, unified, separate Jewish race (usually identified with East European Jewry) from which, however, many members can "pass" as white. In recent years, Jews in this country have often been treated and referred to as "white," particularly by many of the nonwhite races who identify Jews with the privileged group.

5. Minority women live in a double bind, constantly confronted not only with harm "their men" do them, but with strictures against addressing it publicly. Consider the censure by the black community of Anita Hill for her public testimony regarding Clarence Thomas (Chrisman & Allen, 1992; Dworkin, 1992; Morrison, 1992; Phelps & Winternitz, 1992). The dignity of minority women has been a social priority for neither our society nor its minorities.

6. Dershowitz (1991), referring to Israel, but with equal applicability to other Jewish populations.

7. And perhaps Jewish females more than others. "They're not mainstream; we wouldn't think of them," an advertising account executive explained to me, with respect to advertising images, adding that black women are, however, included for the sake of "diversity" and Asian women may be shown in advertising because they are considered "exotic."

8. One thinks of *Julia* (September 1968 through May 1971), about a widowed nurse played by Diahann Carroll (McNeil, 1991, p. 403) and the Robert Culp-Bill Cosby team on *I Spy* (September 1965 through September 1968). Cosby's character was "a Temple graduate, a Rhodes scholar, and a spy whose cover was that of the trainer of a tennis pro" (McNeil, 1991, p. 368).

9. Jewish male characters, too, are subjected to a kind of "orientalization," but only when they are comic characters. Early motion pictures often made Jewish males either buffoons or conniving, greedy stereotypes (Friedman, 1987). Many recent Jewish comic male characters are neurotically frantic. If elements affecting "orientalization" were to be graphed, the graph would have to extend into hyperspace to accommodate dimensions for all the variables: gender, ethnicity, religion, race, socioeconomic status, generation after immigration, and others.

10. Quoting New York City Police Commissioner Theodore A. Bingham, writing in the September 1908 issue of *North American Review*.

11. In fact, it is reported that a founder of the mass communications field, Paul Lazarsfeld, was excluded from desirable academic appointments when he arrived here as a refugee from Austria in the late 1930s, precisely because the word was passed around academe that he was "not our sort." Unwilling to believe in American anti-Semitism, Lazarsfeld believed that the problem must be his German accent.

12. Although the specifics of anti-Semitic paranoia shift about from generation to generation, resolution is never achieved. As a result, Jewish observers have noted (Dershowitz, 1991; Neusner, 1981), to this day Jews feel and behave as continuing guests in this country rather than as full citizens. As recently as the 1992 primaries, Louisiana gubernatorial candidate David Duke urged mass deportation of American Jews. The Anti-Defamation League has recently reported that 20% of the American public admits to anti-Semitic attitudes.

13. In contrast to Miles Silverberg and Joel Fleischman, who mention their Jewishness early and often, and to other male Jewish characters who are openly Jewish from the start even if they do not often dwell on Jewish issues.

14. Even in a theatrical motion picture, in which clues have at most about 3 hours in which to assert themselves, filmmakers may play coy. Sometimes half a film or nearly all of it can go by before we really know for sure that a character is Jewish. For example, in *Fame* we learn Doris is Jewish only when she creates a speech about it; in *Seize the Day* we know the Robin Williams character is Jewish only near the end of the movie, when we see his mother's gravestone engraved with Hebrew letters.

15. Some non-comic male Jews overreact, too, only non-comically and in a carefully motivated manner. Michael Steadman of *thirtysomething* made panicky assumptions requiring his Gentile wife to steady him through a spiritual crisis. Ben Meyer, Rosie's boss on the short-lived *Trials of Rosie O'Neill* (CBS, 1991-1992), facing double binds in his job, worried himself into physical illness.

16. Although we may interpret "half-Jewish" Roseanne Arnold's comic persona as a kind of anti-stereotype—the poor but exuberant non-New-Yorker, who comically threatens her children, serves awful food, and yells when thwarted (rather than playing the martyr or manipulator of the stereotypes). Also, Dr. Lilith Sternin, an ensemble character on *Cheers,* is apparently Jewish, playing against the stereotype by being an "icy" (McNeil, 1991, p. 145), repressed workaholic.

17. Her Jewishness is most explicit in later episodes of 1991-1992, when she refers to her Jewish experience and ethical orientation and when a co-worker asks their supervisor to transfer one of her cases to him because as a Jew she might be biased.

18. The character says she comes from Poland. Most Polish Jews spoke Yiddish. Even when Joel Grey appears as new immigrant Cousin Jacob (November 14, 1992) and sprinkles his speech with Yiddish words, he uses that generic "other" accent. (I note Stuart Ewen's objection [personal communication, March, 1993] that the *Brooklyn Bridge* accent sounds Polish. I wonder, however, how many viewers can tell that.)

Producers avoid Yiddish accents like a kind of cultural plague. For example, the producers of *Star Trek: The Next Generation* had considered making Lt. Worf's adoptive human parents (played by Theodore Bikel and Georgia Brown, and who briefly appear in one or two episodes) Jewish, but decided that would be "too ridiculous" and gave them unspecified, generic accents. Using non-Jewish actors can, moreover, result in jarring mispronunciations, as when Ed Molinaro (playing Mitch Margolis on *Sisters*) calls a *mezuzah* (short *u* as in *look*), a *muh-zooo-zah*.

19. This is not just a matter of lumping together all "otherness," for in that case, one would expect more instances like that of Tess Kaufman, with her additional otherness—being deaf—and more Jewish women as parts of "otherness" ensembles, for example, in sets of black, Jewish, Oriental, and Hispanic characters.

20. Following Jewish law, because he is the offspring of a Jewish mother.

21. On *My Two Dads* (NBC, September 1987-June 1990), Florence Stanley, who has played several Jewish (and several ambiguous) roles, played the judge, whose last name was Wilbur and whose ethnicity/religion I still did not know after months of viewing.

22. After actress Selma Diamond, 1984-1985, died in 1985 and her replacement, Florence Halop, 1985-1986, died in 1986, the next actress in the part was a young black, Marsha Warfield.

23. I am told she briefly reappeared in one additional episode.

24. Angharad Valdivia points out that Elaine, a continuing character on *Seinfeld*, has been allowed only "a string of unsuccessful romantic involvements."

25. Whereas the American Jewish hero leaves Jewish women in order to transcend them and find his fulfillment by becoming absorbed into American civilization, this Israeli Jewish hero leaves his Jewish woman in charge of protecting American civilization (in her capacity as a highly principled district attorney)—while he goes off to protect Israeli civilization.

26. A sign of hope is to be found in a show recently resurrected after a short life and somewhat longer death. Linda Lavin has recently (as of June 1993) reappeared in *Room for Two* (a show that was previously canceled after a few episodes), playing Edie, an apparently Jewish character. As of this writing (June 28, 1993), Edie has just turned down a proposal from Jack, an apparently Jewish character played by Ron Rifkin, who also played Orthodox Jew Ben Meyer on the short-lived *Trials of Rosie O'Neill*), but they remain romantically involved. It is too soon to tell whether *Room for Two* will be revived again and will break the pattern discussed here. It should be noted, also, that these are middle-aged characters with grown children. Perhaps their romantic choices are seen as less crucial than those of younger characters.

27. Although daughters may exist as older siblings when the series begins; the new births are sons, except Rachel Scali's daughter Sara.

28. Except in backstory. Several Jewish men who acquire sons during these series already have had daughters. Stuart Markowitz (*L.A. Law*) has a long-lost teenage daughter who appeared in a few episodes in 1991-1992—wearing, however, a briefly visible cross. Mitch Margolis (*Sisters*) is the father of Teddy's teenage daughter, Cat Margolis, whom he fathered before he became Teddy's sister Frankie's husband and fathered the fetus that Frankie's sister Georgie carries for Frankie as a "surrogate" (*Sisters*, October 24, 1992). From prior seasons, *thirtysomething's* Michael and his Gentile wife, Hope, already have 4-year-old Janey when Hope gives birth to Leo. Interestingly, two out of the four daughters of Jews are named Sara (on *L.A. Law* and *The Commish*)—the name of the Bible's first female Jew.

29. According to traditional Jewish law, the child inherits the mother's religion, not the father's.

30. Thomas Margolis, however, is not Jewish, having been born of a non-Jewish mother. Jewish law gives him the option of choosing to be Jewish when he reaches Bar Mitzvah age.

31. Examples include programs (*Heat of the Night* comes to mind) on which positive, middle-class black female characters, but not male ones, are played only by light-skinned actors.

References

Adler, R. (1983). The Jew who wasn't there: Halakhah and the Jewish woman. In S. Heschel (Ed.), *On being a Jewish feminist: A reader* (pp. 3-11). New York: Schocken.

Alloula, M. (1986). *The colonial harem*. Minneapolis: University of Minnesota Press.

Cawelti, J. (1975). *The six-gun mystique*. Bowling Green, OH: Bowling Green State University Popular Press.

Chrisman, R., & Allen, R. (1992). *Court of appeal: The black community speaks out on the racial and sexual politics of Clarence Thomas vs. Anita Hill*. New York: Ballantine.

Cowan, R., & Perel, E. (1992). Intermarriage and the Jewish world. *Tikkun, 7*(3), 59-64, 94-95.

Dershowitz, A. (1991). *Chutzpah*. Boston: Little, Brown.

Douglas, M. (1966). *Purity and danger: An analysis of the concepts of pollution and taboo*. London: Ark Paperbacks.

Dworkin, R. (1992, October 25). One year later, the debate goes on. *New York Times Book Review*, p. 1.

Eckardt, A. R. (1989). *Black-woman-Jew: Three wars for human liberation*. Bloomington: Indiana University Press.

Faludi, S. (1991). *Backlash: The undeclared war against American women*. New York: Crown Publishers.

Farquhar, E. (1992, May 3). The dowager got a bad rap [Review of the book *Dragon lady: The life and legend of the last empress of China*, by S. Seagrave]. *New York Times Book Review*, p. 12.

Fiedler, L. (1966). *Love and death in the American novel* (2nd ed., rev.). New York: Stein & Day.

Ford, H. (1921, January 1). Jewish control of the American theater. *Dearborn Independent*, p. 8.

Fried, A. (1980). *The rise and fall of the Jewish gangster in America*. New York: Holt, Rinehart & Winston.

Friedman, L. D. (1982). *Hollywood's image of the Jew*. New York: Frederick Ungar.

Friedman, L. D. (1987). *The Jewish image in American film: Seventy years of Hollywood's vision of Jewish characters and themes*. Secaucus, NJ: Citadel.

Gabler, N. (1988). *An empire of their own: How the Jews invented Hollywood*. Garden City, NY: Anchor/Doubleday.

Gitlin, T. (1980). *The whole world is watching: Mass media in the making and unmaking of the New Left*. Berkeley: University of California Press.

Glenn, E. N. (1992). From servitude to service work: Historical continuities in the racial division of paid reproductive labor. *Signs: Journal of Women in Culture and Society, 18*(1), 1-43.

Magnus, S. (1992, Fall). Kol isha. *Outlook*, pp. 7-9, 28. [Available from Women's League for Conservative Judaism, 48 East 74 Street, New York, NY 10021.]

McCombs, M. E., & Shaw, D. L. (1972). The agenda-setting function of mass media. *Public Opinion Quarterly, 36*(2), 176-187.

McNeil, A. (1991). *Total television: A comprehensive guide to programming from 1948 to the present* (3rd ed.). New York: Penguin Books.

Morrison, T. (1992). *Race-ing justice, en-gendering power: Essays on Anita Hill, Clarence Thomas, and the construction of social reality*. New York: Pantheon.

Neusner, J. (1981). *Stranger at home: "The Holocaust," Zionism, and American Judaism*. Chicago: University of Chicago Press.

Neusner, J., Green, W. S., & Frerichs, E. (Eds.). (1987). *Judaisms and their Messiahs at the turn of the Christian era*. New York: Cambridge University Press.

Noelle-Neumann, E. (1973). Return to the concept of powerful mass media. In H. Eguchi & K. Sata (Eds.), *Studies of broadcasting: An international annual of broadcasting science* (pp. 67-112). Tokyo: The Theoretical Research Center, The Radio & TV Culture Research Institute, The Nippon Hoso Kyokai.

Ozick, C. (1983). Notes toward finding the right question. In S. Heschel (Ed.), *On being a Jewish feminist* (p. 125). New York: Schocken.

Patai, D. (1991). Minority status and the stigma of surplus visibility. *Chronicle of Higher Education, 38,* A52.

Pearl, J., & Pearl, J. (1993, October). Television grapples with Jewish identity. *Moment: The Magazine of Jewish Culture and Opinion, 18*(5), 38-45.

Phelps, T., & Winternitz, H. (1992). *Capitol games: The inside story of Clarence Thomas, Anita Hill, and a Supreme Court nomination.* New York: Hyperion.

Plaskow, J. (1990). *Standing again at Sinai: Judaism from a feminist perspective.* San Francisco: Harper.

Pogrebin, L. C. (1982, June). Anti-Semitism in the women's movement. *Ms.,* pp. 45-46.

Pogrebin, L. C. (1991). *Deborah, Golda, and me: Being female and Jewish in America.* New York: Crown.

Roth, P. (1986). *The counterlife.* New York: Penguin.

Said, E. W. (1978). *Orientalism.* New York: Vintage.

Sanday, P. (1981). *Female power and male dominance: On the origins of sexual inequality.* Cambridge, UK: Cambridge University Press.

Scarf, M. (1983). Marriages made in heaven? Battered Jewish wives. In S. Heschel (Ed.), *On being a Jewish feminist: A reader* (pp. 51-64). New York: Schocken.

Sklar, R. (1975). *Movie-made America: A cultural history of American movies.* New York: Vintage.

Weiner, S. (1993, January 22). TV's Jewess problem. *Forward,* pp. 1, 10.

White, D. M. (1950). The gatekeeper: A case study in the selection of news. *Journalism Quarterly, 27,* 383-390.

Whitney, D. C. (1978). *"Information overload" in the newsroom: Two case studies.* Unpublished doctoral dissertation, University of Minnesota.

Appendix 1

Prime-time series of 1991-1992 and 1992-1993 with continuing major male Jewish characters. All have Gentile girlfriends or wives (or, in the case of *Murphy Brown,* employees).

Murphy Brown, CBS
Love and War, CBS
Northern Exposure, CBS
Mad About You, NBC
L.A. Law, NBC
Brooklyn Bridge, CBS
Sisters, NBC

Appendix 2

Prime-time series of 1991-1992 and 1992-1993 with continuing major female Jewish characters.

Seinfeld (NBC). Hero Jerry Seinfeld has a Jewish friend and ex-girlfriend, Elaine.
Reasonable Doubts (NBC). Heroine Tess Kaufman has a Jewish ex-husband, Bruce Kaufman, and a Jewish [Israeli] ex-boyfriend, Asher Roth. No current love interest.
The Commish (ABC). Rachel Scali is wife of Gentile hero Tony Scali.
Cheers (NBC). Dr. Lilith Sternin, wife of Dr. Frasier, one of the ensemble characters, who has now left him.

Appendix 3

Prime-time series from recent years with continuing major Jewish characters, male and female.

My Two Dads (NBC). An apparently Jewish man, Michael Taylor, helping to raise the Gentile daughter of his deceased Gentile ex-girlfriend; played by Paul Reiser, same actor who plays Jewish character in *Mad About You* (Fall 1992). Judge Wilbur, their landlady, played by Florence Stanley, also seems to be Jewish.
thirtysomething (ABC). Michael Steadman, married to a Gentile woman, Hope; one unmarried Jewish woman, Melissa Steadman, unable to get her boyfriends to marry her.
Anything But Love (ABC). Jewish man, Marty Gold, and (apparently) Gentile woman, Hannah Miller (played by half-Jewish Jamie Lee Curtis, herself the product of a union between a Jewish man and Gentile woman, Tony Curtis and Janet Leigh).
Room for Two (ABC). Jewish man Jack, played by Ron Rifkin, and Jewish woman Edie, played by Linda Lavin. Will this series survive this time around?
Trials of Rosie O'Neill (CBS). Heroine's boss is Orthodox Jew Ben Meyer, played by Ron Rifkin, married to a mostly offstage Jewish wife.

12 Watching *Tongues Untie(d)* While Reading *Zami*

Mapping Boundaries in Black Gay and Lesbian Narratives

FRANCES NEGRÓN-MUNTANER

> I have come to believe over and over again that what is most
> important to me must be spoken, made verbal and shared,
> even at the risk of having it bruised or misunderstood.
> Audre Lorde (1984), *Sister Outsider*

A Preface of Location

During the 9 years that I have lived in the United States, I have frequently turned to African American theoreticians, writers, and media makers as

AUTHOR'S NOTE: I would like to thank Angharad Valdivia, Cheryl Wall, and B. Ruby Rich for their useful comments and suggestions for the revision of this chapter.

245

sources of sustenance for my own praxis. Compared to the invisibility and lack of appropriate public forums of discussion on Puerto Rican cultural and political practices, black practices and texts have provided me with a refracted crystal through which to examine my participation as part of a specifically Puerto Rican "diaspora." By producing this "preface of location," I do not imply, as identity disclosures often attempt to suggest, that "if" there were more images, writings, and institutions created by Puerto Ricans for Puerto Ricans, I would not turn to black practices (or any set of others that I may find productive) because I would have already conquered my "own" terrain. Although a context of Puerto Rican "visibility" could well alter and enrich my location and possibilities, I would still not ever fully recognize myself in my "own" (or any other) ethnic, gender, class, or sexually specific context. Thus, it is no doubt one of the assumptions of this intervention that the vitality of any community greatly depends on the quality of its contacts with others. More radically, that it is possible and, indeed, necessary to be an invested voice in struggles and locations that do not necessarily "reflect" one's color, class, gender, and/or sexual practices but instead may invoke practices and discourses of solidarity and community in a larger social context. This last assumption is perhaps one of the most vital legacies of feminism of color in the United States, and a central referent for further dialogue in this chapter. In the following pages, a video by the late black gay videomaker and activist Marlon Riggs (1989), *Tongues Untied*,[1] is "watched" alongside a "reading" of *Zami: A New Spelling of My Name*,[2] a biomythography by poet, writer, and activist Audre Lorde (1982), who died of breast cancer in 1992. In this encounter, some of the stakes of black gay and lesbian representations in relation to a radical politics will be examined and discussed.

The present exploration of two black gay and lesbian identity narratives emerges from several contexts. Around the time that *Tongues Untied* (Riggs, 1989), a video on black gay identity, began to be screened across the country, I found myself working on *Zami: A New Spelling of My Name* (Lorde, 1982). Through this simple "coincidence," watching *Tongues Untied* while reading *Zami*, a potentially fertile terrain for the exploration of identity narratives and their potential political effects was created, because these texts represent two of the most cohesive foundational discourses for black gay and lesbian (respectively) subjectivities. In addition, the tendency of most writing on *Tongues Untied* to constitute a "duplication" (in the sense of enacting effects of the same identity discourses that produced their context), rather than examining how these contexts are produced, also provoked me to undertake this inquiry.[3]

Simultaneously with *Tongues'* popular reception, Audre Lorde was in the process of being canonized by white feminist literary critics as well as actively claimed by black gay and lesbian critics and media makers. Thus the encounter between these two texts, mediated by an(other) subject, promised to produce a different (not privileged) location from which to address the politics of identity raised by these narratives.

The second relevant personal context for this reading is the production of my film *Brincando el Charco: Portrait of a Puerto Rican.* I was already in the process of conceptualizing the film when the *Tongues Untied*/NEA controversy took its course. Although I ultimately abandoned the identity politics premises that sustained my early thinking on *Brincando,* I returned, again and again, to *Tongues* and *Zami* to seek some traces of my discontent; indeed to help me find another way. This second dialogue with the texts produced (for me) a tension between the alleged need for identity discourse in the political terrain and the necessity for a critical examination in relation to the costs of building identity narratives for political action. Perhaps as telling of my own politics as those of the texts (this is always the case, however, in all "critical" inquiries), this encounter also constituted an attempt to understand how identity discourses produce their specific truths and how critical dialogue is essential to promote intersubjective solidarities beyond the historical fragility of identities. In this sense, I invite the reader to travel with me as I mediate these texts; through interruption, identification, seduction, intervention, and distance. As Haraway (1991) has suggested, objectivity, that very debased and historically oppressive notion, can also be constructed not as "truth" but as the very site where subjectivities and practices interact in debate and dialogue.

Preliminaries

Despite the fact that many critics have written about the importance of black lesbian writers in facilitating the black gay literary boom of the late 1980s, there have been remarkably few textual dialogues between black gay and lesbian texts, particularly if these are in different "media." Part of this resistance may be attributed to the gender separatism of gay and lesbian critical communities, which in turn can be partially understood as an unfortunate effect of identity politics, but also of the specialization that dominates in the academy and the fragmentation of audiences, some of which may "watch" but not "read" and vice versa. I would like, however, to point out that although differences in context of production (writing vs. independent video production, in this case) is a relevant category of analysis in exploring these two texts, I will be approaching *Tongues* (Riggs, 1989) and *Zami* (Lorde, 1982) as identity narratives ("texts") employing specific constructions of community. Thus, I am mostly interested in the structure of each narrative, using *Zami* as a "medium" to investigate *Tongues.* In general, I will be using a selective reading of *Zami* as a particular form of identity narrative to facilitate a critical reading of *Tongues Untied,* which, I suggest, constitutes a different form of identity discourse. Last, but not least, despite the fact that almost a decade separates the texts, the process of canonization occurred roughly within the same time period, making both texts somewhat "contemporary." This timing suggests how some gay black male discourses and media practices are both indebted to black lesbian feminists and enjoy a greater potential of becoming culturally central as they involve male rather than female subjects employing hegemonic racial/gender discourses.[4]

Truth, Autobiography, and Myth

Perhaps one of the most provocative ways to "enter" a discussion on *Tongues Untied* "through" *Zami* is to examine the relationship between truth, autobiography, and myth, because both (con)texts' specific relationship to these categories greatly determined the terrain in which these texts were (are) seen/read and critiqued. Also, the claim to truth rather than myth raises important questions about identity politics as a mobilizing strategy, because polarizing identity discourses actively requires the silencing of difference in the service of the possibilities of identity, without recognizing its mythic structure. The claim to truth or myth, thus, has important political implications within the context of this comparison and beyond as each provides different tools for collective empowerment.[5]

Recent commentators on Audre Lorde's (1982) *Zami: A New Spelling of My Name* have suggested that one of the elements making this text critically relevant is its self-conscious blurring of truth and autobiography through non-Western mythmaking (Keating, 1993) and the proliferation of subject positionalities (even under the sign "black lesbian") that the narrative "I" can assume (Kader, 1993). About *Tongues,* however, commentators (including Riggs) seem to underline its "truthfulness," its "realness," and its "biographical" content. Some examples of this last reading can be found in the following critical interventions by Hemphill (1991) and Mercer (1993), respectively:

> The work is grounded in personal testimony from Riggs about his life as a black gay man. His experiences are validated and elaborated through the poetry of ... (1991, p. xxvi)

and:

> The emphasis on authenticity, honesty, and truth-to-experience through personal disclosure is underlined by Riggs's visual presence at the beginning, where he appears nude: a gesture of exposure not only suggesting the vulnerability of revealing one own's story but also establishing the framework of personal disclosure that guides the work as a whole. (1993, p. 245)

The "realist" mode of narrative attributed to *Tongues Untied* has been critically contextualized as part of both African American and gay and lesbian literary and media "traditions." Critics such as Fox-Genovese (1990) have also pointed out the relevance of realist narratives for the study of black women's autobiographies, of which *Zami* is an ambiguous case. Most of this writing, however, seems to naturalize the text's mode of construction rather than engage with its mode of production, creating a form of reflective criticism where the critic "echoes" the text's structure. To suggest that what makes *Tongues Untied* effective, popular, or culturally relevant is its realism, avoids the necessary critical task of investigating how audiences (re)produce realistic effects out of a specific set of representations.

I will stop to consider Mercer's (1993) commentary because it suggests some of the ways that identity narratives regenerate identity discourses at the expense of critical inquiry. The central categories of this commentary: "truth-to-experience," "personal," and "presence," replicate the video's (con)textual premises rather than suggesting the specific ways through which documentary truth is produced in the video. Thus, within a context of watching the video as mythmaking rather than truth, each of these points takes on another meaning. The nudity of Riggs-as-character at the beginning of *Tongues* is not "revealing" of self (this representation is not "given"), but rather (for example) constructive of an effect of "foundation"; of being "born again." The body figures as site of inscription that can, in fact, be made "pure" ("innocent," like an infant) and whole. Because of these naturalizing effects, it is imperative to critically differentiate "Marlon Riggs the producer of *Tongues Untied*" from "Marlon Riggs the narrative voice of *Tongues Untied*," a basic operation that very few critics and journalists proposed in the numerous articles and essays on the subject. It is in this distinction that a first critical move can be established; if not, as spectators we have been completely seduced by the narrative's mythmaking/artifice, not its "truth."

Second, the "presence" of Riggs provides a subjective anchor to establish a narrative stability to *Tongues*, because it is "his" story that produces the narrative effect of closure through the subject's initial state of alienation to his liberation at the end of the video. Thus, Riggs's "presence" creates an effect of "wholeness" and stability even when the story narrates conflict and disjuncture. This disjuncture is ultimately recuperated by the narrative, making the subject's journey a duplication of the narrative's premises ("black men loving black men is the revolutionary act"). Despite the crisis of representation that the subject's conflictive desires produce, the narrative manages to effect a reflection of "ourselves" (black gay male subjects) that attempts to erase rupture and incongruence.

One of Lorde's most significant suggestions for how to critically negotiate texts like *Zami* and *Tongues* is the neologism *biomythography* that accompanies the title of her text and that, remarkably, was not generally applied to *Tongues*. In part, *Zami's* recourse to myth is linked in the narrative to the lack of actual experience of community among black lesbians during the fifties. Thus it "originates" in empirical lack becoming "real" only in the language of African myth:

> I remember how being young and Black and gay and lonely felt.... There were no mothers, no sisters, no heroes. We had to do it alone, like our sister Amazons, the riders on the loneliest outposts of the kingdom of Dahomey. We, young and Black and fine and gay, sweated out our first heartbreaks with no school nor office chums to share that confidence over lunch hour. (Lorde, 1982, p. 176)

While writers engaged with *Tongues*, and the video itself, insist on a transparent relationship between the three categories, *Zami* destabilizes them. "Autobiography" becomes the terrain not of truth but of myth even when critics like Raynaud (1988) locate the impulse toward mythmaking as an attempt to "resolve tensions, to find the intimacy of the newborn, to return to the same" (p. 228). Yet, perhaps what is most productive in *Zami* are the multiple contradictions embedded in the narrative that favor simultaneous essentialist and critical readings; a difficult undertaking with *Tongues*. This does not imply, as we will see later, that *Zami* does not construct its own boundaries (exclusions) of community or does not privilege a specific subjectivity. What it does suggest is that the notion of biomythography is a strategy to construct identity narratives that allow for their own questioning from within, pointing to their potential inclusiveness as political discourses. *Zami* is, among many other possibilities, a text of transformation where the author function (not the actual biographical "author") suffers a radical change, remapping new ("imaginary") possibilities for the reader as a result of the (reading) process. Lorde/writer does not become "Zami" after the text is circulated. The "journey" is one of language; to write "a new spelling of my name" recognizes the mediation of language in constructing communities.

Zami's use of myth is not "pure" in the sense that unlike the function of many myths (understood as either naturalizing of an oppressive order or a rigid social vision) it is neither "stolen speech" (Barthes, 1957) nor essentializing (Eliade, 1957); it is a self-conscious strategy for making a subjectivity "exist" textually. The foundational moment of *Zami* has many centers although it is narratively anchored in a sexual encounter between two African American women characters, Audre and Afrekete (Kitty). Kitty is a mythical figure in the sense that through her a "revelation" is crystallized: the discovery of roots. She is also a medium, a phantom who does not stay to construct but instead disappears. As Eliade (1957) suggests: "The myth proclaims the appearance of a new cosmic situation of a primordial event. Hence, it is always the recital of a creation; it tells how something was accomplished, began to be" (p. 95).

In *Zami*, however, the "primordial" event can also regressively shift locations. Thus, Afrekete's final appearance in the text not only marks her disappearance (the "end") but also leads back to the mother as an "origin" of lesbian desire. That this black mother is positioned at the origin and that one can experience black female sexuality as the most perfect retelling of the myth, does not (and this is one of *Zami's* relevant points of difference with *Tongues*) cancel, expel, or denounce the possibilities of black women loving other women nor does it imply that this maternal origin is stable, as it can be partially substituted by other signs of community (African myth, food, Carriacou, Harlem). Instead, the proposed community of black women functions as a privileged instance of love among women for the narrator because it entails a process of confronting the destructive effects of racism, sexism, and heterosexism (like *Tongues*). In a general sense, *Zami's* most pervasive myth is the gender continuum that functions as a premise for feminism, female solidarity, and a vision for a less oppressive world. The relative broadness and seductiveness of this narrative collides, however, with the text's own relentless insistence and resistance to assuming that identity narratives based on sexuality, race, and/or gender will ever be sufficient for effecting far-reaching social, or even personal, change.

At the same time, it is important within this context that the problematic links between biography, myth, and truth in *Zami* be refocused from the "biographical" perspective, because *Tongues'* case study is particularly productive from this vantage point. Although *Zami* does not exclude or demonize desire between black and white women nor suggest that race is an insurmountable obstacle for achieving solidarity, there is one significant instance of exclusion in *Zami* that parallels that of *Tongues Untied.* Despite the fact that Audre/character ends the book with a "revelation" from a black woman/ goddess and the narrative includes empowering moments of relationships across race, Lorde-the-author's relationship with white men in terms of desire and significance is silenced in Audre-the-character. *Zami's* representation of men suggests that they are insignificant in her life. Yet, if *Zami* were taken to "reflect" Lorde's life—be a "biography"—one could say that *Zami* ends to avoid encountering "Lorde's" marriage to a white man who eventually becomes the father of her two children, one of them a boy. In this sense, the desire for men in her life, albeit partially represented, is excluded from the narrative at the point where it would threaten the unity of the black lesbian subject, defined by her desire for other women and the privileging of the relationships among women over all other forms of relationships. Yet, as a biomythography, *Zami's* strength is not based on its "truth" in relation to the "author's" biography but in its ability to mythically (en)vision a new order of things.

Tongues Untied deploys a different set of relationships among the three categories suggested at the beginning of the section. Through numerous public interventions (including academic, gay, and lesbian alternative publications and the popular press), the video was framed as "truth"; *Tongues* tells the story of Marlon Riggs's "experiences as a black gay man." Thus this autobiographical framing (truth of someone's life) undermines the potential reflexivity embedded in the video's own construction. Although, for example, the speaking subjects are photographed against black backgrounds and speak directly to the camera (working against dominant documentary conventions of "observation"), the assumption of verisimilitude is reinforced by the collusion between the narrative "I" (in the video) and Riggs's social "I" as he and others publicly defended the video ("this is my/his li(f)e"). Thus, despite the representations of, for example, various "different" black gay men, a closer examination suggests that the diverse voices in *Tongues* construct the same overall narrative; black gay male identity must be constructed by the conflation of community and desire. In this sense, *Tongues Untied's* narrative structure and strategies of representation are more closely mythical (in Barthes's [1957] sense) than *Zami's*, to the extent that the video resists "admitting" its constructed truth by attempting to anchor its truthfulness in "reality" (mainly through narrative closure and contextual interventions).

Tongues tells the myth of "being" in a state of fallen grace to finding a unity of subjectivity in the imaginary community of black gay men enacted through performances of speech (i.e., political rhetoric) and collective repetition of discrete acts (i.e., the "snap"). Despite the fact that *Zami* (I will examine this shortly) also places a great burden of faith in language as "matrix" of empowerment, *Tongues Untied* makes a direct connection:

> *I was mute,*
> *tongue-tied,*
> *burdened by shadows and silence.*
> *Now, I speak*
> *and my burden is lightened*
> *lifted*
> *free.*
>   (Riggs, 1989, p. 205)

The journey to speech (public and private) is the result of the struggle to define the "self." This narrative construction evokes psychoanalytical arguments of the role that the symbolic and the law of the father play in defining the illusion of stable subjectivity. Although *Tongues'* narrative can be understood as "talking back" in bell hooks's (1990) sense (form of resistance), "speech" cannot be critically accepted as a sign for "liberation." That the subject is able to accept and articulate the categories of his "subjection" for purposes of contestation is, as this formulation suggests, a contradictory position, not to be confused with "liberation." Speech (language), without a continuous and rigorous critique, can also solidify categories that become exclusionary of other oppressed subjectivities, obscuring possibilities of transformation not contained in them. Intersubjective dialogue, struggling against the conditions that privilege the language-knowledge of some groups over others, is both a more modest and perhaps more desirable political goal.

Following this, *Zami's* faith in language not only rests in "enunciation" but in the capacity for reinvention, in the plasticity of language rather than its consistency. Unlike *Tongues,* however, the relationship to language, because it is linked to both desire and the family space, is not free of contradictions. While language in *Zami* is undoubtedly linked to empowerment, the acquisition of language (which is tied to the mother) is also a contradictory process, an intense source of conflict in the narrative. Thus, for example, the first time that Lorde speaks in *Zami,* the mother attempts to silence her as the white librarian offers to share a story. At the same time that Lorde's "poetry" is linked to the mother ("I am a reflection of my mother's secret poetry as well as her hidden angers" [Lorde, 1982, p. 32]), the actual instance of speech is a rebellion against the mother mediated by a white woman. Significantly, Lorde's speech was "originally" used to declare her desire to read, not talk. The construction of subjectivity is thus linked to the written (representation) rather than to the "oral," with all its cultural connotations of immediacy and transparency exemplified in *Tongues Untied.*

This is an important element to underline, because *Tongues Untied* suggests that same-race/-gender sexuality and (performed/oral) poetry are two of the few strategies for the transformation of reality that do not result in further injury to the oppressed subject. *Tongues'* faith in the power of language is absolute; it bridges the gap between "reality" and "truth" even as it enacts and denies its own artifice. In *Zami,* poetry surfaces when pain and unexpressed frustration and anger find no outlet. Yet this pain is often connected to the loss of a woman Lorde (as narrative voice) loves or needs to connect to, including the mother. In this sense, poetry is a practice deployed against an articulated void; it is always lacking because it attempts to inscribe loss (of the "real") through writing (already a sign of loss). Also, to the extent that poetry is an attempt to represent the mother's language, *Zami* speaks for the mother in the triumph of the written (books) over the oral culture (mother). Again, there is a tense relationship between language as myth and language as producer of empirical reality. The real is only accessible through the symbolic, and the evocation of lived experience as the real is accessed through the memory of another.

Despite the insistence to the contrary, part of the effectiveness of *Tongues Untied* rests not on its "realness" but on its mythic structure; its ability to turn toward the spectators and talk to "us," naturalizing representation with the "real" through image, poetic language, and storytelling. Although Barthes (1957) tends to use the concept of myth to signify ideologically pernicious distortion (a connotation that I am not employing in this context), his comment concerning the clarity of myth is appropriate:

> Myth does not deny things, on the contrary, its function is to talk about them; simply, it purifies them, it make them innocent, it gives them a natural and eternal justification, it gives them a clarity which is not that of an explanation but that of a statement of fact. (p. 143)

Tongues Untied declares the existence of a universal black gay subject and proceeds to map the boundaries of the black gay community with no internal tensions or conflicts produced by difference. In this sense, "the" black gay subject achieves a clarity that no specific subject claiming black gay subjectivity could possibly aspire to. Thus, the mythmaking function of *Tongues* coincides with the discursive founding (a "new order") of a black gay community, radically differentiated from white gay culture and black lesbians as well as distant from cross-racial/-gender desires and influences. It is in the effective uses of the artifice that *Tongues* achieves clarity and power, not because groups do not have "specific practices" but because to render them "whole" requires an attempt to render contradictions "narratable" in a specific way. The effect of truth in *Tongues* and its impact "in the world" is thus less inherent in its language and image ("themselves") and more linked to the investment of gay communities, its organic intellectuals, and the multiple audiences who felt rewarded by the video, accepting *Tongues'* mythic "truths" as True.

Finally, I would like to consider the greatest controversy around the relationship between truth, autobiography, and myth that arose in relation to *Tongues*, because it is perhaps in this debate that the effect of claiming truthfulness in a biomythography suggests the potential political problems in this strategy of representation. The controversy emerged in the pages of Boston's *Gay Community News* as a result of one critic's "discovery" that Marlon Riggs's actual lover of 10 years was white:

> My discovery after seeing the film that Marlon Riggs has a white lover struck me as irony and may leave some feeling cheated. I do not fault Riggs here for his choice of a partner, only for what I see as a deception. Despite his obvious

talent and the positive vibe of the film, one can't help but ask, does he really believe any of this?

If Black men loving Black men is truly "the revolutionary act" as he states at the film's conclusion, then why isn't he acting? And why are we led to believe that his fixation with white men was a phase through which he passed? Certainly, there are many different ways to love Black men, but "coming home," as it is presented in this film, features our primary intimate couplings with other Black men. Clearly, the journey back to ourselves is a process, not an event. (Johnson, 1990, p. 11)[6]

In an interview with Simmons (1991), Riggs admits that the issue of interracial love is "unresolved" but that he does not think he was being misleading, because his search in the video was not for a "lover" but a "community":

For a long time, I thought about this question of incorporating my relationship into the video. If in the end I had said, "Black men loving Black men is a revolutionary act," and had added "now I have a white lover," I would have undercut everything unless I went through another half-hour explaining what that means. . . . So I had to jettison that sort of more personal declaration at the end and really look at it in a more communal sense, which is why I ended with the images of civil rights marches and the community of men marching. (p. 194)

Riggs's declaration thus suggests that he did not articulate a contradiction between a defense of the autobiographical as truth and the mythic as political discourse. As has been suggested, however, many others did point to the problematic slippage of the categories of autobiography, truth, and myth as political strategy. Because Lorde also had intimate relationships with both white men and white women and was not "accused" of "deception," it seems that part of the answer is to be found in the textual and contextual framing of the narrative itself and the specific strategies used to sustain a representation of the black gay community as stable in its desires and political aspirations. Had Riggs called *Tongues* a biomythography and had he not insisted on the autobiographical as a source of Truth value for the video, few would have been disconcerted. If the video had been a mythic vision of a community, there would have been no need for documentary or autobiographical truth. Instead, the biomythography strategy could have allowed for both an invitation to "see" differently (founding a narrative of empowerment for interpellated subjects) and the articulation of "new" subjects in their ambivalence, power, and complexity.

Finally, stemming from my own self-conscious blurring of biography and text, which also acts to interpellate me as a viewer/reader of these texts, both narratives were produced when Riggs and Lorde (subjects outside the narratives) were aware of being ill with fatal diseases. In this sense, the urgency to speak within the text was also a battle against death as the "ultimate" silence. Thus, when Soebnlein (1990) commented in *Outweek* that Riggs's point of departure was "Silence = Death," he was pointing to several elements necessary for contextualizing *Tongues Untied*: the AIDS movement as a political force reshaping gay and lesbian activism, the inscription into language of a specific subjectivity, and the possibility of personal death for the maker (AIDS). In the case of Lorde, she had written specifically on silence as death (long before the use of ACT UP's slogan became generalized). As Lorde comments in *The Cancer Journals* (1980):

I am a post-mastectomy woman who believes our feelings need voice in order to be recognized, respected, and of use. (p. 9)

My silences had not protected me. Your silences will not protect you. But for every real word spoken, for every attempt I had ever made to speak those truths for which I am still seeking, I had made contact with other women while we examined the words to fit a world in which we all believed, bridging our differences. (p. 20)

The fact that Lorde's words were not "of use" to gay men with AIDS during the mid- to late 1980s, making ACT UP's slogan self-generating, continues to underline the still considerable difference between the mobilization (albeit insufficient) generated by AIDS activism and the almost nonexistent advocacy for research, prevention, and social awareness of women with breast cancer. Lastly, disease can further dramatize the intense desire to belong to "the black community" (as mythic origin, family, and symbol of resistance) and to reconcile oneself with the contradictions of birth families. Symbolically, this desire can sometimes be textualized by the use of narrowly defined representations of community as family, at the expense of other socially meaningful interactions.

Mapping Boundaries
in *Zami* and *Tongues Untied*

Cherríe Moraga (1983) has suggested in another context that the notion of women-of-color feminism was more cohesive between the covers of a book than in practice, as tends to be true of most identity discourses. As Baudrillard (1979) suggests, discourses that attempt to "end appearances," ultimately end up by "seducing" themselves as narratives "to better fascinate others" (p. 54), giving way to stories rather than "truth." Despite *Tongues's* and *Zami's* many differences, the identity effect is made possible by similar strategies of exclusions (boundaries of in/out) and selective use of memory (textualized "experience"). Apart from the tendency of many critics to treat identity narratives as parallel to experience (because they may address painful or historically consistent representations of certain experiences, and/or because we may identify with them), identity narratives are no less constructions. In the specific context of the two narratives explored here, it seems relevant to study how each one achieves certain identity effects (cohesion) and how these effects may interpellate their intended subjects (readers and/or spectators).

Lorde's and Riggs's multiple con/textual interventions suggest that both articulated a need for the founding of a black gay (imaginary) community beyond individual lover relationships. This proposed community is also a metaphor for a process of healing from the experiences of pain, racism, sexism, and heterosexism that black gay men and lesbians have endured. hooks (1992) has written that this impulse toward "separatism" is often misunderstood by whites: "All social manifestations of black separatism are often seen by whites as a sign of anti-white racism, when they usually represent an attempt by black people to construct places of political sanctuary where we can escape, if only for a time, white domination" (p. 15).

Both narratives, however, invoke "separatism" in very different ways. Thus, despite the desire for an inclusive African American lesbian community to "come home to," *Zami* self-consciously articulates the symbolic and political use of this narrative and its status as a vision of undetermined and untested potential. In this sense, *Zami* constructs textual spaces of contradiction and ambivalence—despite its "thrust" toward a healing sameness. Before fully engaging with *Tongues,* I will suggest some of the contradictory ways that *Zami* articulates community.

Zami's biomythographic strategy is significantly rooted in the narrative displacements of the central subject onto the body of a mythic African American woman who embodies both sexuality and solidarity as a way of coming home to the black community. Part of the narrative's effectiveness of the journey as trope is the subject's precarious sense of "belonging" as the daughter of emigrant parents. Thus the symbolic location of home in "Africa" (through those cultural practices of the diaspora in the Caribbean) and its actualization in the sexuality of black women with each other contains one of the central premises of *Zami's* identity narrative (and ontology of lesbian desire) as well as the tensions between myth and experience:

> Once *home* was a far way off, a place I had never been to but knew well out of my mother's mouth.... For if we lived correctly, and with frugality, looked both ways before crossing the street, then someday we would arrive back in the sweet place, back *home*. (Lorde, 1982, p. 13)

> When I moved out of my mother's house, shaky and determined, I began to fashion some different relationship to this country of our sojourn. I began to seek some more fruitful return than simple bitterness from this place of my mother's exile, whose streets I came to learn better than my mother had ever learned them.... And there I found other women who sustained me and from whom I learned other loving. (p. 104)

Thus, as these two passages suggest, "home" embodies multiple and often contradictory locations, meanings, and levels of mythmaking. At its most cohesive, "home" in *Zami* is an endless and elusive practice to constitute multiple supportive communities with diverse possibilities for the subject's empowerment.

Despite differences between the founding premises of both texts, Riggs and Lorde (as characters) make journeys to faraway places where a revelation is produced. In Riggs's journey to San Francisco, he finds rejection and alienation. Lorde's travel to México, however, produces a different effect in the subject's quest for visibility and speech. Lorde achieves a sense of visibility by "looking" like everybody else—dark skinned. However, she finds the "comfort" of sameness in difference because, as the narrator suggests, the Mexicans mistake her for a Cuban and call her *la morenita* (the dark one). Furthermore, Lorde's journey provides her with sexual affirmation and a sense of social visibility, although this "reflection" is produced in an encounter with an older white woman.

> It was in Mexico that I stopped feeling invisible. In the streets, in the buses, in the markets, in the Plaza, in the particular attention within Eudora's eyes. Sometimes, half-smiling, she would scan my face without speaking. It made me feel like she was the first person who had ever looked at me, ever seen who I was. And not only did she see me, she loved me, thought me beautiful. This was not accidental collision. (Lorde, 1982, p. 173)

In general, Zami offers a multiplicity of tensions in its construction of the journey to community. Similar to *Tongues,* the text attempts their resolution. Differently, however, *Zami* also textualizes the ambiguities of desire and identity as well as the political necessity of constructing mythic narratives, which provides the tools for the interpellated subjects to question their own constitutive process.

Tongues denies the value of difference; gender differences are largely un-represented and racial differences are demonized. *Zami* acknowledges the productivity of some differences (among women on the racial/sexual axis), warns against others (white heterosexual men), and avoids still others entirely (black gay men). Yet, one of *Zami's* most important contributions to the identity debate is its textual recognition (despite seducing itself into a contra-diction by articulating a mythic future) that differences cannot be ahistorically contained in identity categories or narratives:

> *Being women together was not enough. We were different. Being gay-girls together was not enough. We were different. . . .*
> It was a while before we came to realize that our place was the very house of difference rather than the security of any one particular difference. . . . It was years before we learned to use the strength that daily surviving can bring, years before we learned fear does not have to incapacitate, and that we could appre-ciate each other on terms not necessarily our own. (Lorde, 1982, p. 226)

Even though this conclusion is partly reached through narrating bar lesbian life during the 1950s, *Zami* does establish a hierarchy of differences, some more easily assimilated into a mythic vision of community.

King (1992) has commented on the role of the lesbian bar as a site for exploring identity and difference in *Zami.* The bar "stands for contradictions of identity and solidarity/solitariness," but these identities shift throughout the text (King, 1992, p. 55). The bar (inside) is a point of encounter for the majority white lesbians and the few black lesbians who participate in urban lesbian culture. At the same time, the potential black/white dichotomy is not rigidly defined as women, regardless of race, also assume butch or femme roles. Within these possibilities, Lorde's identifications are not only racial (the recognition that racism defined who was desired in the bar and, in turn, who was desirable) but also in relation to the preferred gender performance: She is ky-ky (neither femme nor butch) and critiques "butchness" as an oppressive sexual/gender performance. In contrast, *Tongues* represents two "kinds" of bars: black gay clubs (the "inside") and the white gay clubs (the "outside"). The "black" bar admits no "internal" differences; there are no distinctions in forms of gender performance or desires. Black men dance, drink, share with each other without any obstacles to same-race/-gender cruising. It is in the (outside) of the white bar that *Zami* and *Tongues* share an antiracist narrative (the "three pieces of ID"). However, the climate produced by racism in the white gay community "spills" (in both texts), mediating the relationships between black gays and lesbians, respectively. Thus, in *Tongues:*

> At the precise moment our eyes should meet, he studies the intricate detail of a building and I check my white sleeves for scuff marks. What is it that we see in each other that makes us avert our eyes so quickly. Do we turn away from each other in order not to see our collective anger and sadness? (Beam, 1986)

And in *Zami:*

> The Black gay-girls in the Village gay bars of the fifties knew each other's names, but we seldom looked into each other's Black eyes, lest we see our aloneness and our blunted power mirrored in the pursuit of darkness. (Lorde, 1982, p. 226)

Despite this strong convergence, the world of *Tongues* is either constructed as a dichotomy (white/black) or as segregated (black). Set almost 30 years earlier, when segregation was a fact for most of the United States, *Zami* constructs fluid, permeable borders where power and resistance are effects of specific practices; shifting depending on context. This narrative difference suggests a feminist (in the historical sense) appropriation of antiracist discourse where racial oppression is not the only axis of the deployment of power.

Following this, it is relevant to consider how "women" and "femininity" figure (or are omitted) from both texts since together with racialized desire, gender figures as a central structuring device in these narratives. As I have mentioned earlier, *Zami* is structured by a discourse of gender solidarity that includes relationships across race. At the same time, the category of "woman" is the privileged site for articulating new communities, acknowledgments, and desires even when heterosexual men (black and white) constitute boundaries of community. In *Tongues,* women are outside discourse, representation, and relevance. Although this may not necessarily be a comment on the "vision" of the video, the few references to women—the representation of drag queens and white men as well as the discursive "repression" of women's voices—do suggest that the masculinization of the world in *Tongues* can be read as a rejection of the feminine, a consistent tendency parallel to the video's distrust of seduction.

Perhaps one of the most unacknowledged instances of both the fluidity of identity and *Tongues'* artificial construction of masculine boundaries is the opening: "Brother to Brother." The repetition of the refrain "brother to brother," together with the images of black men in slow motion, construct the privileged object/subject for the video: a black (later it will be clear) gay man. However, an examination of the source for the phrase *brother to brother* refers the reader to an article written by Beam (1986) in his first anthology on writings by black gay men, *In the Life.* Although Beam's essay indeed addresses black gay subjectivity and survival as his central concern, the essay begins with a quotation from Audre Lorde from her book of essays and speeches, *Sister Outsider* (1984). Thus, after Beam's title, "Brother to Brother: Words From the Heart," two quotes from Lorde follow:

What is most important to me must be spoken, made verbal and shared, even at the risk of having it bruised or misunderstood.

I know the anger that lies inside of me like I know the beat of my heart and the taste of my spit. It is easier to be angry than to hurt. Anger is what I do best. It is easier to be furious than to be yearning. Easier to crucify myself in you than to take on the threatening universe of whiteness by admitting that we are worth wanting each other. [Beam, 1986, p. 230, quoting Lorde, 1984]

[Beam writes] I, too, know this anger. It is the way, sometimes the only way I am granted an audience. It is sometimes the way I show affection. I am angry because of the treatment I am afforded as a Black man. (Beam, 1986, p. 230)

The first time I realized that Lorde's text was embedded in this sequence performed by Hemphill, I tried to find out if Lorde was acknowledged in the final credits: She was not. Once I finished reading Beam's work, I realized that this quote became masculine by virtue of being spoken (performed) by a "male." Although the issue of appropriation is not my essential concern, what the sequence suggests about identity is. The ease with which "women's words," in the context of a strong feminist narrative context, become the words of a man in an equally strong masculinist symbolic world points to an understanding of identity as contextual, and that any attempt to seal the borders of identity is a failed enterprise.

Another instance of (mis)appropriation from Beam, the controversial ending of *Tongues,* is also a relevant site of debate concerning the video's narrative "universalizing" ambition. While in Beam's (1991) essay the phrase "Black men loving Black men is the revolutionary act" (p. 240) is used, its meaning is not closed or overdetermined by same-sex/-race desires. First, Beam's sentence ends with "of the eighties." Thus it is not a universal truth but rooted within the context of black-on-black male violence in urban areas. Given the high levels of violence in black communities across the country, the meaning of "the revolutionary act" can be read as a call to end violence in the black community in general. Beam never made sexuality between black men (gay or not) the revolutionary act (emphasized article in *Tongues*), only a course of action within a specific context and for the broader (imaginary) black community.[7]

In *Tongues,* despite Riggs's comments to the contrary, the most favored reading of the phrase in the text is that of same-sex/-race desire, despite a possible reading that may include an invitation to the talented "tenth" to recognize black gay men as "brothers." However, even assuming the dominant reading of the "brother to brother" call is that of challenging the homophobia of black men (as privileged in the black community by virtue of sexism), *Tongues* does little in challenging the category of "manhood" itself (discursively or structurally). On the contrary, many of *Tongues'* representational choices coalesce to defend gay males as "black men" (like any others). Riggs (1991) has more explicitly articulated the manhood/blackness (community belonging) equation elsewhere:

For in the cinematic and television images of and from black America as well as the lyrics and dialogue that now abound and seem to address my life as a black gay man, I am struck repeatedly by the determined, unreasoning, often irrational desire to discredit my claim to blackness and hence to black manhood. (p. 254)

Tongues' insistence on "manhood" is not very different from the premises of some Black Power ideologies that grounded the struggle for black determination in the "pursuit of manhood" (Powell, 1983). In *Tongues,* there is no critique of gender roles or dominant ideologies of maleness. Riggs mostly uses racism as the distorting force in shaping black men's images of themselves as black, but even more importantly, as men. The assumption that manhood is a value to be defended is not critically examined in the text nor is it defined in any way that suggests difference from dominant constructions of masculinity, except in a limited set of cultural practices represented as "spectacle."

The avoidance of the feminine also points to another relevant question in terms of visual representation. While Mercer (1991) initially criticized, and later re-articulated, a critique of Mapplethorpe's photographs of black male nudes because of their objectification and fetishization of black men, the bodies of white men, in the brief moment they appear in *Tongues Untied,* also appear fetishized, fragmented, objectified, and symbolically feminized. The dichotomy of representation (black vs. white male subjects) suggests that in *Tongues* whiteness is threatening to the cohesion of the black gay subject on two fronts: blurring of gender and bodily fragmentation. White gay men are thus represented as both less than whole (fetishized, fragmented) and feminized as "beautiful bodies" (embodying "perfect" feminine beauty). Following Rose (1986): "We know that women are meant to look perfect, presenting a seamless image to the world so that the man, in that confrontation with difference, can avoid any apprehension of lack" (p. 232).

If the positionality of the black gay male is already constituted as "lacking" by dominant cultures, then the strategy of representing lack in white subjectivity (against the constructed wholeness of the black gay subject) is through the simultaneous representation of black gay men in control of the gaze and white gay men's representation as either fragmented or "perfect" bodies, that is, feminized. At the same time, the feminization of Riggs-as-character is located (and undone) when in allowing himself to be seduced (losing mastery/masculinity) he must retreat and call this moment of seduction "a curse" (I will return to this in the next section). In this context, it is no coincidence that both the young white friend (who seduces) and black transvestites are introduced with music by black women singers (Roberta Flack, Nina Simone, and Billie Holiday), because they are seducing us (as Baudrillard [1979] suggests), by their "weakness" (or their femininity).

A second important instance of the avoidance of the "feminine" is the sequence that begins with the slow-motion image of a drag queen smoking to the rhythms of "Lover Man." In this first part of the sequence, the subject is made object; she doesn't speak except through a woman's singing voice. Again, the issue here is not the privileging of "sync" sound but the exclusion of drag queens from the privilege of voice that the video creates for itself (if the "I" only existed through women's voices, the political implications would be dramatically different). Thus, in the second part of the sequence, following a dissolve, a drag queen is represented walking, literally "talked over" by the voices of Nina Simone and Essex Hemphill. On this occasion, both texts (poetry and lyrics) construct drag queens as devoid of community, love-starved, and submissive to patriarchal notions of femininity. As Goldsby (1993) comments: "Interestingly, Marlon Riggs's *Tongues Untied* (1989) depicts drag queens as pathetic, lovely figures who are ultimately silenced by the subjection to Riggs's narrative 'I' " (p. 114).

Drag queens are thus visually included but not given a voice: They are the boundary where black gay meets black "femininity," a dangerous zone for an identity narrative such as *Tongues*. This representation of femininity can be read with Mulvey's (1985) observations about Hollywood films:

> Woman then stands in patriarchal culture as signifier for the male other, bound by a symbolic order in which man can live out his fantasies and obsessions through linguistic command by imposing them on the silent image of woman still tied to her place as bearer of meaning, not maker of meaning. (p. 804)

As bodies who "perform" their sexuality and gender rather than "be" them ("biologically"), the practice of drag queens suggests a notion of "identity" as a self-conscious play of signs. Masculinity, with its need for "firm" demarcation, cannot represent drag queens except as boundary or fetish. Yet, in consistent logic with sexist thinking, the narrative voice of Riggs points to them as metaphor for home; as nurturers ("a new place better") even when, according to the narrative, they have nothing. To let the queens actually speak would be to contest the dominant "I" who clearly and unambiguously is a black gay man defending his access to manhood/blackness. To assume that drag queens (in general) are interested in defending black manhood and legitimating these dichotomies is to use drag radically for a narrative that does not explore drag as a critique/play of gender/sexual identities with its own set of transformative possibilities.

Despite the silencing of the queens, *Tongues* is most successful when representing identity through various modes of performance; poetry, dance, gestures (snap). In this sense, although *Tongues* is producing an effect of identity through performance, its basis is formulated as community (which is already an effect of representation). What is perhaps lost in this move is the potential for actually questioning the power structures that produce black gay male identity as a form of contestation of heterosexist and racist power structures. The assumption of these categories as inherently liberating obscures the fact that such an identity is carved out of the same power structures it attempts to contest. In this context, the insistence that black gay men are not "women" seems to accept that there is something "wrong" (perhaps disempowering?) about "being" a woman. It ultimately suggests that, with the exception of a few silent queens, gay men are not women and should therefore be part of the community of black men.

One of the most consistent strategies of *Tongues* and *Zami* is the absence of "opposite-sex" same-gender sexuality. In *Zami*, representations of white heterosexual men and women, black heterosexual men and women, white and black lesbians are included, but no gay men characters exist in the narrative. In *Tongues Untied*, as has already been suggested, only heterosexual and homosexual black and white men are represented. Because *Zami* is a more open work, the absence seems more striking there. However, the lack in both narratives, as has been suggested in the examination of Beam's (1991) work, seems to suggest a resistance to including positionalities that can be construed as too "similar" by the dominant culture. Although both narratives need the representation of white men as embodiment of the limits of ideal community, heterosexual blacks, despite the many ambiguities, are representative of "the larger" black community (church, family, neighborhood). Thus the only other group that shares a similar (but not identical) positionality of the speaking "I" is erased. It seems, then, that the inclusion of the "other" queer is also problematic for these identity narratives because these subjectivities (black gay men and black lesbians) can "seem" surprisingly the same, thus questioning the "unique" perspective of each narrative's construction. If gay men, according to the dominant culture, must be somewhat like "women" to be gay men, there is, ultimately, not a major "difference" between them. To have these subjectivities side by side requires a more complex investigation of differences within each gender category and across gender performances, which would threaten the unity of gender that is a basic premise of the speaking subjects in both texts, even when some gestures (*Zami's* claim to have both feminine and masculine desires, *Tongues'* sometimes "effeminate" performances of the snap), the texts attempt ultimately to reaffirm womanhood and manhood, respectively.

Another structuring omission and sometimes romanticization in *Tongues* is social class. *Tongues Untied* dismisses class as a relevant element of black gay subjectivity at the same time that it inscribes a privileged middle-class black gay subjectivity. The only mention of class differences directly articulated as bearing an impact on Riggs's life results in its immediate dismissal. Riggs narrates the story of how blacks in his high school rejected him because they mistook his silence for class "superiority." Yet, Riggs makes consistent reference to his academic achievement, a sign of class privilege and/or upward mobility and an unexamined sign of difference. A second equally compelling instance of middle-class normalization is the definition of a highly desirable date as suggested by a fictional vignette in which a man leaving a message on a date line describes himself as:

> Black Gay Activist, 30's, well-read, sensitive, pro-feminist, seeks same for envelope licking, demonstration companion, dialogical theorizing, good times and hot safe sex.

In this case, a considerable part of what makes a man desirable is his access to Western education connoting a certain degree of class privilege.

A number of other examples making reference to class and poverty also strengthen the middle-class bias of black gay subjectivity in *Tongues Untied*. The first refers to the already described sequence where a drag queen's walk is "talked over" by Hemphill. The construction of the drag queen as silent, love-starved, and "pathetic" is accompanied by the suggestion that she is a prostitute. At the same time, the construction of "prostitution," as ambiguous and complex as it can be, is only invoked here in terms of the skills she is accumulating as a lover in wait for the perfect man. In this sense, there is no acknowledgment of the social and economic context of hustling nor the specific dangers drag queen street prostitutes live with as part of their work.

This does not suggest that, given a sense of choices, someone may in fact prefer sex work to other forms of paid work; however, it is also plausible to ask whether, in this particular representation of this drag queen, the option to do sex work is heavily determined by social class and thus immediately made irrelevant by the text.[8]

In comparison, *Zami* deploys representations of "racism" in a way similar to that of *Tongues,* although class differences and issues of economic survival are central to *Zami's* possibilities of empowerment as a black lesbian. Class, however, is not constitutive of *Zami's* proposed black lesbian subjectivity on the same level as sexuality, race, and gender. In fact, apart from references to times of need in both Lorde's family context and early adulthood, the sign of a working-class lesbian cultural formation, butch/femme relationships, are misread as heterosexist (not feminist) lesbian forms of community. Thus, in *Tongues* as in *Zami,* the bodies of same-gender partners serve as mediators for the arrival of a new home, where class is not constructed as a central category of identity. This home is new to the extent that it allows a previously "invisible" subject to go home "as he is." In this sense, the speaking subject no longer accepts his otherness: "I cannot go home as who I am. When I speak of home I mean not only the familiar constellation but the entire black community. I cannot go home as who I am and that hurts me deeply" (Beam, 1986).

The larger narrative of the potential of women's solidarity makes *Zami* a more ambiguous text in relation to both interracial sexuality and the actualization of a "home" beyond textuality. Even when acknowledging racism among lesbians, *Zami* writes history in order to include interracial lesbian contacts as part of a broader progressive community: "Lesbians were probably the only Black and white women in New York City in the fifties who were making any real attempt to communicate with each other" (Lorde, 1982, p. 179).

Also, despite the construction of "home" as affirming desire between black lesbians, in the context of *Zami's* ambiguities as a narrative it is clear that Lorde never finds a "home" except in writing and the potential encounters with women's bodies, which are always ephemeral. As Kader (1993) suggests: "Within this context, 'home' is recast as a frame of reference—a location with respect to knowledge and meaning. In *Zami,* 'real homes' are temporary, impoverished and uncertain. There is no privileged space, no privileged discourse—only 'the very house of difference' " (p. 191).

Unlike *Tongues, Zami* (although never without contradictions) makes a dual proposition for the founding of a black (women's) community and the necessity to protect and recognize the creative and useful potential of differences. Part of *Zami's* ability to effect a more inclusive discourse stems from its narrative of "women together," because this vision encompasses subjects under a multiplicity of power structures including gender/sexual/racist/classist oppressions. In this sense, Lorde is unable to exclude white women and many heterosexuals. *Tongues,* however, using the axis of race (in a black/white-only dichotomy) and heterosexism (without acknowledging issues of sexism) can create space for only some black gay men (no bisexuals, gender benders, hustlers, etc.). The rare mentions and/or representations of women tend to suggest that there is no "feminist" agenda (as one of the performers says, "I am not your bitch, your bitch is at home with your kids"). This discourse is thus less likely to acknowledge difference as a value.

Finally, before considering the narrative functions of desire in both texts, it is also relevant to suggest that another source of considerable cohesion in *Tongues* is the lack of acknowledgment of the impact of the white gay and lesbian movement in constructing public middle-class black gay subjectivities. While acknowledging that diverse gay and lesbian communities have their autonomous histories, stories, and myths, and that the white gay and lesbian political and cultural imaginary has both denied and cannibalized these for its own purposes, it is also impossible to ignore that the political visibility of particularly middle-class gays and lesbians of color is (at least) linked to the efforts of the contemporary gay and lesbian movement. Thus the dissolve that connects Martin Luther King to members of Gay Men of African Descent suggests an historically misleading continuity, albeit a powerful mythical one. The dissolve symbolically creates a "sameness" of black struggle in the United States, repositioning gays and lesbians (an excluded group from the black heterosexist imagination) into the "black community" (this may be its most useful effect). As its cost, this move avoids coming to terms with the specificities between movements and, perhaps more importantly, their "internal" conflicts and differences.

Although it is true that some of the tactics and rhetoric of the black civil rights struggle of the sixties and hundreds of years of black resistance have had an enormous impact on the articulation of gay liberation, it is no less true that the various post-sixties feminisms and gay liberation discourses are critically important in producing the context for a video like *Tongues Untied* in a more immediate historical sense, a debt that goes entirely unacknowledged by the mythification of continuity.

The Narrative Functions of Desire

Desire is one of the most fertile sites for an investigation of how identity is defined in both texts and the role that sexuality has in stabilizing these identities. Although *Zami's* prologue suggests that, "I have always wanted to be both man and woman, to incorporate the strongest and richest parts of my mother and father within me" (Lorde, 1982, p. 7), Lorde literally "writes off" the father (his impact in her life is described as "distant lighting"). *Zami's* writing of same-sex desire among women is tendentially linked to the deferred desire to engage sexually with the mother and the actual physical experience of having sensual experiences with the mother as a girl (combing of the hair, cooking together). The "maternal" is also the first model for desire as young Audre tries to seduce a new-found playmate, Toni, treating the little girl as her "child" but with the consciousness of her transgression (the taboo to desire and be sexual as/with the mother). In this sense, sexuality among women is always inscribed as a memory of the "primal" connection between mothers and daughters:

> Years afterward, when I was grown, whenever I thought about the way I smelled that day, I would have a fantasy of my mother, her hands wiped dry from the washing, and her apron untied and laid neatly away, looking down upon me lying on the couch, and then slowly, thoroughly, our touching and caressing each other's most secret places. (Lorde, 1982, p. 78)

and:

> Loving Ginger that night was like coming home to a joy I was meant for, and I only wondered, silently, how I had not always known that it would be so. (p. 139)

Despite Zami's rejection of the "law of the father" by invoking the chaos of the maternal relationship, the privileging of the mother-daughter relationship is not equated with an acritical acceptance of the mother's truths. Even here, at the heart of the image, there is difference, as Lorde's mother "is" black but "looks" white.

Tongues represents the law of the father through the symbolic representation of the church, black homophobia, and white (male) racism. There is no "mother" function; with the exception of one reference to the mother (which underlines the narrator's lack of need of a woman in his life), all subjects are self-produced men locked in power struggles. The only symbols that stand for the continuity of community (intergeneration) are also men (King, Turner, Douglass). The sole portrait—of Harriet Tubman—stands almost unreadable "as a woman" among the black (male) cultural icons.

Zami offers several representations of desire between women across racial differences and within them. Differences of class, age, education, and others (alcoholism, mental illness) are also used to construct specific subjectivities. Thus, despite the fact that the connection with Afrekete is privileged by the text in the mythical (symbolic) sense, the contributions of white women in creating a self-affirming context are not erased or eliminated. Despite a broad range of different experiences with women where each character's "circumstances" and "context" make a significant part of the narrative, sexual contact between men and women in *Zami* often leads to disaster for the woman involved and is empty of desire for the narrator. Thus, Lorde recalls her first sexual experience with a boy:

> But four years before, I had to find out if I was going to become pregnant, because a boy from school much bigger than me had invited me up to the roof on my way home from the library and then threatened to break my glasses if I didn't let him stick his "thing" between my legs. (p. 75)

She also becomes pregnant from her (white) boyfriend Peter and must seek an abortion, and the brother of her first landlady makes her watch him masturbate. Lastly, and perhaps most significantly, her best high school friend, Gennie, is sexually molested by her father, resulting in her death by suicide. In comparison, *Tongues* constructs white men "outside" of the community on the basis not of their violence but their desirability. Unlike *Zami*, however, *Tongues* includes black gay men and a general notion of black manhood as part of the "inside" of the mythic community.

Tongues also places desire at the core of the narrative, but the formation of this desire is located elsewhere. Although in *Zami* desire "is a drive from the mother's blood" (Lorde, 1982, p. 256), in *Tongues* there are no fathers, no mothers, no domestic site of desire. Desire appears as an effect of play in the street, generated by the intersubjectivity of boys: thus, it originates in peer culture ("good desire"). The racialization of desire ("bad desire") occurs at a different juncture, as an adolescent and in a racist context. In this sense, the narrative of *Tongues Untied* is predicated on the unresolved and repressed tension between community (articulated as black) and desire for whites (articulated as polluting/threatening to community). Rejection of white men is constructed very differently in *Zami*, where the impact of contact is structured by gender oppression and not desire (Lorde problematically claims that she never felt pleasure in sexual encounters with men). In *Tongues*, the extirpation of desire for white men is an integral part of the subject's journey of "identity" (understanding this to mean a repeated practice). As Butler (1990) comments: "The boundary of the body as well as the distinction between internal and external is established through the ejection and trans-valuation of something originally part of identity into a defiling otherness" (p. 133).

Following Butler, Riggs's identity as a "gay" desiring subject is intimately tied to his desire for white men, a desire that must be extirpated in order for the subject to recognize himself as "what he is":

> A white boy came to my rescue. Beckoned
> with gray/green eyes, a soft Tennessee drawl.
> Seduced me out of my adolescent silence . . .
> He called me friend.
> I fell in love.
> We never touched, never kissed,
> but he left his imprint.
> What a blessing
> his immaculate seduction.
> To feel the beat of life,
> to trust passion again.
> What a joy,
> that it should come from a whiteboy
> with gray/green eyes,
> what a curse.
>   (from *Tongues Untied*)[9]

The language employed in this sequence is clearly articulated within religious terminology and frames the general narrative as one of purification. Thus this seduction, continuing the religious language, constitutes a "fall," a terrible weakness produced by a corrupting desire for white men. Furthermore, seduction is constructed as a curse because while identity constitutes a mirror "reflection" of "sameness," the seduced finds himself in another who is white, polluting the purity of his subjectivity in the process. Yet, as Riggs's own "biography" suggests, it is possible for a subject both to desire white men and affirm the importance of community with other black gay men.

In demonizing desire and questioning the origin of his (Riggs's) love for "vanilla," a narrative inconsistency suggests *Tongues'* difficulties in reconciling desire and community, since the video proposes that the "reason" Riggs desires white men is rooted in the invisibility of black men from gay culture. But, as has already been established by the narrative, desire for white men was an effect of a white adolescent's kindness, prior to forming part of San Francisco's gay culture. Sexual desire and the desire for representation are conflated as a cause/effect relationship introducing a different narrative logic. That a black gay man is (mis)- or (un)represented in gay white culture and thus exoticized or ostracized does not, however, imply that the desire for racial difference is fully explained by this. If that were the case, all black gay men who in some way participate in white gay culture would want only white men. As Rich (1993) has written, racial difference can be an erotic and productive zone of exchange for gays and lesbians. *Tongues'* silence in relation to interracial desire thus seems to sacrifice the film's main impossible value ("truth") for a mythic construction that must erase the traces of ambiguities: "In a film full of courage of coming out of the closet on the subject of queerness, it looked as though Riggs had stayed in the closet on the subject of race (as object of affection, not identity)" (Rich, 1993, p. 333).

This avoidance of representing that which seduces "us" takes an intriguing twist when Riggs-as-narrator suggests by a juxtaposition of him and another black man kissing that a sexual encounter with a black man may have infected him with HIV. As the narrative suggests, however, the "truthful" image would have been of him and a white man. Yet, the taboo on cross-racial relations contradictorily produces the only "seductive" (the cost is death) representation of two black men having sex in the video. In sum, following Baudrillard (1979), "seduction" tends to be represented in "orthodoxies" as "black magic for the deviation of all truths, an exaltation of the malicious use of signs, a conspiracy of signs" (p. 2). In this context, seduction is instead the "white witchcraft" that, conflated with the feminine, ensures Riggs's discourse of identity as a black gay male. Ultimately, *Tongues* attempts to master its "weakness" for white men by resisting to represent (literally see) black and white men in sexual activity.

With and Beyond Identity Narratives

Part of the value of *Zami* as a mapping of community is its persistent slippage and lack of closure between identity and difference. As Kader (1993) has written: "I suspect that Lorde is less interested in 'reconciliation' than in the radical potential of 'difference'—in keeping separate (unmaking) rather than rendering coherent the complexities of identity and history" (p. 184).

It is precisely in these tensions that readers and spectators can mediate a text for a better understanding of the forces that shape our lives. Supporters of a more sophisticated form of identity politics (such as Mercer, 1991) maintain that identity narratives are necessary for the transformation of "I" into "we" and facilitate the location of subjects within discourse ("the past"). This political effect of identity discourses should not, however, obscure the need for a sustained critique beyond the effects of the discourse (even though "we" may identify with it). This is necessary, in great measure because all identity narratives exclude not only their "other" but also many subjectivities within the alleged "sameness." Thus in *Tongues Untied,* for example, the fact that class is never addressed except as a passing (and problematic) reference (re)produces the representational hegemony of middle-class black (mostly "butch") gays over other subjectivities. Also, the political (mythical) potential of (identity) narratives should never be allowed to become the "official" story for any movement since it inevitably contains simplification and loss of memory.

In sum, although it is no doubt "true" that different forms of identity-based struggles have been successful in transforming the lives of interpellated subjects (I am certainly no exception), it is also "true" that these identities carry the seeds of their own self-dissolution, because by stabilizing "itself" any "identity" will begin to implode from within. Affirming identities may continue to be an empowering tool for groups in the practice of achieving concrete political gains. Yet we should never forget that when we accept the categories of our "normalization" (race, gender, sexuality, class) we are also engaging in a contradictory practice. At the same time we may be "expanding" the category to include "us," we are also reifying identities at the expense of other possibilities.

Notes

1. Reprinted by permission from Signifyin' Works.

2. Exerpts from *Zami: A New Spelling of My Name,* copyright © 1982 by Audre Lorde, The Crossing Press. Reprinted by permission.

3. The extensive public discussion around *Tongues Untied* (Riggs, 1989) during the early 1990s was intimately connected to the fact that attacks from the New Right placed the video at the center of a complex controversy over the relationship between the State and the gay and lesbian arts communities, as well as between government institutions and so-called constitutional rights ("freedom of speech"). In this sense, a potentially "subcultural" production was made symbolically central by some powerful crusaders who viewed the video as a sign of American moral and political "decay." Thus, the attack on *Tongues Untied* from the New Right made many gay and lesbian writers, academics, and activists all the more prone to defend and canonize the video rather than examine it critically. It is perhaps now, when the heat is off this particular video, that other dialogues can resume or be continued.

4. Despite a general critical and popular reception that constructed *Tongues Untied's* politics as transgressive, I believe the dichotomous thinking (among other elements) structuring the video makes it much more "mainstream" in terms of American political discourses than Lorde's *Zami,* with its critique of essentialist politics and self-awareness of the mythic nature of its political discourse.

5. I am referring to identity political discourse and not to a specific subject's construction of identity. A butch may be a butch (I will not argue with her), but a hegemonic butch/femme identity discourse (for example) can silence other erotic and community possibilities.

6. Reprinted from Gay Community News with permission.

7. As in a multiplicity of instances throughout the video, *Tongues Untied* tends to incorporate the most essentialized representations of black gay lives to represent a "totality." Thus the video ignores issues of fatherhood, significant relationships with women, spirituality, and the like. One of several possible examples is the verses taken from Alan Miller's "At the Club." The selection used in the video conceals that the suggested erotic encounter between the narrator and the man he cruises is between a gay man and a married (bisexual? closeted?) man in Miller's text.

8. Another instance of the romanticization of poverty is present in Hemphill's (1991) poem "Burnt Beans."

Other dismissals of the oppressiveness of poverty in the lives of black gay men can be located in two of Steven Langley's interventions: "When you find yourself coming up short, do what I do—borrow things from the universe." And at the end of the video, in a revamped new age mode: "You can do what you want to do."

9. Reprinted by permission from Signifyin' Works.

References

Anzaldúa, G., & Moraga, C. (Eds.). (1983). *This bridge called my back: Writings by radical women of color.* New York: Kitchen Table Press.

Barthes, R. (1957). *Mythologies.* New York: Noonday Press.

Baudrillard, J. (1979). *Seduction.* New York: St. Martin's.

Beam, J. (Ed.). (1986). *In the life: A black gay anthology.* Boston: Alyson.

Butler, J. (1990). *Gender trouble: Feminism and the subversion of identity.* New York: Routledge.

Eliade, M. (1957). *The sacred and the profane: The nature of religions.* New York: Harper Torchbooks.

Fox-Genovese, E. (1990). My statue, my self: Autobiographical writings of Afro-American women. In H. L. Gates, (Ed.), *Reading black, reading feminist* (pp. 176-203). New York: Meridian.

Goldsby, J. (1993). Queens of language: Paris is burning. In M. Gever, J. Greyson, & P. Parmar (Eds.), *Queer looks* (pp. 108-115). New York: Routledge.

Haraway, D. (1991). *Simians, cyborgs, and women: The reinvention of nature.* New York: Routledge.

Hemphill, E. (Ed.). (1991). *Brother to brother.* Boston: Alyson.

hooks, b. (1990). Talking back. In G. Anzaldúa (Ed.), *Making face, making soul* (pp. 207-211). San Francisco: Aunt Lute Foundation.

hooks, b. (1992). *Black looks: Race and representation.* Boston: South End.

Johnson, C. A. (1990, February 25-March 3). Not in knots: *Tongues Untied* is the black gay official story. *Gay Community News,* p. 11.

Kader, C. (1993). "The very house of difference": *Zami,* Audre Lorde's lesbian-centered text. In E. S. Nelson (Ed.), *Journal of Homosexuality, 26*(2/3), 181-194.

Keating, A. L. (1993). Myth smashers, myth makers: (Re)visionary techniques in the works of Paula Gunn Allen, Gloria Anzaldúa and Audre Lorde. *Journal of Homosexuality, 26*(2/3), 73-95.

King, K. (1992). Audre Lorde's lacquered layerings: The lesbian bar as a site of literacy production. In S. Munt (Ed.), *New lesbian criticism* (pp. 51-74). New York: Columbia University Press.

Lorde, A. (1980). *The cancer journals.* San Francisco: Aunt Lute Foundation.

Lorde, A. (1982). *Zami: A new spelling of my name.* Freedom, CA: Crossing Press.

Lorde, A. (1984). *Sister outsider.* Trumansburg, NY: Crossing Press.

Mercer, K. (1991). Skin head sex thing: Racial difference and the homoerotic imaginary. In Bad Object Choices (Ed.), *How do I look? Queer film and video* (pp. 169-222). Seattle: Bay Press.

Mercer, K. (1993). Dark and lovely too: Black gay men in independent film. In M. Gever, J. Greyson, & P. Parmar (Eds.), *Queer looks* (pp. 238-256). New York: Routledge.

Miller, A. E. (1991). At the club. In E. Hemphill (Ed.), *Brother to brother* (pp. 72-73). Boston: Alyson.

Moraga, C. (1983). Refugees of a world on fire. In G. Anzaldúa & C. Moraga (Eds.), *This bridge called my back: Writings by radical women of color* (pp. i-iv). New York: Kitchen Table Press.

Mulvey, L. (1985). Visual pleasure and the narrative cinema. In G. Mast & M. Cohen (Eds.), *Film theory and criticism* (pp. 803-816). New York: Oxford University Press.

Powell, L. C. (1983). Black macho and black feminism. In B. Smith (Ed.), *Home girls* (pp. 283-292). New York: Kitchen Table Press.

Raynaud, C. (1988). "A nutmeg nestled inside its covering of mace": Audre Lorde's *Zami.* In B. Brodki & C. Schenk (Eds.), *Life/lines: Theorizing women's autobiography* (pp. 221-242). Ithaca, NY: Cornell University Press.

Rich, B. R. (1993). When difference is (more than) skin deep. In M. Gever, J. Greyson, & P. Parmar (Eds.), *Queer looks* (pp. 318-339). New York: Routledge.

Riggs, M. (Producer, Narrator). (1989). *Tongues untied* [Video]. (Available from Frameline, P.O. Box 14792, San Francisco, CA 94114)

Riggs, M. (1991). Black macho revisited: Reflections of a snap! queen. In E. Hemphill (Ed.), *Brother to brother* (pp. 253-257). Boston: Alyson.

Rose, J. (1986). *Sexuality in the field of vision.* London: Verso.

Simmons, R. (1991). Tongues untied: An interview with Marlon Riggs. In E. Hemphill (Ed.), *Brother to brother* (pp. 189-199). Boston: Alyson.

Soebnlein, K. (1990, April 25). Breaking the gag order. *Outweek,* p. 60.

13 African American Women Between Hopscotch and Hip-Hop

*"Must Be the Music
(That's Turnin' Me On)"*

KYRA D. GAUNT

How do young, intelligent, black women—single mothers, married, working, or seeking degrees of "higher learning"—how do they negotiate participation in a music that has been labeled "male" and appears to be a contemporary example of the subordination of women in our culture? Contrary to popular belief, there are African American women who are fans of rap music. Their voices have been nearly silenced in the wave of criticisms of misogny against rap. This silence will persist as long as we accept the strongly held notion that rap/hip-hop music[1] is exclusively male created and targeted as opposed to being shaped by male and female participation in contradictory and complex ways. Most of the research on women as fans has been overwhelmingly focused on white fandom and white artists from the Beatles to Madonna (see Lewis, 1990, 1992). There are alternative ways of viewing African American women as rap fans other than as objectified, self-degrading, video-dancing, sex-craved, "gold diggers" or "skeezers" (colloquial terms for women after men artists for financial stability or status).

As an African American woman who adores hip-hop music, my experiences as a purchasing fan began in 1989 as a burgeoning student of ethnomusicology, although rap songs have dotted my musical tastes since 1979. My experiences since then have been doused with assumptions from both men and women that female rappers—MC Lyte, Queen Latifah, Yo-Yo, Boss, and even Me'shell NdegeOcello (who is musically more a funkster than a hip-hopper)—are either trying to be like their male counterparts, or that female artists sleep their way into the rap business. These two indictments have become synonymous in many discussions, leaving a lot of "talk" that disqualifies women as "real" rappers and consequently diminishing the significance of and attention to the texts these women create.

> I think they are trying to be like the men [referring to women rappers].
> —Lee, a black, 22-year-old university student

According to Tricia Rose, critics tend multifariously to define rap as "ultra-urban, unromantic, hyper-realistic, neo-nationalist, anti-assimilationist, aggressive Afrocentric impulse" (Rose, 1991, p. 111), and all of these identifications are associated with and represent male points of view. Consequently, people tend to oversimplify the participation of women rappers and fans as their desire to be "one of the boys" (p. 111). Rose demands a more multifaceted analysis of black women's identity and sexuality *even* as they/we listen to gangsta and hardcore styles of rap music so that we do not lose our sexual and gendered identities. Only then can African American women's presence in rap music, with all of its seeming contradictions, begin to be fully visible.

After many defensive maneuvers on my part, I began to seriously contemplate what drew me and possibly other women to rap music. I began to think about my own everyday experiences as a girl within the sphere of girls' musical games. In thinking about games that involved music, I thought of hand-clapping and double Dutch (jump-rope) game-songs. The game-songs we performed beyond the public or mass-mediated realm resemble the music of hip-hop in various ways. For example, the sing-song, declamatory nature of the vocal line, the emphasis on rhythmic punctuation and style, the use of the musical break (or interruption of sound but not musical line), the emphasis on narration and linguistic play, and more. Rap music might be seen as a site for revisiting girls' play for African American women fans and performers, in addition to conventional uses of rap as dance music and a site for cultural and nationalist impulses. In spite of the public opinion about gangsta and hardcore styles of rap music, women have playfully dealt with similar features within their own gendered sphere. Community and camaraderie became the order of the day among neighborhood playmates through the ideas, tunes, and creative rhymes that accompanied hand-clapping games. Double Dutch often used vulgar language and alluded playfully to sexuality, as does rap.

Shawna and Devonne, students at King (a predominantly black elementary school in Los Angeles) described . . . the text of "Mailman, mailman":

I say it a different way. I go:
"Mailman, mailman, do your duty,
Here come the lady with da African booty.
She could do da pompom, she could do the split,
She could do anything to make you split."
That's all. [Shawna, age 8]

And everybody else say:
"Mailman, mailman, do your duty,
Here come the lady with da African booty.
She can do the wahwah, she can do the splits,
She can do anything to make you split, so split!" [Devonne, age 8]
        (Merrill-Mirsky, 1988, p. 213)

In playing these games we used a rapping-style of melody and rhythmically coordinated motions throughout our bodies that represented a way of being black girls. This can provide an alternative avenue to understanding not only the contradictory ways women support and critique male rappers' sexual discourse (Rose, 1994, p. 150), but also how black women's consciousness has been shaped through their own girlhood experiences. So why hasn't this connection ever been apparent before? Why haven't women identified rap music with the games played in some of our pasts?

One reason for this oversight might simply be the persistent reconstructions of femininity and womanhood intersected with race that does not easily allow African American women to express sexuality, vulgarity, anger, or aggression—all key themes in the identity politics of men's expression in rap. Here lies the tension for African American women as fans of a publicly mediated genre like hip-hop music. This chapter will continually draw out the tensions that poise African American women fans and performers between the multiple subjectivities of the realm of hopscotch (and other girls' games) and the culture of hip-hop music. The former is bounded by pre-pubescence, female-authority, and freer expression due to the private and local sites of that expression, while the latter is framed by a consciousness representing African American men and their awareness of expression in a public, white hegemonic context.

Curiously, there is evidence that suggests black girls have constantly participated in spheres of black cultural expression retrospectively or commonly mischaracterized as male. Female expression has often occurred beyond the public sphere, for example, in the practice of "pattin' juba" (a progenitor of "ham-boning" and a probable progenitor of hand-clapping games and black styles of cheerleading):

> On a Maryland plantation, a boy sang the "words of a jig in a monotonous tone of voice, beating time meanwhile with his hands alternately against each other and against his body." The principal "juber rhymer" on that plantation was a girl named Clotilda who improvised the verses for the dancing and recited them in a "shrill sing-song voice, keeping time to the measure . . . by beating her hands sometimes against her sides and patting the ground with her feet." After each stanza, she paused a bit—perhaps to collect her thought for the next improvised stanza—but continued to beat her hands and pat her foot without ceasing. (Southern, 1983, pp. 179-180)

This travel account of black performance from 1859 is recalled in Eileen Southern's unprecedented chronicle, *The Music of Black Americans.* The unusual performance Rutherford documented in his travel log is called *juba* or *pattin' juba*.[2] Pattin' juba became the ham-boning parodied and appropriated as the "Jim Crow"[3] dance of the minstrel stage during the middle of the 19th century. What interests me about Rutherford's account is not only his description of the juba style, which so closely recalls black cheerleading, but also his attention to a black girl as a "master" of style. As early as 1859 black girls were actively participating in cultural expression that is often held up as a male expressive form.

Obscene and vulgar language can be found in the lyrics of hand-clapping games and double Dutch, to later manifestations in black cheerleading and (on the college level) sorority step shows (performances at parties featuring juba-descendent practices). As we get older, the language becomes more explicit than here in the elided linguistic play of an early hand-clapping game known as "Miss Lucy":[4]

> Behind the 'frigerator
> There was a piece of glass
> Miss Lucy fell upon it
> And it went straight up her
> Ask me no more questions
> Tell me no more lies
> The boys are in the bathroom
> Pullin up their
> Fly me up to heaven . . . etc.

Feminist Samplings: Written and Performative Practices Within Cultural Traditions

The most profound intellectual questions emerge out of what seem to be ordinary and commonplace objects of study . . . capable of teaching us that a sideshow can sometimes be the main event (Lipsitz, 1990, p. 20).

> Play me a game like Blind Man's dance
> And bind my eyes with ignorance
> Bump d'bump bump d'bump
>
> Tell my life with a liquor sign
> Or a cooking spoon from the five-and-dime
> And a junkie reel in two/four time
> Bump d'bump bump d'bump . . .
> I'll play possum and close my eyes
> To your greater sins and my lesser lies
> That way I share my nation's prize
> Bump d'bump bump d'bump
> —Excerpt from "Bump d'Bump," by Maya Angelou (1981), And Still I
> Rise, is reprinted by kind permission from the publishers, Virago Press.

In this chapter, I will utilize a mixture of writing styles incorporating poetry, prose, and fiction. Experimental modes of writing have become an attractive and emergent form of writing in culture studies, especially for women writing about culture. Anthropologist Deborah Gordon notes that women have often intermixed autobiography, ethnography, and memoir in their first "feminist" contributions to the field (Gordon, in press). This trend is evidenced in the work of black women writers such as Toni Morrison, bell hooks, June Jordan, and Audre Lorde. This appears to indicate a wide-ranging contemporary trend among women writers as they approach issues by and about women and gender. Gordon suggests that a clear advantage lies in the merging of alternative forms of expression to describe complex cultural practices more fully. Such mergings unflatten and expand academic styles of writing, moving readers toward a more sympathetic understanding of cultural events within a field of "historically situated problems" (Gordon, in press).

I adopt this method of expression in this chapter, not only because of the legacy of feminist or womanist methods of writing the chapter invokes, but also for the sampling aesthetics of hip-hop culture that inform it. Representing this text as a mixture allows a chance to emulate the process of "sampling" portions or entire textures from earlier popular recordings as in hip-hop music or the process of incorporating popular jingles, icons, and cultural themes into African American girls' game-songs. The hand-clapping game-song "Dr. Pepper" is an interesting example of incorporating, or "sampling," a well-known tune from a popular commercial jingle into African American girls' play.[5]

> The history of African-American music and culture has been defined in large measure by a history of the art of signifying, recontextualization, collective memory, and resistance . . . in dialogue . . . through sampling and other revisionary practices. (Rose, 1991, p. 113)

I could claim to identify sampling practices with the postmodernist aesthetic, but the ways in which girls learn their games and the way popular verbal and aural iconography is incorporated into musical style points first to understanding contemporary black musical expression as a product of African American aesthetics and cultural history, rather than from a postmodernist aesthetic.

In discussing the politics of race, gender, and location in the reception and audience of hip-hop music, mixture can serve to unflatten the coded styles and stylized sampling practices of a "black" cultural artistic expression "created and sustained" through the art of sampling that Andrew Goodwin (1990) also identified as a "politics of theft" (p. 271). This politics of theft is used to signify a re-claiming, or re-membering, of musical elements and styles of black performing artists that, for example, dominated black radio versus Top 40 (predominantly white) markets.

The historical web of events and attitudes that surrounds the musical play of African American girls' games and hip-hop music raises many questions about gender socialization and performer-audience dynamics in popular music. In popular music, social and mental constructs about audience and identity are problematized by intersections of race, gender, class, locality, and social power and/or privilege. In any community these compounded intersections are shaped by widespread and subjective interpretations of any shared history and/or identity (Gilroy, 1987, p. 235). Paul Gilroy contends that a "community" can never dictate or ensure that all its members will subscribe to the plural meanings ascribed within or without the group.

"Any Ladies in the House?" Calls and Responses

The familiar "shout out," "Any ladies in the house" or "All the ladies in the house say 'Ho—o' " heard in a variety of black music contexts, calls for the women in the audience to respond sonorously with a scream or with a prescribed response. At a rap music event, women's response qualifies and quantifies their presence through the timbre of their collective voices (i.e., responding collectively in relatively high-pitched hollers or screams), the loudness of their response (i.e., aurally representing their collective size), the length of any response, and through the vibe of their participatory mood. In all these exchanges, women's individual voices are conflated into an ineffable ecstatic response. We might assume that women rappers are attempting to speak for the individual, voiceless women in the rap audience.

Women's raps and my interviews with female rappers display . . . fears of manipulation, loss of control, and betrayal at the hands of men. Women rappers employ many of the aesthetic and culturally specific elements present in male lyrics while offering an alternative vision of similar social conditions. (Rose, 1991)

Figure 13.1. Photographed via video (frame grab) by Kyra D. Gaunt 1995. World Invitational Double Dutch Competition in North Charleston, South Carolina June 16-17, 1995.

Lost my voice?
Of course.

You said, "Poems of
love and flowers are
a luxury the Revolution
cannot afford."

Here are the warm and juicy
vocal cords,
slithery,
from my throat.

Allow me to press them upon
your fingers,
as you have pressed that

bloody voice of yours
in places it could not know to speak,
nor how to trust.

("Lost My Voice? Of Course" from *Revolutionary Petunias &*
Other Poems, copyright © 1972 by Alice Walker, reprinted by
permision of Harcourt Brace & Company)

Alice Walker wrote this poem, titled "Lost My Voice? Of Course. / for
Beanie*" (Walker, 1972, p. 44). The asterisk she inserted after Beanie leads the
reader to a subscript, and obviously back to a past when he was "*A *childhood*
bully." The ideals of the so-called Revolution, whether the black power ideologies of the 1960s or the b-boy politics of hip-hop culture, involve a
polarization of the male and the female, the masculine and the feminine. This
bi-polarized "disorder" is irreconcilable, leaving women (as fans and rappers)
as well as men little or no room to talk openly about the dimensions of
women's subjectivity and participation in rap music.

Understanding Women's Discourse
in the Context of Rap Discourse

I want to explore women's discourse about the music and lyrics of rap
within the contested discourse that encircles rap as music. Is there a critical
space allowed for women as subjects rather than objects in the all-too-often
hostile discussions about lyrical misogyny and the objectification of women's
"tits and asses" in rap videos and product packaging? The answer is found in
deconstructing the words we use to describe and talk about rap music. How
is it that the commonly precipitated response from women rap fans, "I like
the beat, but I don't listen to the lyrics," has been interpreted as some kind of
complicity with the subordination of women? This response and others are
rarely interrogated within the context of the hostile public discourse surrounding black men and around rap as a musical complex (vs. its reduction
to lyrics or disqualifications as "real" or "good" music).

The contradictory ways that women hip-hop fans critique and support
male rappers' sexual discourse is apparent in fan responses found in Rap
magazines (e.g., *Rap Pages* and *Source*).[6] Among the more common responses
to "misogynistic" raps, one finds women who claim they would never admit
to liking the music because it "downs" or objectifies women through its lyrics.

Certain songs (e.g., "Bitches Ain't Shit" by Dr. Dre) seem to "talk bad" about women. Yet, what often follows these critiques is a contrasting interest or appreciation for a song which they often express in a savory-tone claiming "but it's the jam" or "cuz' the beats are slammin'." This is reminiscent of a different moment when young teenagers on Dick Clark defined the "goodness" of a song by its beat. Such complex responses hint at the denial, limitation, or maladaption of women's paarticipation and pleasure as fans in and of hip-hop. This leads to the contradictory denial of the lyrics by women while they are seemingly driven by constructions of some irresistible, "primitive" beat. Such contradictions lead to several mischaracterizations of female fans. On the surface their response can be reduced by their preference for the "beat" as having limited appreciation for anything more than the most elemental part of the music. In intellectual classical criticism of pop music and black music, the "beat" or rhythm is more generally viewed as the simplest musical element in composition and creativity (anyone can do it), and the grossest erotic or sexually constructed aspect of popular music.

The idyllic intellectualized hip-hop fandom found among many African American men rarely focuses on the "beat" or in turn the danceability of the music, but focuses on the skill and authority of the rapper almost at the expense of considering the value of the musical dimensions of the art. Inter-pretations of such responses by women are also biased by the perception that black, African-derived music lacks the kind of melody one finds in Beethoven or, more contemporarily, Sting.[7] The overwhelming perception of beats, rhythm, and the controversial use of sampling has led many to believe that rap is not music (including some of its fans). All these factors and perceptions clutter the way women's responses to rap music are interpreted. "Rap lyrics are a critical part of a rapper's identity, strongly suggesting the importance of authorship and individuality in rap music" (Rose, 1994, p. 95). The more women deny the lyrics of rap for the sake of the "beat," the more readily they can be dismissed as groupies and sex objects. Residual Victorian ideals of white womanhood, perceptions about black women and their bodies, and notions of black nationhood as a struggle over patriarchy further complicate our understanding of African American women's fandom.

Most people are not conversant with even one way of talking about the formal and aesthetic aspects of music. This is ultimately why articles on rap in major newspapers only focus on the lyrics of Snoop Doggy Dogg, Public Enemy, or MC Lyte. What else can they communicate to a poorly conversant music public? How do you describe for a newspaper deadline the interaction of meter and rhythmic units of time and a particular flow of those rhythms that defines part of Snoop's style? How do you describe the way rap music is constructed when the general public does not accept, nor can they verify to themselves or others, whether it is music or not? This is really a useless debate. Music is being made, like it or not.

Consequently, the music is overlooked, distorting even more women's role and participation in rap. There was a popular song during the 1980s that featured an incessant chorus of female voices chanting "must be the music" as the lead (male) singer replied "That's turnin' me on." This song signifies many of the tensions raised in confronting the issues of representation, performer-audience dynamics, and contextual analysis of African American women's fandom. If we imagine that women are articulating this thought—"Must Be the Music (That's Turnin' Me On)"—it could be interpreted in a number of ways. It could be a denial of the lyrics of rap for the attraction of the music. It could be a veiled disclosure signifying women's access to sexual excitement through both the music (i.e., through listening and dancing) *and* the lyrics (including the "vulgar" language).

Lisa Lewis has developed a form of textual analysis for female address in videos that can be adopted for further analysis of African American women's rap fandom. The textual practice involves two interrelated sign systems—access and discovery. *Access signs* appropriate the privileged experiences of boys and men (rap music), and *discovery signs* refer to and celebrate distinctly female modes of cultural expression and experience (girls' games). The reception of rap music can then be used in the fandom of African American women as a sign of "access" and of "discovery" (Lewis, 1990, p. 109) of their own sexual desire and gender identity. Therefore African American women, like any other fans, as Lisa Lewis has stressed, are drawn to both "extra-textual and textual details" (Lewis, 1990, p. 156).

Obscuring (Performing) the Masculine and the Feminine

> The bass drum[8]
> the foundation of black sound,
> That big drum's masterful sound
> the Mother drum
> —She—
> the master drum,
> upon which He often improvises and is called—
> the master drummer.

He makes Her skins talk, He speaks through Her songs
They are voiced drums ringing bass heavy and intricate
the heart of the music
the heart of the ritual.
She—Phat and unflattened,
bringing together her music,
her sexuality

—

A music full with Her childhood

Might male tongue/drums sing our sidewalk games?
A girl-song language from hand and hip, jump, and skip-rope about
Miss Lucy and Miss Mary Mack
and Little Sally Walker
(all of whom were young and single and
in some ways free from the subordination of becoming a "lady")
Free of being de-moralized,
of being accused the matriarch,
free of upsetting the "natural" order of the Black family.
—Kyra D. Gaunt

The mediation between the access and discovery signs found in rap music for African American women is illustrated through obscured boundaries between masculine signs ("hardness," the street, theft, sex, penetration, etc.) and feminine signs (softness, romance, commitment, children, the female body, etc.) in the lyrics of female rappers, the dress of both performers and fans, and the masculine and feminine musical constructions that are now a part of the rap aesthetic. Many African American women rappers are consciously and unconsciously obscuring their private positions on issues of gender and sexuality within black performance contexts. It is rare to hear Queen Latifah respond as pointedly as she does here in any of her recorded raps.

But you know what? There's a double standard out there. Me and [MC] Lyte have groupies. We could literally do a buncha niggers in every place we went to. We could say, "Oh, that nigga right there is fine, BOOM, I'm gettin' him," then ask him backstage. But if I did that, would I be a woman or would I be a hoe? Y'all can stick your shit in 20 different people and still be men. (Chambers & Morgan, 1992, p. 117; reprinted by permission from *Essence*)

Inherent in Latifah's response is envy. Envy of the social freedom men appear to have and the sexual freedom they enjoy. She speaks of a lack of access to the sexual privileges men in rap have enjoyed as a result of their gender.

In analyzing one of Latifah's more popular rap songs, "Come Into My House," I observed that her use of language slyly vacillates around signs of access and of discovery relative to dancing, women's sexuality, and power. This is achieved primarily through the constructed image of Latifah as a reigning black queen. This notion appears to turn the existence of a monarchical king on its head, but Latifah's lyrics show their command through her lyrical allusions to sexuality while constantly denying the erotic as the dominant subtext.

In one of her most popular recordings from 1989 on Tommy Boy Records, Queen Latifah welcomes listeners into her "house" where she potentially entertains dancers listening to the song as a house music mix in a club (personal Walkman listeners, home stereo listeners, street boombox listeners, etc.). Her "house" is defined as a "Queen-dom," a place ruled not by a king, but a queen in her femaleness envisioning a female monarchical rule. This place she says is open to all who come in order to dance or groove to the music as an escape of a sort. She invites those who've had a hard day, to escape the former ruler of the day (read: work or labor). A house where work is not about labor or housework but pleasure subverting the work of the day for the work of the nightclub.

Throughout the incessant refrains of the chorus we hear Queen Latifah exclaim, "Give me body!" The entire song acts as a counter-narrative inviting us to another world, not only where wage labor work is subverted, but where the body is privileged as an expression of individualized dance shared with an audience and Latifah, who urges everyone to "move." Latifah clearly understands the multiple meanings of the body in Rap music, in dance music, and from perspectives and worlds other than her own. As if in response to those concerns, criticisms, and misunderstandings by outsiders, she explains in her lyrics that expression of the body is not an "erotic interlude" negating perceptions of the female (and the male) body in the performance of sexualized dances found in black nightclubs. The Queen reminds us further that this so-called erotic interlude, "moves multitudes" whether she is alluding to the power and history of black dance music in the United States and throughout the world, or the power of her music to make you and others dance doesn't matter. Throughout the rap song, Queen Latifah challenges ideas about women in control and their ability to deal with power. The idea of her power is represented in slippery polysemic meanings that suggest being able to fight "blow for blow" yet, also hint at the power relations in the performance of oral sex or a "blow job." Here Latifah emphatically states that she can take and give some and "still rise," alluding to a famous poem by Maya Angelou that in one line asks does a woman's "sassiness" upset you? She creates her rap performance within the contested terrain of women's lived and talked about experiences particularly related to issues of power and physical might and power in bed.

She concludes the third and final verse with a hope that her lyrical display has "aroused" her third-person plural/singular audience and reiterates that it *is* (not "was") an open invitation to "Come Into My House"—the title of this song. Latifah re-interprets a conventionally female domain, the house, into her "queen-dom" set in a non-conventional and often sexualized context for women—nightclubs—which are perceived as male-dominated or controlled spaces privileging male DJs, male artists, male MCs, and even male pleasure. Nightclubs always offer one night a week as "ladies night" where women get free admission, but the marketing strategy often involves baiting more men to come into a house full of women. Conversely, women are attracted to such nights with the idea that more men will attend as well. In Latifah's song "Come Into My House," she celebrates her "queen-dom" and femaleness in a sign of discovery as described earlier, while privileging certain dimensions of maleness for herself as a woman occupying and employing strategies that are male and female.

This popular hip-hop/house-dance tune, "Come Into My House," appears to subtly blur the line between women as sexual objects and women as subjects of sexual encounters or power struggles. The background lyric sung by Latifah imperceptibly alternates between "Don't make me wait" and "Don't make ya wait" during the pulsating, repeated groove marked by a confidently punctuated bass line ascent heard in the introduction, the choruses, and the conclusion of the song. This oscillation between pronouns characterizes a change from waiting with anticipation to teasing whomever is waiting, which blurs the representation of Latifah's meaning between signs of access and of discovery. Musically, the segments that feature this oscillation are formal transitional spaces. Rather than being marginalized by the versification of the song, the intro, the choruses, and the conclusion are desirable spaces for audience participation, vocally or dance-wise. In the context of club dancing, the real activity, or significance of physical expression, occurs in these spaces of "marginality"—the introduction, the chorus, the bridge, and so forth. In these moments the lyrics are secondary to the music, and other activities and responses, including dancing, are foregrounded. These are the same musical spaces in which samples are found in earlier recordings and placed in new hip-hop texts.

Contributing Strands to Hip-Hop Culture

The study and exploration of black girls' games, if viewed as a musical site in U.S. popular culture, might uncover a means of learning black musical style, a musical style that is highlighted by the use of call-and-response, syncopation, dance, individuality within collectivity, improvisation, and subtle movements and nonverbal expressiveness within musical time. In public sites this play appears to be socially segregated. But in the company of siblings and playmates of the opposite sex, in the privacy of the home, in a "closed" community or street block, or away from the eye/spy of adults (in children's exclusive sites, i.e., the bus stop or at recess), play is not always segregated. Girls' games were and in many cases continue to be situated "out in left field" for boys.

> CAROL MERRILL-MIRSKY: Is it true that girls do this (handclapping) more than boys?
>
> BOYS: Yes.
>
> CM: Why?
>
> DARYL: Because they're girls' games. They make 'em up. We don't. We don't play 'em.
>
> NATHANIEL: 'Cause they girls.
>
> MARVIN: 'Cause they have more excitement.
>
> NATHANIEL: We like the Beastie Boys. No, we play kick ball, and they like to play handball and hand games 'cause they don't have a area that they have fun in. [Daryl, Nathaniel, Marvin, age 8] (Merrill-Mirsky, 1988, p. 73)

This interview of boys in Los Angeles elementary schools was conducted for a 1988 dissertation on ethnicity and gender in children's musical play. The brief exchange reveals boys' awareness of gender boundaries, but it also reveals their "transgressing" those boundaries. Merrill-Mirsky also provides the girls' perspectives on the division of play by gender.

> It's like other things. We don't play with G.I. Joes. It's [handclapping games] something girls do and boys don't. [Jasmine, age 10]

In fourth grade, a few boys played hopscotch, but as they get older they want to be more normal. [Celeste, age 12]

We bring it (games with song) to school. And then everybody learn how to do it. Even the boys. They copy what we do. When we be dancin', when we be doin' this (demonstrates), the boys go (exaggerates movements). They be teasin' us. They just jealous because they don't know how to do it. [Devonne, Shawna, Shaquanna, Bridget, age 8] (Merrill-Mirsky, 1988, p. 73)

This last collective response highlights the girls' ownership of the production and dissemination of these games. Their statements emphasize their competency as well. Boys, in girls' opinions, do not know how to play their games as well. It also calls attention to boys' fears of fully participating in the girls' space through movement and song. While boys parody girls' behavior through grotesque imitation, they also learn the games, albeit through mockery.

Merrill-Mirsky itemizes some key characteristics distinguishing girls' play from boys' that were revealed in her study of 298 children, of which only 18 were boys. The Los Angeles schools studied were dominated by either African Americans, Latino Americans, or new immigrant ethnic groups. Girls' games tend to involve choral activity, songs, and rhymes; rhythmic play, linguistic play, motor activity involving various body parts, solitary practice, competition between individuals rather than groups (but that competition is usually indirect), well-defined and multiple stages of play, much in-game waiting, turn-taking in ordered sequences, and play in private areas. Boys tended to exercise power tactics such as bodily strength and contact, use of larger spaces, larger groups in their activities, well-defined outcomes with winners and losers clearly labeled, a continuous flow of activity, games that last longer, fantasized or actual conflict between groups or teams, aggressive negotiations for play, and play in public areas (Merrill-Mirsky, 1988).

The mocking of girls' games by boys allows them never "really" to engage in girls' play under the threat that they might be viewed as "girls" in the eyes of other boys. So their full participation would have to take place outside the public view and public play sites of other boys. Boys also develop their own gendered linguistic games (sometimes also involving musical declamation) that are similar to the rhyming and turn-taking of girls' games. These everyday performative expressions have several names, such as "rapping," "capping," "the Dozens," or "toasts."

Such raps or toasts often involve bravado and stylistic expression in lyrics, rhyme, and delivery even when re-telling a common version or re-casting an old one to fit the times. Often lyrics might develop around a string of abilities: "the bed tucker, the cock plucker, the motherfucker," and so on. Ordinarily, as part of the sport or skill of the play, a performer of this street ritualized practice would refer derogatorily to a listener's family and the listener themselves (or whomever the lyrical display is directed at) and the performer would elevate their own family members and themselves both in very creative ways. For example, "I might not be the best in the world, but I'm in the top two and my brother's gettin' old. Ain't nothing bad about you but your breath" (H. R. Brown, 1969/1990, p. 354). In explaining the art of "The Dozens," H. Rap Brown says it could go on for hours, and that "some of the best Dozens players were girls" in his youth (pp. 354-355). I cannot personally recall experiences among "girl" friends that involved the Dozens.

Documentation of the Dozens by anthropologists in the 1960s led to it being defined as the art of "verbal dueling" among black males, not unlike the practice of memorizing texts from the latest raps and improvising (or "freestyling") has been commonly defined as the experience of male fans of hip-hop. Anthropologists framed these games as "duels," which is a much more provocative way of characterizing male activity than as play. Break-dancing crews were labeled gangs by the police and other onlookers, and their performances were represented as mock fights or duels among former gang members; this seems to obliterate any interpretation of the art form as competitive dance, which has been characteristically defined as a sign of feminine or female expression.

The Dozens and other similar linguistic games, or duels, as well as contemporary male artists' raps, tend to diminish the melodic variation of song (best characterized by R&B songs) to something closer to speech, though still melodically inclined. Women rappers (Queen Latifah, Salt 'n' Pepa, TLC, Me'shell NdegeOcello), unlike their male counterparts, tend to employ singing as well as rapping in their performances. It has been commonplace to hear fans discriminating between rappers according to the absence or presence of song or song-like (more pitch-defined or melodic) rapping. Therefore, if men rarely use more melodic styles of rapping and are seen as the progenitors of rapping as an expressive cultural form, then women rappers who use more melodic styles are depreciating their authenticity as rappers. MC Lyte, the female duo BO$$, and Yo-Yo rarely if ever use a style of rapping that resembles song in any way. This is more than likely due to a lack of ability to sing well, rather than any attempt to construct themselves as "authentic." Nevertheless, artists whose style is more declamatory than song-like are often perceived as more "hardcore" than others. The presence of singing often reminds hip-hop fans of another category of black popular music, R&B (e.g., Luther Vandross, Anita Baker, and Boyz II Men) that has very different musical aesthetics, often signifying romance (a feminized representation). For women, romance and sex(uality) are often inextricable.

> The codes marking gender difference in music are informed by the prevalent attitudes of their time . . . music does not just passively reflect society; it also serves as a public forum within which various models of gender organization (along with many other aspects of social life) are asserted, adopted, contested, and negotiated. (McClary, 1991, pp. 7-8)

Several studies and articles have acknowledged a gender division that exists in the consumption, and equally in the marketing, of popular music styles. Most have asserted that rhythm 'n' blues and its antecedent rock 'n' roll (from Louis Jordan and Wynonie Harris to Bill Haley and Elvis Presley), heavy metal, and rap have been constructed as masculine hegemonic sites of production, representation, and consumption. Musics assumed to be produced for women and girls are displayed through a dominant code of *romance*—translated into the "feminization" and manipulation of musical sound. In black popular music this is exemplified best in R&B music with romantic ballads composed and sung by Luther Vandross, whose supple baritone melodies articulate caressing, finesse, and even exciting erotic flourishes through an up-close-and-personal bedroom voice. "Girls [and women] are encouraged from all directions to interpret their sexuality in terms of romance, to give priority to notions of love, feeling, commitment, the moment of bliss" (Frith & McRobbie, 1990, pp. 378-379). Unlike the codes of romance in popular music and R&B, girls' games and rap music allow African American women an avenue for the discovery of sexuality and experiences that are not connected to conventional notions of women's roles.

Might hip-hop's music be re-weaving rhythms
from double Dutch and the "kiss my ass" languaging of football and basketball
sideline cheers
where dark- and light-brown girls stomp their feet
and clap their hands
expressing themselves through black stomped cheers

—a stylized sort of dance—
beyond the gaze on our short-skirted, shiny legs
grounded in saddle shoes and polyphonic rhythms
that put your hands on your hips
and make your back-bone slip,
so you can shake it to the east,
shake it to the west,
shake it to the very one
ya love the best.

we shake it from ourselves

from remembrances of "eeny-meeny pepsa deeny" handclappin'
and "Teddy bear, teddy bear touch the ground" jump-ropin'.

Maybe this is why women can find a space for themselves in Snoop Doggy
Dogg and TuPac,
Black Sheep and Boss
and not be "trying to be" like men.

Are we being a bit hysterical about "women on display" whether they be
cheerleaders
or hip-hop "ho's" [I smell the mud of a gangsta show]?

Look beyond the gaze
Beyond the frame that constructs women as sexually desirable to men.
See what's behind women's participation
From the inside, rather than from the masculinized gaze that orients our lens.

Lyrics from an old English game-song (not exclusive to black girls), "Skip to My Lou," are used in a modern rap-song by the group Leaders of the New School. This New York City-based hip-hop group, which would easily be classified within the realm of "hardcore," is comprised of four young black men in their early twenties. Lead rapper Busta Rhymes, whose tongue is distinctly dance hall/reggae-flavored, opens with the lyrics from a girls' game and calls what he's engaged in a "hopscotch game."

The use of lyrics from an old English game-song (not exclusive to black girls), "Skip to my lou," and male rappers mentioning being involved in a "funky hopscotch game" in a contemporary rap-song seems quite odd. The group *Leaders of the New School*, based in New York City, who can be classified within the realm of "hardcore," is comprised of four black men in their early twenties. Lead rapper, Busta Rhymes, those rap tongue sounds of the rough and rugged stylings of dancehall/reggae, opens the single "What's Next"[9] with references to girls' games. Might this be men accessing the privileged space and play of women and girls? The answer is not clear, but there is obviously more going on than assumptions that Rap music is about discovering and privileging male expressivity. This single and the album it appeared on were not very successful. This may indicate that this blurring of gender lines is not as acceptable as the "hardcore," "misogynistic" representations that are more commonly heard about in the hip-hop world. Albeit simplistic to accept this as the sole reason for the lack of success of Leaders of the New School's second album, my point is that Rap is both male and female in very complex and contradictory ways.

Busta Rhymes urges the listener to join and follow along in his funky hopscotch game that is meant to be very playful and maybe a bit child-like with its references to "skip to my lou" and hopscotch. The line borrowed closely reflects the melody of the game-song "skip-to my lou" which at the very least indicates an awareness of its original context as a children's game. I should note here also that often when these games are instituted within school settings, boys and girls engage in this game. However, given the identity politics of Rap artists and rap personas, this would clearly qualify as a "girl's game-song." It must be recognized here that I am not inclined to conclude from any of my musings about girls' games and Rap that Rap comes *from* girls and their games rather than boys as is often perceived. On the contrary, I am interested in understanding what the use of such expressions found in some-what isolated and gendered performances demonstrate about a shared web of cultural elements and practices that begin to make divisions between the gender spheres permeable.

Understanding and acknowledging the transmission of girls' games is important here. The invitation by Busta Rhymes is not blurred through its adoption of the lyrics of a girl's game-song, mainly because the original melodic material is not there. The language is adopted, not the music. Nothing about the music in the opening of this rap song aurally references the musical language of girls' games. The borrowing from a feminine sphere is muted through the absence of the melodic material. Yet, a blurring of gender remains, considering that the implied audience of rap music address is predominantly male for sound recordings and videos. Even the reference to baking and stuffing is odd, given conventional gender roles. It must be recognized here that I am not particularly inclined to imply that rap comes from girls and their games. Rather, I am interested in understanding that the mutual expressions found in each performative practice demonstrate the sharing of a web of cultural elements and practices that appear to make divisions between the gender spheres permeable.

A curious aspect of girls' games concerns their transmission. These games are typically passed on solely among children and remembered from age-group to age-group without much adult intervention. My mother and I can recall many of the same games, though hers were from her segregated upbringing and mine from a de-segregated one. During my mother's late teen years there was a similar case of borrowing from what most have considered a "female" sphere. The soul recording "Walkin the Dog" by Rufus Thomas was a popular black dance of the time that was "outlawed" from public display because it was too vulgar, as maintained in my mother's stories about growing up in Maryland outside of Washington, D.C. In a recent interview conducted for my research on this topic, an account was related to me that resembled my mother's tale about the Thomas song and the dance associated with it. A 46-year-old African American woman from Detroit recalled that, "you could get kicked out of school for doing that dance." I asked her if she remembered the opening lines to the song, because we had ended the interview and were reminiscing about young women's sexuality and the games they once played. The opening lines of the song quote verbatim the text of an age-old, cross-cultural girls' hand-clapping game, "Miss Mary Mack":

Mary Mary
All dressed in black
Silver buttons all down her back . . .

Maybe men use girls' games to draw women's attention to their music. Once again the melodic material is recast and subverted. Maybe the inclusion of words from our former games keep us "turned on" or tuned in to rap music.

Alternative Hip-Hop Expressions:
Examples of Black Women's Performance

New artist Me'shell NdegeOcello (pronounced "en-day-gay-o-chel-lo") is probably considered an "alternative" African American artist for a number of reasons. Her alternative status is underscored by her ability to play several "conventional" instruments, her complementary use of both rapping and

Figure 13.2.

singing, her displacement of the "conventional" norms of female expression in her lyrics, and, finally, because she's a woman—as opposed to a man—who controls the production of her own music. NdegeOcello is also bisexual, and it is this information that truly blurs the definitions implied by our heterosexual assumptions about female sexuality and about male hegemony of rap and popular styles of music.

NdegeOcello is a new artist on Madonna's newly formed Maverick recording label. She is a versatile artist who brings her own compositions and a strong funk style of bass playing to her work. *Plantation Lullabies* (1993), her debut album, features her virtuosity on a variety of instruments while performing her own original compositions. What's unusual about her as a popular *musician* is the fact that her primary instrument is the bass. The playing of the electric bass in popular and jazz styles has been typically associated with male artists from Larry Graham (Sly Stone, Graham Central Station), who invented the slap bass technique, to Jaco Pastorius (Weather Report), whose distinctive style has marked much of the bass playing in fusion and New Age music.

The first single from NdegeOcello's debut album for Maverick, "If That's Your Boyfriend (He Wasn't Last Night)," stimulated negative responses from many of my male colleagues and friends. Their comments often began, "I hate that song . . . " followed by concerns about the lyrics rather than the music, which has typically been the subject of intellectual discourse among male fans from rock to hip-hop (for a definition of rock see Frith & McRobbie [1990, p. 373]). I was left thinking that their reactions, as well as similar reactions from female friends, were related more to a disrupted sense of the sexual propriety of a woman; an unacceptable hetero- (or bi-) sexual expression within which female sexuality is expressed. Note the lyrics to this rap:

> now i'm the kind of woman i'll do almost anything
> to get what i want i might play any little game
> call me what you like but you know it's true
> you're just jealous cause he wasn't with you
> don't mean no harm, i just like what i see
> and it ain't my fault if he wants—me
> got what i want and the feeling was right
> if that's your boyfriend he wasn't last night
> (*If That's Your Boyfriend* [*He Wasn't Last Night*] [Me'Shell Johnson]
> © 1993 WB Music Corp., Maverick Music Company, Me'Shell Ndege'Ocello
> & Luna Bird Publishing. All rights administered by WB Music Corp. All
> rights reserved, used by permission.)

Had NdegeOcello been a man, one wonders just how "alternative" this expression would seem. If, according to Frith and McRobbie (1991), certain rock genres construct masculinity as a sexually exclusive environment dependent on the absence of women, might not Me'shell be privileging its opposite: an aggressive, dominating, and boastful expression of sexual control and hardness in a female exchange about a shared sexual partner. One expects a male bass (electric) guitar player, a male seducer, male bravado. NdegeOcello deconstructs the acceptable romantic conventions of a woman as musician and disrupts and blurs the range of acceptable heterosexual expressions.

African American Women and Hardcore: "You Acting Womanish"[10]

Generally, in mainstream (and slightly beyond mainstream) black popular music, black audiences are rarely invited to expand definitions of black women's sexuality. From Aretha Franklin, Dionne Warwick, Gladys Knight and her Pips to the extravaganza of girl/women groups that have marked the recording industry, this has rarely been confronted publicly. Women artists who did not conform to "norms" of female expression (i.e., codes of romance minus sexual agency) were not played on black or white daytime radio. Nevertheless, Millie Jackson, considered a "raunchy" foul-mouthed artist, attracted an "underground" black audience beyond the realm of the charts. Millie Jackson's "vulgar" and assertive expression of female sexual agency was displayed through a rough-edged and risqué rap-like style. She made a career out of the celebration of female/adult sexual pleasure. She performed at the height of the underground musical periods of funk and soul from which hip-hop artists have constructed their sampled textures. If Tricia Rose's assertion that hip-hop sampling indicates the importance of collective identities and group histories is correct, these collective and group images have concealed and overlooked the authority and individuality of female artists like Jackson (Rose, 1994).

Hip-hop culture is defined by its coded associations with the street. The street is a domain through which girls and women play and work, but loitering there may eclipse their "female" gender and/or sexuality. The trope of the street has served as a critical sign of adolescent and adult male discourse in rap music since its inception. This trope of the street was adopted by MTV following the appearance of Michael Jackson's *Beat It* in 1983 (Lewis, 1990). The street became an overarching sign system for male discourse, male competitiveness, and contemporary expressions of paramilitary organization (gangs). This system of coding valorized street-corner activities and leisure as a distinctly male domain. So the street as a code for masculinity tends to restrict the full expression of women as women without some form of re-gendering (from woman to man), thereby implying disruptions of heterosexual "norms."

Rap duo BO$$ [Boss], two women hailing from the inner city of Detroit, must be the ultimate enigma for the women protesting against gangsta rap in Congress. The duo (a rapper and a DJ) completely blur the discrete categories of female and male, feminine and masculine, through both the trope of the street and the tropes of gangsta expressions. Their nom de guerre, BO$$ with the dollar signs in place of the final consonants, signifies authority and privilege through its association with the workplace, the home, and of course the power of stepping up to the microphone, commanding the mike as a rapper. Most of these connotations imply male identities, but ironically, and in slippery ways, suggest the often dreaded dominance of the black matriarch symbolized so often about black women and the black family.

BO$$ attempt to ascribe contradictory signs around themselves, simultaneously privileging access to male experience (i.e., rap artist/star, money maker, etc.), but also reclaims the positive values of independence and control black women experience as heads of single-parent households (where the absence of a male head of household is often a dilemma and a reality). It is a contradictory identity, but one that can appeal to conventional male fandom and female fandom in its polyvocality. The dollar signs also represent rap's capitalistic rhetoric about "gettin' paid," accruing capital and fame. But even the significance of accruing capital can be contradictory in BO$$'s lyrics. For example, in their lyrics from the single "Deeper" (SONY, 1993), they speak of being "heavy" or deeply involved in Rap while they are "frontin' singers." Things are so "tense" Lichelle (the voice of the duo) raps that her dollars "ain't makin' no fucking sense."

This can be interpreted as BO$$ being deeply committed to or involved with rap while they exceed the fame and fortune of singers (once again the negation of singing and/or R&B). The final expression here is a doubly ironic one. She is tense as a result of both how much money she is making and the manner in which she is making that money—as a rapper, musician, or popular star with its contestations between work and leisure. She is also a female rap artist who's making it big. This excerpt is taken from the second track on BO$$'s 1993 debut album. This track, "Deeper," is accompanied by a sample excerpting the hyper-romantic chorus hook of 1970s R&B artist Barry White singing "Deeper, deeper." Barry White's rich, velvet, subterranean voice underscored his place as the king of romantic mood music long before Luther Vandross emerged in the late 1980s. White offered his female and male fans a musical setting for addressing woman's desire. Deep or low male voices penetrate deeply into the consciousness of female R&B fans, just as the deep and low sub-woofer bass sounds that emanate from rap music penetrate the consciousness of hip-hop fans.

BO$$ has been criticized among/in fan conversations I have been privy to for her own low-sounding voice. Many complain that she sounds too much like a man—too "butch," too masculine.

Again, in the lyrics of "Deeper" the duo speaks to their own image as women through claiming the identity of "a hard bitch" who won't soften up in response to questions made by men's voices in the song. Lichelle raps that she's tried being cool (read: softer than a "hard bitch") but she gets caught up

Figure 13.3.

in the harder image when she goes to clubs. At one point she says "I'm just like you" to the anonymous, "everyman" male voice who intermittently questions her pose throughout the track. Lichelle's rap is full of "excessive" language, language marked by irreverence for what is decent public discourse, black street or vernacular language that is more commonly acceptable among men than women. So the women of BO$$ are just like male rappers. Is this a good or a bad implication? Neither and both depending on your perspective on gangsta rap in this case. Ultimately, BO$$ demonstrates women *can* access the male "gangsta" pose.

Women in gangsta rap can adopt the male voice and the male dress and use male privilege and space to deconstruct codes of gender identity as a sign of access, but it is a sign of constant struggle that remains unsettling for male and female fans. BO$$ further problematizes notions of authenticity and image in the rap music industry. On the first track of her compact disc, a "personalized" exchange from her answering machine is framed in an unusual call-and-response structure of the outgoing and incoming message. Music accompanies the outgoing message recorded by rapper Lichelle of the duo, and the unaccompanied incoming message is left, we are to assume, by her real mother.

Women in gangsta rap can adopt the male voice and male dress and use male privilege and space to deconstruct codes of gender identity as a sign of access, but it is a sign of constant struggle that remains unsettling for male and female fans and artists. Lichelle, the voice and personality of BO$$ begins problematizing the social identity of gangsta rappers and female gangsta rappers simultaneously from the very start of their debut compact disc. Recalling the proverbial "ships in the night," the first track is an impersonal exchange between gangsta rapper (and daughter), Lichelle, in a pre-recorded outgoing message. This message, which is musically-accompanied, projects the virtual quality of any CD. It is followed by an unaccompanied, incoming message left by her older-, crackly-voiced mother. The sounds of her voice leads the listener to believe in the actuality of her identity—this really is Lichelle's mom.

The style of the outgoing message is distinctly "hardcore"—indelicately extolling "I don't give a fuck, not a single fuck, not a single solitary fuck." Lichelle quickly ends her curious tirade and asks the caller to leave a message and she'll get back to them. A sterile beep is heard. Lichelle's mom says hello. There is a pregnant pause. She begins to chastise her daughter for having such an offensive message on her machine. She had raised her daughter with better manners than that. Her mother reminds her of the "cultural" upbringing she "paid for" in order to raise her "right" (i.e., dance school, piano lessons, Catholic School for 12 years). The "gangsta stuff" is not a mother's anticipated reward for such effort. There is silence. She then concludes as if nothing unusual had happened, "O.K. . . . call your Mom. Bye."[11]

The struggle here between the social roles that women are supposed to play out is represented as a struggle between mother and daughter, the teacher of respectable ways of being and the rebellious student. Her mother calls up religious up-bringing, money, and education as testament to the extent to which Lichelle was raised "right" as a proper young lady. In the end, her mother must resign her protest to asking her daughter to call her back. So many issues of control, socialization, and role expectations about gender are immediately represented through this unique introduction to BO$$'s debut recording.

Conclusion

Leslie Segar, one of hip-hop's most successful choreographers, whose dance reflects training in gymnastics, jazz, aerobics, and technical dance, reflects the importance of remembering the past in understanding the regeneration in the present. She notes in an article in *Rap Pages* that contemporary hip-hop choreographers (who are primarily women) learn much about the art of presentation and style from "the old school" (a street metaphor for styles from the not-too-distant past) that includes breakdancing, African dance, tap dance, and even jump rope ("Hip-Hop's Fly Choreographers," 1993). Girls' game-songs appear to play a significant and subconscious role in the development of black musical and dance style for the everyday and the professional performer. Segar's recollections of jump rope are a testament to that development.

> *Like Ntozake's colored girls in red and black and blue*
> *Dancing their way into their dark phases of womanhood*
> *Through unseen performances of girls in the hood*
> *In silence for so long*
> *they can't recognize the sound of their voices*

> *My dear (little Sally Walker)*
> *To the front of the stage for this woman's main event.*

> *So how do we girls get from "Mary Mack" to Hip-hop queens*
> *(not Brooklyn or the Bronx but Latifah and Lyte)?*
> *While Alice Walker and Queen Latifah tell black men*
> *they better do right by us,*
> *I try to re-member the musical moments of our coming to age.*

> *The ring games.*
> *The clapping games at the school bus stop at 8:30 every morning at*
> *Courthouse Square apartments.*
> *Co-ordinatin our hands and hips*
> *with tongues in rubato*
> *(that means adjustin the speed to the accuracy of our movements*
> *and returning to the fast tempo once past the hard part).*
> *You know! When you do the back-to-front hand clap and start the pattern all*
> *over again. These are the*
> *games that young black girls learn*

grade after grade
pattin' juba
generation after generation
mary mackin'
they taught us rhythm and black style and inspired the fetish for cheerleading
(for me not so much in school, but in the neighborhood league where black girls,
in a mostly white school district, could make up their own cheers).
Those, too, are passed down from grade to grade.
—"And we're big B-I-G, and we're bad B-A-D, and we're boss
B-O-SS B-O-SS Boss" while polyphonic limbs weave a hocket full of individual
rhythms
as the words of cheers bump upAgain-stEach other
in stomps and claps of harmonious calls and responses
between foot and mouth and clapped hands and hips.

How can we begin to understand the role rap and hip-hop plays in black girls'
and women's lives if we don't remember
the b-girl moves of our long lean and shiny legs in double Dutch and hopscotch?
The scoopin up of sixies in jacks and the bump-bump of tetherball at recreation
daycamps
that baby-sat black summers in the park.

[dreamily:] Love songs . . .
and Luther . . .
cannot do what those things did for our dark brown and car'mel bodies
or our lunar rhythms takin' form in short skirts, pom-poms, saddle shoes and
new sized bra.

Although hip-hop music is a communicative social performance produced, and possibly sustained, primarily by boys and men, this music and all forms of contemporary music performance have the capability of reflecting and restructuring the social relationships and interactions in culture. Ethnomusicologist Ruth Stone (1982) suggests that such cultures can only be understood for their nuances, subtleties, and ambiguities in creation of an audio phenomenon. She adds that musical events are dynamically shaped and created by the selection and manipulation, or the "minute turning of experience," of everyday life. What results is often quite different than everyday life or the representations found in popular culture. What results is a "special" manipulation of social relations (Stone, 1982, p. 136).

The special manipulation of the social relations found in hip-hop music is only apparent in considering women's fandom. I wanted to find a culturally expressive angle that bridged conventional gender boundaries accepted in hip-hop music to date. We can no longer afford to accept the black and white or the male and female as discrete spheres of contemporary popular culture. With overwhelming (though not exhaustive) attention to African American men in hip-hop, and given the limited amount of research investigating the musical lives of African American women in hip-hop and other contemporary popular cultures, I hope this chapter begins to diminish perceptions of men as the sole progenitors of black style. I hope this also encourages the study of women in "other" cultural contexts as well. For me, this chapter represents the beginnings of an exploration into an ethnomusicological study of African American women's musical lives that will complement the previous work accomplished on male fandom and white female fandom.

> *I*
> *am a black woman*
> *tall as a cypress*
> *strong*
> *beyond all definition still*
> *defying place*
> *and time*
> *and circumstance*
> *assailed*
> *impervious*
> *indestructible*
> *Look*
> *on me and be*
> *renewed.*
>
> (Mari Evans, 1970; *I Am a Black Woman*, published by
> Wm. Morrow & Co., 1970, by permission of the author)

Notes

1. I use the terms *rap* and *hip-hop* interchangeably throughout this chapter, but I prefer to use the term *hip-hop* to emphasis a larger cultural network of artistic expression including rap, DJ practice, digital sampling, breakdancing, and graffiti. At times, I use the term *rap* to mean the category of recorded music since 1979.

2. The term *juba* can be traced to one of the largest African language families, Bantu, in which *juba* or *duiba* means to pat, beat time, the sun, the hour. In U.S. slave culture it came to identify an African dance step recorded in South Carolina and the Caribbean. The dance step eventually was called the "Charleston" and became popular among whites (Robinson, 1990, p. 216).

3. Term denoting the systematic practice of discriminating against black people since the mid-1800s. The first stock character of minstrel shows was Jim Crow, a parody of an old black slave who was observed doing a juba dance and song.

4. It should be noted here that girls from a variety of cultural backgrounds play similar hand-clapping games that bear the same lyrics (i.e., Dr. Pepper, Mary Mack, Miss Lucy), but often differ in the way the lyrics are syncopated and turned into melody, and in the way they are "rhythmatized" in the body. The universality of the lyrical themes among girls throughout the country is an interesting subject of study. My interest, however, lies in understanding black women's musical experiences in everyday and popular culture.

5. As you read this text, be aware that certain written details (the use of hyphenation, lower case/upper case letters, "misspellings") are part of a larger, conscious, aesthetic desire on the author's part. Hopefully, actual "typos" will not interfere with my intent to convey a sense of verbal and oral articulations (sound, intonation, nuance, tempo, and rhythm) indigenous to my experience with black English vernacular (BEV).

6. See Rose (1994, p. 150) for a discussion of this issue concerning the contradictory ways of women as rappers. Also, see fan response in Posey (1993, p. 5)

7. In a special devoted to the history of rap on MTV (June 8, 1989), Sting (formerly of The Police) and Paul McCartney (formerly of The Beatles) converse about the lack of originality, the bragging about money, and how this emergent art form is the first black music they haven't liked. Sting: "They are not very original. . . . Is it music if anyone can do it?" (cited in Costello & Wallace, 1990, p. 83).

8. Within this chapter I have woven strands of my own poetry involving thoughts about women/girls, musical practice, and audience reception. To avoid confusing the reader, my original poetry hugs the right margin of the text to represent visually a change of voice and style.

9. From the single "What's Next?", *Time: The Inner Mind's Eye, the Endless Dispute with Reality* (Elektra Records, 1993).

10. **Womanist** 1. From *womanish*. (Opp. of "girlish," i.e., frivolous, irresponsible, not serious.) A black feminist or feminist of color. From the black expression of mothers to female children, "You acting womanish," that is, like a woman. Usually referring to outrageous, audacious, courageous, or *willful* behavior. Wanting to know more and in greater depth than is considered "good" for one. Interested in grown-up doings. Acting grown up. Being grown up. Interchangeable with another black folk expression: "You trying to be grown." Responsible. In charge/*Serious* (Walker, 1983, p. xi).

11. Transcribed by K. D. Gaunt.

References

Angelou, M. (1981). *Poems.* New York: Bantam Books.

Brown, H. R. (1990). Street smarts. In A. Dundes (Ed.), *Mother wit from the laughing barrel: Readings in the interpretation of Afro-American folklore* (pp. 353-356). Jackson: University of Mississippi Press. (Reprinted from *Die nigger die,* by H. Rap Brown, 1969, s.l., Dial Press)

Chambers, G., & Morgan, J. (1992, September). Droppin' knowledge: A rap roundtable (with MC Lyte, Queen Latifah, Chuck D of Public Enemy, Q-Tip of Tribe Called Quest, Heavy D, and KRS-One). *Essence,* pp. 83-85, 116-118, 120-121.

Costello, M., & Wallace, D. F. (1990). *Signifying rappers: Rap and race in the urban present.* New York: Ecco Press.

Evans, M. (1970). *I am a Black woman.* New York: Morrow.

Frith, S., & McRobbie, A. (1990). Rock and sexuality. In S. Frith & A. Goodwin (Eds.), *On record: Rock, pop, & the written word* (pp. 371-389). New York: Pantheon. (Reprinted from *Screen Education, 29,* 1978)

Gilroy, P. (1987). *"There ain't no black in the Union Jack": The cultural politics of race and nation.* Chicago: University of Chicago Press.

Goodwin, A. (1990). Sample and hold: Pop music in the digital age of reproduction. In S. Frith & A. Goodwin (Eds.), *On record: Rock, pop, & the written word* (pp. 258-274). New York: Pantheon. [Reprinted from *Critical Quarterly, 30*(3), 1988]

Gordon, D. (in press). Feminist anthropology and the writing of culture. In R. Behar & D. Gordon (Eds.), *Women writing culture/Culture writing women.* Berkeley: University of California Press.

Hip-hop's fly choreographers. (1993, August). *Rap Pages,* 48-51.

Lewis, L. (1990). *Gender politics and MTV: Voicing the difference.* Philadelphia: Temple University Press.

Lipsitz, G. (1990). Popular culture: This ain't no sideshow. In *Time passages: Collective memory and American popular culture* (pp. 3-20). Minneapolis: University of Minnesota Press.

McClary, S. (1991). *Feminine endings: Music, gender, and sexuality.* Minneapolis: University of Minnesota Press.

Merrill-Mirsky, C. (1988). *Eeny meeny pepsadeeny: Ethnicity and gender in children's musical play.* Unpublished doctoral dissertation, University of California, Los Angeles.

Posey, C. (compiler). (1993, August). On the street. *Rap Pages,* p. 5.

Riddell, C. (1990). *Traditional singing games of elementary school children in Los Angeles.* Unpublished doctoral dissertation, University of California, Los Angeles.

Robinson, B. (1990). Africanisms and the study of folklore. In J. E. Holloway (Ed.), *Africanisms in American culture* (pp. 211-224). Bloomington: Indiana University Press.

Rose, T. (1991). Never trust a big butt and a smile. *Camera Obscura, 23,* 109-131.

Rose, T. (1994). *Black noise: Rap music and black culture in contemporary America.* Hanover, NH: Wesleyan University Press, University Press of New England.

Shange, N. (1977). *For colored girls who have considered suicide/When the rainbow is enuf.* New York: Macmillan.

Southern, E. (1983). *The music of Black Americans: A history* (2nd ed.). New York: Norton.

Stone, R. (1982). *Let the inside be sweet: The interpretation of music event among the Kpelle of Liberia.* Bloomington: Indiana University Press.

Walker, A. (1972). *Revolutionary petunias & other poems.* New York: Harcourt Brace Jovanovich.

Walker, A. (1983). *In search of our mothers' gardens* (p. xi). San Diego, CA: First Harvest/Harcourt Brace Jovanovich.

Name Index

309

Subject Index

About the Contributors

Carolyn M. Byerly is Assistant Professor in the Media Studies Department at Radford University in Virginia, where she teaches classes in newswriting, international communications, and critical theory of news. Her research is concerned with the ways in which marginalized groups, including those in Third World nations, use mainstream media to advance their political agendas. She has published in the European journal *Development* and in *Journalism Educator*. Her chapter "Feminism, News Frames, and the Dialectics of Gender Relations" is forthcoming in M. Meyer's *Representations of Women in Popular Culture*. She completed her doctoral and master's degrees in communications at University of Washington, and her bachelor's degree in social sciences at University of Colorado. Her professional background is in print journalism, government public information, and nonprofit community public relations.

Lisa M. Cuklanz holds a Ph.D. in Communication Studies from the University of Iowa and is currently Assistant Professor of Communication at Boston College in Chestnut Hill, MA. She served as Chair of the Feminist Scholarship Division of the International Communication Association from 1992 to 1994 and is on the editorial board of *Communication Quarterly* and *Communication Education*. Her research interests include news coverage of social change and public policy issues, and discursive constructions of rape and sexual harassment. Her recent publications include the article "Truth in Transition: Discursive Constructions of Character in the Rideout Rape in Marriage Case" (in *Women's Studies in Communication,* 1993), and book chapters "Male Is to Female as _____ Is to _____: A Guided Tour of Five Feminist Frameworks for Communication Studies" (with K. Cirksena) in L. Rakow's *Women Making Meaning: New Feminist Directions in Communication* (1992), and "Mainstream News Frames: The Hill/Thomas Hearings," in P. Siegel's *He Said, She Said, We Listened: Communication Perspectives on the Hill/Thomas Hearings* (forthcoming). She is currently working on an analysis of mainstream U.S. news coverage of NAFTA.

Kasennahawi Marie David is a Traditional Mohawk within the Iroquois Confederacy. Born and raised in Kanehsatake, she still volunteers her time at the community radio station, CKHQ. Her participation includes on-air duties, as well as reporting on community news and events, and participating in organizing fundraising activities for the station. Her part-time, job-sharing position as a Curriculum Technician at the Resource Center, a branch of the Kanehsatake Education Center, allows her and the other two women she works with to continue to put their time in at the radio station. As part of the curriculum, she has written several stories for children based on the Mohawk community, three of which have been published by the Resource Center. As a journalist, she has written articles for Native publications, including *Native Beat,* a national monthly newspaper originating out of Ontario, and *The Eastern Door,* a biweekly newspaper published in Kahnawake. Her interests include following the struggles of other Indigenous Peoples, as well as other minority groups. For David, networking is a good way to publicize the issues that are important to the Traditional people of the Mohawk Nation.

Katherine Toland Frith is Associate Professor in the School of Communications at The Pennsylvania State University and has been the Professor-In-Charge of the Advertising major for the School. Her areas of research interest are international advertising and environmental issues in advertising. She has been the recipient of two Fulbright awards: She spent the 1986-1987 academic year as a Visiting Fulbright Professor at Institute Technology MARA in Malaysia; in 1993 she taught in the School of Art and Design at Institute Technology Bandung in Indonesia. Prior to receiving her Doctorate in Education at the University of Massachusetts in Amherst, she was a writer at a number of large advertising agencies in New York, including: J. Walter Thompson, N. W. Ayer, and Grey Advertising. Most recently she worked at InterAdmark in Jakarta, Indonesia—a Dentsu affiliate. She has published articles in *Media Asia, Journalism Quarterly, Current Issues and Research in Advertising* and has written chapters for *Advertising Management Casebook, The Publicity Process,* and *Early Adolescence: Perspectives on Research, Policy and Intervention.* Before coming to Penn State University she taught in the Department of Journalism at Iowa State University.

Kyra D. Gaunt is a doctoral candidate in the ethnomusicology program at the University of Michigan. She holds several degrees in classical voice performance and has performed extensively in a variety of popular, jazz, and gospel music contexts. In addition to performing, she has taught several courses in black popular recorded music since 1920, African American women and feminism, and Western art music for non-majors. Her research interests include gender and the black music experience since 1970, analysis of hip-hop music and sampling practice as an extension of earlier musical aesthetics, oral histories and ethnographies of black music in everyday experience, and contemporary African American music and women's sexuality. She recently completed a series of biographical articles for the upcoming publication of *The Encyclopedia of African-American Culture and History.* She is an active member of the Society for Ethnomusicology and the International Association for the Study of Popular Music. She currently hosts an original radio program at an alternative college FM station in Ann Arbor called "Third World Diva Girls" that features the music and written word of women of color from around the world.

Marina Heung is Assistant Professor in the Department of English at Baruch College-CUNY, where she teaches courses in film, Asian literature, Asian-American literature, and writing. Her articles on the representation of gender, race, cultural ideologies, and mother-daughter relationships in film and Asian-American literature have appeared in *The Journal of Popular Film and Television, Film Criticism, The Michigan Quarterly Review, Cinema Journal,* and *Feminist Studies.* Her essay on "Family Romance of Orientalism" appeared in *Genders(21).* She recently completed her term as founding chair of the Asian/Pacific/American Caucus of the Society for Cinema Studies.

Bette J. Kauffman received her Ph.D. in Communications from the University of Pennsylvania in 1992. She has received awards for her still photography, and has professional experience in videography, journalism, and public relations. Her publications include an article on feminism and ethnography in *Communication Theory;* biographical pieces for the forthcoming reference work, *Women in World History;* and a book chapter on women artists and social identity. She is currently writing *Woman Artist: Communicating Social Identity,* based on her doctoral dissertation, as well as pursuing the intersections of class and gender in new research on women and hunting. She teaches in the School of Communications at The Pennsylvania State University, in the areas of critical cultural studies, visual communications, and qualitative research methods.

Susan Kray earned her Ph.D. in Communication at the University of Illinois at Urbana-Champagne in 1991. Her research focuses on women in high-technology workplaces and on ways in which our culture excludes and stigmatizes minority women. Research on which this chapter is based was supported by the American Association of University Women, through a Beckman Fellowship. Her current research, sponsored by the Beckman Fellowship and by an NEH Summer Fellowship, centers on stigmatized images of Jewish women and Judaism in spiritual self-help literature, particularly the work of feminist Christians and neo-pagans, and in the work of Christian feminist theologians and scholars.

Rashmi Luthra is Assistant Professor of Communications at the University of Michigan-Dearborn. She has published articles on social marketing of contraceptives, the use of sex determination tests for selective abortion in India, and the Indian immigrant press in the United States. Luthra teaches courses in international communication, critical media studies, and women's studies.

Isabel Molina Guzmán is a doctoral candidate at the Annenberg School for Communication. She was a master's candidate at the school from 1992 to 1994. Guzmán's master's thesis dealt with the social construction of race and the communication of race as a sign among Spanish-Caribbeans living in the United States.

Marguerite Moritz is Associate Professor in the School of Journalism and Mass Communication at the University of Colorado. She has written extensively on depictions of lesbians and gays in the media and is currently working on a comparative study of civil rights for lesbians and gays in Denmark, the Netherlands, and the United States. She also writes on media representations of women in Eastern Europe. Before taking a faculty position, she worked as a television news producer and documentary maker for NBC's Chicago television station.

Frances Negrón-Muntaner is a Philadelphia-based researcher, writer, and filmmaker. She has studied film at Temple University (M.F.A.) and is currently a doctoral candidate in Comparative Literature at Rutgers University. She has published in many journals and newspapers in Puerto Rico and the United States, including *Alba de America, Heresies, Radical America, Sinister Wisdom, Conditions, The Evergreen Chronicles, Center for Puerto Rican Studies Bulletin, Jump Cut, The Independent,* and *Mairena.* She is the editor of the first collection of Latino poetry in the Delaware Valley, titled *Shouting in a Whisper* (1994). She was codirector and coproducer of the award-winning film *AIDS in the Barrio: Eso no me pasa a mi/That Could Not Happen to Me.* She is currently completing a narrative film on Puerto Rican identities, *Brincado el Charco: Portrait of a Puerto Rican,* and an experimental video commission for television, *Puerto Rican I.D.*

Beverly Nelson is the mother of two teenage children and has always lived in Kanehsatake. When the idea of a Mohawk-run community radio station was introduced in 1984, she readily signed up as a volunteer and stayed with it as she learned all facets of broadcast radio. Through the years, she was an on-air announcer, producer, writer, sales rep, and manager. She has finally left CKHQ to pursue work in other fields outside her community, but she will always hold close to her heart the people she worked with and learned from at Kanehsatake Mohawk Radio, "The Heart of the Community."

Jasmine Paul graduated from The Pennsylvania State University in 1994 with a B.A. in Media Studies and a B.A. in Women's Studies. Her previously published work includes three articles in *The Individualist Perspective,* published by Penn State's Philosophy department. She has also had several poems published by *The Wayfaring,* an independent literary magazine. Her work in visual media includes directing and editing a video program, "The Art of Oppression," which has been incorporated into the Women's Studies curriculum. She is currently enrolled in the Film Studies Graduate Program at the University of California, Los Angeles.

Lorna Roth is Assistant Professor in the Communication Studies Department at Concordia University in Montréal, Québec (Canada), where she teaches a variety of courses related to development, policy, and cross-cultural communications. She has been actively involved in broadcasting policy analysis and consulting with First Nations and multicultural/multiracial groups since the late 1970s and is presently completing a book on the development of First Peoples' Television Broadcasting in the Canadian North.

Angharad N. Valdivia teaches and researches multicultural and international communications issues at the Institute of Communications Research at the University of Illinois at Champaign-Urbana. She has published articles on gender and the press during the Nicaraguan revolution and continues to work on the issue of voice and postcolonial women. In particular, she is concluding a study on Rigoberta Menchu. Her current work focuses on issues of women of color in the United States, including a critique of active audience studies and analysis of Latina actress Rosie Pérez. She is a former co-chair of the Feminist Scholarship Interest Group, and remains active in communications and women's studies organizations.

DATE DUE

NOV 27 1998			
DEC 15 1998			
MAY 05 2000			
MAR 03 2005			